International Law and Organization

THE LIPPINCOTT SERIES
IN INTERNATIONAL POLITICS

under the editorship of
STEVEN MULLER
Cornell University

International Law and Organization

An Introductory Reader

edited by

RICHARD A. FALK
Princeton University

WOLFRAM F. HANRIEDER
University of California, Santa Barbara

Philadelphia · New York
J. B. LIPPINCOTT COMPANY

Richard A. Falk
for
his son, Christopher

Wolfram F. Hanrieder
for
Demetrios P. Agretelis

Contents

INTRODUCTION

I

The achievement of a proper appreciation of the role played by international law and organization in the conduct of international relations requires, above all else, a realistic sense of context. It is essential to take full account of the primary fact that the elements of power (or the capabilities to exert influence) in the international system are predominantly controlled by the governments of the principal nation-states. As a result, the only systems of order that can arise in international society presuppose high degrees of decentralization. If we can understand and accept the consequences of decentralization in international society, then we can proceed with benefit to compare the relatively centralized systems of legal order that have developed in national societies.

This basic comparison between the social and political structure of national and international society underlies a proper appreciation of the role of international law and organization. Such a comparison discourages the tendency to transplant domestic legal rules and institutional procedures into the quite different milieu of international life. Frequently the study of international law and organization has been hindered by the dual temptation (1) to measure its success as a legal order by the degree to which it resembles domestic legal order, and (2) to equate strengthening international law and organization with the adoption and growth of international variants of domestic law systems and domestic political institutions. To rely upon a domestic model to appraise the working of law and organization at the international level neglects the *distinctive features* of a decentralized legal system and overlooks the fact that transplanting centralized institutional practices to a decentralized setting is not likely to improve the quality of international order.

One need only refer to the long record of hopes and disappointments associated with the work of the International Court of Justice (ICJ) to illustrate this point. The wide-spread disappointment of

1

legalists resulting from the small role that has been so far played by the ICJ is misplaced. This disappointment arises only from a false expectation built upon an unsound analogy to the important role played by courts in domestic legal order.

The same reasoning applies when we evaluate the performance of international organizations. The unwarranted expectation that the United Nations could persistently deter or regulate violent conflict and channel forces of change into institutional structures ignores the decentralization of power and purpose in the international system and, as well, invokes standards of performance that are not fully met even by domestic political systems. We wish to emphasize, then, that it is essential to begin the study of international law and organization by stressing the decentralized character of international society. A question highlights the form of inquiry: how can we explain the operations of law and organization in a social system that lacks a government?

An additional consequence of relying on a domestic legal-institutional model is the unfortunate tendency to consider international law and organization as being almost exclusively concerned with the *restraint of behavior.* Hence, some analysts even question the legal character of international law because it lacks regular enforcement mechanisms such as an international police force or effective sanctions. Of course, centralized enforcement is one of the areas in which a decentralized system appears, almost by definition, to be most deficient. So, however, is a giraffe deficient in the ways of man. And further, so is man deficient in the ways of a giraffe, in height and speed and non-aggressiveness. To comprehend international legal order (the intermeshed system of law and organization) is above all to appreciate it for what it is and to acknowledge what it is not.

In this regard, the *role of communication* is very significant. A principal role of international law and organization is to facilitate communication among national actors to permit these actors to identify and implement their common interests and to reduce the mutually destructive risks that result from the pursuit of adverse interests. In the nuclear age bitter enemies retain a pervasive need to communicate reassurance to one another in periods of heightened tension and crisis. The Hot Line providing a telecommunications link between the United States and the Soviet Union illustrates the role of international law in facilitating communication among rivals to avoid a catastrophe spiralling out of international misunderstanding.

The United Nations can be aptly appreciated only if it is understood to provide a forum for interstate communication in a decentralized social order. During the Arab-Israeli War of June, 1967, the Security Council provided a forum where belligerent opponents could maintain contact and implement their converging interests in terminating violence at the earliest possible stage through mutual adherence to a cease-fire. Because national pride and morale were inhibiting factors, it is doubtful whether the Arab countries could have assented to a cease-fire agreed upon by direct interstate communication with Israel; thus, the United Nations apparently played a crucial role in this crisis situation that probably could not have been effectively played by traditional forms of international diplomacy. The role of the United Nations in the Middle East is a failure only for those observers who project false expectations about the capacity of an international organization to restrain force in situations where one or more states perceive national interests to require the use or threat of military power. As we have said, these expectations are false because military power in *any* social system can only be managed in relation to the will and capability of the power-wielders, and in international society, states remain the predominant power-wielders. But the disappointment of false expectations with regard to restraints on force should not undermine our appreciation of reasonable expectations with regard to sustaining processes of communication.

States as bureaucratic entities are rule-oriented. This fact assures the automatic implementation of decisions made by international organizations in routine circumstances. Moreover, international organizations have their own bureaucracies that frequently promulgate rules within the explicit or implicit latitude set by member states. This "bureaucratic decision-making" often takes place without specific legislative authorization by the representative bodies of international organizations. Secretariats, commissions, or individual international civil servants may interpret rules in new ways, issue statements on particular topics and establish committees for their study, or initiate and shape resolutions and other proposals for consideration by the organization's representative body. Not only are national and international bureaucracies linked in important ways, but the interplay of the two levels of bureaucracy often generates subtle innovative pressures that gradually modify the nature and functions of an international organization.

The rule-orientation of national bureaucracies also assures the routine application of international law except in unusual circumstances. Usually it is not worthwhile for a state to violate rules of international law. And often, in the event of violation, the possibility of retaliation and reprisal exists quite independent of the relative power of states. For example, the embassy personnel of the United States government in Kinshasa is just as vulnerable to abuse as are the diplomats of the Congo government stationed in Washington.

The logic of reciprocity protects the Congolese diplomats from abuse in the United States despite the great superiority of American power. Since the issue of abusing a diplomat is not normally a _casus belli,_ even a small state has the necessary capability to deter violations of rules of international law by a superpower. The effectiveness of international law depends in this instance also on the distinctive workings of a decentralized legal system.

II

In dividing these readings into a section on "law" and another on "organization" we do not imply the existence of two distinct subject-matters. On the contrary, law and organization are complementary aspects of a single process that seeks to stabilize international relations through the evolution of an agreed framework of permissible behavior. The perspective of law helps to identify the limits of permissible international behavior. The perspective of organization emphasizes the role of institutional arenas in clarifying and modifying what is permissible in given situations, in responding to allegations of impermissible behavior, and in administrating international programs of aid and welfare. International organizations also play an ever-expanding role in facilitating cooperation among states in a wide variety of activities that include regional economic integration, the promotion of global trade, the conservation of ocean resources, the control of pollution, the demilitarization of outer space, and the maintenance of effective global communication and transportation.

One finds that international jurists have been for centuries dedicated to the task of limiting the use of force in world politics. In the late Medieval period when the Christian nations dominated the world and when the rich legacy of Roman Law was fresh in the minds of lawyers, an attempt was made to rest a universal legal order upon the widespread assent accorded natural law. It was hoped that the moral and legal principles of natural law jurisprudence would create an adequate substitute for the unifying authority successfully provided by the Roman Church in its role as an "international organization" in the period before the Reformation. The split in Christendom that culminated in the Reformation was not regarded by jurists as creating an insuperable obstacle to the acknowledgment of common standards of restraint; the nations dominant in international affairs remained Christian and shared a common cultural and moral heritage. This assumption of a universal consensus on norms was clearly reflected in the seventeenth century peace proposals—some utopian, some more realistic—for the integration of Western Europe, for an all-European union, for a trans-Atlantic community, or for the union of all Christian states. This early optimism about international law and the more guarded hopes for some type of international institution recurs in every period of human crisis and is powerfully present after every collective trauma of mankind. This internationalist sentiment has generally failed to grasp the hard fact that the profession of common values does not necessarily assure the presence of common interests. *why not?*

Such a failure of understanding remains widespread. Observers often attribute the presence of international discord to the special quality of the conflict between communist and democratic values and thereby overlook the pervasiveness of conflict throughout the history of international relations. In addition to disagreements over political values, other bases of international conflict presently exist, including fierce competition for scarce resources, for limited space, and for maximum power and prestige. The aggregate of these conflicts constitute the global struggle that we identify as the cold war.

The behavior of European nations in the expansionist centuries that led to World War I made it evident that rules or norms, no matter how agreeable their sound and sentiment, are unable by themselves to contain the pursuit of wealth, power, and prestige within an agreed and peaceful framework of behavior. Neither rules supposedly based on the will of God nor those that were said to follow from the universal mandate of reason proved capable of effectively restraining the conduct of sovereign states. The resort to force by aggressive nations was a decision that appeared to depend far less upon national attitudes toward the justice of the cause than upon the presumed superiority of national armaments. Deterrence by adequate military counter-force, rather than reliance on an available valid rule of restraint, was quickly acknowledged as essential for the security of peacefully inclined nations.

However, despite their refusal to be bound by rules governing the exercise of national power, states were willing to support legal regimes and rudimentary international institutions seeking to regularize diplomatic, maritime, cultural, financial, and commercial transactions across national frontiers. In contrast with the rules of just war deduced from divine will or projected by human reason, the authority of law over this subject matter of routine interaction arose from the observable behavior of nations. This behavioral basis for legal authority possessed the special advantage of reinforcing the pretensions of sovereign prerogative, since national governments at that time were eager to consolidate their internal power, and to subdue feudal lords. Such a network of legal regulations permitted the development of convenient and predictable standards for routine, but significant matters and did not interfere with the state's quest for maximum

aggressor

power, prestige, and wealth. International law in the nineteenth century gradually acknowledged that a state's use of military force was
a matter of national discretion, subject only to moral restraints that
might in theory, but seldom appeared in practice to impinge upon
the conscience of the sovereign rulers. War was not ignored, but
its threat was resisted mainly by the diplomacy associated with
the maintenance of a balance of power. Such a system of order
depends upon the logic of deterrence and upon flexible alliance patterns. The formation of new coalitions must operate whenever a
potential threat to the existing international structure is posed by an
aggressor nation. This balancing approach achieved considerable international stability in the century before the French Revolution. In
this period the balance of power system was essentially non-institu-
tionalized. The "classical" balance of power system limited the role
of force in European politics quite successfully, even though the permissive attitude toward the use of international force shocked those
pious sensibilities who wanted war condemned, as well as avoided or
limited. In the period between the Congress of Vienna (1815) and
World War I, the logic of deterrence required increasing institutionalization, in part because the international system possessed diminishing opportunities for the flexible shifting of alliance patterns. At the
same time, the negotiating habits acquired by the practice of "congressional diplomacy" gradually paved the way in the latter part of
the century for the establishment of cooperative international institutions to regulate postal services, promote public health and sanitation,
prohibit slave trading and foster countless other joint endeavors.

These functionally limited international organizations were neither
designed for, nor capable of, meeting such ambitious tasks as the
maintenance of peace through the procedures and institutions of
collective security. Nonetheless, conceptions of international law
remained relevant to the use and limitation of international force.
Instead of mobilizing the combined power of the community against
a nation that waged war without a just cause, as was the intention of
the pre-Grotian tradition, international law attempted to restrict the
scope and to limit the methods of warfare. Neutrality laws delimited
the scope of belligerency with considerable precision, and the laws of
warfare developed standards to prevent unnecessary suffering for
combatants and civilians. In such an international system, war functions as a permissible political technique and allows a nation to coerce
changes in the *status quo:* war has a legislative function. Attempts to
eliminate force from world affairs frequently overlook the extent to
which war has acted as a progressive energy in world history and
usually neglect the need to find alternative peaceful mechanisms to
assure social change. To eliminate military force and its threat with-

But only by eliminating [?] will other avenues be found.

out a provision for peaceful change would impose a dangerous, and very likely, an undesirable rigidity upon international relations; moreover, it would tend to insulate and secure existing patterns of injustice. Even the constitutional documents of the League of Nations (The Covenant) and the United Nations (The Charter) contain provisions that acknowledge the responsibility of a global international organization to guide forces of change into peaceful channels.

The acceptance of the idea that legal obligation in world affairs depends upon national consent (as manifested by practice and agreement) led jurists interested in enlarging the province of international law to study the processes by which consent was manifested. Human suffering, economic waste, and the developing military technology of warfare inspired a variety of projects to persuade states to give their sovereign consent to a body of rules that would guarantee peace. This juridical approach reached its highwater mark at the Hague Codification conferences on the laws of war held prior to World War I (1899, 1907). Consent to external authority, however, proved no more compatible with the egocentric energies of sovereignty than had the obligations posited by the natural law school. It became evident that states were unwilling to bind themselves on crucial matters and that they would not even abide by prior consent if a legal obligation was later perceived as running seriously contrary to national interests.

Rules of war pertaining to naval operations and blockade, such as "visit and search," were abandoned soon after the submarine became an important military weapon. The popular interpretation of this development is misleading. The refusal to "visit and search" enemy merchant ships did not represent a denial of the legal character of international obligations. Rather, the abandonment of "visit and search" practice illustrates the extent to which important legal obligations can suffer from technological obsolescence. The technological and social environment needs to reinforce legal and organizational norms that come into conflict with strong political pressures. When this support is absent or removed, then it is unlikely that actors will continue to obey the rule, especially if maintaining the rule is more advantageous for one set of actors than for another.

If the legal rule deals with a trivial issue, continuing adherence to it is more likely. One reason for adherence is that once rules have been fed into the bureaucratic process they operate to control foreign offices and other administrative institutions until repudiated by political decision-makers. Rules and standards governing routine subject matter can achieve effectiveness without community reinforcement. The relevant governments officially and automatically obey. In contrast, obligations that bear upon national security require effective centralized sanctions of reliable decentralized deterrents. Without this implementation of the rule, no state, no matter what it pledges, can be relied upon to give up its discretionary right to use force to promote national objectives.

The League of Nations combined the collective techniques of the balance of power system with the rudimentary formalities of a supranational legal structure. As in the early formulations of natural law, the organized community claimed control over those nations that were guilty of behavior that was collectively determined aggression. Community response systems seek to confront an aggressor with overwhelming military capabilities brought to bear on behalf of a victim of aggression. In contrast, the idea of neutrality as a strategy to limit warfare avoids the identification of which side is the "aggressor" and which side the victim, and seeks to contribute to international order by sustaining the neutral status of non-belligerents, thereby hoping to confine the scope of violence. It is hardly necessary to point out that the League's ambitions far exceeded the willingness of major nations to give up sovereign control over military decisions. The United States refused to participate formally in the League at all; other principal nations participated, but only nominally. However, despite these failings, the League did settle several minor conflicts that might have otherwise embroiled major nations.

In addition to collective security arrangements, the Permanent Court of International Justice was established in 1920 to give nations a reliable way to settle their conflicts with one another. One approach to world peace attributed the outbreak of war to the absence of dignified alternatives to force, rather than to ambition or malice. Techniques of adjudication, mediation, arbitration, good offices, and negotiation attempted to provide the international environment with a range of pacific settlement procedures.

The post-World War I effort to eliminate war also led to the widely ratified Treaty for the Renunciation of War (Pact of Paris or Briand-Kellogg Pact signed in 1928) and to the Anti-War Treaty of Rio de Janeiro (1933), expressing the solemn will of nations to limit the use of force in international affairs to purposes of individual or collective self-defense. A declaration of this kind is not likely to achieve a significant impact on behavior. Subsequent events have shown how little weight is attached by national governments to solemn declarations of this sort. Nevertheless, formal pledges may help to mobilize world public opinion. In addition, they provide officials with standards that may be useful if it becomes necessary to condemn resort to war or to urge self-restraint. The continuous endeavor to arrive at a definition of aggression embodies a similar belief that the maintenance of world peace is fortified by agreed standards of restraint on the use of military power.

Conferences, agreements, and proposals that seek a partial or complete disarmament or the proscription of certain methods of warfare (such as the use of poison gas) are also within the province of international law and organization. The disarmament approach aims to reduce or eliminate the capacities of nations to wage international war. It is a natural way to implement declarations of renunciation and to carry out the collective responsibility for maintaining the peace.

World War II increased interest in approaches to peace that depended upon international law and organization. The development of nuclear weapons has stimulated an intense interest in disarmament and arms control, and the prospect of a nuclear war has intensified the search for alternatives to war as a means to resolve conflicts, to contain aggressors, and to achieve social change. However, a legal-institutional control of force presupposes that the social environment provides adequate reinforcement. The insufficiency of this reinforcement explains the current skepticism about prospects for world government and about extravagant peace movements that promise to bring the rule of law reliably into the relations of sovereign states. States continue to rely mainly upon unilateral defense systems, bolstered by regional military groupings of the like-minded, and they continue to exhibit an alarming willingness to use force assertively and unilaterally to achieve their international ends. So long as national power and sovereign animus dominate the international scene, the realistic contributions of international law and international organizations to peace must be understood as modest and marginal.

III

There are, then, two opposing currents in the contemporary stream of international life. First, *vital contacts* between nations that depend mainly upon decentralized legal-institutional control to achieve a degree of international order; centralized approaches to vital contacts (for example, United Nations, disarmament, pacific settlement procedures, collective security, definition of aggression, war crimes trials) provide scant hope of coping with either the national capability or disposition to wage war. Our conception of law and organization needs to be wide enough to encompass clearly the decentralized normative patterns based upon mutual self-restraint, reciprocity, and tacit rules of the game. In other words, to avoid irrelevance or legalism on the level of vital contacts, international law and international organizations must envision their role as one of blunting the stark confrontations that arise from the mutual deterrence postures, upon which major actors continue to rely for their ultimate security interests. Although often by subtle means, these ordering processes clearly help to keep international conflict within manageable limits. The possession of nuclear weapons by cold war antagonists has led to the growth of a complex and crucial regime of decentralized norms that may yet be able to spare us the disasters of nuclear warfare. It is imperative that nations perceive these decentralized norms, accord them fidelity, and acknowledge the dependence of national interests upon minimum international stability. Here the function of international law and organization is not primarily to provide a restraint system replete with effective sanctions, but rather to moderate hostile responses. For example, during the Cuban Missile Crisis of 1962 the American claims were couched in legal terms, which in turn encouraged the Soviet Union to respond in this restrained rhetoric rather than feeling obliged to use the language of and adopt the rigid attitudes associated with sovereignty and national honor. By "technicalizing" messages sent by the adversaries, international law helped to structure communication during a crisis situation.

The enormous international volume of *routine contacts* that concern many people and that presuppose effective and fair administration is the second dimension of international order.* The realm of routine contact is removed from the field of general awareness. This everyday subject-matter has generated a legal-administrative substratum of international relations and leads to specialized requirements for legal and administrative know-how relevant to a vast range of international transactions. The effectiveness of the legal regime available to conduct routine contacts is facilitated by the rule-oriented behavior of the principal supervisory institutions, mainly domestic and supranational tribunals and foreign offices equipped with legal and technical advisers. Some authors have recently alleged that the security which law and organization afford to routine transactions has become jeopardized by the inexperience and non-bureaucratic orientation of some governments in the new nations.

It is doubtful that routine contacts will "spill-over" to the realm of vital contacts so long as effective world order rests on the deterrent effect of retaliation rather than on authoritative and persuasive insti-

---

* The distinction between routine and vital matters is itself fluid and subtle. The status of property is routine in the relations among capitalist nations but vital in the relations between a capitalist and a socialist nation, especially if the socialism is of the Soviet or Chinese variety. If a vital matter can be fed into the bureaucratic process, then it has the possibility of eventually attaining the stability of a routine matter. One could even envisage such a transformation of Arab-Israeli relations if formulas to govern the use of the Suez Canal and quotas for maximum annual Israeli immigration could be successfully negotiated.

tutional procedures and capabilities. Nevertheless, international public order performs critical services by improving the moral, psychological, and physical capacity of the world community to deal with local conflicts that, if not dealt with effectively, might escalate into a nuclear war. This underlines the importance of recognizing that international law and organization, however conceived, are not autonomous instruments of social control. These ordering instrumentalities depend for effectiveness upon suitable forms of implementation in each instance and upon an overall capacity to adapt to a highly dynamic international environment.

PART I
INTERNATIONAL LAW

1. INTERNATIONAL LAW AND ASSUMPTIONS ABOUT THE STATE SYSTEM

By WILLIAM D. COPLIN

MOST writers on international relations and international law still examine the relationship between international law and politics in terms of the assumption that law either should or does function only as a coercive restraint on political action. Textbook writers on general international politics like Morgenthau,[1] and Lerche and Said,[2] as well as those scholars who have specialized in international law like J. L. Brierly[3] and Charles De Visscher,[4] make the common assumption that international law should be examined as a system of coercive norms controlling the actions of states. Even two of the newer works, *The Political Foundations of International Law* by Morton A. Kaplan and Nicholas deB. Katzenbach[5] and *Law and Mini-*

Reprinted by permission of the author and *World Politics,* XVII (No. 4, 1964), 615-635.

[1] Hans J. Morgenthau, *Politics Among Nations* (New York 1961), 275-311. The entire evaluation of the "main problems" of international law is focused on the question of what rules are violated and what rules are not.

[2] Charles O. Lerche, Jr., and Abdul A. Said, *Concepts of International Politics* (Englewood Cliffs, N.J., 1963), 167-87. That the authors have employed the assumption that international law functions as a system of restraint is evident from the title of their chapter which examines international law, "Limitations on State Actions."

[3] J. L. Brierly, *The Law of Nations* (New York 1963), 1. Brierly defines international law as "the body of rules and principles of action which are binding upon civilized states in their relations. . . ."

[4] Charles De Visscher, *Theory and Reality in Public International Law* (Princeton 1957), 99-100.

[5] Morton A. Kaplan and Nicholas deB. Katzenbach, *The Political Foundations of International Law* (New York 1961), 5. In a discussion of how the student should observe international law and politics, the authors write: "To understand the substance and limits of such constraining rules (international law), it is necessary to examine the interests which support them in the international system, the means by which they are made effective, and the functions they perform. Only in this way is it possible to predict the areas in which rules operate, the limits of rules as effective constraints, and the factors which

mum World Public Order by Myres S. McDougal and Florentino P. Feliciano,[6] in spite of an occasional reference to the non-coercive aspects of international law, are developed primarily from the model of international law as a system of restraint. Deriving their conception of the relationship between international law and political action from their ideas on the way law functions in domestic communities, most modern writers look at international law as an instrument of direct control. The assumption that international law is or should be a coercive restraint on state action structures almost every analysis, no matter what the school of thought or the degree of optimism or pessimism about the effectiveness of the international legal system.[7] With an intellectual framework that measures international law primarily in terms of constraint on political action, there is little wonder that

---

underlie normative change." Although the authors are asking an important question—"Why has international law been binding in some cases?"—they still assume that international law functions primarily as a direct restraint on state action. For an excellent review of this book, see Robert W. Tucker, "Resolution," *Journal of Conflict Resolution,* VII (March 1963), 69-75.

[6] Myres S. McDougal and Florentino P. Feliciano, *Law and Minimum World Public Order* (New Haven 1961), 10. The authors suggest that if any progress in conceptualizing the role of international law is to be made, it is necessary to distinguish between the "factual process of international coercion and the process of authoritative decision by which the public order of the world community endeavors to regulate such process of coercion." This suggestion is based on the assumption that international law promotes order primarily through the establishment of restraints on state actions.

[7] There are a few writers who have tried to approach international law from a different vantage point. For a survey of some of the other approaches to international law and politics, see Michael Barkun, "International Norms: An Interdisciplinary Approach," *Background,* VIII (August 1964), 121-29. The survey shows that few "new" approaches to international law have developed beyond the preliminary stages, save perhaps for the writings of F. S. C. Northrop. Northrop's works (e.g., *Philosophical Anthropology and Practical Politics* [New York 1960], 326-30) are particularly significant in their attempt to relate psychological, philosophical, and cultural approaches to the study of law in general, although he has not usually been concerned with the overall relationship of international law to international political action. Not mentioned in Barkun's survey but important in the discussion of international law and politics is Stanley Hoffmann, "International Systems and International Law," in Klaus Knorr and Sidney Verba, eds., *The International System* (Princeton 1961), 205-38. [See page 89.] However, Hoffmann's essay is closer in approach to the work by Kaplan and Katzenbach than to the approach developed in this article. Finally, it is also necessary to point to an article by Edward McWhinney, "Soviet and Western International Law and the Cold War in a Nuclear Age," *Canadian Yearbook of International Law,* I (1963), 40-81. Professor McWhinney discusses the relationship between American and Russian structures of action, on the one hand, and their interpretations of international law, on the other. While McWhinney's approach is basically similar to the one proposed in this article in its attempt to relate international law to politics on a conceptual level, his article is focused on a different set of problems, the role of national attitudes in the contemporary era on ideas of international law. Nevertheless, it is a significant contribution to the task of analyzing more

skepticism about international law continues to increase while creative work on the level of theory seems to be diminishing.[8]

Therefore, it is desirable to approach the relationship between international law and politics at a different functional level, not because
international law does not function at the level of coercive restraint,
but because it also functions at another level. In order to illustrate
a second functional level in the relationship between international law
and politics, it is necessary to examine the operation of domestic law.
In a domestic society, the legal system as a series of interrelated
normative statements does more than direct or control the actions of
its members through explicit rules backed by a promise of coercion.
Systems of law also act on a more generic and pervasive level by
serving as authoritative (i.e., accepted as such by the community)
modes of communicating or reflecting the ideals and purposes, the
acceptable roles and actions, as well as the very processes of the
societies. The legal system functions on the level of the individual's
perceptions and attitudes by presenting to him an image of the social
system—an image which has both factual and normative aspects and
which contributes to social order by building a consensus on procedural as well as on substantive matters. In this sense, law in the
domestic situation is a primary tool in the "socialization"[9] of the
individual.

International law functions in a similar manner: namely, as an
institutional device for communicating to the policy-makers of various
states a consensus on the nature of the international system. The
purpose of this article is to approach the relationship between international law and politics not as a system of direct restraints on state
action, but rather as a system of quasi-authoritative communications
to the policy-makers concerning the reasons for state actions and
the requisites for international order. It is a "quasi-authoritative"
device because the norms of international law represent only an
imperfect consensus of the community of states, a consensus which
rarely commands complete acceptance but which usually expresses
generally held ideas. Given the decentralized nature of law-creation
and law-application in the international community, there is no
official voice of the states as a collectivity. However, international
law taken as a body of generally related norms is the closest thing

---

clearly the relationship between international law and politics.
   [8] See Richard A. Falk, "The Adequacy of Contemporary International Law:
Gaps in Legal Thinking," *Virginia Law Review*, L (March 1964), 231-65, for
a valuable but highly critical analysis of contemporary international legal
theory.
   [9] See Gabriel A. Almond and James S. Coleman, eds., *The Politics of the
Developing Areas* (Princeton 1960), 26-31, for an explanation of the concept
of socialization.

to such a voice. Therefore, in spite of the degree of uncertainty about the authority of international law, it may still be meaningful to examine international law as a means for expressing the commonly held assumptions about the state system.

The approach advocated in this article has its intellectual antecedents in the sociological school, since it seeks to study international law in relation to international politics. Furthermore, it is similar to that of the sociological school in its assumption that there is or should be a significant degree of symmetry between international law and politics on the level of intellectual constructs—that is, in the way in which international law has expressed and even shaped ideas about relations between states. It is hoped that this approach will contribute to a greater awareness of the interdependence of international law and conceptions of international politics.

Before analyzing the way in which international law has in the past and continues today to reflect common attitudes about the nature of the state system, let us discuss briefly the three basic assumptions which have generally structured those attitudes.[10] First, it has been assumed that the state is an absolute institutional value and that its security is the one immutable imperative for state action. If there has been one thing of which policy-makers could always be certain, it is that their actions must be designed to preserve their state. Second, it has been assumed that international politics is a struggle for power, and that all states seek to increase their power. Although the forms of power have altered during the evolution of the state system, it has been generally thought that states are motivated by a drive for power, no matter what the stakes. The third basic assumption permeating ideas about the international system has to do with maintaining a minimal system of order among the states. This assumption, symbolized generally by the maxim "Preserve the balance of power," affirms the necessity of forming coalitions to counter any threat to hegemony and of moderating actions in order to avoid an excess of violence that could disrupt the system.

[10] The following discussion of the assumptions of the state system is brief, since students of international politics generally agree that the three assumptions listed have structured most of the actions of states. This agreement is most complete concerning the nature of the "classical" state system. The author is also of the opinion that these assumptions continue to operate today in a somewhat mutated form. (See his unpublished manuscript "The Image of Power Politics: A Cognitive Approach to the Study of International Politics," chaps. 2, 4, 8.) Note also the agreement on the nature of classical ideas about international politics in the following: Ernst B. Haas, "The Balance of Power as a Guide to Policy-Making," *Journal of Politics*, XV (August 1953), 370-97; Morton A. Kaplan, *System and Process in International Politics* (New York 1957), 22-36; and Edward Vose Gulick, *Europe's Classical Balance of Power* (Ithaca, N.Y., 1955).

It is necessary at this point to note that an unavoidable tension has existed between the aim of maintaining the state and maximizing power, on the one hand, and of preserving the international system, on the other. The logical extension of either aim would threaten the other, since complete freedom of action by the state would not allow for the limitation imposed by requirements to maintain the system, and a strict regularization of state action inherent in the idea of the system would curtail the state's drive for power. However, the tension has remained constant, with neither norm precluding the other except when a given state was in immediate danger of destruction. At those times, the interests of the system have been subordinated to the drive for state survival, but with no apparent long-range effect on the acceptance by policy-makers of either set of interests, despite their possible incompatibility. The prescriptions that states should be moderate, flexible, and vigilant[11] have been a manifestation of the operation of the system. Together, the three basic assumptions about the state system have constituted the conceptual basis from which the policy-makers have planned the action of their state.

I. Classical International Law and the Image of the State System

Almost every legal aspect of international relations from 1648 to 1914 reinforced and expressed the assumptions of the state system. State practices in regard to treaties, boundaries, neutrality, the occupation of new lands, freedom of the seas, and diplomacy, as well as classical legal doctrines, provide ample illustration of the extent to which the basic assumptions of the state were mirrored in international law.

The essential role of treaties in international law reflected the three assumptions of the state system. First, treaty practices helped to define the nature of statehood. Emanating from the free and unfettered will of states, treaties were the expression of their sovereign prerogatives. Statehood itself was defined in part as the ability to make treaties, and that ability presupposed the equality and independence usually associated with the idea of the state. Moreover, certain definitive treaties, like those written at the Peace of Augsburg (1515) and the Peace of Westphalia (1648), actually made explicit the attributes of statehood. The former treaty affirmed the idea that the Prince had complete control over the internal affairs of the state,

---

[11] See Gulick, 34; and for a discussion of the principles of moderation, flexibility, and vigilance, *ibid.*, 11-16.

while the latter emphasized that states were legally free and equal in their international relationships.[12] Even the actual wording of treaties expressed the classical assumption about the sanctity of the state. Whether in the formal references to the "high contracting parties" or in the more vital statements about the agreement of sovereigns not to interfere with the actions of other sovereigns, treaties were clear expressions of the classical idea of the state.[13]

Treaty law also contributed to the evolution of the classical assumption regarding the maintenance of the international system. Both explicitly and implicitly, treaties affirmed the necessity of an international system. Whether or not they contained such phrases as "balance of power," "just equilibrium," "universal and perpetual peace,"[14] "common and public safety and tranquillity,"[15] "public tranquillity on a lasting foundation,"[16] or "safety and interest of Europe,"[17] the most important treaties during the classical period affirmed the desirability of maintaining the international system.[18] Also, many treaties reaffirmed earlier treaty agreements, contributing to the idea that the international system was a continuing, operative unity.[19] Therefore, treaties usually reminded the policy-maker that the maintenance of the international system was a legitimate and necessary objective of state policy.

Finally, treaties affirmed the necessity and, in part, the legality of the drive for power. The constant juggling of territory, alliances, and other aspects of capability was a frequent and rightful subject of treaty law. Treaties implicitly confirmed that power was the dynamic force in relations between states by defining the legal criteria of power and, more important, by providing an institutional means, subscribed to by most of the members of the system, which legalized certain political transactions, such as territorial acquisition and dynastic exchange.

A second state practice which contributed to the classical assumptions about the state system was the legal concept of boundaries. Inherent in the very idea of the boundary were all three assumptions

[12] For the effects of the two treaties, see Charles Petrie, *Diplomatic History, 1713-1939* (London 1949), 111; David Jayne Hill, *A History of Diplomacy in the International Development of Europe* (New York 1924), 603-6; and Arthur Nussbaum, *A Concise History of the Law of Nations* (New York 1961), 116.

[13] E.g., *The Treaty of Ryswick, 1697* in Andrew Browning, ed., *English History Documents,* VIII (New York 1963), 881-83.

[14] *Treaty of Ryswick,* Article I, in *ibid.*

[15] *Barrier Treaty of 1715,* Article I, in *ibid.,* Vol. X.

[16] *Treaty of Vienna, 1713,* in *ibid.,* Vol. VIII.

[17] *Treaty of Quadruple Alliance, 1815,* in *ibid.,* Vol. XI.

[18] Leo Gross, "The Peace of Westphalia, 1648-1948," *American Journal of International Law,* XLII (January 1948), 20-40. [See page 45.]

[19] For a treaty which expressed the necessity of keeping prior obligations, see *Treaty of Aix-la-Chapelle, 1748,* in Browning, ed., Vol. X.

of the classical system. First, the boundary marked off that most discernible of all criteria of a state's existence—territory.[20] A state was sovereign within its territory, and the boundary was essential to the demarcation and protection of that sovereignty. Freedom and equality necessitated the delineation of a certain area of complete control; the boundary as conceptualized in international law was the institutional means through which that necessity was fulfilled. Second, the boundary was essential for the preservation of the international system.[21] After every war the winning powers set up a new or revised set of boundaries which aided them in maintaining order by redistributing territory. More important, the boundary also provided a criterion by which to assess the intentions of other states. Change of certain essential boundaries signified a mortal threat to the whole system, and signaled the need for a collective response.[22] Finally, the legal concept of boundaries provided a means through which the expansion and contraction of power in the form of territory could be measured. Since the boundary was a legal means of measuring territorial changes, international law in effect reinforced the idea that the struggle for power was an essential and accepted part of international politics. All three assumptions of the state system, therefore, were mirrored in the classical legal concept of boundaries.

Another international legal concept which reflected the assumptions about the state system was the idea of neutrality. The primary importance of neutrality law lay in its relation to the classical emphasis on the preservation of the international system. The practice of neutrality was an essential element in the mitigation of international conflict because it provided a legitimate means of lessening the degree of violence in any given war (by reducing the number of belligerents) and also made those involved in a war aware of the possibility of hostile actions from outside should the conflict weaken the participants too greatly. In short, the legal concept of neutrality implied that the actions of states must remain moderate and flexible in order to preserve the state system.[23]

There were other aspects of international legal practice which substantiated the assumptions of the state system. For instance, since the sixteenth century the law pertaining to the occupation of new lands

[20] See John H. Herz, *International Politics in the Atomic Age* (New York 1962), 53, for a discussion of the role of territory in the classical state system and the international legal system.

[21] See Hoffmann, 212, 215, for a discussion of the way in which territorial settlements in treaties aided stability within the system. He calls this function part of the law of political framework.

[22] E.g., the English and French attitude toward Belgium.

[23] For a discussion of the role of neutrality in the balance of power system, see McDougal and Feliciano, 391-413.

and to freedom of the high seas constituted a vital aspect of international law, and provided "legitimate" areas in which the struggle for power could take place.

From the outset, most of the non-European areas of the world were considered by the great powers to be acceptable arenas for the struggle for power. International legal practice made it easy for states to gain control of land overseas by distinguishing between the laws of occupation and the laws of subjugation. This distinction made it easier for powers to extend control over non-European territorial expanses because it enabled states to "occupy" territory legally without actually controlling it.[24] Through the laws of occupation, international law confirmed the assumption that colonial expansion was part of the struggle for power.

The law of the high seas also contributed to the idea of the struggle for power. The expansion of trade, military power, and territorial domain was, throughout almost the entire history of the state system, greatly dependent upon the free use of the high seas. The laws of the sea were designed so that maximum use could be made of this relatively cheap mode of transportation. Like the laws of occupation of non-European territory, sea law helped to keep the distribution of power among European states in continuous flux.[25]

Therefore, both the laws of the seas and the laws governing the occupation of new lands were instrumental in "legalizing" areas for conflict. Given the assumption that states always maximize their power, a free sea and the easy acquisition of non-European lands provided the fluidity needed for the states to struggle for power. Moreover, both sets of laws removed the area of conflict from the home territory, thus enabling states to increase the scope of their struggle without proportionately increasing its intensity.[26]

A final category of international law which reinforced the assumptions about the state system was the law of diplomacy. The legal rationalization behind the rights and duties of diplomats (i.e., since diplomats represent sovereign states, they owe no allegiance to the receiving state) emphasized the inviolability of the state which was an essential aspect of the classical assumptions.[27] At the same time,

---

[24] L. Oppenheim, in H. Lauterpacht, ed., *International Law* (New York 1948), I, 507.

[25] The attempt to control a "closed sea" was sometimes a bid by a powerful state to freeze the status quo—e.g., Portugal's control of the Indian Ocean in the sixteenth and seventeenth centuries (Nussbaum, III).

[26] Analysts have argued over whether colonialism reduced or exacerbated international antagonism. Without settling the argument, it seems safe to say that the struggle for colonies was a more spectacular and relatively less dangerous system of conflict than was competition for European land.

[27] For the relationship of the assumption of statehood and the functioning

the very fact that even semi-hostile states could exchange and maintain ambassadors emphasized that all states were part of a common international system.[28] Finally, the classical functions of a diplomat—to make sure that conditions are not changing to the disadvantage of his state and, if they are, to suggest and even implement policies to rectify the situation—exemplified the rule of constant vigilance necessary in a group of states struggling for power. Therefore, in their own way, the laws of diplomacy expressed all three of the assumptions of the state systems.

The assumptions of the state system were reinforced not only by the legal practices of states but also by the major international legal theories of the classical period. Three general schools of thought developed: the naturalists, the eclectics or Grotians, and the positivists.[29] In each school, there was a major emphasis on both the state and the state system as essential institutional values. Whether it was Pufendorf's insistence on the "natural equality of state,"[30] the Grotians' concept of the sovereign power of state,[31] or Bynkershoek and the nineteenth-century positivists' point that treaties were the prime, if not the only, source of international law,[32] the state was considered by most classical theorists to be the essential institution protected by the legal system. At the same time, almost every classical writer on international law either assumed or argued for the existence of an international system of some kind.[33] Along with Grotians, the naturalists maintained that a system of states existed, since man was a social animal. Vattel, probably the most famous international lawyer in the classical period, asserted that a balance of power and a state system existed.[34] Even the positivists of the nineteenth century assumed that there was an international system of some kind. This

---

of diplomatic immunities, see a discussion of the theoretical underpinnings of diplomatic immunities in Ernest L. Kelsey, "Some Aspects of the Vienna Conference on Diplomatic Intercourse and Immunities," *American Journal of International Law,* LXXXVIII (January 1962), 92-94.

[28] Morgenthau, 547.

[29] For a discussion of the precise meaning of these classifications, see Nussbaum.

[30] *Ibid.,* 149.

[31] Hugo Grotius, *The Rights of War and Peace,* ed. with notes by A. C. Campbell (Washington 1901), 62.

[32] Cornelius Van Bynkershoek, *De dominio maris dissertatio,* trans. by Ralph Van Deman Mogoffin (New York 1923), 35.

[33] De Visscher, 88. For similar interpretations of classical and pre-twentieth-century theorists, see Walter Schiffer, *The Legal Community of Mankind* (New York 1951), chap. 1; or Percy E. Corbett, *Law and Society in the Relations of States* (New York 1951).

[34] Emeric de Vattel, *The Laws of Nations* (Philadelphia 1867), 412-14.

is apparent from their emphasis on the balance of power,[35] as well as from their assumption that relations between nations could be defined in terms of legal rights and duties.[36]

Therefore, there was a consensus among the classical theorists of international law that international politics had two structural elements: the state, with its rights of freedom and self-preservation; and the system, with its partial effectiveness in maintaining a minimal international order. That the theorists never solved the conflict between the idea of the unfettered sovereign state, on the one hand, and a regulating system of law, on the other, is indicative of a conflict within the assumptions of the state system,[37] but a conflict which neither prevented international lawyers from writing about an international legal order nor kept policy-makers from pursuing each state's objectives without destroying the state system.

Although the norms of classical international law sometimes went unheeded, the body of theory and of state practice which constituted "international law as an institution" nonetheless expressed in a quasi-authoritative manner the three assumptions about international politics. It legalized the existence of states and helped to define the actions necessary for the preservation of each state and of the system as a whole. It reinforced the ideas that vigilance, moderation, and flexibility are necessary for the protection of a system of competing states. And finally, international law established a legalized system of political payoffs by providing a means to register gains and losses without creating a static system. In fact, this last aspect was essential to the classical state system. With international law defining certain relationships (territorial expansion, empire-building, etc.) as legitimate areas for political competition, other areas seemed, at least generally in the classical period, to be removed from the center of the political struggle. By legitimizing the struggle as a form of political competition rather than as universal conflict, international law sanc-

---

[35] G. F. Von Martens, *The Law of Nations: Being the Science of National Law, Covenants, Power & Founded upon the Treaties and Custom of Modern Nations in Europe,* trans. by William Cobbett (4th ed., London 1829), 123-24.

[36] Almost all of the nineteenth-century positivists assumed that relations between nations were systematized enough to allow for a system of rights and duties. E.g., William Edward Hall, *A Treatise on International Law* (Oxford 1904), 43-59; Henry Wheaton, *Elements of International Law* (Oxford 1936), 75. Wheaton does not discuss duties as such, but when he talks about legal rights he distinguishes between "absolute" and "conditional" rights. According to Wheaton, the "conditional" rights are those resulting from membership in the international legal system. This formulation implies the existence of corresponding duties.

[37] See Von Martens, 123-34, for the intellectual and legal problems growing out of the assumption that states may legally maximize power but that they also have a responsibility "to oppose by alliances and even by force of arms" a series of aggrandizements which threaten the community.

tioned a form of international system that was more than just an anarchic drive for survival.

II. CONTEMPORARY INTERNATIONAL LAW AND THE ASSUMPTIONS OF THE STATE SYSTEM

As a quasi-authoritative system of communicating the assumptions of the state system to policy-makers, contemporary international law no longer presents a clear idea of the nature of international politics. This is in part a result of the tension, within the structure of contemporary international law itself, between the traditional legal concepts and the current practices of states. International law today is in a state of arrested ambiguity—in a condition of unstable equilibrium between the old and the new. As a result, it no longer contributes as it once did to a consensus on the nature of the state system. In fact, it adds to the growing uncertainty and disagreement as to how the international political system itself is evolving. The following discussion will attempt to assess the current developments in international law in terms of the challenges those developments make to the three assumptions of the state system. It is realized that the three assumptions themselves have already undergone change, but our purpose is to show where contemporary international legal practice and theory stand in relation to that change.

THE CHALLENGE TO THE STATE AND THE SYSTEM

The current legal concept of the state is a perfect example of the arrested ambiguity of contemporary international law and of the threat that this condition represents to the assumptions of the state system. On the one hand, most of the traditional forms used to express the idea of statehood are still employed. Treaty-makers and statesmen still write about "respect for territorial integrity," the "right of domestic jurisdiction," and the "sovereign will of the high contracting parties." Moreover, most of the current substantive rights and duties, such as self-defense, legal equality, and territorial jurisdiction, that are based on the assumption that states as units of territory are the irreducible institutional values of the system continue to be central to international legal practice.[38] On the other hand, certain contemporary developments contrast sharply with the traditional territory-oriented conceptions of international law.[39] With the growth of international

---

[38] E.g., Charles G. Fenwick, *International Law* (New York 1952), chap. II.
[39] For a survey of current challenges to traditional international law, see Wolfgang Friedmann, "The Changing Dimensions of International Law,"

entities possessing supranational powers (e.g., ECSC), the legal idea
of self-contained units based on territorial control lacks the clear
basis in fact that it once enjoyed. Many of the traditional prerogatives
of the sovereign state, such as control over fiscal policy,[40] have been
transferred in some respects to transnational units. While the development of supranational powers is most pronounced in Europe, there
is reason to believe, especially concerning international cooperation
on technical matters, that organizations patterned on the European
experience might occur elsewhere.

Another significant manifestation of ambiguity in the territorial
basis of international law is found in the post-World War II practice
of questioning the validity of the laws of other states. The "act of
state doctrine" no longer serves as the guideline it once did in directing the national courts of one state to respect the acts promulgated in
another.[41] Once based on the assumption of the "inviolability of the
sovereign," the "act of state doctrine" today is the source of widespread controversy. The conflicting views of the doctrine are symptomatic of the now ambiguous role of territoriality in questions of
jurisdictional and legal power. Although these developments in current legal practice are only now emerging, they nonetheless can be

---

Columbia Law Review, LXII (November 1962), 1147-65. Also, see Richard A.
Falk, *The Role of the Domestic Courts in the International Legal Order*
(Syracuse 1964), 14-19, for a discussion of the fact that while there is a growing "functional obsolescence" of the state system, the assumptions of the state
system continue to operate for psychological and political reasons.

[40] E.g., Articles 3 and 4 of the *Treaty Establishing the European Coal and
Steel Community* (April 18, 1951).

[41] For an excellent discussion of the legal and political problems related to
the question of the "act of state doctrine" in particular, and of territorial
supremacy as a concept in general, see Kenneth S. Carlston, *Law and Organization in World Society* (Urbana, Ill., 1962), 191-93, 266-69. Also, for a discussion of the problem in a larger framework, see Falk, *Role of the Domestic
Courts.* Since World War II, states, especially on the European continent,
have found increasingly broader bases to invalidate the effect of foreign laws.
Traditionally, states have refused to give validity to the laws of other lands for
a small number of narrowly constructed reasons (e.g., refusal to enforce penal
or revenue laws). Today many states have declared foreign laws invalid for a
variety of reasons, the most important being the formulation that the national
court cannot give validity to a foreign law that is illegal in terms of international law (see *"The Rose Mary Case," International Law Report* [1953],
316ff.), and the most frequent being a broad interpretation of "sense of public
order" (see Martin Domke, "Indonesian Nationalization Measures Before Foreign Courts," *American Journal of International Law,* LIV [April 1960], 305-
23). The most recent case in American practice, the *Sabbatino* decision
(Supplement, *International Legal Materials,* III, No. 2 [March 1964], 391),
appears to reaffirm the traditional emphasis on the territorial supremacy of the
national legal order in these matters, but is actually ambiguous. On the one
hand, the Opinion of the Court applied the "act of state doctrine" in declaring the Cuban law valid, but on the other hand, the Court stated that "international law does not require application of the doctrine."

interpreted as a movement away from the strictly and clearly defined legal concept of the state that appeared in classical international law.

Other developments in contemporary international law represent, theoretically at least, a challenge to the assumption that the state and its freedom of action are an absolute necessity for the state system. Most noticeable has been the attempt to develop an international organization which would preserve a minimal degree of order. Prior to the League of Nations, there had been attempts to institutionalize certain aspects of international relations, but such attempts either did not apply to the political behavior of states (e.g., the Universal Postal Union) or did not challenge the basic assumptions of the state system (as the very loosely defined Concert of Europe failed to do). As it was formulated in the Covenant and defined by the intellectuals, the League represented a threat to the assumptions of the state system because it sought to settle once and for all the tension between the policy-maker's commitment to preserve his state and his desire to maintain the state system by subordinating his state to it through a formal institution.

Proponents of the League saw it as a means to formalize a system of maintaining international order by committing states in advance to a coalition against any state that resorted to war without fulfilling the requirements of the Covenant. If it had been operative, such a commitment would have represented a total revolution in the legal concept of the state as an independent entity, since it would have abolished the most essential of all sovereign prerogatives, the freedom to employ coercion. However, the ideal purpose of the League, on the one hand, and the aims of politicians and the actual constitutional and operational aspects of the League, on the other, proved to be quite different. Owing to certain legal formulations within the Covenant (Articles 10, 15, 21) and the subsequent application of the principles (e.g., in Manchuria and Ethiopia), the hoped-for subordination of the state to the system was not realized.[42]

Like the League, the United Nations was to replace the state as the paramount institutional value by establishing a constitutional concert of powers. However, it has succeeded only in underscoring the existing tension between the drive to maintain the state and the goal of maintaining the system. In the Charter itself, the tension between

---

[42] For a useful discussion of the relationship between the idea of collective security and the assumption of the balance of power system, see Inis L. Claude, *Swords into Plowshares* (New York 1962), 255-60; and Herz, chap. 5. It is necessary to make a distinction between the theory of collective security, which certainly would challenge the basic assumptions of the state system, and its operation, which would not.

the state and the system remains unresolved.[43] Nor does the actual operation of the United Nations provide a very optimistic basis for the hope that tension will be lessened in the future.

In terms of international law, regional organizations constitute a mixed challenge to the traditional relationship between the state and the system. Although certain organizations represent an attempt to transcend the traditional bounds of their constituent members on functional grounds, this does not necessarily mean that those members have rejected the state as a political form. In reality, if regional organizations represent any transformation at all in the structural relationship between the state and the system, they constitute an attempt to create a bigger and better state, an attempt which is not contrary to the traditional assumptions of the state system. In spite of the fact that some organizations are given supranational power and present a challenge in that sense, most of the organizations are as protective of the sovereign rights of the state as is the United Nations Charter (e. g., the OAS Charter) or are not regional organizations at all, but military alliances.[44]

A more serious challenge, but one somewhat related to the challenge by regional organizations, is the changing relation of the individual to the international legal order. In the classical system, international law clearly relegated the individual to the position of an object of the law. Not the individual, but the state had the rights and duties of the international legal order.[45] This legal formulation was in keeping with the classical emphasis on the sanctity of the state. Today, however, the development of the concepts of human rights, international and regional organizations, and the personal responsibility of policy-makers to a higher law not only limit the scope of legally permissible international action but, more important, limit the traditional autonomy of the leaders of the state over internal matters.[46] The idea that the individual rather than the state is the

43 Compare Articles 25-51, or paragraphs 2-7 in Article 2, for the contrast between system-oriented and state-oriented norms.

44 This is not to say that regional organizations do not represent a challenge to the concept of the state on psychological or social grounds. Obviously, the type of allegiance to a United Europe would be different in kind and degree from the traditional allegiance to a European state. However, in terms of the challenge to the legal concept of the state, regional organizations still adhere to the idea that the constituent members are sovereign in their relationship with states outside the organization.

45 See Corbett, 53-56, for a discussion of the place of the individual in classical international law.

46 Most modern writers have noted that the individual no longer stands in relation to international law solely as the object (e.g., Corbett, 133-35, or Friedmann, 1160-62), though they are agreed that, to use Friedmann's words, "the rights of the individual in international law are as yet fragmentary and uncertain."

unit of responsibility in the formulation of policy has a long intellectual tradition;[47] however, it is only recently that the norms associated with that idea have become a part of international law.

Although the role of the individual in international law is small and the chances for its rapid development in the near future slight, it represents a more vital challenge to traditional international law and to the assumptions of the state system than either international or regional organizations. Since the principle of collective responsibility (of the state) rather than individual responsibility has traditionally served as the infrastructure for the rights and duties of states,[48] the development of a place for the individual in the international legal system that would make him personally responsible would completely revolutionize international law. At the same time, by making the individual a higher point of policy reference than the state, the development of the role of the individual represents a challenge to the assumption once reflected in classical international law that the preservation and maximization of state power is an absolute guideline for policy-makers. The evolving place of the individual in the contemporary international legal system, then, is contrary to the traditional tendency of international law to reaffirm the absolute value of the state.

THE CHALLENGE TO THE CONCEPT OF POWER

One of the most significant developments in international law today relates to the assumption that states do and should compete for power. In the classical period, international law, through the legal concepts of neutrality, rules of warfare, occupation of new lands, rules of the high seas, and laws of diplomacy, reinforced the idea that a struggle for power among states was normal and necessary. Today, many of these specific legal norms still apply, but the overall permissible range of the struggle for military power[49] has been limited by the concept of the just war.

The idea of the just war is not new to international law. Most of the classical writers discussed it, but they refused to define the con-

[47] According to Guido de Ruggiero, *The History of European Liberalism* (Boston 1959), 363-70, the liberal conception of the state has always assumed that the individual was the absolute value, though this idea has not always been operative.

[48] For an excellent discussion of the role of collective responsibility in international law, see Hans Kelsen, *Principles of International Law* (New York 1959), 9-13, 114-48.

[49] Although the military struggle today is considered to be only one aspect of the struggle for power, it is the one most closely related to the problem of order in both the classical and the contemporary system, and therefore the most crucial in the relationship between law and politics.

cept in strict legal terms and usually relegated it to the moral or ethical realm.[50] The nineteenth-century positivists completely abandoned the doctrine with the formulation that "wars between nations must be considered as just on both sides with respect to treatment of enemies, military arrangements, and peace."[51] However, with the increased capability of states to destroy each other, a movement has grown to regulate force by legal means.

This movement developed through the Hague Conventions and the League of Nations and, in some respects, culminated in the Kellogg-Briand Pact of 1928. Today, the just war is a more or less accepted concept in international law. Most authors write, and most policy-makers state, that aggression is illegal and must be met with the sanction of the international community. The portent of this formulation of the assumption regarding power is great since, theoretically at least, it deprives the states of the range of action which they once freely enjoyed in maximizing their power and in protecting themselves. If the only legal justification for war is self-defense, or authorization of action in accordance with the Charter of the United Nations,[52] then a war to preserve the balance of power or to expand in a limited fashion is outlawed. While the traditional formulation of international law provided a broad field upon which the game of power politics could be played, the new formulations concerning the legal use of force significantly limit and, one could argue, make illegal the military aspects of the game of power politics.[53] The freedom to use military power, once an essential characteristic of sovereignty and an integral part of international law, is no longer an accepted international legal norm.

The concept of the just war directly challenges the assumptions of the state system, because it implies that the military struggle for

[50] See D. W. Bowett, *Self-Defense in International Law* (Manchester 1958), 156-57; and Nussbaum, 137, 153-55, 171.

[51] See Nussbaum, 182-83. Also see Ian Brownlie, *International Law and the Use of Force by States* (Oxford 1963), 15-18.

[52] Actually, the range of action provided by the contemporary formulation, especially regarding the authorization in accordance with the United Nations Charter, could be broad and could conceivably take in "balancing" action if the deadlock in the Security Council were broken. The reason for this is the very ambiguous mandate for Security Council action spelled out in the Charter. It is possible under this mandate to call the limited "balancing" action, typical of the eighteenth century, an action taken to counter a "threat to the peace." Nonetheless, given the current stalemate within the Security Council, and the nature of the General Assembly actions to date, it is safe to conclude that contemporary international law has greatly limited the wide-ranging legal capacity that states once had in deciding on the use of force.

[53] See Brownlie, 251-80, for a discussion of the contemporary legal restrictions on the use of force. Also see Kaplan and Katzenbach, 205, for a discussion of the just-war doctrine and its compatibility with the balance of power system.

power is no longer a normal process of international politics. No longer does international law legitimize the gains of war, and no longer do policy-makers look upon war as a rightful tool of national power.[54] This is not to say that states do not use force in their current struggles or that the doctrine of the just war would deter them in a particular case. However, the doctrine does operate on the conceptual level by expressing to the policy-makers the idea that the use of force is no longer an everyday tool of international power politics. In terms of the traditional assumption about the state's natural inclination to maximize power, the contemporary legal commitment to the just-war doctrine represents a profound and historic shift.

III. International Law and the Reality of Contemporary International Politics

Contemporary international legal practice, then, is developing along lines which represent a threat not only to traditional concepts of international law but also to the assumptions of the state system. The sporadic developments in international and regional organizations, the evolving place of the individual in the international legal system, and the doctrine of the just war are manifestations of the transformation occurring today both in the structure of international law and in attitudes about the state system. Actually, of course, the traditional conceptions of international law and the classical assumptions about international politics are not extinct.[55] Rather, there is in both international law and politics a perplexing mixture of past ideas and current developments. The only thing one can be sure of is that behind the traditional legal and political symbols which exist today in a somewhat mutated form, a subtle transformation of some kind is taking place.

It is not possible to evaluate the line of future development of the assumptions about the state system or the international legal expression of those assumptions from the work of contemporary theorists of international law. The most apparent new expressions are those

---

[54] Certainly, technological developments have been primarily responsible for the rejection of war as a typical tool of international power. In this case, as in most, international legal doctrine mirrors the existing attitudes and helps to reinforce them.

[55] As in the past, international lawyers are still concerned with definitions and applications of concepts of territorial integrity, self-defense, and domestic jurisdiction, and policy-makers are still motivated by the traditional ideas of state security and power. However, the traditional political and legal symbols have been "stretched" to apply to current conditions. For a development of this position see Coplin, chaps. 4 and 8.

that propose increased formalizations of world legal and political processes.[56] On the other hand, much international legal theory today seems to be dedicated to an affirmation of the traditional assumptions of international politics. Political analysts like Hans Morgenthau,[57] E. H. Carr,[58] and George F. Kennan, [59] and legal theorists like Julius Stone,[60] P. E. Corbett,[61] and Charles De Visscher,[62] are predisposed to "bring international law back to reality."

This trend toward being "realistic" occupies the mainstream of current international legal theory,[63] and to identify its exact nature is therefore crucial. Many writers who express this viewpoint seem to fear being labeled as overly "idealistic." They utter frequent warnings that international law cannot restore international politics to order,

[56] E.g., Arthur Larson, *When Nations Disagree* (Baton Rouge, La., 1961); or Grenville Clark and Louis B. Sohn, *World Peace Through World Law* (Cambridge, Mass., 1960). These theorists and others who fall under this classification are "radical" in the sense that what they suggest is antithetical to the assumptions of the state system as traditionally developed. These writers are not necessarily utopian in their radicalism. This is especially true since adherence today to the traditional assumptions might itself be considered a form of (reactionary) radicalism. However, the radical scholars, in the sense used here, are very scarce, especially among American students of international law. Today there is a very thin line separating the few radical scholars from the more numerous radical polemicists of world government.

[57] Morgenthau writes (277): "To recognize that international law exists is, however, not tantamount to assessing that . . . it is effective in regulating and restraining the struggle for power on the international scene."

[58] E. H. Carr, in *The Twenty Years' Crisis, 1919-1939* (London 1958), 170, writes: "We are exhorted to establish 'the rule of law' . . . and the assumption is made that, by so doing, we shall transfer our differences from the turbulent political atmosphere of self-interest to the purer, serener air of impartial justice." His subsequent analysis is designed to disprove this assumption.

[59] George F. Kennan, *Realities of American Foreign Policy* (Princeton 1954), 16.

[60] Julius Stone, *Legal Control of International Conflict* (New York 1954), introduction.

[61] Corbett, 68-79, 291-92.

[62] De Visscher writes (xiv): "International law cannot gather strength by isolating itself from the political realities with which international relations are everywhere impregnated. It can only do so by taking full account of the place that these realities occupy and measuring the obstacle which they present."

[63] The programs of the last two annual meetings of the American Society of International Law exemplify the way in which the concern for reality (as power) has come to dominate international legal theory. In the 1963 program, the relationship between international law and the use of force was not discussed by international legal theorists but by two well-known writers on the role of conflict in international politics. The 1964 program manifested the same tendency. It centered on the question of compliance with transnational law, a topic treated in a sociopolitical framework by most panelists. This point is not to be taken as a criticism of the two programs, both of which were excellent and very relevant, but as proof of the assertion that the mainstream of contemporary theory of international law is significantly oriented to the role of power.

but, on the contrary, can exist and flourish only after there is a political agreement among states to maintain order. In short, it is assumed that international law cannot shape international political reality, but can merely adjust to it. Although there are complaints of too much pessimism in current legal theory,[64] most writers, given the initial predisposition to avoid "idealism," do not heed them.

The desire of contemporary theorists to be "realistic" has been crucial to the relationship between contemporary international law and the assumptions of the state system. In their effort to achieve realism, current theorists have not examined their traditional assumptions about international politics. When they talk about adjusting international law to the realities of power, they usually have in mind the traditional reality of international politics. Today, a large share of the theoretical writing on international law that is designed to adapt law to political reality itself is rapidly becoming outmoded. Much contemporary international legal theory, then, has not contributed to the development of a new consensus on the nature of international politics but instead has reinforced many of the traditional ideas.

In order to understand more fully the relation of international law to world politics, it is necessary to do more than examine law merely as a direct constraint on political action. The changes in the conceptual basis of international law that are manifested in current practice and, to a lesser extent, in current legal theory are symptomatic of a series of social and institutional revolutions that are transforming all of international politics. To conclude that international law must adjust to political reality, therefore, is to miss the point, since international law is part of political reality and serves as an institutional means of developing and reflecting a general consensus on the nature of international reality. In the contemporary period, where the international legal system is relatively decentralized, and international politics is subject to rapid and profound development, it is necessary to avoid a conceptual framework of international law which breeds undue pessimism because it demands too much. If international law

---

[64] Many writers, even realists like Morgenthau (*op.cit.*, 275) and others like McDougal and Feliciano (*op.cit.*, 2-4), decry the modern tendency toward "cynical disenchantment with law," but it is obvious from their subsequent remarks that they are reacting more against the "utopianism" of the past than the cynicism of the present. There have been a few who have attacked the "realist" position on international law (e.g., A. H. Feller, "In Defense of International Law and Morality," *Annals of the Academy of Political and Social Science*, vol. 282 [July 1951], 77-84). However, these attacks have been infrequent and generally ineffective in starting a concerted action to develop more constructive theory. For another evaluation of the "realist" trend, see Covey T. Oliver, "Thoughts on Two Recent Events Affecting the Function of Law in the International Community," in George A. Lipsky, ed., *Law and Politics in the World Community* (Berkeley 1953).

does not contribute directly and effectively to world order by forcing states to be peaceful, it does prepare the conceptual ground on which that order could be built by shaping attitudes about the nature and promise of international political reality.

2. BRINGING LAW TO BEAR ON GOVERNMENTS

By ROGER FISHER

IT has long been suggested that nations could adjust their conflicts of interest amicably and live in peace forever if they would
only conform their conduct to international law. As the world situation has become more explosive, the prospect of a world under law
has become more fashionable and there is increasing talk of the
"rule of law." But much of the arguments for extending the rule of
law to international relations remains "on an inspirational and
rhetorical level that does not permit underlying difficulties to come to
the surface."[1] While the Senate considers repeal of the Connally
amendment,[2] by which the United States reserved the right to decide
independently whether a dispute concerning itself was within the
jurisdiction of the International Court of Justice, discussion of an
international order is pursued with renewed vigor. It is important
that this discussion be approached realistically, with an eye to what
is now possible, and not lose itself in references to a distant goal.
For any decision on the Connally amendment must deal with an issue
which may well be called *the* problem of international law: why
governments comply with law.

Most lawyers hold in common a view of international law which
runs somewhat as follows: There is a great difference between
positive law—law with a policeman behind it—and so-called international law. International law is a body of vague rules for the attention of the political scientist and the amusement of the law student

This paper is a revised version of a talk given at Boston University Law
School on November 17, 1960. Reprinted by permission of the author and *The
Harvard Law Review*, 74, 1130-1140 (1961). Copyright 1961 by The Harvard
Law Review Association.

[1] Fuller, *The Forms and Limits of Adjudication* 18 (limited pub., 1959).
[2] Declaration by the President of the United States of America, August 14,
1946, Respecting Recognition by the United States of America of the Compulsory Jurisdiction of the International Court of Justice, para. 2(b), 61 Stat.
1218, T.I.A.S. No. 1598.

not much interested in law. It should not be confused with real law, which, as Mr. Justice Holmes pointed out, is "the articulate voice of some sovereign or quasi-sovereign that can be identified,"[3] and "does not exist without some definite authority behind it."[4] Law is the command of a sovereign backed by force. And however much it is hoped that nations will abide by acknowledged rules some day, they do not now; nor can they ever be compelled to do so, at least in the absence of world government. Only woolly thinking would confuse positive law enforced by our courts—our Constitution, our civil and criminal laws—with the moral directives which go by the name of international law.

So runs the party line of the profession.[5] But Holmes, who was one of its ardent supporters, also commended to us a "reconsideration of the worth of doctrines which for the most part still are taken for granted without any deliberate, conscious, and systematic questioning of their grounds."[6] He would surely approve the reappraisal of accepted doctrines in the light of a developing understanding. It is time to ask ourselves whether the notion of law as the command of a sovereign is a useful one for the solution of problems of international order.

We are interested in why governments comply with law, why they comply with court decisions. The process by which domestic law is brought to bear upon governments may have general application and be relevant to the international problem. The command theory of law, which was used to distinguish the law that *is* from the law that *ought to be,* was evidently developed out of an examination of the typical private action for a tort or on a contract. If a court declared that Doe must pay Roe a stated amount, the sheriff and the marshall stood ready to enforce the judgment with the full power of the state. This was the situation envisioned by Austin when he spoke of laws as commands. His definition of law did not apply to rules restraining the behavior of the state itself which Austin referred to as rules of "positive morality."[7] The "power of the government," he said, "is incapable of *legal* limitation."[8] It followed that a government had neither legal rights nor legal duties.

A sovereign government . . . may appear in the character of defendant, or may appear in the character of demandant, before a tribunal

---

[3] Southern Pac. Co. v. Jensen, 244 U.S. 205, 222 (1917) (dissenting opinion).
[4] Black & White Taxicab & Transfer Co. v. Brown & Yellow Taxicab & Transfer Co., 276 U.S. 518, 533 (1928) (dissenting opinion).
[5] See, *e.g.,* Briggs, *The Cloudy Prospects for 'Peace Through Law,"* 46 A.B.A.J. 490 (1960).
[6] Holmes, *The Path of the Law,* 10 Harv. L. Rev. 457, 468 (1897).
[7] I Austin, *Jurisprudence* 267-71 (5th ed. 1885).
[8] *Id.* at 263.

of its own appointment, or deriving jurisdiction from itself. But from such an appearance of a sovereign government, we cannot infer that the government lies under legal duties, or has legal rights against its own subjects.[9]

Within such a theory, international law is clearly no more than positive morality. But much of the modern law school curriculum besides international law would have to be similarly characterized. Courses in constitutional law, administrative law, and tax law, to name only a few, deal in large part with limitations on governmental action or involve the Government as a party to a dispute in courts deriving jurisdiction from itself. More than sixty per cent of the cases in which the Supreme Court handed down opinions during its 1959 Term adjudicated rights and duties of the federal government.[10] We can suspect that a definition of law which excludes so much may not be useful today.

But we are not concerned here with a mere matter of definition. Whether or not we are content to call all these areas of law "positive morality," the fact remains that a large part of our courts' work lies in these very areas. Whether or not governments are theoretically capable of legal limitation, they do regularly submit to adverse court decisions. I suggest that we lawyers, in uncritically accepting the command theory and applying it to international law have ourselves been guilty of woolly thinking. I suggest that in denying the status of international law because there is no apparent sovereign issuing the commands, we show a limited understanding of how a court system operates in its relations with a government. In blandly assuming that all law rests on superior force, we have ignored the cases in which the government loses a judgment and honors it.

Is organized force essential to such compliance? Clearly it is not. When a judgment is entered against the United States in the Court of Claims, no superior sovereign compels Congress to vote an appropriation. The judgment is paid because that is the law; but the law is not the articulate voice of a superior sovereign. When, in the *Youngstown* case,[11] the Supreme Court ordered the Secretary of Commerce to return the steel mills which the President had ordered him to seize, the Court had no regiments at its command. But despite the fact that the Supreme Court sitting in Washington had no greater force at its command vis-àvis the Government than does the International Court of Justice sitting at the Hague, the steel mills were returned.

[9] *Id.* at 287–88.
[10] See *The Supreme Court, 1959 Term,* 74 Harv. L. Rev. 81, Table III (1960).
[11] Youngstown Sheet & Tube Co. v. Sawyer, 343 U.S. 579 (1952).

The more closely one examines law within this country and within others, the less significant seems the element of force. Even such hard, positive laws as the criminal and tax laws depend ultimately on compliance with them by the Government, and the general pattern is one of compliance. To be sure, Congress on perhaps a dozen occasions, has failed to honor a judgment of the Court of Claims.[12] But the Government, which is never without funds or absent from the jurisdiction, has a far better record than the private judgment debtor. This record, even if less than perfect, demonstrates that a pattern of governmental compliance can be secured without a supragovernmental police force.

Moreover, even where the organized force of a superior sovereign is available it may be difficult to make a government comply. If a government is not persuaded to obey by other reasons, superior force alone may not be enough. In *Virginia v. West Virginia*[13] the Supreme Court had before it the continuing failure of the West Virginia legislature to raise and appropriate the funds needed to pay Virginia that share of its public debt which West Virginia had undertaken upon becoming a separate state. Assuming that the United States Army was at the Court's disposal, what should the Army do to enforce the judgment? Should it seize the state capitol and sell it at auction? Should it raise funds at the point of a gun? If so, from whom? However effective force or the threat of force may be when applied to an individual, it is difficult to bring force to bear on a political enterprise which offers no obvious point of application.[14] So long as a rule runs only to a political entity rather than to individuals, a superior power must face the problem of trying to apply force to an abstraction.

If it is not the threat of force which induces governmental compliance with domestic law, it is not the absence of force which explains why our Government feels less strongly bound by international law than, for example, by the Constitution. Nor does an explanation lie in the fact that international rules are generically more vague than constitutional rules. They are not. Nor can we look for an answer in our Government's denying the binding nature of international law. It does not. Nor is an answer to be found in the assumption that the Government will comply more readily with rules benefiting citizens than with those benefiting foreigners. The due process clause protects citizen and alien alike.

What is the difference, then, between a judgment of the Court of Claims and a judgment of the International Court? Is it merely that

[12] See Note, 46 Harv. L. Rev. 677, 685–86 n.63 (1933).
[13] 246 U.S. 565 (1918).
[14] The West Virginia controversy was settled by the party states. See W. Va. Acts Ext. Sess. 1919, ch. 10, at 19.

the United States accepted the jurisdiction of the former one hundred years ago and has not yet really accepted the jurisdiction of the latter? The question is worth exploring. An understanding of the factors inducing governmental obedience to domestic law may shed light on the problem of securing obedience to international law. We should not expect to find factors that guarantee obedience. Governments do not always obey rules. In a given case, what are considered vital interests may lead a government to break the law just as they may persuade an individual to steal. The question, rather, is: What are the forces which tend to induce obedience, the elements which impart strength to the law? Knowing that these elements are in fact strong enough to bring about general governmental compliance with domestic law, we will want to appraise their ability to bring about governmental compliance with international law.

In considering whether to respect a rule, one factor which a government takes into account is the danger of external consequences should it not respect the rule. Even where there is no organized superior sovereign power to compel obedience, a government is not free to ignore the conduct and attitudes of those with whom it must deal. The United States Government, considered as an entity, respects the Constitution partly because it fears the retaliatory action which might be taken by the citizens if it did not. A focal point for such retaliation might be the polls. And the Government respects the right to vote, influenced in part, perhaps, by fear of more violent action if it were denied.

Internationally, the most significant forces external to a government are not its own citizens but other nations. Before a government decides to break a rule of international law, it must consider the possible reaction of other states. It is not only the immediate reaction of the states most affected by the breach that is relevant; the effect on what may be called world public opinion must also be considered. Thus, should the United States consider resumption of espionage flights over the Soviet Union in violation of Soviet and international law, an intelligent decision could not ignore three factors external to the government: (1) political criticism within the United States; (2) the possibility of direct retaliation by the Soviet Union; and (3) the likelihood of an adverse reaction among our allies and the uncommitted nations. These considerations are analogous to those which an individual must weigh before deciding to disregard domestic law. Although they do not result from the organized will of a superior sovereign, they are not wholly unpredictable and arbitrary. There are rules about punishing rule-breakers; an injured state cannot engage in excessive retaliation without itself weighing the consequences.

Some rules of international law have long been maintained largely by the pressure of these external forces. If the Soviet Union catches a foreign diplomat photographing military installations in violation of Soviet law, he is not punished, but rather is declared *persona non grata* and politely asked to leave the country. Presumably, a major factor inducing this respect for the international rule of diplomatic immunity is the desire of the Soviet government for similar treatment of its diplomats by other countries. Similarly, in the arms-control field, one force—in many cases, the most important force—causing a country to respect a treaty or other form of restraint is apprehension of the various external consequences of not respecting it. Such apprehension keeps limited wars limited. It is a force that can be used to cause respect for rules limiting preparation for war.

In addition to these pressures from outside, there are internal forces influencing government action. One of these is comparable to that which supports individual respect for law. Man is by and large a moral creature who is usually anxious to believe that what he does is not only practical but right. Individual moral standards may differ, but it is nonetheless true that each of us is influenced by his idea of what he ought to do. An individual will frequently respect a rule simply because he believes that the rule ought to be respected, without appraising his chances of being caught and without a Machiavellian weighing of the pros and cons.

A government is made up of such individuals, and this fact tends to cause governmental respect for law. The strength of this moral force depends on matters of both procedure and substance. It depends on how the rule was established, including such things as the solemnity with which the obligation to respect it was assumed. It depends also on the degree to which the rule coincides with the moral views of the individual officials in the government affected. A rule against assassination of foreign officials might be respected for reasons going beyond a cold calculation of the consequences. On the other hand, rules requiring the officials of one country to inform on their colleagues might be broken because of moral scruples despite a recognized theoretical advantage in compliance.

These pressures from possible external consequences and from internal morality which induce governmental conformity to rules are comparable to those affecting individual behavior. But there are special internal factors which operate on a government which are either not present or are insignificant in the case of an individual. These are at the heart of our problem.

First, a government is an institution which is dedicated to promoting respect for law. In the domestic sphere a government recognizes that rules are necessary for the avoidance of collisions of interest and that it has an affirmative stake in the creation and maintenance of law. But this law-creating and law-maintaining function is less well recognized in the international field. In the United States, the chief legal officer concerned with domestic law, the Attorney General, conceives of his job as the promotion of law and justice. In contrast, the comparable official concerned with international law, the Legal Adviser to the State Department, has rarely considered his job in that light. He has seen himself not as an "Assistant Secretary for International Law," whose job is to promote law in the international area, but rather as a kind of house counsel, whose function is to keep the Department out of trouble.

But whatever views particular officials may have of their offices, it is clear that all governments undertake to create and maintain a legal order. One way to promote such an order is for the government itself to respect laws applicable to it. To the extent (but only to the extent) that a government recognizes that its long-run interests require it to promote a legal order in the international arena, such recognition will tend to create respect for international rules as a means of fulfilling that objective.

A second consideration which is peculiarly applicable to governments is that they have a greater interest in the fair and wise settlement of disputes than in advancing their immediate financial or institutional position. Until 1863, when Congress empowered the Court of Claims to enter judgments against the United States,[15] the Government could "win" every case simply by congressional failure to vote a private bill. But it was perceived, however dimly,[16] that to win any

[15] Act of March 3, 1863, ch. 92, 12 Stat. 765 (now 28 U.S.C. §§ 1491–1505 (1958)).

[16] A tie vote in the Senate was broken by the Vice-President. Views uttered by opponents of the Court of Claims are strangely similar to those uttered today by opponents of the International Court of Justice. Senator Hale of New Hampshire prefaced his remarks by declaring:

> I think, sir, when some future Gibbon shall write the history of the decline and fall of the great Republic, and shall give the indications which marked its progress to decay, one of them will be that about the year of grace 1863 the Thirty-Seventh Congress took it into their head that they were wiser than everybody that went before them, and departed from all the precedents established by their fathers, and started out on new, untried, and extravagant theories and notions.

He went on to object:

> But, sir, we are going to give this new Court of Claims power that we have denied and that our fathers have denied always to any and every Court . . .

CONG. GLOBE, 37th Cong., 3d Sess. 310 (1863).

particular case was less important for the Government than to resolve all cases by a demonstrably fair means. Decisions based on executive or legislative discretion must always be justified on the merits; a claim that has been three times rejected may have to be reconsidered. And the possibility of discrimination is great. But if a private claim is determined according to judicial procedure—if it has had its day in court—the Government is protected from political criticism, whether the criticism is that the claim should or should not have been paid. In some respects a judicial decision is like an administrative decision. The government has referred a question of policy to persons qualified to decide it. And having obtained a decision, the government follows it simply because the decision has been made, for reasons not unlike those which cause it to follow a decision of, say, the Secretary of Agriculture.

The political interests of a government may in some cases be particularly well served when the decision is against the government. The judicial process may enable the government to lose an argument gracefully and according to principle. Responsibility for an unpopular but necessary action can often be passed to the courts and immunized from partisan attack. A judicial decision may provide the executive with a good excuse for doing what it would have to do anyway.

These considerations might well apply to decisions of an international court. The international interests of a government may be advanced more by having a matter decided fairly than by refusing to concede the point involved. If the status of China in the United Nations could be submitted to the International Court, a sensible solution might be achieved with far less disadvantage to the United States than would be involved either in abandoning a tenaciously held position under political pressure or in indefinitely prolonging an unsatisfactory situation. Similarly, although the Guantanamo Naval Base may be secure for the present, it is clear that the United States could not insist forever on maintaining a military base against the wishes of the local government. Eventually this country might be better served by abandoning its Cuban base pursuant to an order of an international tribunal, which might provide for the removal of property and payments by the Cuban government, than by lingering on until pushed out by other means. Thus, internationally as well as domestically, situations may arise in which compliance with law is not coerced but proceeds directly from self-interest.

There is a final and significant way in which a government's reasons for complying with rules of law differ from those of an individual. A government is a complex structure comprising a great many individuals, a structure which depends for its very existence on respect for rules. Every individual in the government has many rules applicable to him. Some of these rules demand obedience to superiors. But others, which in the United States include the Constitution and statutes, lay down substantive law. These latter speak not merely to the Government as a whole; they speak also to individual officials and are regarded by each of them as being binding directly upon him. Thus, it is a risky business for a superior to direct his subordinates to disregard a particular rule. Each subordinate will be subjected to conflicting pressures and there is no guaranty of the result. A high official cannot command the breaking of rules without undermining respect for rules generally. And it is upon obedience to rules that his authority to command depends.

This analysis applies to any government. The situation in the Congo vividly attests the weakness of governments whose officials do not respect law. In sharp contrast, the government of the Soviet Union is highly organized and rule-respecting. It is a mistake to think of that government as lawless, and commanding obedience from its officials only at the point of a pistol. No one is holding a pistol to the head of the man who holds the pistol; that man is complying with rules.

Once a rule has become intertwined in the governmental fabric the government is no longer free to ignore it. Once subordinate officials recognize a particular legal rule as being just as binding upon them as is the concept of obedience to the orders of their superior, it will be difficult for the government to ignore that rule. In the United States, rules created by treaty or executive agreement are thought to be binding on officials only through the presidential chain of command. If the President directs disregard of a treaty obligation, subordinate officials tend to think of that as a matter for his decision alone, and, therefore, tend to respect the decision he has reached. If the treaty obligation were incorporated into a statute or constitutional amendment, the President and the Government as a whole would find the treaty far more difficult to ignore. Such action would require a collective decision to break one rule while respecting another.

One can see how such a procedure might operate even in the arms-control field. Should a treaty provide for the abolition of nuclear stockpiles the most complete inspection system that could be devised would be inadequate to guarantee that no weapons remained hidden. But it might be possible to create a structure of rules within each country that would satisfy other countries that there was no evasion of the agreement. The treaty obligation might be incorporated into the national constitutions. The citizens of each country might constantly be reminded by public notices and official speeches that it was their individual duty to notify United Nations officers of any hidden weapons. Rewards might be offered to those who discovered weapons and punishment threatened to those who concealed them. With such a massive effort to develop rules recognized as personally binding by a great number of people, each government would have created significant forces supporting compliance with the international obligation. In addition to the risks of retaliation and adverse world reaction due to the likelihood of detection under such circumstances, it might be difficult to bring about a governmental decision to act against officially declared government policy.

No absolute guaranty can be given that a government will always respect a rule. We have no guaranty that our Government will always respect the Constitution or the decisions of the Supreme Court. But by seeking to understand why governments so generally obey domestic law, we shall be better able to undertake the task of securing respect for international law. Current efforts to deal with pressing international issues, such as the jurisdiction of the International Court and the arms race, are being hamstrung by antiquated dogma about what law is and by an insufficient realization of why governments comply with it. No more in the international than in the domestic sphere should the argument be heard that governments must be lawless because they cannot be coerced.

Great! Why is a G more lawless i'lly than domestically? It isn't
why do G's obey domestic l?

3. THE PEACE OF WESTPHALIA, 1648–1948

By LEO GROSS

THE acceptance of the United Nations Charter by the overwhelming majority of the members of the family of nations brings to mind the first great European or world charter, the Peace of Westphalia. To it is traditionally attributed the importance and dignity of being the first of several attempts to establish something resembling world unity on the basis of states exercising untrammeled sovereignty over certain territories and subordinated to no earthly authority.

The next attempt, the settlement of Vienna of 1815 and the Congress of Aix-la-Chapelle of 1818, which in a sense completed the former, gave birth to that loose system of consultation between the Great Powers known as the Concert of Europe. Born of the cataclysm of the Napoleonic Wars and anchored in the Protocol of the Aix-la-Chapelle of November 15, 1818, the Concert provided some sort of a self-appointed directing body for the maintenance and manipulation of that balance of power on which the European peace precariously reposed for about a hundred years. Uncertain in its foundations, devoid of much organization or continuity, it was characterized as much by the devotion of the Great Powers which composed it to the policy of a free hand as it was, in consequence, by the absence of definite commitments. Consultation and conference on problems of mutual interest was a frequent practice but no obligation of the Great Powers. It was precisely this flexibility, frequently regarded and praised as the chief virtue of the concert system, which ultimately brought about its ruin at a moment when it was most desperately needed. The policy of free hands reaped a large harvest in World War I.

Faced with the devastating results of World War I and the bankruptcy of the Concert, the Paris Settlement of 1919, without essentially departing from the Peace of Westphalia, attempted a novel solution, drawing for its inspiration on the Concert, the Hague Peace Conferences, the experience of the nineteenth and twentieth centuries

Reprinted by permission of the author and *The American Journal of International Law,* 53, 1-29 (1959).

in non-political international collaboration, and the wartime collaboration between the Allied and Associated Powers. It produced the League of Nations, in which the member states assumed certain commitments to coöperate in various fields and, above all, without abolishing the right of war, *jus ad bellum,* to establish "the undertakings of international law as the actual rule of conduct among governments." It is a moot question whether the failure of the League should be attributed to a defective legal technique in organizing international security or to a kind of fatal and gradual relapse of the Great Powers into the traditional methods of consultation untrammeled by and frequently in open disregard of their obligations under the Covenant. The climax in this process of degeneration was reached in 1939 when alliances were hurriedly tossed around and when Poland, though attacked by Germany on September 1, 1939, found it convenient to manifest its contempt of the League of Nations by not even appealing to it under Article 10 of the Covenant, and when Great Britain and France went to the assistance of Poland not because they were legally bound to do so by the Covenant but because they felt in honor bound to fulfill their obligations as allies in Poland. Thus World War II started in the customary way, even as if the League were non-existent; as a consequence the League was doomed.

Critics of the United Nations Charter point out that it includes some of the elements of the League organization and that it relies even more heavily than did the League on the notion of consultation, on limited obligations in the political, and the method of voluntary coöperation in the non-political, field. The Charter proclaims that the organization is based on the sovereign equality of all the members only in order the firmer to establish the hegemony of a group of Great Powers. On the other hand, in Articles 24 and 25, the principal framers of the Charter almost obtained what the Concert never succeeded in obtaining, namely, the recognition by the lesser nations of the preëminent position of the Great Powers as the guardians of international peace and security. In spite of this and other important indications of a new approach to the problem of international security and relations, the Charter at first glance would seem to have left essentially unchanged the framework of the state system and of international law resulting from the Peace of Westphalia.

Thus the Peace of Westphalia may be said to continue its sway over political man's mind as the *ratio scripta* that it was held to be of yore. What is the explanation of this curious phenomenon? In view of this continued influence of the Peace of Westphalia, it may not be amiss to discuss briefly its character, background and implications.

It should be clear from the outset that the actual provisions of the Treaties of Osnabrück between the Empire and Sweden, and of

Münster between the Empire and France and their respective confederates and allies, have undergone more than one substantial change in the course of time. The political map of Europe as outlined in these Treaties is no longer. It should be noted, however, that the chief political idea underlying the Franco-German settlement of 1648 has undergone relatively little change. Then the axiom of French politics was, as it appears to be today, that the best guarantee of French security lies in a divided and impotent Germany, and that this division and impotence must be secured by appropriate provisions such as those which gave France a right to intervene when necessary in order to vindicate the principle of the sanctity of treaties.

The Thirty Years' War had its origin, at any rate partially, in a religious conflict or, as one might say, in religious intolerance. The Peace of Westphalia consecrated the principle of toleration by establishing the equality between Protestant and Catholic states and by providing some safeguards for religious minorities. To be sure, the principle of liberty of conscience was applied only incompletely and without reciprocity.[1] The religious Peace of Augsburg of 1555 and the rule *cujus regio ejus religio* were confirmed. With a view to alleviating the lot of religious minorities, however, the Treaty of Osnabrück provided that[2] ". . . subjects who in 1627 had been debarred from the free exercise of their religion, other than that of their ruler, were by the Peace granted the right of conducting private worship, and of educating their own children, at home or abroad, in conformity with their own faith; they were not to suffer in any civil capacity nor to be denied religious burial, but were to be at liberty to emigrate, selling their estates or leaving them to be managed by others."

Moreover, in an effort to assure equality between Catholic and Protestant members of the German Diet, the Treaty of Osnabrück laid down the important rule that in matters pertaining to religion[3] ". . . a majority of votes should no longer be held decisive at the Diet; but such questions should be settled by an amicable 'composition' between its two parts or *corpora*. . . . In the same spirit of parity it was agreed that when possible there should be equality of consulting and voting power between the two religions on all commissions of

[1] Sir A. W. Ward, *The Peace of Westphalia,* The Cambridge Modern History, Vol. IV, 1934, p. 416: ". . . the provision made for individual freedom in the exercise of any of the recognized religions was insufficient; and from the dominions of the House of Austria as a whole; Protestant worship was deliberately excluded." But see Yves de la Brière, *La Société des Nations?,* 1918, p. 57.

[2] Ward, work cited, p. 412. See also Andrea Rapisardi Mirabelli, "Les Congres de Westphalie," 8 *Bibliotheca Visseriana* (1929), p. 75.

[3] Ward, work cited, p. 414; Mirabelli, work cited, pp. 13, 76.

the Diet, including those *Deputationstage* which had come to exercise an authority nearly equalling that of the Diets themselves."

The principle of religious equality was placed as part of the peace under an international guarantee.[4] The Peace of Westphalia thereby established a precedent of far-reaching importance. One or two illustrations may be in order. The Constitution of the Germanic Confederation of June 8, 1815, which forms part of the Final Act of the Congress of Vienna of June 9, 1815, stipulates in Article XVI that the difference between the Christian religions should cause no difference in the enjoyment by their adherents of civil and political rights, and, furthermore, that the German Diet should consider the grant of civil rights to Jews on condition that they assume all civic duties incumbent on other citizens.[5] By the time the Congress of Berlin convened the principle of religious tolerance had become so firmly established that the delegate of France, M. Waddington, could make the following statement: [6]

> Mr. Waddington believes that it is important to take advantage of this solemn opportunity to cause the principles of religious liberty to be affirmed by the representatives of Europe. His Excellency adds that Serbia, who claims to enter the European family on the same basis as other states, must previously recognize the principles which are the basis of social organization in all states of Europe and accept them as a necessary condition of the favor which she asks for.

The representatives of Great Britain, Germany, Italy, Austria-Hungary, and of the Ottoman Empire concurred in the view propounded by M. Waddington and the Congress acted accordingly in the case of Serbia, Montenegro, and Rumania.

---

[4] Mirabelli, work cited, p. 13: *Mais une circonstance ultérieure—importante au point de vue international—c'était que le principe de l'égalité des confessions (basé jusqu'alors sur la tolérance des Princes, ou sur des lois révocables) prenait alors la forme d'engagement international, fixé conventionnellement par les traités et pour cela assuré par leur force et leur durée.*

[5] 2 *British and Foreign State Papers*, 1814–1815, p. 132. The Final Act of Vienna and its Annexes include several interesting provisions designed to ensure freedom of religion. A particularly illuminating example is to be found in Article II of the Annex to the Treaty between the King of the Netherlands and Austria of May 31, 1815, which reads: *Il ne sera rien innové aux Articles de cette Constitution qui assurent à tous les Cultes une protection et une faveur égales, et garantissent l'admission de tous les Citoyens, quelle que soit leur croyance religieuse, aux emplois et offices publics.* Work cited, p. 141.

[6] Protocol of June 28, 1878. 69 *British and Foreign State Papers*, 1877–1878, p. 960; English translation from the "Letter addressed to M. Paderewski by the President of the Conference (M. Clemenceau) transmitting to him the Treaty to be signed by Poland under Article 93 of the Treaty of Peace with Germany" of June 24, 1919. 112 *British and Foreign State Papers*, 1919, p. 226. See also George A. Finch, "The International Rights of Man," in this JOURNAL, Vol. 35 (1941), p. 662.

This precedent was relied upon by the Principal Allied and Associated Powers in submitting to Poland the Treaty of June 28, 1919, concerning the protection of minorities. In his covering letter to M. Paderewski, the President of the Paris Peace Conference stated that "This treaty does not constitute any fresh departure," and continued as follows:[7]

It has for long been the established procedure of the public law of Europe that when a state is created, or even when large accessions of territory are made to an established state, the joint and formal recognition by the Great Powers should be accompanied by the requirement that such State should, in the form of a binding international convention, undertake to comply with certain principles of government.

The latest step in this long line of evolution is represented by the United Nations Charter, the Preamble of which declares that the peoples of the United Nations are determined "to reaffirm faith in fundamental human rights, in the dignity and worth of the human person, in the equal rights of men and women, and of nations, large and small," and, "to practice tolerance and live together in peace with one another as good neighbors." It is one of the basic purposes of the United Nations to achieve international coöperation "in promoting and encouraging respect for human rights and for fundamental freedoms for all without distinction as to race, sex, language, or religion." If the efforts of the United Nations are crowned with success by the adoption of an international bill of the fundamental rights of man, they will have accomplished the task which originated in the religious schism of Europe and which had found its first, albeit an inadequate, solution on an international basis in the Peace of Westphalia.

Another aspect of the Peace of Westphalia which exercised considerable influence on future developments relates to the guarantee of the peace itself. Both treaties declare that the peace concluded shall remain in force and that all parties to it "shall be obliged to defend and protect all and every article of this peace against anyone, without distinction of religion."[8] This was by no means a new departure. As Van Vollenhoven pointed out, the promise of guarantee in the treaties of 1648 merely followed earlier precedents.[9] Nevertheless this guarantee of the observance and the execution of an agreed international transaction, including as it did clauses of a constitu-

[7] See letter quoted in the preceding note.
[8] Text from Article CXXIII of the Treaty of Münster, in *A General Collection of Treatys,* Vol. I, 1710, p. 36.
[9] See C. Van Vollenhoven, *The Law of Peace,* 1936, p. 85.

tional character, as far as the Empire was concerned, came to assume in the following decades an overriding significance. It was pointed out that "no guarantee was more important or has been more often referred to than that included in the treaties of Westphalia."[10]

"These treaties contain clauses by which Sweden and France not only make peace with the Emperor on certain terms, but pledge themselves to their allies, the subordinate German Princes, that they will ensure that the privileges and immunities conferred on the Princes and free cities of Germany in the treaty shall be upheld and maintained. This is constantly referred to in later treaties as the guarantee for the execution of the terms of the treaty and, as Sir Ernest Satow has pointed out, it continued to be regarded as valid almost down to the outbreak of the French Revolution. Here, again, the fact of the guarantee was of the highest importance in ensuring that the treaties should be observed and that they should continue to hold their place as part of the general European System."

For the first time Europe thus received "what may fairly be described as an international constitution, which gave to all its adherents the right of intervention to enforce its engagements."[11] That this attempt to guarantee effectively a peace so laboriously achieved was not wholly successful needs hardly to be emphasized.[12] In this respect the Settlement of Westphalia is in good company with many other international instruments of historical importance.

In addition to the guarantee, the Settlement of Westphalia formulated certain extremely interesting rules for the peaceful settlement of disputes and collective sanctions against aggressors. Thus the Treaty of Münster, in Articles CXIII and CXXIV stipulates that[13]

> if it happens that any point should be violated the Offended shall before all things exhort the Offender not to come to any Hostility, submitting the Cause to a friendly Composition, or the ordinary Proceedings of Justice. Nevertheless, if for the space of three years the Difference cannot be terminated, by any of those means, all and every one of those concern'd in this Transaction shall be oblig'd to join the injur'd Party, and assist him with Counsel and Force to repel the Injury, being first advertis'd by the Injur'd that gentle Means and Justice prevail'd nothing; but without prejudice, nevertheless, to every one's Jurisdiction, and the Administration of Justice comfortable to the Laws of each Prince and State; and it shall not

[10] Sir James Headlam-Moreley, *Studies in Diplomatic History,* 1930, p. 108. The statement quoted in the text continues, as follows:

[11] David Jayne Hill, *A History of Diplomacy in the International Development of Europe,* Vol. II, 1925, p. 602; but see La Brière, work cited, p. 67.

[12] Christian L. Lange, *Histoire de l'Internationalisme,* Vol. 1, 1919, p. 498.

[13] From Articles CXXIII and CXXIV of the Treaty of Münster, in work cited. C. Van Vollenhoven, "Grotius and Geneva," 6 *Bibliotheca Visseriana,* p. 72.

be permitted to any State of the Empire to pursue his Right by Force and Arms; but if any difference has happen'd or happens for the future (between the states of the Empire), every one shall try the means of ordinary Justice, and the Contravener shall be regard as an Infringer of the Peace. That which has been determin'd (between the States of the Empire) by Sentence of the Judge, shall be put in execution, without distinction of Condition, as the Laws of the Empire enjoin touching the Execution of arrests and Sentences.

This was a "novel feature"[14] in international treaty and peace-making. The provisions for a moratorium of war, the settlement of disputes by peaceful means, and for individual and collective sanctions against the aggressor, after a delay of three years, although proclaimed primarily for the Empire, the members of which had been given their sovereign rights to conclude treaties of alliance, have nevertheless served as a model for numerous subsequent treaties.[15] They constitute, in a sense, an early precedent for Articles 10, 12, and 16, of the Covenant of the League of Nations. Writers on the subject, of course, have not failed to point out the shortcomings of the above-quoted provisions which admittedly were serious.[16]

The grave dislocations in the social and economic life of Europe caused by the long war prompted the delegates to the Congress of Westphalia to discuss means designed to facilitate reconstruction. For this purpose two clauses were inserted in the Treaties of Münster and Osnabrück. One aimed at restoring freedom of commerce by abolishing barriers to trade which had developed in the course of the war, and the other intended to provide a measure of free navigation on the Rhine.[17] In this respect, as in many others, there is apparent the particular character of the Westphalian peace which distinguishes it sharply from routine peace treaties and which points out its kinship with the great peace settlements of 1815 and 1919.

As the above rapid survey of some of the salient features of the Peace Settlement of 1648 discloses, the actual terms of the settlement, interesting and novel as they may be, would hardly suffice to account for the outstanding place attributed to it in the evolution of international relations. In order to find a more adequate explanation it would seem appropriate to search not so much in the text of the treaties themselves as in their implications, in the broad conceptions on which they rest and the developments to which they provided impetus.

[14] Van Vollenhoven, *The Law of Peace*, p. 86; see also p. 88.
[15] Van Vollenhoven, *The Law of Peace*, p. 86.
[16] Lange, work cited, p. 498. More definite provisions for arbitration were included in the Treaty between Spain and the United Provinces signed at Münster on January 30, 1648. See Van Vollenhoven, work cited, p. 88.
[17] Mirabelli, work cited, p. 84.

In this order of ideas it has been affirmed that the Peace of Westphalia was the starting point for the development of modern international law.[18] It has also been contended that it constituted "the
first faint beginning of an international constitutional law" and the
first instance "of deliberate enactment of common regulations by concerted action."[19] In this connection the special merits of the work of
Grotius have been stressed. On the one hand it has been argued that
"Grotius adapted the (old) Law of Nature to fill the vacuum created
by the extinction of the supreme authority of Emperor and Pope."[20]
On the other hand it has been affirmed that Grotius developed a system of international law which would equally appeal to, and be
approved by, the believers and the atheists, and which would apply
to all states irrespective of the character and dignity of their rulers.[21]
It can hardly be denied that the Peace of Westphalia marked an
epoch in the evolution of international law. It undoubtedly promoted
the laicization of international law by divorcing it from any particular religious background, and the extension of its scope so as to
include, on a footing of equality, republican and monarchical states.
Indeed these two by-products of the Peace of 1648 would seem significant enough for students of international law and relations to
regard it as an event of outstanding and lasting value. It would seem
hazardous, however, to regard the Settlement of Westphalia and the
work of Grotius as more than stages in the gradual, though by no
means uniform, process which antedates and continues beyond the
year 1648.[22] As to the contention that Grotius filled the vacuum created by the deposition of Pope and Emperor, more will be said about
this in a different context.

Closely related with the stimulus to international law is the
impetus said to have been given by the Peace of Westphalia to the
theory and practice of the balance of power. Indeed, the existence of
a political equilibrium has frequently been regarded as a necessary

[18] Paul Fauchille, *Traité de Droit International Public*, Vol. I, Pt. I, p. 75;
see also P. H. Winfield, *The Foundations and the Future of International Law*,
1941, p. 18.

[19] F. S. Dunn, "International Legislation," 42 *Political Science Quarterly*
(1927), p. 577.

[20] Winfield, work cited, p. 20.

[21] W. Van der Vlugt, "L'Oeuvre de Grotius et son Influence sur le Dével-
oppement du Droit International," 7 *Recueil des Cours* (1925), p. 448; Mirabelli, work cited, pp. 54, 92. But see John N. Figgis, *From Gerson Grotius,
1414–1625*, 1916, p. 284, n. 13. This merit is now claimed for Gentili: A. P.
Sereni, *The Italian Conception of International Law*, 1943, p. 114, "His first
merit lies in having cleared the field of international law from the dogmas of a
particular religion and of having distinguished the juridical from the ethical
and political aspects of the problems debated."

[22] Van Vollenhoven, *The Law of Peace*, p. 1; Mirabelli, work cited, p. 7;
Sereni, work cited, p. 124.

condition for the existence of the Law of Nations.[23] It has also become virtually axiomatic that the maintenance of the state system depends upon the preservation of a balance of power between its component and independent parts.[24] There is substantial evidence for the fact that while the principle of the balance of power had been evolved prior to 1648,[25] the Peace of Westphalia first illustrates its application on a grand scale. The operation of the maxim *partager pour équilibrer*[26] can be traced in the territorial clauses of the Treaties of Münster and Osnabrück. This is notably the case in those referring to the aggrandizement of France and Sweden, to the independence of the United Provinces, of the Swiss Confederation, and to the consolidation of about nine hundred units of the Empire into about three hundred. Henceforth, in the organization of Europe resulting from the Peace, *tout repose sur la convenance de balancer les forces et de garantir les situations acquises par l'établissement de contrepoids.*[27] It is interesting to note that the advocacy of a political equilibrium in the literature of the Renaissance has been interpreted as having the character of a protest against the rival principle of a universal monarchy.[28] It was argued, in effect, that the freedom of all states would be brought about as a result of the establishment of a political equilibrium.[29] In this sense the balance of power doctrine forms an important part of that body of political thought which came to fruition in the Peace of Westphalia. It assumed, thereby, increased significance and prestige.

Of even greater importance than any of these particular aspects of developments of the Treaties of Osnabrück and Münster were the general political ideas, the triumph of which they apparently consecrated in the mind of man. The Peace of Westphalia, for better or worse, marks the end of an epoch and the opening of another. It represents the majestic portal which leads from the old into the new

[23] Oppenheim, *International Law*, 4th ed., edited by Arnold McNair, Vol. I, 1928, p. 99; but see La Brière, work cited, pp. 62, 68.

[24] Van Vollenhoven, work cited, p. 91.

[25] Mirabelli, work cited, p. 10. See E. Kaeber, *Die Idee des europäischen Gleichgewichts in der publizistischen Literatur vom 16. bis zur Mitte des 18. Jahrhunderts*, 1907, pp. 8, 20.

[26] Charles Dupuis, *Le Principe d'Equilibre et le Concert Européen*, 1909, p. 23.

[27] Dupuis, p. 22; see also pp. 12, 20, and 21; La Brière, work cited, pp. 60, 62.

[28] Lange, work cited, p. 133: *Au fond le principe d'équilibre implique une protestation contre le principe de l'Empire universel.* A publication in the year 1632 espoused the notion of the *système des contrepoids* and argued that the King of France *tiendra la balance du monde en ses mains, qu'il a apporté du Ciel. Kaeber*, work cited, p. 32.

[29] Kaeber, work cited, p. 41; G. L. Comte de Garden, *Histoire Générale des Traités de Paix*, Vol. I, 1848, pp. 246, 250.

world.[30] The old world, we are told, lived in the idea of a Christian commonwealth, of a world harmoniously ordered and governed in the spiritual and temporal realms by the Pope and Emperor.[31] This medieval world was characterized by a hierarchical conception of the relationship between the existing political entities on the one hand, and the Emperor on the other.[32] For a long time preceding the Peace of 1648, however, powerful intellectual, political, and social forces were at work which opposed and, by opposing them, undermined, both the aspirations and the remaining realities of the unified control of Pope and Emperor. In particular the Reformation and the Renaissance, and, expressive of the rising urge of individualism in politics, nationalism, each in its own field, attacked the supreme authority claimed by the Pope and the Emperor. The combined impact of these centrifugal forces could not, in the long run, be resisted solely by the writings of the defenders of their authority. To maintain the claims it would have been necessary to display a real overpowering authority. Neither the Pope nor the Emperor, however, was at that time in the position to restrain effectively the centrifugal tendencies. The latter was ultimately forced to abandon all pretenses on the field of battle and the former's protest against the Peace of Westphalia, the Bull *Zel Domus* of November 26, 1648,[33] failed to restrain the course of history. In the spiritual field the Treaty of Westphalia was said to be "a public act of disregard of the international authority of the Papacy."[34] In the political field it marked man's abandonment of the idea of a hierarchical structure of society and his option for a new system characterized by the coexistence of a multiplicity of states, each sovereign within its territory, equal to one another, and free from any external earthly authority.[35] The idea of an authority or organization above the sovereign states is no longer. What takes its place is the notion that all states form a world-wide political system

[30] Robert Redslob, *Histoire des Grands Principes du Droit des Gens*, 1923, p. 223.

[31] Dupuis, work cited, p. 9: *Le moyen âge avait revé d'organiser l'Europe sur la double base de l'unité de la chrétienté et de la hiérarchie des pouvoirs. Le pape et l'empereur, placés au sommet de la société internationale devaient, en théorie, maintenir l'unité, en se partageant la domination dans l'ordre spirituel et dans l'ordre temporel; ils devaient, en même temps, sauvegarder les droits de tous, en offrant un recours suprême contre les abus auxquels se pouvaient livrer les mille détenteurs de la souveraineté morcelée par régime féodal.* See also Julius Goebel, *The Equality of States*, 1923, p. 22.

[32] Van der Vlugt, work cited, p. 448.

[33] J. Du Mont, *Corps Universel Diplomatique du Droit des Gens*, Vol. VI, Part I, 1708, p. 463.

[34] John Eppstein, *The Catholic Tradition of the Law of Nations*, 1935, p. 192; see also p. 325.

[35] Sir Paul Vinogradoff, "Historical Types of International Law," 1 *Bibliotheca Visseriana* (1923), p. 45.

or that, at any rate, the states of Western Europe form a single political system.[36] This new system rests on international law and the balance of power, a law operating between rather than above states and a power operating between rather than above states.

It is true that the powers assembled at the Congress of Westphalia paid homage to the old conception of world unity by proclaiming in the preamble of the Treaty of Münster that it was made *ad Christianae Reipublicae salutem* and in that of the Treaty of Osnabrück *au salut de la Republique Chrestienne*.[37] Nevertheless, there is a notable lack of consensus in the appreciation of the major implications of the Peace of Westphalia. According to one view the old system was simply superseded by a modern, the present political, state system, a world-wide system.[38] On the other hand the view is also held that the Peace of Westphalia marks a decisive date in the history of the disorganization of the public law of Europe.[39] In this order of ideas it was argued that the system inaugurated by the Peace, while it may be new, was "as utterly remote as possible from a juridical order founded on a common respect for law";[40] and that in spite

[36] Van Vollenhoven, *The Law of Peace*, p. 81.

[37] Du Mont, work cited, p. 450, 469.

[38] Van Vollenhoven, work cited, p. 81; G. F. de Martens, *Traité de Droit International*, Vol. I, 1883, p. 117; similarly Paul Fauchille, work cited, p. 75. Fauchille underscores *la reconnaissance par les Etats européens de la solidarité de leurs intérêts politiques, . . . dans l'application de l'idée qu'un certain équilibre politique était l'un des facteurs* de la paix; Oppenheim, work cited, p. 69; H. Treitschke, *Politics* (English translation), Vol. II, 1916, p. 569; Montagu Bernard, *Four Lectures on Subjects Connected with Diplomacy*, 1868, p. 6; T. J. Lawrence, "The Work of Grotius as a Reformer of International Law," *Essays on Some Disputed Questions of International Law*, 1885, p. 189; Edwin L. Borchard, "International Law," 8 *Encyclopaedia of the Social Sciences*, 1935, p. 169; James Bryce, *The Holy Roman Empire*, 1866 (revised edition), p. 372; see also Mirabelli, work cited, p. 8; Jacob ter Meulen, *Der Gedanke der Internationalen Organisation in seiner Entwicklung, 1300–1800*, 1917, p. 24; Hill, work cited, Vol. III, p. vii; same, Vol. II, 1906, pp. 599, 604; Wolfgang Windelband, *Die auswärtige Politik der Grossmächte in der Neuzeit. Von 1494 bis zur Gegenwart*, 4th ed. (1936), p. 126 f.; see also Singer, "Völkerrechtsgeschichte," *Wörterbuch des Völkerrechts*, edited by Strupp, Vol. III, 1929, p. 193; Dupuis, work cited, pp. 13, 21; T. A. Walker, *A History of the Law of Nations*, 1899, Vol. I, pp. 147 and ff.; The Collected Papers of John Westlake on Public International Law, ed., by L. Oppenheim, 1914, pp. 55 ff.; E. H. Carr, *Nationalism and After*, 1945, p. 1.

[39] de la Brière, work cited, p. 58.

[40] Same, p. 53. The passage quoted with approval in Van Vollenhoven, at p. 83, appeared in the following context: *Dans leur modalités politiques et diplomatiques, en effet, les tractations de Westphalie portent le caractère d'un empirisme tellement brutal, tellement immoral, tellement incohérent, qu'on est en droit de les proposer aux négociateurs futurs de la paix du XXe siècle comme un parfait exemple des erreurs et des fautes dont il faudra désormais nous préserver à tout prix. Bien plus, dans son principe même (et c'est là surtout que nous voulons en venir), le règlement européen adopté à Münster et à Osnabrück constituera la première application général et solonnelle de la*

of all the appearances of the birth of a new international society of nations "even the germ of such a society was likely to be absent under a system in direct opposition to any impingement upon the sovereign independence of each individual state."[41] Which of these conflicting views is accurate? The answer is difficult in the extreme for the materials regarding the basic problems of the origin of our state system lack coördination and clarity[42] and all the necessary sources are not readily available. For these reasons the following remarks are necessarily tentative and intended to indicate rather than to solve the problems connected with the rise of the modern state system and the particular role of the Peace of Westphalia in this vital process.

The imperial authority, the gradual weakening of which is sometimes said to have set in as early as the Treaty of Verdun of 843, probably received a serious blow in the course and as a result of the Great Interregnum (1254–73) on the one hand, and the rise of independent or quasi-independent communities in Italy and of national states in England,[43] Spain and France, on the other. The discovery of the New World and the extension of intercourse between the Western Christian and Eastern non-Christian world provided those opposing the claim of the Emperor to universal dominion with arguments of considerable persuasiveness. The Great Schism in the Church (1378–1417) and the rise of sects and eventually of the Reformation weakened correspondingly the authority of the Pope. These developments in the secular and spiritual fields which finally culminated in the Thirty Years' War and the Peace of Westphalia, were reflected in and stimulated by contemporaneous political thought.

One of the early opponents of the Emperor was Bartolus of Sassoferrato, who drew a fine distinction between the *de jure* overlordship of the Emperor and the *de facto* existence of *civitates superiorem non recognoscentes.*[44] The formula, said to be of French origin, was later cast by Baldus in a sharper form: *Rex in regno suo est Imperator regni sui.*[45] In that sentence, observed Professor Barker, "we may

---

politique d'équilibre, système diplomatique aussi radicalement éloigné que possible de l'ordre juridique, fondé sur le respect du droit des tous, qui est aujourd'hui le très noble objectif des promoteurs de la 'Société des Nations.'

41 Van Vollenhoven, *The Law of Peace,* p. 93.

42 Professor Sereni's book referred to above constitutes a recent and useful contribution.

43 Sir Henry Maine, *Ancient Law,* 1930, p. 129, Pollock's Notes, to the effect that the Kings of England never owed or rendered any temporal allegiance to the Empire. Figgis, work cited, p. 213 suggests that "the dream of a universal state had disappeared with the failure of Charles V to secure the Empire for his son."

44 Sereni, work cited, p. 59.

45 Same, note 11.

hear the cracking of the Middle Ages."[46] Bartolus, however, in spite
of his insistence on the *de facto* independence of Italian city states,
still recognized the Empire and the Emperor as the Lord of the world
albeit on an idealistic or spiritualistic plane.[47] In France a similar
movement against the universalistic claims of both Emperor and
Pope was on foot. The development of the theory of sovereignty by
Bodin may be regarded as marking the end, on the doctrinal level, of
the efforts to throw off the overlordship of the Emperor and vindicate the independence of states.[48] This movement was not unopposed.
Imperialist writers continued to defend and support the claims of the
Emperor. Their argument was, broadly, that being of divine origin,
the rights of the Emperor existed irrespective of their actual exercise.
No voluntary abandonment, not even an express grant, was susceptible of impairing them. As late as the seventeenth century, imperialist
lawyers repeated the claim that the King of France, like other
princes, was of right, and must forever remain, subject to the Roman
Emperor.[49]

While some of the jurists of the sixteenth century questioned with
increasing boldness the claim of any single potentate to be *totius
orbis dominus*[50] others combined their opposition with the exposition of a new positive doctrine, that of an international community
of states. This doctrine is admittedly of ancient origin. The conception of the entire human race forming a single society goes back to

[46] Ernest Barker, *Church, State, and Study,* 1930, p. 65.

[47] Sereni, p. 60: "All the cities, however, all the states, are in Bartolus'
mind coordinated within the empire. The emperor is the Lord of the world:
to deny it would be heresy. . . . Thus the superiority of the empire over the
cities is admitted on a purely ideal plane. Bartolus' elevation of the empire to
the function of a spiritual institution amounts to a complete denial of its
political authority, in accordance with the reality of the age. The empire is
envisaged by Bartolus as the necessary universal society, in which all the
powers of Christendom must co-operate. In Italy, Dante, Marsilio of Padua,
Cino da Pistoia, and many other political thinkers, jurisconsults, and poets had
invoked the authority of the empire on the same ideal plane. The empire was
to have been the unifying force of the Christian world, to have appeased all
discords, suppressed wars and reprisals, affirmed the reign of peace and justice
on the earth. For Bartolus as well as for these other Italians the empire was
then but a messianic dream, an ideal aspiration." Cf. also Sir Paul Vinogradoff, work cited, p. 43.

[48] Maine, work cited, p. 129: "Modern National sovereignty may be regarded, in a general way, as a reaction against both the feudal and the imperial conceptions. Rules of the Middle Ages, as and when they felt strong
enough, expressly or tacitly renounced both homage to any overlord and submission to the Emperor."

[49] Bryce, work cited, p. 243. Sereni, work cited, p. 65, n. 33. "As late as the
end of the sixteenth century there were still Italian jurisconsults who en-
deavored to maintain the supremacy and the universality of the authority of
the pope and the emperor."

[50] Walker, work cited, p. 149.

the Stoa and the teachings of the early church fathers.[51] It experienced a revival in the works of some of the early writers of international law, notably those of Victoria, Suarez, and Gentili. They denied, on the one hand, the claim of the Emperor to exercise temporal jurisdiction over princes,[52] and affirmed, on the other, the existence of an international community governed by international law.

Victoria, in a famous passage arguing the binding force of laws made by a king upon the king himself, irrespective of his will, and of pacts entered into by the free will of the contracting parties upon them, declares:[53]

> From all that has been said, a corollary may be inferred, namely: that international law has not only the force of a pact and agreement among men, but also the force of a law; for the world as a whole, being in a way one single State, has the power to create laws that are just and fitting for all persons, as are the rules of international law. Consequently, it is clear that they who violate these international rules, whether in peace or in war, commit a mortal sin; moreover, in the gravest matters, such as the inviolability of ambassadors, it is not permissible for one country to refuse to be bound by international law, the latter having been established by the authority of the whole world.

Gentili referred with approval to the teachings of the Stoics that[54]

> the whole world formed one state, and that all men were fellow citizens and fellow townsmen, like a single herd feeding in a common pasture. All this universe which you see, in which things divine and human are included, is one, and we are members of a great body. And, in truth, the world is one body.

And again, he declared:[55]

> Now what Plato and those expounders of the law say of private citizens we feel justified in applying to sovereigns and nations, since the rule which governs a private citizen in his own state ought to

---

[51] Barker, work cited, p. 62; James Brown Scott, *The Law, the State, and the International Community*, Vol. II, 1939, p. 255.

[52] Walker, work cited, p. 149; Sereni, work cited, pp. 64, 115.

[53] Relectio of the Reverend Father, Brother Franciscus de Victoria Concerning Civil Power, a translation by Gwladys L. Williams. In James Brown Scott, *The Spanish Origin of International Law*, 1934. Appendix C, p. xc.

[54] Alberico Gentili, *De Iure Belli Libri Tres,* translation of the edition of 1612 by John C. Rolfe, *The Classics of International Law,* edited by James Brown Scott, 1933, p. 67. See also Sereni, work cited, p. 64.

[55] Gentili, work cited, p. 68. Affirming that it is right to make war upon pirates, Gentili says: "And if a war against pirates justly calls all men to arms because of love for our neighbor and the desire to live in peace, so also do the general violation of the common law of humanity and the wrong done to mankind. Piracy is contrary to the law of nations and the league of human society": p. 124.

govern a public citizen, that is to say a sovereign or a sovereign people, in this public and universal state formed by the world. As a private citizen conducts himself with reference to another private citizen, so ought it to be between one sovereign and another, says Baldus.

Suarez' conception of the international society is expounded in the following "perhaps the most memorable passage of the 'Law of Nations.' "[56]

The rational basis . . . of this phase of law consists in the fact that the human race howsoever many the various peoples and kingdoms into which it may be divided, always preserves a certain unity . . . enjoined the natural precept of mutual love and mercy; a precept which applies to all, even to strangers of every nation.

Therefore, although a given sovereign state, commonwealth, or kingdom, may constitute a perfect community in itself consisting of its own members, nevertheless, each one of these states is also, in a certain sense, and viewed in relation to the human race, a member of that universal society; for these states when standing alone are never so self-sufficient that they do not require some mutual assistance, association, and intercourse, at times for their own greater welfare and advantage, but at other times because also of some moral necessity of need. This fact is made manifest by actual usage.

Consequently, such communities have need of some system of law whereby they may be directed and properly ordered with regard to this kind of intercourse and association; and although that guidance is in large measure provided by natural reason, it is not provided in sufficient measure and in a direct manner with respect to all matters; therefore, it was possible for certain special rules of law to be introduced through the practice of these same nations. For just as in one state or province law is introduced by custom, so among the human race as a whole it was possible for laws to be introduced by the habitual conduct of nations. This was the more feasible because the matters comprised within the law in question are few, very closely related to natural law and most easily deduced therefrom in a manner so advantageous and so in harmony with nature itself that, while this derivation (of the law of nations from the natural law) may not be self-evident—that is, not essentially and absolutely required for moral rectitude—it is nevertheless quite in accord with nature, and universally acceptable for its own sake.

It is this conception of an international society embracing, on a footing of equality, the entire human race irrespective of religion and form of government which is usually said to have triumphed in the seventeenth century over the medieval conception of a more re-

[56] James Brown Scott, *The Spanish Conception of International Law and of Sanctions,* 1934, p. 90. The English translation of the above quotation from Suarez, *De Legibus,* Book II, Ch. XIX, paragraph 9, is taken from Scott, *The Law, the State, and the International Community,* Vol. II, p. 257.

stricted Christian society organized hierarchically, that is, on the basis of inequality. As the dominating political position of the Roman Emperor had gradually but decidedly declined in the centuries and decades preceding the Peace of Westphalia, it is probably correct to say that the Peace merely finally sealed an existing state of affairs. Lord Bryce said that the Peace of Westphalia "did no more than legalize a condition of things already in existence, but which, by being legalized, acquired new importance."[57] It is probably also true, in a broad sense, that with the Congress of Westphalia the various states entered into the legal concept of a *societas gentium* which had long before been established by the science of natural law.[58] It is equally correct that the so-called Grotian Law of Nature school continued to expound the concept of a society of states. Christian Wolff's idea of a *civitas gentium maxima* is a noteworthy and well-known example. A sideline of this type of thinking and writing is represented by the writers who in one form or another, on a restricted or universal basis, advocate the establishment of a more definite society of states than in their view appeared to be actually in existence. One might mention as representatives of this school of thought Dante, Pierre Dubois, George of Podebrad, Erasmus, Emeric Crucé, Sully, William Penn, the Abbé de Saint-Pierre, Rousseau, Jeremy Bentham, Immanuel Kant, William Ladd, William Jay, Elihu Burritt, Saint-Simon, Jean de Bloch, A. H. Fried, J. Novicov, and others. To some extent their writings should have served as evidence that the *pluriversum* which emerged in the sixteenth and seventeenth centuries was not quite an international community and that the states did not always behave as members of one body politic.

Be that as it may, it would seem not altogether unjustified to observe that the development of international law, a determining factor of any conception of an international community, did not come to a standstill with the Peace of Westphalia. It would seem possible to distinguish at least three trends of thought on the subject of the binding force of international law prior to 1648. In Victoria one might discern the attempt to base international law on an objective foundation irrespective of the will of the states and to conceive international law as a law above states. In Suarez the objective foundation is at least overshadowed if not replaced by a subjective foundation in the will of the states. Suarez presented the *jus gentium* as a law between states.[59] In Gentili, of whom it has been said that he had

---

[57] Bryce, work cited, p. 372; Mirabelli, work cited, p. 15 ff.

[58] Ter Meulen, work cited, p. 34.

[59] Walker, work cited, p. 155; Introduction by Coleman Phillipson to Gentili in the above-quoted edition, p. 23a, n. 4.

taken the first step towards making international law what it is,[60] namely, almost exclusively positive, international law still appears to be based on natural reason and derived from a law of nature superior to the nations.[61] Gentili's doctrine "marked progress because it affirmed the existence of an autonomous system of rules of law distinct from the precepts of religion and ethics and directed at regulating international relations according to abstract principles of justice."[62] But what, precisely, we may ask, was the nature of that autonomy? An indication of its meaning may perhaps be gleaned from Gentili's doctrine of the just war. One of the essential conditions of a just war is that it must be waged for a just cause. Gentili affirms that war may be waged with justice on both sides.[63] He is said to come close to Machiavelli's opinion that all necessary wars are justified.[64] But who decides whether there is a just cause, whether the necessity is of such a nature as to justify war? The answer to this question must obviously be of decisive importance for the understanding not only of Gentili's doctrine of just war but equally for his conception of international law. Now it is extremely interesting to note that the decision "concerning the lawfulness of war is on the whole left to each belligerent."[64] If this is an accurate interpretation of Gentili's doctrine, then the autonomy of international law would seem to assume a deeper meaning. It would indicate not merely the independence of international law from the precepts of civil law, religions, and ethics. It would also seem to indicate that the contents of international law as well as the existence or non-existence of international law depends upon the insight of the states concerned, or, to use a modern phrase, upon the will of the states.[65]

[60] T. E. Holland, *Studies in International Law*, 1898, p. 23.

[61] Sereni, p. 107: "With Gentili there thus begins the naturalistic conception of international law, later accepted by Grotius."

[62] Sereni, p. 107.

[63] Gentili, Book I, Ch. VI, p. 31.

[64] Sereni, p. 109.

[65] Gentili, while affirming that "some law of nature exists," stressed the difficulty involved in discovering "what that law is and how we shall prove that it is this or that"; Book I, Ch. I, p. 5. His reasoning on this subject, particularly at p. 7, is illustrative of the difficulty inherent in any law of nature doctrine. Gentili seems to accept the agreement of states, not necessarily of all states, and usage, as a test of the existence of rules of international law: p. 8. See Phillipson's *Introduction*, p. 22a. It is also interesting to note that in discussing arbitration of dispute between sovereigns Gentili starts from the proposition that the sovereign has no earthly judge." Book I, Ch. III, p. 15. Having referred to a number of arbitrations, he says: "But why do I multiply examples, as if any one could not call to mind a great number of such occurrences in every age? Why, to be sure, in order that those who avoid this kind of contest by arbitration and resort at once to the other, that is, to force, may understand that they are setting their faces against justice, humanity, and good precedent, and that they are rushing to arms of their own free will, because they are unwilling to submit to any one's verdict": p.16.

Grotius and several subsequent writers still maintain natural or divine law alongside of customary law as a source of international law. It would seem, however, that with Grotius the accent begins to be transferred from the Law of Nature or divine law to that branch of human law which "has received its obligatory force from the will of nations, or of many nations."[66] Zouche, the "second founder of the Law of Nations," rather than Grotius, is called the father of positivism for the emphasis given by him to customary international law.[67] Without any attempt to trace the development of the doctrine of the will of states as the basis of international law, it may be useful to conclude this brief survey with a few remarks about Vattel. Vattel, regarded as a Grotian, still maintains the distinction between different types of branches of the Law of Nations. Within the positive law of nations, based on the agreement of nations, he differentiates three divisions: the voluntary, the conventional, and the customary law. The voluntary law proceeds from their presumed consent, the conventional law from their express consent, and the customary law from their tacit consent. Positive international law is distinguished from the natural or necessary law of nations which Vattel undertakes to treat separately. In order to understand the respective functions of natural and positive international law Vattel draws the following distinction:

> But after having established on each point what the necessary law prescribes, we shall then explain how and why these precepts must be modified by the voluntary law; or, to put it in another way, we shall show how, by reason of the liberty of nations and the rules of their natural society, the external law which they must observe towards one another differs on certain points from the principles of the international law, which, however, are always binding upon the conscience.

With these nice distinctions in mind one may ask legitimately what precisely is the role of these branches of the law of nations with respect to the conduct of states in relation to one another. Vattel leaves no doubt about it, for he declares that while the necessary law is at all times obligatory upon the conscience, and that a nation must never lose sight of it when deliberating on the course it must pursue in order to fulfill its duty, it must consult the voluntary law "when there is question of what it can demand from other states."[68] It may

[66] Grotius, *De Jure Belli Ac Pacis*, Translated by Francis W. Kelsey, *The Classics of International Law*, Edited by James Brown Scott, Vol. II, 1925, Book I, Ch. I, paragraph 14. Phillipson's *Introduction*, p. 22a.

[67] L. Oppenheim, *International Law*, 5th ed., edited by H. Lauterpacht, 1937, Vol. I, p. 87.

[68] E. Vattel, *The Law of Nations*, translated by Charles G. Fenwick, *The Classics of International Law*, Edited by James Brown Scott, Vol. III, 1916, p. 9.

not be unreasonable to conclude that according to Vattel only those rules of the law of nations which proceed from and are based on the consent of states are enforceable in international relations. This rather significant feature of Vattel's doctrine, it is believed, may not have entirely escaped the attention of diplomats to whom it was addressed, and it may, therefore, account at least partially for his immense popularity. But Vattel's international law is no longer above but beside the diplomat.[69]

Although he does not rank as a strict positivist, Vattel prepared the ground for the era of uninhibited positivism. He helped to establish, precisely because of his popularity, perhaps more than any of his predecessors or successors, the consensual character of international law and to reduce natural law from the function of supplying an objective basis for the validity, the binding force, of the law of nations to the function of supplying rules for filling gaps in positive international law. This distinction between the dual function of natural law in relation to the law of nations is not always observed and yet it would seem to deserve close attention.

The development of international law along the lines indicated above, was bound to influence the concept of an international society of states. In the course of time it became purely formal. *Ubi ius, ibi societas.* Those who argued the existence of a law of nations accepted the use, though rarely more, of the phrase, "Family of Nations." In the period following the Peace of Westphalia the development of international relations would seem to have followed decidedly not the conception of an objectively founded international law and community of Victoria but that indicated in the teachings of Suarez, if indeed it be accurate to assume an essential difference between their doctrines.[70] From the 18th century and, in particular from Vattel

[69] Albert de Lapradelle's introduction to the above edition of Vattel, Vol. III, p. liv: "Writing for courts and for the leaders of nations, he could only place law beside diplomacy as wise counsel; he could not set it above diplomacy as a strict rule."

[70] Scott, *The Spanish Conception of International Law and of Sanctions,* 1934, p. 91: "If the two passages (quoted above in the text), however, be compared from the standpoint of international law, the statement of Suárez seemed to lack that sense of ultimate completeness which always seems to have been in the mind of Victoria; his is not merely an international community with law, but it is an international community with a power to create law and to punish the violations of that law. It may well be that the presence of law in Suárez' community implies both the right consciously to create and the power to preserve that law inviolate; but neither the right not the power are express, as in the case of Francis of Victoria's international community. For does not Victoria say expressly that the *jus gentium* has 'the force of a pact and agreement among men'? Whereas Suárez implies in the succeeding chapter of this very book that the law of nations may have been introduced simply through 'usage and tradition, . . . and without any special and simultaneous compact or agreement on the part of all peoples.' This con-

onward, however, there can be no doubt as to the trend of the development. It was predominately positivist and consensual. The will of states seems to explain both the contents and the binding force of international law. The concept of the Family of Nations recedes in the background.[71] To have paved the way for this development by liquidating, with a degree of apparent finality, the idea of the Middle Ages of an objective order of things personified by the Emperor in the secular realm, would seem to be one of the more vital aspects of the consequences of the Peace of Westphalia and of its place in the evolution of international relations. Viewed in this light the answer to the question formulated above cannot be doubt-ful. Instead of heralding the era of a genuine international community of nations subordinated to the rule of the law of nations, it led to the era of absolutist states, jealous of their territorial sovereignty to a point where the idea of an international community became an almost empty phrase and where international law came to depend upon the will of states more concerned with the preservation and expansion of their power than with the establishment of a rule of law. In the period immediately following the Peace, of the objective validity of international law there may be some doubt. Of the subjective character of much of modern international law there can hardly be any doubt.[72]

It may be said, by way of summary, that on the threshold of the modern era of international relations there were two doctrines with respect to the binding force of international law and the existence of an international community of states. The doctrine of Victoria is characterized by an objective approach to the problem of the binding

---

ception of Suárez looks to an inorganic association; Victoria's conception looks to an organized society, with a law of nations having the force of a pact, the obligations of which are enforceable, not merely under the law of nations but under the natural law."

71 Lapradelle, as cited, p. liv: "It would be vain to look in his work for a reflection of the fine passage of Suárez on the solidarity of nations; but, on the other hand, it would be too much to require in a diplomat of the end of the eighteenth century, even though he were permeated with the spirit of the Encyclopaedia, the same freedom of speech as in a monk of the sixteenth. Vattel, who does not develop to any great extent the idea of arbitration, would probably have no place as an organizer of the society of the future."

72 Emphasizing the destructive character of Vattel's elegant doctrine of the law of nations, Van Vollenhoven concludes: "Henceforth, there will be not merely no positive law, even on a limited scale, there will be not merely the claims of the governments to a limitless sovereignty; from that time onward there will be a nominal law of peace, exacting in character, elaborated in detail, full of celestial principles and unctuous rhetoric, but one that is rendered utterly futile by the reservation, ceaselessly reiterated, that it is for the sovereign states to judge the extent to which those principles and that rhetoric shall bind them in the sphere of reality." *The Law of Peace*, p. 107 f. See also J. L. Brierly, The Law of Nations, 1936 (2d ed.), p. 32.

force of international law and by an organic conception of the international community of states. The other doctrine, characterized by the voluntaristic conception of the binding force of international law, is adumbrated in the work of Suarez.[72a] It is developed in the writings of Gentili, Grotius and Zouche, and it breaks to the fore in the work of Vattel who, emphasizing the independence rather than the interdependence of states, wrote the international law of political liberty.[72b] The growth of the voluntaristic conception of international law is accomplished by a weakening of the notion that all states form and are part of an international community. It is still very strong in the writings of Suarez and Gentili, although it seems to have assumed a character different from that attributed to it by Victoria. The test of the strength of the community doctrine may be said to have come in the seventeenth century. The liquidation of the universalistic claims of the Empire and the recognition of a multiplicity of states wielding the same powers as those hitherto reserved for the Emperor should have created a political and juridical condition favorable for the establishment of a genuine society of states. The opportunity which may have existed at the end of the Thirty Years' War for substituting a new order based on the impersonal supremacy of international law for the old order based on the personal supremacy of the Empire, was not, however, utilized. Instead of creating a society of states, the Peace of Westphalia, while paying lip service to the idea of a Christian commonwealth, merely ushers in the era of sovereign absolutist states which recognized no superior authority. In this era the liberty of states becomes increasingly incompatible with the concept of the international community, governed by international law independent of the will of states. On the contrary this era may be said to be characterized by the reign of positivism in international law. This positivism could not admit the existence of a society of states for the simple reason that it was unable to find a treaty or custom, proceeding from the will of states, which could be interpreted as the legal foundation of a community of states. In the nineteenth century, after Napoleonic

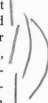

[72a] Joseph Delos, *La Société Internationale et les Principes du Droit Public*, 1929, p. 229 f: *Considérable dés son vivant, traditionnelle aujourd'hui encore, l'oeuvre de Suarez a dépassé de beaucoup le cercle des théologiens. Suarez est, lui aussi, l'un des Fondateurs du Droit International, le plus connu peut-être, et l'un de ceux qui ont le plus influé sur les destinées de la doctrine. Son rôle dans de conflit du Droit à fondement objectif et du Droit subjectif, nous semble avoir été décisif à plus d'un égard. Son oeuvre offre de plus le cas topique que nous cherchions: elle permet de saisir, à un moment donné, et particulièrement important, puisqu'il se place aux origines mêmes du monde moderne, la cause du mal dont souffre la science politique internationale: la substitution du point de vue volontariste au point de vue du Droit à fondement objectif.*

[72b] Lapradelle, as cited, pp. liv, lv.

wars, there may be discerned in the Congress and Concert system the beginning of a conscious effort to establish a community of states based on the will of all states or at least on the will of the Great Powers. The Hague Peace Conferences, the League of Nations and, we may confidently assert, the United Nations are further stages in this development cognizable by positive international law.

This reaction against the unrestrained liberty of states, recognized as self-destructive in its ultimate implications was accentuated by a reaction against the prevailing voluntaristic conception of international law. The attempts to provide international law with an objective foundation, without, however, abandoning altogether the will of states doctrine, are illustrated by Bergbohm's and Triepel's theory of the *Vereinbarung*. A radical departure from the consensual view of international law is characteristic of Kelsen's theory of the initial hypothesis, and of the recent revival of natural law thinking in the field of international law. Other writers follow this trend away from the purely consensual nature of international law by emphasizing the role of *pacta sunt servanda* as the fundamental norm in international law. Others still suggested that international law is based on the maxim *voluntas civitatis maximae est servanda*.[73] The sociological interpretations of the binding force of international law should not be forgotten in this connection. It is common to all these schools of thought that they strive to vindicate for international law a binding force, independent of the will of the states and to substitute for the doctrine that international law is a law of coordination, the old-new doctrine, that international law is, and, if it is to be law, must be, a law of subordination, that is, a law above states.

An international law thus conceived could be interpreted as a law of an international community constituting a legal order for the existing states. It would seem doubtful, however, whether this result can be achieved without the creation of some new institutions or the strengthening of existing institutions. It was pointed out that the efforts to establish the binding force of international law independent of the will of states are bound to cause international lawyers to advocate the creation of an international legislature or, as a very minimum, of an international tribunal endowed with compulsory jurisdiction over disputes between states. While the creation of an international legislature would be concomitant with the formation of a super-state "the objective ascertainment of rights by courts is one (manifestation of the legal nature of international law) which could be effected within the frame of the existing practice and doc-

[73] H. Lauterpacht, *The Function of Law in the International Community*, 1933, p. 421. A brief survey of recent doctrine on international law will be found on p. 415.

trine of international law."[74] The absence of an international court
of justice with compulsory jurisdiction over disputes between states
does not merely strain the legal character of international law to the
breaking point. In truth, it would seem to jeopardize altogether the
conception of international law as a body of rules governing the
conduct of states.

The history of the past three hundred years tends to show that
international law, increasingly separated from its roots in right
reason and natural law and deprived of its sources of objective and
heteronomous validity, could but inadequately perform the task
which devolved upon it following the disappearance of the secular
rule of the Empire and its aspiration to be the Universal Monarchy
envisioned by Dante. Such an international law, rugged individualism
of territorial and heterogeneous states, balance of power, equality of
states, and toleration,—these are among the legacies of the Settlement of Westphalia. That rugged individualism of states ill accom-
modates itself to an international rule of law reënforced by necessary
institutions. It would seem that the national will to self-control which
after a prolonged struggle first threw off the external shackles of
Pope and Emperor is the same which *mutatis mutandis* persists today
in declining any far-reaching subordination to external international
controls. It was one of the essential characteristics of the League of
Nations and it is one of the chief weaknesses of the United Nations.

The approaching tercentenary of the Peace of Westphalia would
seem to invite a thorough reëxamination of the foundations of international law and organization,[75] and of the political, economic, ideological and other factors which have determined their development.
It may not be unreasonable to believe that such a broad inquiry,
along with important insights into the forces which have shaped in
the past and which shape at present the course of international law
and organization, might also yield some precise data regarding the
ways and means of harmonizing the will of major states to self-
control with the exigencies of an international society which by and
large yearns for order under law.

[74] Lauterpacht, p. 426.
[75] Such a revision has been proposed by Dr. Lauterpacht in a different context: p. 437.

4. THE "SATISFIED" AND "DISSATISFIED" STATES NEGOTIATE INTERNATIONAL LAW: A CASE STUDY

By ROBERT L. FRIEDHEIM

PEACE will be achieved, virtually all Western leaders say upon issuing a general statement on foreign policy, when all men learn to obey a common law. The achievement of world peace through world law is a popular solution to the problems of world politics of our times. However, creating a viable international law that all or even most states are willing to obey has proved difficult.

An examination of the two United Nations Conferences on the Law of the Sea held in Geneva in 1958 and 1960 will help illuminate some of the difficulties in creating a law to which there is common consent —and therefore in employing law as the road to peace.

This article will address itself—by an analysis of the content of the debates at Geneva—to the different attitudes that representatives of states and bloc groups brought to the negotiating table. Because the difference in attitudes was so sharp, the conferences proved to be less successful than hoped for by advocates of world law. Not only were participants split on the question of the substantive content of the law, but they also differed on the nature of the international system, present and future, and on the proper means of negotiating law in a United Nations-sponsored conference, which is itself a special political area with distinctive characteristics.

I

The first set of attitudes to be considered is that of those states at the law of the sea conferences who were dissatisfied with the legal status quo. They cannot all be labeled "new states," although most were. Although many were, not all were "revolutionary states" who

Reprinted by permission of the author and *World Politics*, XVIII (No. 1, 1965), 20-42.

felt compelled to "export their ideological impetus."[1] Nor can they be described as lacking an international-law tradition, because the Latin American states, which are included in this category, are very much in that tradition. Rather, the common factor was that these states were "have-not" states, most of whom were located in the southern half of the world, and most of whom believed that their interests were not served by present concepts of international law. This is not an unusual position for those who consider themselves underdogs to take. However, the verbal vehemence with which they expressed their revolt against the past trend of international law seemed to shock those participants in the conferences who were "satisfied" with international law. This antagonism resulted in a clash of wills on many important issues, with each side seemingly incapable of understanding the attitudes and modes of operation of the other.

The "dissatisfied" were heavily represented at the law of the sea conferences. The core of this category was composed of states that in the United Nations General Assembly are associated with the Asian-African, Arab, and Latin American caucusing groups and the anti-colonial common-interest group.[2] These constituted fifty-four of the eighty-six states represented at the first conference, and fifty-six of the eighty-eight at the second. In addition, some of the members of the underdeveloped common-interest group who were not also members of the regional and anticolonial groups felt discriminated against under present concepts of international law.[3]

The key attitude expressed by the dissatisfied states was a strong, conscious, and often expressed belief that the conference process was a *political* process. They clearly understood that their operations were to be guided by practices usually known collectively as parliamentary diplomacy. This meant bloc organization, bloc voting, bloc-sponsored

---

[1] Richard A. Falk, "Revolutionary Nations and the Quality of International Legal Order," in Morton A. Kaplan, ed., *The Revolution in World Politics* (New York 1962), 323.

[2] Although the Soviet-bloc states are members of the anticolonialist group, a full discussion of their conduct must be omitted for reasons of space. However, it should be pointed out that the Soviet-bloc states should not be classified as "dissatisfied." Although often allied with the dissatisfied, the Soviet bloc did not participate in the all-out assault on law *per se* so characteristic of the dissatisfied states. The positions adopted by the Soviet Union (and her satellites) at the conferences were typical of a conservative revolutionary state ambivalently trying to accomplish two ends—on the one hand, export of revolutionary principles and harassment of cold-war enemies; on the other, a genuine attempt to negotiate commonly accepted legal principles in areas where important material interests would be protected if normative behavior could be enforced. For a discussion of conservative revolutionary states, see Falk, 315.

[3] The reader should not assume that the characteristics ascribed to a category of states created for purposes of analysis are wholly applicable to all states that generally fall into that category.

proposals, bloc-sponsored candidates for the elective offices of the conferences, and bloc attempts to manipulate the rules of procedure. The groups of the dissatisfied were the most organized, evident, and self-conscious at the conferences. Mr. Ahmed Shukairi, chairman of the Saudi Arabian delegation, was very outspoken in referring to the Arab states "attending the conference . . . as a voting group."[4] Other instances of frank references to blocs are too numerous to list. The dissatisfied took advantage of their numbers by frequently sponsoring multinational proposals.[5]

Probably the major reason why the dissatisfied considered the conference process as political and why a considerable number of representatives reflecting this position demonstrated great parliamentary skill was the large proportion of dissatisfied delegations which had as representatives men with recent General Assembly experience. Twenty of the dissatisfied states had at least one representative (five states had several) who was not only a "professional diplomat" but also—in Philip Jessup's phrase—a "professional parliamentarian."[6] Three other delegations had senior advisors who learned the art of parliamentary maneuver in the General Assembly.[7]

This is not to say that the dissatisfied controlled the conferences either by dominating a majority of the votes taken or by getting a majority of their proposals accepted. While the incidence of bloc voting was relatively high among the dissatisfied groups, so were the absence rates of members which reduced the number of total votes the group cast. None of the dissatisfied except the underdeveloped group was among the groups that most frequently voted with the majority. But their evident, organized efforts constantly harassed their opponents, and frequently forced them either to water down or to withdraw proposals opposed by the dissatisfied bloc. Even more important was the ability of the dissatisfied groups to mobilize their numbers to dominate voting on key proposals. While their general record for effectiveness was not good, they could point with satis-

---

[4] United Nations Conference on the Law of the Sea, *Official Records,* Vol. III, First Committee (A/CONF. 13/39), 4th meeting, par. 30. Hereafter all citations from the records, documents, or reports of both UN Conferences on the Law of the Sea will be made with the official UN document number.

[5] See, for example, A/CONF. 13/C.5/L.6 (19 "dissatisfied" sponsors), A/CONF. 13/C.3/L.65, 66, 66/Rev. 1 (12 sponsors, A/CONF. 19/C.1/L.2/ Rev. 1 (18 sponsors), A/CONF. 19/C.1/L.6 (16 sponsors), A/CONF. 19/L.9 (10 sponsors), among many others.

[6] "International Negotiations Under Parliamentary Procedure," *Lectures on International Law and the United Nations* (Ann Arbor, University of Michigan Law School, 1957), 419.

[7] These figures were compiled from the list of delegations to the Conferences on the Law of the Sea and to Sessions XII, XIII, XIV, and XV of the General Assembly.

faction to several successful attempts to block passage of the various United States proposals for a six-mile territorial sea and a twelve-mile contiguous fishing zone, and to force elimination from a British proposal of a fifteen-mile limit on the use of straight baselines. They could also point to more positive victories such as enlarging to twenty-four miles the baseline to be drawn from headland to headland in delimiting bays, forcing through an Indian proposal which gave the coastal state "sovereign" rather than exclusive rights over the continental shelf, and gaining majorities for several proposals sponsored jointly by Asian-African and Latin American states which increased the authority of the coastal states over fishing in waters off their coasts.

The satisfied states were annoyed by the political strategy used by the dissatisfied. But they were profoundly shocked by the dissatisfied's analogous assumption—that the *subject matter* to be dealt with in the conferences should also be political. The dissatisfied made frequent reference to the General Assembly resolution that allowed political factors to be considered in formulating the law of the sea: "[The conferences] should take into account not only the legal but also the technical, biological, economic, and political aspects of the problem."[8] These states early in the first conference made it evident that they understood this to mean carte blanche to fight for furthering what they conceived of as their own interests. While this motive was not uncharacteristic of most participating states and groups, the dissatisfied seemed more conscious of their interests and more outspoken in defending them.

A statement by the Vietnamese delegate, Mr. Buu-kinh, in a debate on the continental shelf, can scarcely be plainer: "His delegation would prefer to see the criterion of depth alone retained, particularly as the waters off its own shores were relatively shallow and did not reach a depth of 200 metres for more than 200 miles."[9] The Mexican delegate, Mr. Gomez Robledo, in discussing a Canadian proposal on reservations to any convention signed as a result of the conference, was equally candid: "Representatives wishing to permit reservations had been reproached for defending national interests; but they were attending the conference for that very purpose."[10] Or, as Mr. Caabasi of Libya flatly remarked about a United States proposal on the breadth of the territorial sea: ". . . His delegation had voted against the United States proposal because it contained provisions which were contrary to his country's interests."[11]

[8] General Assembly Resolution 1105, XI Session, par. 2. For example, see A/CONF. 13/42, 19th meeting, par. 33.
[9] A/CONF. 13/42, 11th meeting, par. 14.
[10] A/CONF. 13/38, 9th plenary meeting, par. 34.
[11] *Ibid.,* 14th plenary meeting, par. 66.

Since these dissatisfied states were so insistent and outspoken in asserting that the conference process was a political means of attaining their own national interest, they were no less definite in assigning to the states opposing them the same self-interested motives. For example, Dr. Alfonso Garcia Robles of Mexico, advocating a broad belt of territorial sea, ascribed to the narrow-seas advocates the motive of sheer self-interest. He ignored entirely any reference to traditional historic and legal doctrines of freedom of the seas: "It had been suggested that the States whose fleets carried almost all the world's maritime transport should be asked why they opposed the extension of the breadth of the territorial sea to twelve miles. He could not see what would be the point in putting such a question. Gidel* had given the answer when he had stated that a dominant factor in the dispute was the inequality of sea power; the greater a State's sea power, the more it would tend to limit the breadth of its territorial sea, for it had no need to look to international law for means to exercise special powers over a broad zone of sea adjacent to its coasts. Unfortunately, the maritime powers, which were usually also fishing powers, were not confining themselves to exercising special powers in the areas of sea adjacent to their coasts, but were only too often attempting to exercise them in the territorial sea of other countries, too."[12]

Just as these states saw the conference process in terms of politics and their own interests, so they regarded international law. They saw it as a cloak, a set of ideas used to camouflage self-interest, the domination by the few of the many. Nothing could be more candid than these remarks by Dr. Jorge Castaneda of Mexico: "Rigid adherence to the traditional rules of international law could prove disastrous to all concerned, for the traditional rules on the regime of the sea had been created by the great Powers for their own purposes before many major problems had arisen and before the birth of the new states which now formed the majority."[13]

The same theme was repeated again and again by delegates of many of the dissatisfied states. For example, Mr. Ba Han, of Burma: ". . . In the past international law had been a body of rules and usages adopted by powerful states. However, the international situation had changed and new sovereign independent states had emerged, keenly conscious of their liberty."[14] Mr. Ulloa Sotomayor, of Peru: "Rules of international law had sometimes been unilaterally created in the interests of great powers; it was therefore reasonable for certain rules

---

* Gilbert Gidel was a noted French international lawyer regarded as the foremost modern authority on the law of the sea. [Editors' note]

[12] A/CONF. 19/8, 10th meeting, par. 12.

[13] A/CONF. 13/41, 13th meeting, par. 22.

[14] A/CONF. 13/39, 4th meeting, par. 6.

of law to be initiated by small States in their legitimate interests. . . . It was inadmissible that a sort of colonialism of the high seas should be allowed in the name of freedom of the seas."[15] Mr. Diallo, of Guinea: "With regard to 'historic rights,' . . . the concept was nothing other than a manifestation of the right of the strongest and a vestige of colonialism, which [Guinea] would oppose in all its forms. To perpetuate those rights would be a grave injustice to the young States that were struggling not only for political but also for economic independence."[16]

This attitude was not exclusive to the more vociferously dissatisfied anticolonial states, but also affected even friends and allies of the West. For example, Mr. Vu Van Mau of Vietnam observed that the purposes of the first United Nations law of the sea conference had been ". . . to single out from a mass of unilateral practices anarchically applied those which corresponded to rules of law, so that they could subsequently be adopted to the new needs of mankind and to the aspirations of emergent States."[17] And the Iranian delegate, Mr. Dara, said emphatically, "A great many delegations would not accept servitude to the large maritime Powers which wished to fish in the waters of the other States."[18]

These views of the dissatisfied are, in effect, a denial of the entire history and body of international law. Several Latin American delegates did in fact deny that the great international-law writers of the past had ever had anything more in mind than protecting the interests of the states or organizations to which they owed allegiance. As Mr. Melo Lecaros of Chile put it, ". . . The rise and development of the law of the sea had been prompted by one single factor: interest. Political or economic interest had always prevailed in defining the law of the sea through the centuries. Grotius had not argued for the freedom of the seas simply as an intellectual concept, but to defend the interests of the Dutch East India Company. Selden's sole aim in refuting Grotius had been to defend England's interests. Things had changed very greatly since that time. The rule of law had been extended, but it was impossible to overlook the fact that the reason for the existence of law was interest. Law had been created by man for the use of man."[19] Mr. Llosa of Peru also felt it necessary to tilt against Hugo Grotius, the very "father of international law," who, he said, ". . . did not write a work on international law but a treatise to vindicate the claims of the Dutch East India Company, by whom he

[15] *Ibid.*, 5th meeting, par. 13.
[16] A/CONF. 19/8, 18th meeting, par. 6.
[17] *Ibid.*, 3rd meeting, par. 6.
[18] A/CONF. 13/38, 20th plenary meeting, par. 70.
[19] A/CONF. 19/8, 14th meeting, par. 13-14.

had been retained, to freedom of navigation and trade."[20] So international law had moved in the wrong direction from the outset!

The dissatisfied states were acutely aware of the factor of time in regard to international law. The new states among the group, those who often set its tone and behavioral pattern, were quite naturally very conscious of their own recent independence and separate national existence. They demanded that international law take them into account, and consider their interests and desires; they demanded participation and the right of consultation in formation of international law. Among innumerable statements of this attitude are the following two examples. Mr. Subardjo of the Philippines: ". . . The law of nations must take into account the fact that since the Second World War former dependencies and colonies in Asia and Africa had achieved the status of sovereign States."[21] And Mr. El Bakri of Sudan: "Those who had described the present conference as the third to codify the law of the sea, counting the Hague Codification Conference of 1930, had overlooked one of the major developments which had taken place since 1930, namely, the number of countries that had become independent and which, with their different outlook, had taken their rightful place in the international community. In considering the problem of the breadth of the territorial sea, full account must be taken of the changes in institutions and ideas that had supervened during the past thirty years, and the final solution would have to accord with the contemporary spirit of social and political progress."[22]

A close and perhaps necessary corollary of this extreme self-consciousness is that the new states and their allies did not recognize, and would not consider binding upon themselves, that law which was created before they became independent states. Expressions of this attitude at the conferences abound. Mr. Bocobo of the Philippines: ". . . The newer countries valued their freedom above all else and refused to accept certain rules of international law evolved before they had attained statehood."[23] Mr. Loutfi of the United Arab Republic: ". . . The majority of the new countries that had gained their independence since [the Hague Conference of 1930] had adopted a limit in excess of three miles. Their argument that the three-mile rule constituted a principle of international law was thus devoid of substance."[24] Mr. Ba Han of Burma ". . . could not accept the suggestion that abandonment of the three-mile rule was a concession. That

---

20 A/CONF. 13/41, 23rd meeting, par. 11.
21 A/CONF. 13/39, 7th meeting, par. 1.
22 A/CONF. 19/8, 19th meeting, par. 14.
23 A/CONF. 13/39, 50th meeting, par. 1.
24 *Ibid.*, 21st meeting, par. 4.

alleged rule had been established by others at a time when his own country, for one, was completely helpless under foreign rule."[25]

There was an impatience with, rather than a reverence for, age and tradition, a feeling that the old laws should be swept away or re-molded so that the newer states could help create new laws for new conditions. In stating Afghanistan's position on the access of land-locked states to the sea, Mr. Tabibi remarked: "Besides, many of [the international instruments in question] were very old and an historic conference such as the present should replace them by others which would contribute to the development of international law, particularly since the signatories of the instruments relating to the rights of land-locked countries were mainly European countries."[26] Mr. Hekmert, explaining Iran's vote against a United States-proposed amendment to the International Law Commission draft, stated that he ". . . agreed with the arguments against the proposed [amendments]. The International Law Commission, in whose proceedings he had taken part, had not forgotten the existence of the 1884 Conventions when it drew up articles 62 and 65. It had nevertheless felt that the provisions embodied in those articles were more in line with twentieth-century conditions. The group of Afro-Asian states now numbered more than thirty, whereas, in 1884 there had not been more than five or six independent states in that part of the world. In the days of the 1884 Convention international law had been largely a matter of concern to western countries. It was important that it should now be applicable and accepted on a world-wide basis."[27]

The keynote, the driving force, of this attitude was the need for change. Change for these states replaced history and tradition as a commander of respect. Symbolic were the remarks of the Korean delegate, Mr. Kim: "Several representatives had stressed how useful the three-mile limit had been in the past—at a time when it had been consistent with prevailing conditions. But those conditions had changed, and the three-mile limit was no longer adequate. Korea . . . earnestly hoped the Conference would adopt a principle better adapted to the varying conditions obtaining in the different parts of the world."[28] Consistent with their enthusiasm for change, the dissatisfied states were fond of calling those who were satisfied with the main aspects of international law "conservatives," while their own group was labeled "progressive."

Their devotion to change in international law was based on political, economic, and, particularly, technological changes in world con-

[25] A/CONF. 13/38, 14th plenary meeting, par. 51.
[26] A/CONF. 13/43, 8th meeting, par. 32.
[27] A/CONF. 13/40, 31st meeting, par. 24.
[28] A/CONF. 13/39, 15th meeting, par. 14.

ditions: "Legal rules had to develop at the same pace as modern technology"; and "existing rules might no longer be practical because of changed conditions." But it is clear that such statements were only a rationalization for a more profound sentiment. Without being fully aware of it, the dissatisfied states had returned to an older concept: law equated with justice, and further, with justice defined in relation to themselves. The older foundations of international law, having been established before the independent existence of these states, when they were "completely helpless under foreign rule," without regard for their welfare, could not be regarded as just; and since the law was unjust, it must be changed. Any change, in their view, was therefore a change for the better.

Justice to themselves was paramount, and it was elevated to the level of principle. But while they treated certain matters as principles, they rarely handled them in legal terms. They preferred to emphasize strictly political doctrines—coastal rights, wider areas of sea control —and to have these issues stated as vaguely as possible. In their practical, pragmatic, nonhistorical manner, they had no use for doctrine *qua* doctrine. Legal doctrine was for them political; they made no distinction in bargaining between legal matters and any other international problem. A speech by Mr. Quarshie of Ghana illustrates well the paradoxical concern for "principle" (justice) and disregard for law: "The African States, which had seen their continent divided among the great Powers without the consent of the populations concerned, found it difficult to understand the moral arguments now advanced against the division of the sea. That division was essentially a practical matter. The needs of shipping varied according to the region, and a 200-mile limit might be suitable in one place but unsuitable in another. Requirements also varied with time; for instance, the contiguous zone was now far more important than it had been in the past."[29]

The dissatisfied states, then, tended to use "doctrine" and "principle" not as bases for consistent legal philosophy, but, somewhat opportunistically, to attain their own political-economic ends, which they considered "justice." Frequently this resulted in absurd inconsistencies, but these states were not concerned with doctrinal purity— as U Mya Sein of Burma remarked characteristically, "There was an over-emphasis on legal niceties."[30] A good example of this was the position the dissatisfied states took on the issue of sovereignty.

Of all the juridical concepts developed in the long history of international law, the most meaningful to the dissatisfied states was sov-

[29] A/CONF. 13/38, 21st plenary meeting, par. 21.
[30] A/CONF. 13/42, 19th meeting, par. 33.

ereignty.[31] They defined the concept very rigidly so that no external political unit, nor any obligation made, could deprive them of their sovereign rights as they defined and understood them. Sovereignty to them was a symbol of their independence. The dissatisfied were not, however, concerned with the development of a logical theory about the symbol, but rather with the preservation of the facts for which the symbol stood. They pressed ardently for sovereignty over the continental shelf, for control of fisheries off their shores as an extension of their sovereignty, and for a wider belt of territorial sea in which to exercise their sovereignty. These states were also adamant opponents of any scheme that conveyed to an international court or arbitral group compulsory jurisdiction over questions touching upon a state's sovereignty. They were concerned with the preservation of their own sovereignty even at the risk of impinging upon the sovereignty of other states. Afghanistan, Bolivia, Ghana, Indonesia, Laos, Nepal, Paraguay, Saudi Arabia, Tunisia, and the UAR (among nineteen sponsors), all ardent supporters of an absolute theory of state sovereignty, were able to introduce with no qualms a proposal that would give a landlocked state an absolute right of transit across the territory of a coastal state, thereby possibly impairing the sovereignty of the latter.[32] India, a leading advocate of sovereignty of the coastal state over its continental shelf, making no attempt to explain away the seeming inconsistency of her position, introduced a proposal that would prevent the "sovereign" coastal state from "building military bases or installations [on] the continental shelf."[33] Thus sovereignty was not treated as a juridical idea to be developed so that the same legal rules would be applicable to all states equally; it was, instead, appropriated by the dissatisfied as a means of maintaining tactical freedom. This was typical of their opportunistic use of legal doctrine and principles.

The significance of the dissatisfied states' wholly *political* attitude toward international law was that these nations were unable to differentiate between political and legal reality. They assumed, incorrectly, that political reality was identical with legal reality. These states, firm opponents of the three-mile territorial sea, assumed and pronounced it politically "dead and buried" when "two of its traditional champions had withdrawn their support."[34] However, while it is probably true that the three-mile limit is no longer politically

[31] See the general debates of the Fourth Committee for views of the dissatisfied on sovereignty. A/CONF. 13/42, 1st meeting–29th meeting.

[32] UN Doc. A/CONF. 13/C.5/L.6

[33] UN Doc. A/CONF. 13/C.4/L.57.

[34] A/CONF. 13/39, 53rd meeting, par. 17. For other death pronouncements see *ibid.*, 54th meeting, par. 1 and 15; 55th meeting, par. 35; A/CONF. 19/8, 20th meeting, par. 26.

viable—that is, there is very little chance of its being accepted by
states that do not already adhere to it—it is not true that it is dead
and buried in legal terms. As long as states that had traditionally held
to the three-mile rule continue to affirm it, it will be the rule applied
by them off their coasts and in their courts. Moreover as Mr. André
Gros, representative of France, pointed out, it "was the only rule
that did not need express recognition by the international community."[35]

The dissatisfied states also tended to assume that a resolution,
sponsored by ten of them, establishing a twelve-mile fisheries zone
was already part of international law, without any conference adoption. This presumption was based upon the willingness of opponents
to consider the measure as a political possibility, a point for negotiation—that is, it was politically viable, but certainly not established
international law.[36] On the other hand, at times the dissatisfied states
were unwilling to recognize as international law that which had just
been adopted by a majority of states. After a Swiss proposal on
questions of landlocked countries had been adopted, the dissatisfied
states, which had supported an unsuccessful nineteen-power proposal
because it created new rights to overcome past injustices to land-
locked states, claimed the contents of that defeated proposal to be
"the existing rules of international law."[37] Thus, insistence upon the
exclusively political nature of proposals which they wanted codified,
led these states to a position in which communication with the more
legally oriented nations was difficult and negotiation virtually impossible.

A few final characteristics of this attitude should be mentioned.
The dissatisfied states displayed a typical "have-not" distrust of the
expert. He was identified with the colonial powers, the West, and
was therefore somewhat feared and resented. Mr. Quarshie of Ghana
expressed the psychological reaction of the underdeveloped states to
Western technical expertise: "Ghana feared the exploitation of its
fishing resources and threats to its security; it sought a solution which
would guarantee it a maximum freedom from exploitation and
threats. Its fears could not be allayed by exhibitions of technical
knowledge or outright dismissal of its views. In consultation, the
main point often lay less in the validity of the argument itself than in
the reaction to that argument."[38] The Mexican delegate, Mr. Gomez
Robledo, also expressed well the resentment of the learning and
expertise of international-law specialists of older, and especially of

[35] A/CONF. 19/8, 20th meeting, par. 12.
[36] Ibid., 12th plenary meeting, par. 24.
[37] A/CONF. 13/43, 25th meeting, par. 40-43.
[38] A/CONF. 19/1, 25th meeting, par. 22.

European, states: "... Although the Mexican delegation had the greatest respect for recognized experts in international law, it should be remembered that the Conference was not a university but an assembly of sovereign states. Furthermore, every country in the world could now inform itself as to the true meaning of sovereignty and no state had a monopoly of learning on the matter."[39]

Along with their fear of the expert went an unwillingness to commit themselves to legal details on the exercise of rights and duties under consideration at the conferences. Legal detail was viewed by them as a trap for the inexperienced or the unwary. In part, the reason that they preferred vaguely general statements to more exact definitions of legal rights and obligations was their lack of technical expertise. The dissatisfied states constantly feared that their agreement to a detailed proposal would create obligations for them that their negotiators could not perceive. Moreover, agreement on detailed solutions to problems in the law would have reduced their tactical mobility, which they did not wish to have happen. Relatively weak in power terms, they saw as their main protection from the physically powerful states both the ability to avoid being permanently obligated to perform required acts and the ability to perform acts not yet sanctioned by law. They preferred that legal rights and obligations be no more than moral imperatives—broad legal obligations that should be fulfilled but whose enforcement is backed only by the sense of obligation of the affected state itself. Since their sense of obligation to the idea of law is weak, the law is weak. As a result of their preference for vagueness, many provisions sponsored by dissatisfied states embodied in the conventions, should they come into force, will present new ambiguities for states to continue to dispute.

II

Those states with an international-law tradition manifested a behavioral pattern very different from that of the dissatisfied states. This group included all states represented that had a Western European political tradition—some twenty-three states in all. The core of the category was composed of the Western European, Benelux, European Community, and Scandinavian caucusing groups, and the NATO common-interest group. Usually voting with these groups were the "White Commonwealth" states, five European states not represented in the General Assembly, and Israel. In addition, the votes of five United States cold-war allies—Japan, Pakistan, and the

[39] A/CONF. 13/38, 9th plenary meeting, par. 60.

Republics of China, Korea, and Vietnam—could frequently be counted upon by the satisfied.

Although heavily outnumbered, the states in this category can be said statistically to have dominated the conferences. All the satisfied groups were able to command the votes of their members approximately eighty percent of the time on substantive issues. They also had an outstanding record of voting with the majority on both substantive and procedural issues. With additional votes coming from the five non-UN-member European states and the five United States cold-war allies, the satisfied voted with the majority on forty-three of sixty-six roll-call votes on substantive issues, and on ten of twelve votes on procedural issues. Another significant index of the "success" of the satisfied was the high percentage of proposals made by its members that were adopted by the conferences. Eighteen states each proposed more than two percent of the total number of amendments adopted. Of these states, fourteen were either in the satisfied category or were states such as Japan and Pakistan that ordinarily voted with the satisfied.

It should be noted, however, that statistics on the law of the sea conferences do not tell the whole story of the successes and failures of the satisfied. Although they controlled a majority of the votes taken, and proposed most of the amendments accepted, the satisfied failed to gain majorities for their proposals on *key issues* such as the breadth of the territorial sea and fishing rights in areas beyond the territorial sea. They failed here because they were unable to persuade the dissatisfied that the measures desired also guarded the interests of the dissatisfied. The failure can be laid in large part to the fact that the satisfied couched their arguments in terms of traditional law—which the dissatisfied did not recognize and would not accept—instead of in terms of more realistic political-economic bargaining. Although their political positions at the conferences were not uniform—ranging from flexibility on the part of the United States and the United Kingdom to extreme conservatism and legalism on the part of continental powers such as France and the Federal Republic of Germany—still they shared a common belief that international law exists, that it is fundamentally just, that it provides a hope for adjustment of interests as well as protection of interests. They showed clear agreement with the broad background of sea-law doctrine and its cornerstone, freedom of the seas. Many states showed great pride in their past roles as formulators of international law: the Dutch continually invoked Grotius and Bynkershoek; the Spanish, Vitoria; the French, their great international lawyers.

Naturally, the satisfied relied heavily upon technical experts to staff their delegations. Twenty satisfied states had one or more legal experts from their government legal departments, foreign offices, or leading universities as full representatives at the conferences. Eighteen of the satisfied also had as representatives men from their ministries of food, fisheries, transportation, navy, communications, and commerce. In addition, all of them brought to Geneva large delegations of advisers with legal or technical expertise. On the other hand, only five of the satisfied states—Australia, Canada, Greece, Italy, and Spain—had as representatives diplomats with recent experience in the political practices of the General Assembly.

Unfortunately the satisfied states' concept of law interfered with their understanding the process by which law must be negotiated in a contemporary international setting. They did not act as if they understood that the political process by which substantive questions are negotiated will itself help shape the results. In particular, many of the satisfied refused to admit that conferences with legal subjects on the agendas are political—that they provide forums in which agreements are forged by states when they believe that such agreements protect their mutual interests. Moreover, United Nations-sponsored conferences are legislative in nature. That is, they operate under the rules of parliamentary diplomacy, and decisions depend upon forming majorities. In such an arena, it is extremely difficult, and perhaps impossible, to create a majority that will vote for and be willing to be bound by what it believes to be an abstractly perfect legal or administrative formula. The satisfied tended to view the conferences as an opportunity to promulgate a legal code consistent with their international-law doctrine. They viewed apprehensively the possibility that past law and the international-law tradition were only two factors among the many that would be considered in creating conventions to which a majority of states could agree politically. Such conventions would add to mere codification an element of progressive development—that is, the creation of new rules of international law—which the satisfied delegates deplored.

The remarks of Swedish delegate, Mr. Sture Petren, illustrate precisely the reluctance of the satisfied to accept the notion of progressive development: "Mr. Petren . . . emphasized the difference between the 'progressive development' of international law and its 'codification.' In practice, the development of law and its codification could not easily be separated. . . . Any conventions which might be drafted by the Conference, whether they related to the codification or the development of law, would therefore be of a mixed nature, containing both old rules of law and new ones. These two kinds of law had not at all the same legal effect. The old rules, if they were based on customary law, bound all mankind independently of the new conventions to be concluded, whereas the new rules, which would come into being only through the conventions, would bind only those states which signed and ratified those conventions. Other states would not be bound to recognize or observe them. The Swedish delegation therefore felt that the Conference should proceed with caution, and should not depart too radically from existing law."[40]

The satisfied delegates were not averse to using political tactics at the conference; in fact they were quite skilled at forming voting groups, making bloc proposals, lobbying, and manipulating the rules of procedure. All the while they were publicly deploring the very use of such tactics by others and implicitly apologizing for finding it necessary to use them themselves. One after another satisfied delegate took the floor to excoriate blocs and bloc voting. They felt issues should be handled as ideas "on their merits." Typical was a British appeal to de-emphasize national and bloc interests for "wider considerations."[41]

Another major blunder of the satisfied states was their failure to answer the charge of the dissatisfied that the former were interested in preserving the present law because it protected their own interests. It is true that their interests did coincide with their doctrinal views. Their key doctrine, freedom of the seas, while theoretically opening the seas to all, in practice can only be exploited by those who have existent navies and merchant fleets. The satisfied states are the biggest shippers, have the biggest surface fleets, have large, important trade and fishing interests. But the satisfied states could have answered this accusation in political and economic terms, and have declared that freedom of the seas is open-ended and in fact generous to small powers, since without it the powerful could physically control large areas of the sea.

Dumbfounded by the attack of the dissatisfied on what the satisfied regarded as a liberal concept, the latter fell back on rigid, legalistic defenses. At times this tactic was used politically simply to discourage change. But the evident dismay of many satisfied delegates indicated that they could not understand the need to answer this attack by different tactics and different language. All they could do was deplore the attack on the law of the sea. For example, Dr. Max Sorensen of Denmark felt that ". . . a trend which, over the past few decades, had weakened rather than strengthened the authority of the international law of the sea should be halted, and Denmark would cooperate wholeheartedly with other nations in restoring the authority of the law."[42]

There were exceptions. Occasionally one of the less powerful states with an international-law tradition such as New Zealand, Greece,

[40] A/CONF. 13/39, 6th meeting, par. 1-2; see also par. 24-25; 18th meeting, par. 10.
[41] A/CONF. 13/39, 53rd meeting, par. 10.
[42] *Ibid.*, 4th meeting, par. 10.

Switzerland, Australia, or Sweden,[43] would defend the law of the sea not only as useful for the great seagoing powers, but also as valid for lesser and developing states. (Of course, these nations were themselves in the international-law tradition, and the law of the sea did serve their interests to some extent.) And, although they did not always act accordingly, both the United Kingdom and the United States occasionally recognized that explaining international-law doctrine in traditional terms did not appeal to the newer dissatisfied states, but only contributed to their suspicion and fear of the West.[44]

But these were only exceptions; the rule was a rather inflexible legalism and refusal to answer the dissatisfied states' political attack against the norms of traditional international law. The satisfied states had come to the conference not to adjust interests but to argue law. They did so to the detriment and sometimes to the exclusion of political-economic questions. The Federal Republic of Germany, for example, refused to recognize that fishery conservation was a problem and therefore refused to sign the convention on that subject.[45] Germany also consistently doubted the validity of the idea of the continental shelf in international law. Most of the satisfied states shared this belief. There is of course a legal case for this position; that is, the concept of the continental shelf is not of ancient lineage and is not therefore part of customary international law. In that case, they insisted, their consent was necessary to bring the concept of the shelf under law binding on them. But when they reluctantly did accept the idea of the shelf, it seemed no compromise to the proponents of the shelf concept, since it had accumulated sixteen years of state practice by those states with an active interest in exploring or exploiting the shelf. By adopting a legally sound but extraordinarily conservative position, and then agreeing to no more than had been in practice for years, they gave their negotiating techniques an air of hollow unreality and empty legalism.

Too often delegates of satisfied states would not even concede any necessary relationship between law and politics. They saw law as an abstract perfectible entity, divorced from the compromises required by the politics of competing state interests. Consider the following remarks of Professor Paul de la Pradelle, the Monacan delegate: ". . . It was difficult to disentangle the law of the sea from the accretions imposed by national sovereignty. He hoped that one day the

[43] *Ibid.*, 9th meeting, par. 10, 18; 16th meeting, par. 18; 17th meeting, par. 11; 44th meeting, par. 11, respectively.

[44] A/CONF. 13/43, 21st meeting, par. 40. See also Loftus Becker, "Some Political Problems of the Legal Advisor," *Department of State Bulletin,* XXXVIII (May 19, 1958), 835; and U.S. Senate, Committee on Foreign Relations, *Conventions on the Law of the Sea,* Hearings, 86th Cong., 2nd sess. (Washington, January 20, 1960), 5.

[45] A/CONF. 13/38, 18th plenary meeting, par. 74-77.

compromise formulae produced by the 'diplomacy of the sea' would give place to a true law of the sea, in harmony with the [United Nations] Charter."[46] Little wonder that the satisfied states were unable to cope with problems of negotiating legal subjects at a conference which was, after all, a political arena!

Just as the political emphasis of the dissatisfied states led them to fear detail in drafting and to eschew expert opinion and technical arguments, so the legal emphasis of the satisfied states led them to a firm reliance on just such techniques. Because these primarily Western states had interests in many diverse aspects of activities dealing with the sea, and had the necessary legal and technical resources, they submitted a large number of very detailed proposals. One difficulty for these states as a group was that there were often numerous competing proposals from states with similar outlooks. One of the many examples of very detailed proposals is a Dutch revision of the International Law Commission Draft Article on the continental shelf. The original paragraph 2 read: "Subject to the provisions of paragraphs 1 and 5 of this article, the coastal state is entitled to construct and maintain on the continental shelf installations necessary for the exploration and exploitation of its natural resources, and to establish safety zones at a reasonable distance around such installations and take in those zones measures necessary for their protection."[47]

This sentence was expanded by the Dutch to read: "Subject to the provisions of paragraphs 1 and 5 of this article and within the limits mentioned in article 68, the coastal state is entitled to construct and maintain or operate installations and other devices in the said areas necessary for the exploration and exploitation of their natural resources. The said installations and other devices shall be surrounded by a safety zone of 50 metres radius prohibited for all vessels except exploration and exploitation craft. A group of such installations and devices shall be considered as one unit if the distances are less than half a nautical mile. Entrance into such units is forbidden for all ships of more than 1,000 registered tons, except exploration and exploitation craft. If such a unit is more than 10 nautical miles long, a fairway of one nautical mile wide shall be provided in the middle, and properly marked, without prejudice to paragraph 5. The area inside such units shall be a prohibited anchorage."[48] Like many other detailed proposals, the Dutch draft alienated several of the Netherlands' natural allies. In this case, the United Kingdom also proposed an amendment whose purpose was the same as the Dutch amendment, differing only in length and wording. The

46 A/CONF. 19/8, 23rd meeting, par. 17.
47 UN Doc. A/3159.
48 UN Doc. A/CONF. 13/C.4/L.22.

result was a quibble among states whose position was basically the same.

Submission of competing amendments to the same article, differing only in detail, was characteristic of the satisfied states at the conferences. Only infrequently would a legal specialist from one Western state agree that another's handling of details was technically correct and sufficiently comprehensive to cover all contingencies. This often meant that states of similar outlook which submitted proposals differing only in detail would maintain their competing proposals into the voting stage, instead of uniting to back one of the texts. As a result, it became difficult to get a detailed proposal adopted. When no agreement on details could be reached among these states, the committee or the conference adopted the most general proposal or the original International Law Commission text. While the desire of the legally sophisticated to write comprehensive codes is understandable, it would have been much more to the point to put greater effort into forming a consensus on basic issues. Without such a consensus, it is impossible to negotiate on details.

When the satisfied states tended to submit detailed proposals, their justifications and explanations for the proposals were of course complex legally and technically. These remarks were not, could not be, directed to the delegates from the dissatisfied states who most needed convincing. The dissatisfied delegates were never shown why certain proposals were not contrary to their interests and could indeed have been interpreted in the interest of all. Because the dissatisfied, suspicious of the satisfied states' position at the outset, were never sufficiently convinced by the arguments of the satisfied states' delegates, they tended automatically to oppose changes in the International Law Commission draft proposed by satisfied states. For example, it is difficult to see how a change requested by the United Kingdom in the definition of a pirate ship or aircraft should have been contrary to the interests of the dissatisfied. The International Law Commission draft had defined such craft by a clause of "intent"—that is, a craft was a pirate ship if "it is *intended* by the persons in dominant control to be used for the purposes of committing"[49] an act of piracy. The British desired to make the definition of fact; a pirate ship is one "which has been used to *commit* any acts of piracy."[50] Characteristically, another satisfied state, Italy, submitted another similar proposal.[51] Neither delegation clearly explained the legal difference between intent and act. Both proposals failed; the International Law Commission text was adopted.

[49] UN Doc. A/3159 (italics added).
[50] UN Doc. A/CONF. 13/C.2/L.83 (italics added).
[51] UN Doc. A/CONF. 13/C.2/L.81.

The satisfied states placed reverent reliance upon expert opinion, particularly that of the great French expert on law of the sea, Gilbert Gidel, who was a delegate to the first conference. Great resentment was expressed by delegates of the satisfied states, the French in particular, when the dissatisfied states used a statement of Gidel's, taken out of context from a work written in 1934, to attack the three-mile limit: "La prétendue regle des trois milles a été la grande vaincue de la Conférence."[52] M. Gros, the chief French delegate, attacked the newer states for misquoting Gidel and mishandling expert opinion.[53] Furthermore, he informed them that, while expert opinion by its very nature is free of national or group bias, Gidel's opinion had the added authority of being practically synonymous with the position of the French Government.[54] Ironically, and sadly for those states who revered the opinion of Professor Gidel and the experts, Gidel's proposed revision of the International Law Commission definition of the high seas, a masterpiece of drafting exactness, failed of adoption. This could not have eased the resentment felt at the "misuse and abuse" of expert opinion.

Another tendency of Western and international-law-minded states was, not surprisingly for those legally oriented, to re-argue decided cases in international law. In particular, the *Lotus Case* and the *Anglo-Norwegian Fisheries Case* were dissected by Western international lawyers at the first conference.[55] Politically, this was a waste of time. Legally, the differences between the respective positions were important, but no matter how the lawyers differed on the interpretation of the court's ruling, they and the states they represented felt bound by that ruling. The tendency to argue the legal niceties of the case often made them neglect the importance of convincing the dissatisfied of the basic validity of the court's ruling and its worthiness to be included in the draft articles on the law of the sea under negotiation.

III

From this article it may be concluded that the results achieved by the Conferences on the Law of the Sea, like those of any United Nations-sponsored international conference, were dictated by the will-

---

[52] Gilbert Gidel, *Le Droit international public de la mer*, Vol. III, *La mer territorial et la zone contiguë* (Paris 1934), 151.

[53] A/CONF. 13/39, 37th meeting, par. 16-20.

[54] A/CONF. 13/42, 17th meeting, par. 36.

[55] See, for example, A/CONF. 13/39, 5th meeting, par. 35; 9th meeting, par. 23; 17th meeting, par. 18; 28th meeting, par. 15.

ingness of the participating states to create essentially political agreements. States or groups of states which assume that a specialized subject matter such as international law should not be subject to the political rough-and-tumble associated with parliamentary diplomacy, but dealt with logically within the broad lines of its past development, are bound to be disappointed by results achieved in a conference.

Indeed, one conclusion that might be drawn from the study of attitudes of dissatisfied states at the law of the sea conferences is that future conferences would be useless for codifying and developing law because of the hostility of dissatisfied states toward international law, a remnant of their European and imperialist past. Their concern with sovereignty, their suspicion of legal details, their wholly political attitude—all make it unlikely that they will be willing to agree to universal norms. By characterizing international law as an institutionalization of the values of the "top dogs" of the European-centered past, the dissatisfied seemed to demonstrate that they could not conceive that states might value law for its normative quality. They could not acknowledge that states have in the past compromised in negotiating legal subjects in order to create a pattern of orderly relationships even though their interests might not be fully served by such norms, or even that order itself may be to the interest of a state.

This attitude of the dissatisfied bodes ill for the possibility of creating universality in the law in our time. If, however, this is to be an end actively sought, international conferences, or some other United Nations-sponsored device, will probably be necessary to gain consent of the dissatisfied.[56] And if conferences are to be used for this purpose, it must be recognized, and not merely ruefully as Mr. Petren of Sweden did, that "progressive development" is guided by political considerations and that the results of a conference will be an undifferentiated mixture of "progressive development" and "codification." No purpose is served by deploring a "diplomacy of the sea" and distinguishing it from a true "law of the sea."

The course of attempting to achieve universality by means of conferences presents the satisfied with knotty problems. To avoid utter

---

[56] Alternative schemes, such as allowing the General Assembly to declare codes of customary law, or giving legislative power to an enlarged Security Council or to a special majority in the General Assembly, would not avoid those problems in negotiating that became obvious at the law of the sea conferences. Legal rules under these schemes would still have to be negotiated under parliamentary diplomacy. For these schemes see Jorge Castaneda, "The Underdeveloped Nations and the Development of International Law," *International Organization*, XV (Winter 1961), 38-48; and Arthur N. Holcombe, "The Improvement of the International Law-Making Process," *Notre Dame Lawyer*, XXXVII, Symposium (1961), 16-23.

failure, the satisfied must alter their outlook on international law and on negotiating it.

The burden of responsibility for bringing conferences dealing with international law to successful conclusions rests with the states most devoted to international law. This does not mean that these states should make drastic changes in the law or sacrifice vital interests merely to foster agreement for agreement's sake. What is necessary is a recognition on the part of satisfied states that an international conference is a forum in which political negotiations must not be looked upon with distaste, and a determination on their part to find common interests, and to make real attempts to talk to other participants in terms which all understand. Such changes in attitude—if forthcoming—are no guarantee of success; indeed, they may only hasten failure by more clearly demonstrating the real reasons for disagreement. But a realistic appraisal of the conference process as a political process is the only approach which will make success even remotely possible.

5. INTERNATIONAL SYSTEMS AND INTERNATIONAL LAW

By STANLEY HOFFMANN

THE purpose of this essay is twofold. First, it proposes to undertake, in introductory form, one of the many tasks a historical sociology of international relations could perform: the comparative study of one of those relations which appear in almost any international system, i.e., international law.[1] Secondly, this essay will try to present the rudimentary outlines of a theory of international law which might be called sociological or functional.[2]

International law is one of the aspects of international politics which reflect most sharply the essential differences between domestic and world affairs. Many traditional distinctions tend to disappear, owing to an "international civil war" which projects what are primarily domestic institutions (such as parliaments and pressure

Reprinted from *The International System*, edited by Klaus Knorr and Sidney Verba (Princeton: Princeton University Press, 1961), pp. 205-237. Reprinted by permission of the author and Princeton University Press. Copyright 1961© Princeton University Press.

[1] See some suggestions in my *Contemporary Theory in International Politics*, Englewood Cliffs, N.J., 1960, pp. 174ff.

[2] These adjectives are borrowed from Julius Stone, "Problems Confronting Sociological Enquiries Concerning International Law." *Recueil des Cours de l'Académie de Droit International*, Vol. 89 (1956), 1, and Hans J. Morgenthau, *Dilemmas of Politics*, Chicago, 1958, ch. 11, respectively. The only additional recent works which try to establish a political sociology of international law are Charles de Visscher's *Theory and Reality in Public International Law*, tr. by P. E. Corbett, Princeton, N.J., 1957; Percy E. Corbett's *Law in Diplomacy*, Princeton, N.J., 1959; B. Landheer's "Contemporary Sociological Theories and International Law," *Recueil des Cours* . . . , Vol. 91 (1957), 1, and, to some extent, John Herz's *International Politics in the Atomic Age*, New York, 1959, and Morton A. Kaplan's and Nicholas Katzenbach's "The Patterns of International Politics and of International Law," *American Political Science Review*, LIII (September 1959), pp. 693-712—the last two pieces being more concerned with politics than with law. The present essay, which supplements an earlier piece on "Quelques aspects du rôle du Droit International dans la politique étrangère des Etats" (Association Française de Science Politique, *La Politique étrangère et ses Fondements*, Paris, 1954, pp. 239-77), will itself be expanded into a volume on *International Law in World Politics*.

groups) into world politics, and injects world-wide ideological clashes into domestic affairs. International law, like its Siamese twin and enemy, war, remains a crystallization of all that keeps world politics sui generis. If theory is to be primarily concerned with the distinctive features of systems rather than with the search for regularities, international law becomes a most useful approach to international politics.

This paper will examine the relations between international law and international systems, first in general terms, and subsequently in more concrete form, with evidence derived from history. Finally, in the light of such a historical presentation, I will examine briefly two of the main politico-legal problems raised by international law.

I

Most theories of domestic politics start from the ideal-type of (1) a community—i.e., an unconditional consensus on cooperation, a belief in a common good (however vague) and in the precedence of this common good over particular interests; and (2) an organization, the State, which has created this community or was established by it, and is endowed with the monopoly of the legitimate use of force. The theory of international politics must start from the ideal-type of a milieu in which (1) the behavior of the members ranges from, at best, that of partners in a society (who cooperate on a limited number of issues, rarely unconditionally, and give primary allegiance to themselves, not the society) to that of accomplices in chaos: the social group made up of the states is always on the verge of being a fiction; and (2) there is no monopoly of power, over and above that possessed by the members. Thus, whereas procedures for cooperation, for the creation and expression of consent, exist both in domestic and in world politics, the permanent possibility of free and legitimate recourse to violence remains the mark of international relations.

This simple and banal point of departure is of decisive importance both for the understanding of international law and for the delimitation of international systems.

(a) Law is a body of rules for human conduct established for the ordering of a social group and enforceable by external power. Domestic law orders the national group by acting directly on the individual citizens and by regulating all the problems which are deemed to be of social importance; it is enforced by the power of the state, exerted directly on individuals. By contrast, international law suffers from three forms of precariousness. The first is its low degree of institutionalization. The second is its unique substance. In the domestic order, which regulates a great mass of individuals, law is an instrument of homogeneity. The international legal order regulates a small number of subjects. Consequently, its law is a law of differentiation, which vacillates from the Charybdis of universality at the cost of vagueness, to the Scylla of precision at the cost of heterogeneity. The scope of the subject matter is limited by the reluctance of the subjects to submit themselves to extensive regulations and by the inefficiency of premature regulations: hence the numerous gaps in the body of rules. The third weakness is the limited amount of solidity or authority in international law. I do not refer here to efficiency in Kelsen's meaning of the term, for it is true that most forms of international law are obeyed, but to the effect of the following factors: the obscurities or ambiguities which mar existing rules, since they are established by the subjects themselves; the fact, analyzed by de Visscher, that the greatest solidarities exist in matters which least affect the power and policies of the subjects and vice versa; the fact that, in Julius Stone's words, international law is the one legal order which provides for its own destruction by the mere force of its own subjects.[3]

(b) An international system is a pattern of relations between the basic units of world politics, which is characterized by the scope of the objectives pursued by those units and of the tasks performed among them, as well as by the means used in order to achieve those goals and perform those tasks. This pattern is largely determined by the structure of the world, the nature of the forces which operate across or within the major units, and the capabilities, pattern of power, and political culture of those units.[4]

One of the main tasks of a historical sociology of international politics is the delimitation of such systems: where does one system begin or end, in space and in time? It is with the limits in time that I am concerned here. As Raymond Aron has observed, periodization is always both necessary and dangerous: the historian is free in his choice of criteria but should refrain from attributing to those he chose consequences which only empirical evidence could prove.[5] The criteria I would propose are what I would call the *stakes of conflict.* A new system emerges:

---

[3] *Legal Controls of International Conflict,* New York, 1954, p. 1.

[4] Such a definition corresponds to accepted definitions of domestic political systems, which are characterized also both by the scope of the ends of politics (the limited state *vs.* the totalitarian state, the welfare state *vs.* the free enterprise state) and by the methods of organizing power (constitutional relations between the branches of government, types of party system).

[5] Raymond Aron, "Evidence and Inference in History," *Daedalus,* Vol. 87 (Fall 1958), pp. 11-39.

(1) When there is a new answer to the question: what *are* the units in potential conflict?—i.e., when the basic structure of the world has changed (as in the passage from the city-state system to the Roman Empire; from the Empire to the medieval system; from the medieval hierarchy to the modern "horizontal" system of multiple sovereignties).

(2) When there is a new answer to the question: what *can* the units do to one another in a conflict?—i.e., a basic change in the technology of conflict. Such a change may also bring about a transformation in the basic structure of the world: as John Herz has reminded us, the gunpowder revolution ushered in the era of the "impermeable" territorial state. Even within the same type of basic structure, a fundamental innovation in the technology of conflict changes the nature of the international system: the atomic revolution has rendered obsolete previous "multiple-sovereignty" systems because it meant the passage from a relative to an absolute power of destruction, and consequently the end of great-power "impermeability." An effective diffusion of nuclear power would mean another system still.

(3) When within a single state of the technology of conflict there is a new answer to the question: what do the units *want* to do to one another? Here, we try to distinguish systems according to the scope of the units' purposes, and to the techniques the actors use in order to meet their objectives or to prevent their rivals from achieving theirs.

If we combine those sets of criteria, we come to a fundamental distinction between two types of systems: stable ones and revolutionary ones. A stable system is one in which the stakes of conflict are limited, because the relations between the actors are marked by moderation in scope and means. Whatever the world's basic structure and the state of the technology of conflict, the units act so as to limit the amount of harm they could inflict upon one another. In a revolutionary system, this moderation has disappeared. When one major actor's decision to discard it coincides with or brings about a revolution in the technology of conflict, or a change in the basic structure of the world, or both, the system is particularly unstable.[6] In other words, a stable system is one in which the life or the essential values

---

[6] The *number* of violent conflicts does not intervene in these definitions. A stable period may be marked by frequent wars as long as they remain limited in objectives and methods. A revolutionary period may not necessarily be marked by all-out, general war, if the technology of conflict introduces a mutual interest in avoiding the total destruction such a war would entail; but as long as this restraint does not bring back moderation in the purposes and means of conflicts other than all-out war, the system remains largely a revolutionary one, although it disposes of an element of stability—a fragile element, given all the other circumstances.

of the basic units are not constantly in question, and the main actors agree on the rules according to which the competition will take place; a revolutionary system is one in which the incompatibility of purposes rules out such an agreement.

For each kind of basic structure in the world, and each kind of technology of conflict, we may obtain the ideal-type of a stable system by asking what are the conditions from which moderation in scope and means is most likely to follow. Actual historical systems at times meet all those conditions, but often they do not; and they are, of course, marked by constant change in all their elements. Those changes (1) do not affect the system at all if they do not hurt or remove the essential conditions of stability; (2) merely weaken the system by making it operate in less than ideal conditions, if they do cripple some of those conditions but without destroying the moderation in scope and means; (3) ruin the system altogether if such deterioration, instead of leading to temporary disturbances, brings about a breakdown in moderation, a revolution in the technology of conflict or in the basic structure of the world.

Whether a change which affects the essential conditions of stability damages the system decisively or not depends on the circumstances. A breakdown requires the collapse of a large number of such conditions. This can happen either (1) when one of the main actors decides to overthrow the system, and succeeds in removing so many of the conditions of stability that the system does indeed collapse— i.e., when this actor's move leads not simply to *any* kind of conflict, but to a revolutionary one; or (2) when a previous deterioration leads to a conflict which might not start as a revolutionary one, but becomes one because it develops into a decisive additional factor of disruption. In both cases, the end of a stable system is marked by a general war.[7]

In the world of multiple sovereignties before the invention of absolute weapons, it was the balance-of-power system which brought stability into international politics: i.e., a pattern of relations among states which through shifting alliances and the use of various diplomatic techniques tends to limit the ambitions of the main actors, to

---

[7] Besides making the fundamental distinction *between* stable and revolutionary systems, we have to distinguish *among* stable and *among* revolutionary ones. Here our criteria should be, in addition to the basic structure of the world and the state of the technology of conflict: (1) in the case of stable systems, the kind of *means* used by the actors in their competition and cooperation: cf. below, the distinction between the stable system which preceded the French Revolution and the stable system which followed the Congress of Vienna; both were "balance of power" systems, but the latter was more institutionalized than the former; (2) in the case of revolutionary systems, the type of *objective* for which the conflicts take place (religious allegiance, form of government).

preserve a relative equilibrium among them, and to reduce the amount of violence between them. The ideal conditions for such a system are as follows:

(1) Conditions related to the structure of the world: a greater number of major states than two; a relative equilibrium of power among them; the existence of a frontier, a prerequisite of the kind of flexibility that a balancing system needs.

(2) Conditions related to transnational forces: technological stability; a common outlook among the leaders of the major states, provided either by a similarity of regimes, or by a common attitude toward religion, or by similar beliefs about the purpose of the state. Such an outlook allows for horizontal ties as strong as, or stronger than, the political ties which attach those leaders to their domestic community; a common conception of legitimacy can thus develop.

(3) A condition related to the domestic situation within the major actors: the existence of a political system in which the state exercises only limited control over its citizens' international loyalties and activities.

(4) The outcome of these conditions is a system in which the objectives of the major actors remain limited to moderate increases in power or prestige, and in which many of the tasks which can be performed through the processes of world politics remain beyond the pale of those politics. The means used by the major units in their mutual relations are coalitions designed to prevent any single actor from disrupting stability, either by rewarding him for his cooperation or by punishing him for his misbehavior, without, however, making it impossible for him to cooperate again.

The ideal conditions for stability can be defined as *evenness* in the situation of the major units—just as a large degree of identity in the members of the state is necessary for the emergence of the general will. Conversely, the process of deterioration which leads to disturbances within the system and might provoke its breakdown beyond a certain point can be summed up as the reintroduction of unevenness or *heterogeneity*.[8] This process includes the appearance of the following conditions:

(1) In the structure of the world: irrepressible ambitions of individual rulers;[9] ambitions kindled by a disparity in power between a

---

[8] See the little-known but brilliant analysis by Panayis A. Papaligouras, *Théorie de la Société internationale*, Geneva, Graduate School of International Studies, 1941.

[9] They do not, by themselves, destroy the balancing system but they make its operation uncertain, and increase the likelihood of "in-system" wars, which may in turn destroy the system if other essential conditions for an ideal balance have also disappeared, or if the logic of war destroys previous limitations on the instruments of conflict.

major actor and its neighbors or other major units; the end of the frontier, which increases the likelihood of, and the stakes in, direct clashes between the major units.

(2) In the forces which cut across those units: a technological revolution, which leads to instability when it produces a race; the destruction of transnational ties, either under the impact of domestic integration which inevitably submits diplomacy to greater internal pressures, or because of an ideological explosion set off by a disparity of regimes or beliefs.

(3) In the domestic situation of the major units: strong integrative trends leading to nationalism; the expansion of state control over the foreign activities of the citizens either for economic or for ideological purposes.

(c) Let us turn now to the relation of international law to various international systems. International law can be studied as a product of international systems and as a repertory of normative theory about each one of them. On the one hand, it is shaped by all the elements which compose an international system:

(1) It reflects the structure of the world. The nature of the actors determines whether the law of the system is the "law of coordination" made by territorial states, or the external public law of an empire, or whether it will disappear altogether as it did during much of the medieval period. The size of the diplomatic field determines the degree of universality of the legal order. The degree of unity of international law and the efficiency of a good deal of its provisions depend on the existence, duration, and seriousness of a relationship of major tension.

(2) International law reflects the forces which cut across the units. Technology is of considerable importance: the intensity or density of legal relations between the actors depends largely on the state of the arts. The unity and authority of the legal order depend on the presence and number of transnational ideologies and conceptions of legitimacy.

(3) The domestic situation of the major units is relevant here also. International law has always reflected the pattern of power and the political culture of the main actors.[10] The development of law by treaties and the reception of rules of international law within the various units depend on the provisions of constitutions and on the decisions of domestic courts.

(4) Finally, international law reflects the relations among the units. It is shaped by the scope of those relations: the breadth and the nature of the subject-matter regulated by law according to the

---

[10] See Corbett, *op.cit.*, especially chs. 1-3.

range and character of the goals which the units try to reach and of
the tasks they try to perform. In particular, the rules of law often
express the policies of the major units. Moreover, customs and
treaties always both reflect the methods by which the units try to
meet their objectives, and regulate at least some of the techniques
used in the process.

On the other hand, if we turn from empirical systems to normative
theory, we find in theories of international law a critical assessment
of international systems from the viewpoint of world order. In any
political system, order is achieved if the following three requirements
are met: (1) security—i.e., dealing with the problem of conflict by
assuring the survival and safety of the members of the system; (2)
satisfaction—i.e., dealing with the problem of assent, and obtaining
it through constraint or consent; (3) flexibility—i.e., dealing with
the problem of change (which is crucial, since assent is never
definitive or total), by establishing procedures capable of absorbing
shocks and of channeling grievances. In a world divided into numerous units, order is always threatened. Legal theorists have constantly
asked whether order was possible at all; if so, whether the system
was capable of ensuring it; and if not, what kind of measures were
necessary to obtain order. On the whole, in each period, there have
been three types of reactions: the deniers, who question either the
possibility or the desirability of a stable legal order; the utopians,
who also question the effectiveness of the existing system but propose
to substitute a radically different one; the adjusters, who try to show
how and to what extent order can be established or preserved within
the existing system. We learn a great deal about the nature and
operation of a given international system if we study the range of
disagreements among those three groups; the more stable the system,
the narrower this range.

Since international law constitutes the formal part of whatever
kind of order reigns and expresses the more lasting interests of the
actors—their long- or middle-range strategy, rather than their daily
tactics—the link between the solidity or authority of international
law and the stability of the international system is both obvious and
strong. The basic function of international law is to organize the
coexistence of the various units: this presupposes that their existence
is assured. In stable systems, it is possible to distinguish three kinds
of international law:[11]

(1) The law of the political framework—i.e., the network of
agreements which define the conditions, and certain of the rules,

[11] See George Schwarzenberger, *Power Politics,* New York, 1951, ch. 13;
and Hans J. Morgenthau, *op.cit.,* pp. 228-29.

of the political game among the states. By conditions, I refer to such provisions as the settlement of borders after wars, the main alignments expressed in treaties of alliance, the holding of periodic conferences among major powers; by rules, I refer to provisions which determine the mutual commitments of states, or the procedure for the settlement of major disputes.

(2) The law of reciprocity, which defines the conditions and rules of interstate relations in areas which affect less vitally the power and policies of the states. This is the large zone in which states can be assumed to have a mutual and lasting interest in common rules: the zone of predictability, on which the competition of the actors in politically more sensitive areas rests and depends. We can distinguish two kinds of laws of reciprocity: first, the law of delimitation which defines the respective rights and privileges of states, in peacetime over such matters as diplomatic relations, territory, and people, in wartime over weapons, military objectives, non-combatants, etc.; second, the law of cooperation, which regulates joint interests, particularly in commerce.

(3) The law of community, which deals with problems which can best be handled, not on the basis of a reciprocity of interests of states understood as separate and competing units, but on the basis of a community of action independent from politics: problems of a technical or scientific nature for which borders are irrelevant.

This distinction is sound and legitimate in a stable period, for when the survival of the players is insured, a hierarchy of interests becomes possible. The law of the political framework deals the cards with which the players try to reach such objectives as greater power, or prestige, or the triumph of ideals; the law of reciprocity provides the underpinning of national security and defines those functions and attributes of the state which are not put at stake in the political contests. But in a revolutionary system, the distinction between these two kinds of law becomes extremely fuzzy, for when survival is not assured, the limits which the law of reciprocity sets to states' privileges or jurisdiction become obstacles to their quest for greater security and power, while cooperation over joint interests is replaced by conflict or competition which challenges previous rules. In such a system, the power and policies of states are directly involved in almost every aspect of international activity.[12] Thus, in

---

[12] Scholars may argue that important mutual interests still exist and that states have little to gain by turning the zone of predictability into a battlefield. The trouble is that what seems irrational to the scholar from the viewpoint of international society seems rational to the statesman from the viewpoint of his own national calculation, given the peculiar logic of such calculations in fiercely competitive situations. An "objective" common interest might not be

a revolutionary system, the great bulk of international law partakes of the somewhat shaky authority of the law of the political framework.

The difference in the solidity of law in revolutionary and stable systems is reflected in the contrasting impact of political change on law. Changes which do not destroy a stable system have no lethal effect on the legal order, precisely because customs and agreements express, as I have put it, strategic rather than tactical interests. To be sure, the body of rules reflects such changes if they are of sufficient magnitude: in particular, the disappearance of some of the essential conditions for an ideal stable system has repercussions on the law of the political framework, which is the most sensitive to such tremors; it may also leave its mark on the law of reciprocity, because certain kinds of agreements become increasingly rare, or codification more troublesome, or difficulties appear in the discharge of treaties. However, the law of reciprocity may continue to develop even when the ideal conditions for stability are not present anymore (as was shown by the flowering of such law just before World War I), precisely because it reflects mutual interests which the fluctuations of politics do not impair so long as the stable system lasts. Also, while the essential moderation in the scope and means of international relations continues, the gaps and uncertainties of law do not become factors of disruption: in the areas which are not regulated or in which the rules are ambiguous, a purely political decision or interpretation by the states concerned will be needed but, given the system, no destructive effects are likely to follow.

In a revolutionary system, however, gaps and ambiguities become wedges for destruction or subversion of the international order in the interest of any of the actors. The absence of any agreement on the rules of the game, the increase in the stakes of conflict, the reign of insecurity for the actors, mean that political changes will have the following impact on international law: (1) just as old theories and concepts outlive the system which justified them, old regulations which have become obsolete nevertheless continue to be considered valid (although they are less and less respected) because of the increasing difficulty in agreeing on new rules, or because the old ones serve the interests of some of the contending units; (2) new problems thrown up by political or technological change often remain unregulated, for the same reasons; (3) new regulations appear which constitute attempts to deal with some of the changes but turn out to

---

perceived by the antagonists and, even if it is, there remains an abyss between such understanding and a formal legal agreement which would sanction it. On these points, see Kenneth Waltz, *Man, the State, and War,* New York, 1959, pp. 192ff.

be incompatible with the new system; and (4) since international systems change essentially through general wars, the collapse of previous laws of war is usually the first effect of the change on the legal order.

This conglomeration of ruin, gaps, and "dysfunctional" old or new rules denotes the major areas of friction and tensions in world politics during the lifetime of revolutionary systems and particularly in periods of passage from one system to another.

Thus, it is in balance-of-power systems that the authority of international law has been greatest: as Oppenheim has stated in his treatise, the existence of the balance is a condition of the flourishing of authoritative international law. However, this condition is at the same time a limitation.

(1) Even when the balance functions under optimum conditions. the political framework may remain largely unregulated. We have to distinguish between systems in which the balance is more or less automatic or mechanical, and systems in which it is institutionalized to a greater degree—a distinction among stable systems based in particular on the law of the political framework (see n. 7).

(2) Even when the balance functions under optimum conditions, it operates sometimes at the expense of law. In a system of "sovereign" states, the principles of equality and consent are essential to the legal order. But the daily practices of the balance may conflict with these norms: a preponderance of power often forces small or even isolated large states to assent to measures which go against their objectives or detract from the formal equality of all the units.

(3) Among the many power configurations which characterize the relations of the major units in balancing systems, there is one which threatens the solidity of· international law (especially that of the political framework) more permanently. When the optimum conditions are met, the most likely resulting combination is the "mechanism of imbalance"—a coalition of a majority of the main actors against an isolated would-be disrupter; but when those conditions are not all present, there may come into being an opposition of blocs of comparable strength, so that alignments stiffen instead of remaining flexible, with a tendency to shift. The authority and unity of international law may then be imperiled.

II

I will try now to support the preceding generalizations by examining briefly three concrete examples of relations between international systems and international law.

(a) The first example, which I want to mention very briefly, is that of international law during the balance-of-power system which lasted from the Peace of Westphalia until the French Revolution.

The balance could operate effectively because the treaties of Westphalia had redistributed territory in such a way as to create a number of major states capable of neutralizing each other, and had also removed the poisonous element of religious conflict. Within the main units, mercantilism and absolutism weakened gradually. New transnational ties developed: the "corporate identity" of monarchs, diplomats, and officers across borders led to a consensus on the legitimacy of the balance, just as the community of European intellectuals produced a consensus on the values of the Enlightenment. The result, politically, was a mechanical balance, with frequent disturbances due either to the fact that a state could never be sure in advance whether or when others would try to stop it, or to individual ambitions. Hence numerous limited wars occurred: stylized wars of position which affected only rarely the civilian population.

Although there was little international law of the political framework, the law of reciprocity developed in a way which reflected both the moderation and the volatile character of a balancing system. On the one hand, in the area of trade, statesmen came to realize that law was the best technique for obtaining an increase in national wealth and power (as in past mercantilist practice), but with safety; the idea of a harmony of interests replaced the previous expectation of conflict, hence numerous measures to protect commerce at sea, especially in wartime. Neutrality became for the first time altogether possible, a good bargain, and a subject of legal regulation. On the other hand, the balance imposed limits to the development of law. The preservation of the system required at the end of wars practices which restored the equilibrium among the major powers at the expense of small states; those compensations proved that the norm of territorial integrity was efficient only as long as it was backed by force, and that it was subordinated to the operations of the balance. Also, there were gaps wherever rules would have restricted state power too sharply: maritime warfare remained anarchical, and no adequate procedure for the settlement of disputes developed, except for rare and delicate instances of arbitration.

The response of theory to these developments was most interesting. In the previous revolutionary system, a big gap had separated destroyers of the medieval dream of unity, like Machiavelli, creators of new dreams like Crucé or Sully, and the numerous would-be rescuers of the medieval theory, who reasserted the supremacy of natural law and the doctrine of just war, but secularized the former, hedged in the latter with qualifications, and came to recognize the existence of an international law created by the will of states. Now, in a system of increasing moderation, the gap narrowed. Even deniers of the efficiency of "covenants without the sword" showed that self-restraint might prevent a war of all against all. At the other pole, the Kantian utopia also reflected a new optimism: the problem of establishing order among the states was going to require essentially a change in the regimes but not the end of the division of the world into separate units, and it would be solved by the invisible hand of history. The theorists in the middle, still trying to save the idea of a legal community of mankind, gradually gave up natural law as its cement—a retreat which would have been taken as an invitation to and a confession of chaos in the preceding period, but which could now be accepted without anguish, for a positivistic emphasis on the fundamental rights of states as the foundation of order did not seem necessarily self-defeating any longer. The expectation of a harmony of interests had been fed by the system.

Its collapse was sudden and took the form of a swift chain reaction. (1) The decisive factor was the change in France's regime—a fact which shows that the study of international systems must extend to the analysis of the political ones they include. (2) The revolution, in turn, destroyed previous transnational links: the heterogeneity of regimes introduced an explosive element into Europe, and after a brief period of idealistic pacifism—a revulsion against the balance, that sport of kings—the revolutionaries, turning to Messianism, lit the fuse. (3) This attempt to destroy old regimes everywhere in turn removed another essential condition of the balance; nationalism in France led to the imposition of full government control on its citizens' acts and thoughts. (4) Next, the previous equilibrium among the major powers was destroyed by the French victories—an incentive to exploit unevenness even further. (5) Then, Napoleon's ambitions produced the first modern instance of total power politics, based on an ideological inspiration, and waged by total domestic and international means. (6) A further series of changes in the previous conditions of stability resulted: constant shifts in the map of Europe, a transformation of the domestic order of many of the actors, who moved away from feudal absolutism to defeat France's nationalism with its own weapons, the creation of two opposed ideological camps. Consequently, previous international law was thoroughly disrupted: the law of neutrality collapsed; wars of total mobilization, movement, and extermination of civilians replaced the ballet of limited wars. We have here the example of a system breaking down because of the deliberate attempt by one of its major actors to destroy it, and because of this actor's capacity to succeed for a while by exploiting the dynamism of revolution.

(b) Let us examine now the international system of the nineteenth century, its fate and its impact on international law. The defeat of the force which had destroyed the previous system—France—and the apparent collapse of French-inspired ideals seemed to make a return to stability possible. The victors of 1815 decided to restore a balancing system, for they saw in it the pattern which could best ensure such stability, by giving security to the main powers, providing the greatest amount of flexibility, and obtaining the assent of all, including France, on whom only a far tighter organization of her enemies than they were capable of maintaining could have imposed a punitive peace with any chance of success.

Some of the victors, however, wanted a new kind of balancing system; what is interesting here is the discrepancy between intention and performance. Specifically, although England was willing to return to a mechanical balance, Austria and Russia wanted to extend the scope and means of world politics: whereas the eighteenth-century balance had excluded intervention in domestic affairs, Metternich and Alexander now wanted an organized balancing system which would include in its concept of legitimacy a formula for domestic order, and dispose of means of enforcement against the rise of liberal and nationalist forces. The international law of the political framework would have become an explicit and powerful instrument of the big powers' common policy of preserving the Vienna order, both in its international *and* in its internal aspects. But this was not to happen, for it soon appeared that a voluntary system of cooperation was too weak to control developments within nations which a previous balancing system had already been powerless to prevent. In other words, so extensive a community could not be created by superstructural means alone: the failure of the Holy Alliance proved that an effective new balancing system could be obtained only through a return to moderation in scope and means, not through an ambitious extension.

In the beginning, almost all the conditions for a successful balance were present. (1) The structure of the world was marked by a double hierarchy: first, there was a distinction between a civilized core and a frontier; secondly, within the core, there was a hierarchy between small and large states. No permanent relation of major tension emerged until after 1870. (2) In the core area, technology expanded but never to such a degree as to give to one major actor power of life and death over another. Despite the clash of political ideologies, supranational ties persisted: the dominant ideologies were themselves either supranational or favorable to the maintenance of bonds between national elites; the "Internationale" of diplomats allowed for a consensus on the rules of the game. (3) Although regimes were far from identical, the limited state developed everywhere. The conduct of foreign affairs could be divorced from domestic passions. Constitutionalism, marked by the legalization of public affairs and by the growth of the judicial apparatus, made notable advances. Liberalism led to a separation between state and society.

Consequently, the relations among states were once again characterized by moderation in scope and means. The moderation in scope was twofold. First, the number of tasks performed by the processes of world politics was limited to conflict and political accommodation. The failure of Metternich's hope meant that, within the core area, domestic developments were not a legitimate object of international politics: the "neutrality of alignment"[13] necessary to the effectiveness of the balance required neutrality toward regimes as well, which remained possible as long as internal revolutions made no attempt to disrupt the international system. The separation of state and society removed another vast zone from world politics—the field of private transnational activities, especially economic ones. Secondly, the objectives of the major units also remained moderate in scope: they sought limited increments of power and influence within the core area; they avoided on the whole the destruction of the actors' value systems or national existence in this area. As for moderation in means, it was shown by the return to limited wars, the practice of non-intervention within the core area, the multiplication of international conferences of all kinds.

In this system, international law—the law of the European core area—played all three of the roles described above, within the limits previously defined. The law of the political framework was the law of the Concert: as the instrument of the society of the major powers for the supervision of small states and the control of the individual ambitions of each member, it consecrated the power relations which developed for such purposes. Hence the prevalence of the legal techniques of neutralization and internationalization. They implied an agreement on common abstention from, or common action in, a given area or problem; they resulted from the consensus on moderation and cooperation rather than all-out isolated moves.[14] But since this law was a balancing technique, not a way of overcoming the balance, its development was hemmed in by the usual limitations. Many rules merely expressed the independence of states in such a system: for instance, the principle of unanimity in Concert meetings. Law was violated whenever the maintenance of the system required it—i.e., at both ends of Concert activities: the composition of the meetings violated the principle of equality, and the process of enforce-

---

[13] See Kaplan and Katzenbach, *op.cit.*
[14] For a more detailed analysis, see the author's *Organisations internationales et pouvoirs politiques des Etats*, Paris, Colin, 1954, part 1.

ment often twisted the independence, integrity, or free consent of small powers. Finally, there were major gaps in the law of the framework, as exemplified by the purely voluntary character of Concert meetings and by the total freedom to resort to war. Moreover, these limitations and violations became far more dangerous for world order during two periods: the 1850's, when the balance was too fluid—i.e., the mechanism of imbalance did not function, owing to the divisions or passivity of a majority of the big powers— and the last years before World War I, when the hardening of the blocs produced arteriosclerosis in the Concert.[15]

The law of reciprocity was a projection of the constitutional state into world affairs, a reflection of mutual interests, and a product of the balancing system, which curtailed states' objectives. The law of delimitation became firmly established. The law of cooperation progressed considerably in two areas: commerce, where the retreat from mercantilism opened a "depoliticized" zone for free trade and for the free establishment of aliens; the settlement of disputes, as states became willing to resort to judicial procedures in a variety of cases: either cases involving private citizens in the "depoliticized" area, or even cases which involved state interests directly, but which the actors found convenient to send to arbitration because the balance had made resort to force less profitable, or because the development of domestic legal institutions had given greater prestige to legal than to diplomatic mechanisms. But in all its branches the law of reciprocity suffered from the same weakness as the law of the political framework. The different standards for the treatment of foreigners applied by the major states to "civilized" nations and to backward areas showed the limit of the norm of equality. The treatment of debtors by creditor nations proved that the law often identified right with might. "Depolitization" came to an end either whenever citizens ran into trouble abroad and appealed to their country of origin, or when a dispute fell within one of the numerous areas excluded by reservations in arbitration treaties. Spectacular failures at the Hague Conferences left many gaps in the laws of war and for the settlement of disputes. Again, these weaknesses became more severe when the Concert did not function well; at the end of the period, a return to protectionism, tariff wars, and the failure of the London Conference on maritime warfare were signs of deterioration.

The branch of the law of reciprocity which reflected best all the elements of the system was the law of war and neutrality. First, since war was a legitimate method of settlement of disputes, and law did

---

[15] It was in 1871 that Russia denounced the Black Seas provisions of the Paris Treaty, in 1908 that Austria annexed Bosnia-Herzegovina.

not try to curtail the ends which sovereignty served but only to regulate the means which it used, war was entitled to a *status*: it received a legal framework, which distinguished sharply between peace and war (hence the need for a declaration at one end, a formal treaty at the other), and between international and civil strife. Within this framework, both the means and the various categories of war victims were regulated. Secondly, since total war practices were banned by the balance, and war had once again become a method of settlement of disputes but not a way of eliminating one's antagonist, war was considered to be merely a *moment;* it was a dispute between states, not individuals: hence the customs and court decisions on the effect of war on treaties and, more importantly, the crucial distinction between the combatants and non-combatants in war, between the duties of the neutral state and those of neutral citizens. Furthermore, it was a political dispute, not an interruption of economic processes: hence the protection of the neutral trader, who was maintaining the continuity of these processes, and the inviolability of as much of the belligerents' private property as was possible, both at sea and in occupied territory.

The law of community expanded also through countless conferences, conventions, and even institutions; it regulated an increasing number of administrative and technical functions.

Consequently, the law of the nineteenth-century balancing system presented two sides. In matters which affected directly the power and the policies of the major states, law was the transcription of the balancing process in normative terms, the expression of a system in which each state submitted to law insofar as the rules were backed by the pressure of superior force. In other matters, law grew out of the restrictions to which power, in a liberal century, consented for the development of non-political forces of reciprocity and for the devaluation of borders. One result of this double role of law was a fairly effective system of world order. Security was achieved in the core area, especially for the major actors; lesser ones bought survival at the cost of supervision, and, often, partial sacrifices of sovereignty. The Concert tried to preserve flexibility by acting to legalize and harness revolutionary changes. Assent was never complete, but as long as the major powers preferred, or had no choice but to prefer, the maintenance of the system to the gains they might hope to reap by destroying it, this was enough.

Another result was a new rapprochement among the three groups of theorists who coexisted in this period. They agreed on three crucial points: first, the possibility of avoiding chaos; secondly, the basic character of the state as the foundation of world order (and the definition of the state in terms of will); thirdly—and paradoxically—

the weaknesses of international law in the world as it was: an admission which, as in the previous stable period, could be made because of the general moderation of world politics. Even deniers such as Hegel believed in a European family or a "higher praetor" which would prevent the warring states from turning inevitable war into inexpiable hate. Even the visionaries no longer dreamed of supranational utopias: they thought that the world was moving toward a community of harmonious nation-states, thanks to free trade and public opinion. The positivists could deal with the previously avoided problem of the basis of legal obligation, and come up with auto-limitation, *Vereinbarung*, or an indivisible community of interests, without feeling that these were circular answers. At the end of the previous period, the positivists, stressing the differences between international and municipal law, and the individual rights of the state, had sounded almost like the cynics. Now, on the contrary, it was the positivists and the visionaries who were close, as Walter Schiffer has shown.[16] Both groups saw a new world almost without power, and failed to realize that the retreat of power from certain spheres had been the result of a highly political balancing process—which was at its most rigid, and in its death throes, just when the theorists believed that the millennium was arriving.

The deterioration of the system had, once again, started with a change in the domestic order: but this time it was a change which occurred in most of the major units and the deterioration was gradual, not sudden, and not deliberate. (1) The emergence of the modern nation state weakened some of the essential conditions for an ideal balance: for in such a unit, the population is mobilized around national symbols, and the development of the machinery of the state re-enforces internal integration at the expense of transnational ties: after 1870, the army's weight in domestic affairs increased everywhere, and pushed the nation toward imperialism. (2) Consequently, there came about a change in the structure of the world which almost obliterated the difference between disturbances within the system and destruction of the system: the end of the frontier. (3) The horizontal links between the major powers were progressively weakened by the rise of mass nationalism, the success of philosophies of conflict and of national or racial superiority, and the acts of nationalities' movements which sought allies among the major powers. The legitimacy of states which were not based on the national principle was being challenged: thus international legitimacy concerned itself again with domestic affairs, and with this new dimension heterogeneity returned to the system. (4) As a result, the

---

16 *The Legal Community of Mankind,* New York, 1954.

relations between states took on new and threatening aspects. The very frequency of disturbances, due to the uncertainty of the balance, created a climate of dissatisfaction in which small powers tried to escape from the control of bigger ones. The big states, also looking for an exit, could agree only on temporary adjustments which would not tie their hands for the future, but which in turn infuriated the small powers. In such a climate, the freezing of the balance after Bismarck's departure meant the end of "neutrality of alignment" and the replacement of the hierarchical system of the Concert with a vertical one, in which blocs composed of large *and* small states were facing each other. Hence a switch in means—the decline of the Concert, the return to arms races—and an increase in scope: the sphere of economic affairs became vital again for international politics. It was another change in means: the resort to general war, which dealt the death blow to the system: for the "technical surprise" of World War I, to use Aron's expression, destroyed all remaining restraints on means, and the logic of the war made the objectives of states once again incompatible and increasingly more universal.

(c) Lastly I would like to discuss the relation of international law to world politics in the present revolutionary system.

The essential elements of the present system are as follows: (1) The structure of the world is characterized by one consolidation and two deep transformations. On the one hand, the diplomatic field, which had been gradually extended and unified by the previous system, embraces the whole world for the first time. On the other hand, two conflicting movements have destroyed the double hierarchy of the nineteenth century: bipolarity has replaced the multiplicity of major actors (and put an end to the mechanism of imbalance); the splintering of the former frontier into a large number of new units has obliterated the distinction between the core area and the rest.

(2) A gigantic technological revolution has led to a race toward industrial power, and not been accompanied by the restoration of any universal transnational links. The diversity of regimes, "isolationist" reactions in many nations (especially the new ones) against the intrusion of foreign affairs into all spheres of life, the tendency of the major forms of regimes to project and promote themselves throughout the world have resulted both in the absence of any clear and extensive conception of international legitimacy, and in huge ideological rivalries. New transnational links have emerged as a consequence of the latter, but they are divisive, competitive, and often negative solidarities.

(3) The spiritual and temporal control of the state on the citizens has increased everywhere. Just as the old territorial essence of sovereignty was becoming obsolete, the spreading ethics of nationalism

and the universal practice of public welfare have given to sovereignty an incandescent "personal" core.

(4) The outcome is a series of revolutionary changes in the scope and means of world politics. Concerning the former, there is no longer any "depoliticized" zone of major importance. The collapse of empires has made the question of economic development, once dealt with by private investment or behind the walls of the empires, one of the biggest issues of world politics. Nor is there any more a separation of domestic and international affairs: the logic of intervention, either to enforce some degree of conformity within one's own camp or to subvert the adversary's, has spread throughout the whole world and made the diffusion of political "ways of life" one of the tasks performed by world politics.[17] Consequently, the objectives of states have expanded in such a way that the full realization of the goals of one unit or bloc would often involve the physical or moral death of another actor or camp, and such goals include blueprints for domestic as well as for international order. As for means, they have never been as varied: "total diplomacy" ranges from highly institutionalized military alliances to economic warfare, from propaganda to a host of international organizations; quasi-Doomsday machines and traditional limited wars coexist with revolutionary guerrilla wars. There is one moderating force which makes this revolutionary system an original one: the possibility for one power alone to inflict unacceptable damage on its enemies, however numerous, makes a return to the principle of imbalance unlikely in case of a new multipolar system, but it also makes the actors hesitate far more to resort to violence than the dynamism of a revolutionary system would otherwise allow. Hence the appearance of a highly delicate and uncertain restraint.

Thus, by comparison with the pre-1914 system, the present one is marked both by extraordinary and continuing changes, and by great complexity.[18] Such changes and such complexity have had an enormous impact on international law; the European-made legal order of

---

[17] Many of the difficulties of the UN operation in the Congo stem from the attempt to distinguish between the domestic and the international aspects of the crisis—an exercise in fiction.

[18] We speak of a "loose bipolar system" in which "bloc actors" tend to become more important than unit actors—but at the same time the rate of obsolescence of strategies and the diffusion of nuclear power challenge such a view. Inversely, we refer to the fragmentation of the old frontier into multiple new sovereignties—but at the same time the necessities of the struggle against colonialism and for development might lead to the gradual emergence of "bloc actors" there. We discuss the atomic age but, as Herz has observed, many interstate relations are still in a pre-atomic phase. We have both a revolutionary system, and a tacit agreement on one rule of the game—the avoidance of total war.

the past could not be stretched to the dimensions of the new system without major cracks.

Let us look first at the impact of the changes. It has been threefold. In the first place, huge chunks of the traditional body of rules have been destroyed. This destruction has four aspects.

(1) Basic distinctions which translated into the legal order the restraints of the balancing system have lost any meaning or justification in the present one. The distinction between matters of domestic jurisdiction and matters regulated by international law has practically vanished, in a period when the choice of a regime largely determines the international conduct of a state. The distinction between the civilized nations and the others is challenged by the new states' objections to many traditional rules (e.g., in regard to territorial waters or even about diplomatic representation). The distinction between private acts, for which the state is not responsible, and public acts has been destroyed by intervention or subversion by "private" groups manipulated by their governments, or by the growing importance of transactions which a large foreign or international "private" company concludes with a state. The distinction between war and peace has been replaced by what Philip Jessup has called situations of intermediacy: a period of irreconcilable oppositions, ideological clashes, *and* fear of total war could not but engender wars without declaration, armistices without peace, non-belligerency without war, and help for insurgents without recognition of belligerency.

(2) Consequently, many of the traditional rules have been destroyed by massive violations. Numerous provisions on war and neutrality could not outlive the technological and political conditions of the nineteenth century, nor could the law which forbade states to help foreign insurgents or subversives. Similarly, many of the rules which governed territorial jurisdiction have vanished: instead of a fairly clear distinction among a number of separate zones and the sharp definition of the conditions in which state power could be exercised in each of them, there are now blurred, overlapping, and multiplying zones. The size of those on which states claim rights has augmented; the claims themselves have steadily expandnd, even over the open seas, and often through unilateral moves. Traditional rules on the treatment of foreign property have been very generally disregarded. Those changes have been the reflection of all the transformations in the international system: the increase in the number of nations has often led the least viable or secure ones to demand the fullest amount of control over the biggest amount of space; the technological revolution has provoked a rush into air space; the decline of the old transnational consensus has affected the freedom of the seas; the modern welfare state, and the totalitarian regimes,

have tried to grab resources wherever possible and to remove previously accepted restrictions on territorial sovereignty; the cold war
has led to U-2 flights, to weapon tests in the ocean, and has added
military overtones to the struggle about the breadth of the territorial
seas; the anticolonial revolution has been one of the prime movers in
this struggle and in the spread of expropriation; the Arab-Israeli conflict has had repercussions on canals and straits.

(3) Many of the gaps in the body of rules have become opportunities for chaos. The silence of international law on the upper limits of
air space may lead to dangerous and conflicting claims. International
law has little to say about most of the modern methods of propaganda, subversion, and intervention short of the actual use of force.
Nor did it foresee that traditional privileges of domestic jurisdiction,
such as the right of a state to grant its nationality, to regulate the
conduct of aliens, to treat its own citizens as it sees fit, and to recognize new states or governments, would be used as weapons in the
struggle between the states. Here we find what is probably the best
example of the different meaning for world order of gaps in stable
and revolutionary systems. In the nineteenth century, recognition was
deemed a privilege, not a duty, but no arbitrary consequences followed because, on the whole, very simple tests were applied: a
double check of whether the state existed or whether the government
was in control, and whether it accepted the existing framework of
international law and politics. Since the latter was flexible enough,
and contained no requirements about regimes or alignments, there
were few instances of trouble. Today, the same privilege has become
a nightmare, because of the collapse of the old consensus on international legitimacy—so that states use criteria of recognition which
are tests of conformity to their own concept of legitimacy—and also
because of the appearance of a new dimension of legitimacy: the
nature of the regime or the way in which it came to power. This
is as true in the case of the anticolonial conflict as it is in the cold
war. Finally, international law has nothing to say about most of the
new weapons which have appeared since 1914.

(4) Some of the traditional rules which are still standing have
become much more uncertain in their operation because of changes
in the international system. Principles dealing with state immunities
were established at a time when the state did not engage its "majesty"
in trading or manufacturing activities; court reactions to those developments have been conflicting and subject to shifts. The validity of
intervention at the request of a foreign government becomes dubious
when there is a domestic contest about the legitimacy or legality of
this government. Treaties reflect the forces of disintegration which
have appeared in the world: the increase in the number of states has

led either to the "individualization of rules" through reservations, or to the use of expressions as vague as, say, "genuine link" in the recent Geneva provision dealing with flags of convenience, or to conflicts between obligations accepted by the same nation in agreements which regulate similar matters but bind different groups of states. Domestic reactions against the increasing scope of treaties have brought about difficulties in ratification and moves such as the Bricker offensive. Clashes between new transnational solidarities explain the problem of the colonial clause. The intensity of interstate conflicts has made resort to the *rebus sic stantibus* argument more frequently than ever.

Thus, much of present international law, precisely because it reflects a dead system, is obsolete. But changes in the international system have had a second kind of effect on international law: some of the rules which are supposed to be valid today are premature. These are rules which express attempts at imposing a new scheme of world order which purported to draw the lesson from the ultimate failure of the balance-of-power system, but proved to be thoroughly unfit for the present revolutionary world. There were essentially two types of efforts.

(1) On the one hand, there was an attempt to give to the law of the political framework a far bigger scope than in the past, by curbing states' sovereignty in matters as vital as the settlement of political disputes and the resort to war. The conduct of states would have been subordinated to rules administered by international organization. The success of this effort *presupposed* a stable world which would not be racked by profound ideological splits, in which a basic homogeneity of regimes and beliefs existed, and in which the transnational forces of public opinion and "world parliamentarism" would keep disputes at a reasonably low pitch. The fundamental flaw of the formula was in the ambiguous nature of international organization: it is an "as if" international community, which leaves the basic character of the world system unchanged, and in which decisions are still made by the states. Consequently, its success depends entirely on the universe outside—i.e., on whether there is a system of basically satisfied, democratic units tied together by a common concept of legitimacy; if not, the organization itself has no power to bring such a world about. If such a happy world does not exist at the start, its indispensable establishment thus depends on the ability of the major powers to bring it to life—an ability which is totally missing. As a result, a new and dangerous gap has come to plague world order: the gap between the Charter provisions and practices on disputes (i.e., the power of the UN organs is limited to frequently ineffective recommendations), and the Charter's sweeping ban on the use of force: a gap which encourages states to devise

highly refined techniques of offensive short of force, and drives those which are the victims of such tactics to disregard the ban.[19] The attempt to revert to a "just war" concept has proved to be impossible or absurd in a world of conflicting legitimacies.

(2) The other type of effort was a direct projection, into the international sphere, of the legal relationships which exist between groups or individuals in a constitutional state. The resort to international jurisdiction for the settlement of many disputes, an international protection of human rights, the establishment of a criminal code thanks to which the punishment of warmakers would be the judicial side of a coin whose political side was the outlawry of war—all these measures reflected the utopia of a legal community of mankind, and they have suffered a fate even worse than the fictitious political community. International adjudication can be effective only when international relations are not fundamentally at variance with the conditions which exist within a liberal state: when there is a large zone of private activities uncontrolled by governments, when the objectives of states are not so incompatible as to rule out a joint resort to the judge. The prevalence of the desire to change the law over mere disagreements on interpretation, the opposition in the values of the major ideological camps, have provoked a decline of the role of the World Court and a full-scale revolt against adjudication. Human rights are unlikely to receive adequate international protection at a time when the core of sovereignty is the link between the state and its subjects.

Out of the dialectic of the obsolete and the premature, contemporary international law has managed to show a third kind of effect of the changes in the international system; there are some pieces of evidence of a "third way" which is neither a return to the old system, nor a realization of the Wilsonian utopia, but the elaboration of rules which correspond to the few elements of stability in the present system. Although Charter provisions are used by all states as instruments for the enhancement of their own interests, procedures and institutions which correspond to the general desire to avoid total war have been developed by the U.N. Although the competition of East and West for the allegiance of the "Third World" tends to become constantly more intense, it remains on the whole peaceful; consequently, an international law, and numerous international organs, of technical assistance and economic development have appeared: they

---

[19] See, for instance, the arguments of D. W. Bowett in *Self-defense in International Law*, New York, 1958, pp. 145ff., and Julius Stone in *Aggression and World Order*, Berkeley, Calif., 1958, ch. 5. Contra, Joseph Kunz, "Sanctions in International Law," *American Journal of International Law*, LIV (April 1960), pp. 324-47.

correspond to the convergent interests of all three camps in channeling some of those measures through the procedures of an "universal actor." On the ruins of the nineteenth-century law of reciprocity, a few new conventions of delimitation and cooperation have been signed, dealing with the "humanitarian" side of war, or with the continental shelf, or with the joint exploitation of sea resources, or with the Antarctic.

This is not much. Some of those developments (e.g., the continental shelf) reflect a very traditional agreement on increasing, not curtailing, states' powers. The UN apparatus against the extension of conflicts remains an improvised one: contemporary internationalization of trouble spots, designed to avoid direct intervention by one of the super-powers, remains an *ad hoc* practice, despite efforts at turning it into a general rule, and East-West mutual interests in preventing nuclear war have expressed themselves in parallel unilateral measures but not in firm agreements. Only in the area of community—scientific research, health, communications—have the obstacles been few. Nevertheless, such developments suffice to make contemporary international law look like Janus: it has one face which announces chaos, and one which promises order.[20]

Not only does contemporary law thus bear the marks of all the changes in the international system: it reflects also the heterogeneity of the present system—indeed, of every element of this system; hence a permanent contradiction between such heterogeneity and the formal homogeneity of a legal system whose members are supposedly equal.

(1) Contemporary law reflects the heterogeneity of the structure of the world. Although the nation-state is the basic unit and the common aspiration of men more than ever before, there is a major disparity between states which meet the traditional criteria of statehood—a population, a territory, a government—and those which are essentially governments still in search of their nation—governments which operate within explosively artificial borders.[21]

(2) Present-day law reflects the asymmetry of domestic regimes: the difficulties met by various attempts at codification, or at regulating international trade, air communications, and raw materials, or at establishing common standards of inspection for arms control have shown how much the attitudes of a welfare state and a free enter-

---

[20] Similarly, during the period which preceded the peace of Westphalia, every legal development was ambiguous, for it destroyed the previous unity of the Civitas Christiana and the secular authority of the Church, but at the same time brought into shape the modern territorial state through a succession of wars.

[21] See Rupert Emerson, *From Empire to Nation,* Cambridge, Mass., 1960, ch. 6.

prise state and, even more, those of an industrialized and of an underdeveloped country differ in international economic matters, or how radically a democracy's and a totalitarian state's conceptions of secrecy diverge.

(3) Contemporary law reflects the heterogeneity of the system with respect to those forces which cut across the units. Technological unevenness has left its mark: it is from the underprivileged states mainly that pressure has come for a legal regulation of space problems; the opposition of nuclear "haves" and "have-nots" has limited the effectiveness of international cooperation for the peaceful uses of nuclear energy. As for ideological asymmetry, even though Soviet international law appears to differ little in its *rules* from Western law, there are most significant variations in the interpretation of, and the general attitude toward, law which correspond to the differences in the nature of the regimes;[22] in particular, there is a considerable difference in the attitude of each camp toward the use of force within its sphere. Efforts at negotiating various agreements on human rights have shown the incompatibility of the main competing conceptions of world order on crucial issues.

(4) Present-day law reflects numerous contradictions in the relations between the units. In the first place, it shows traces of a basic clash which affects the policy of every state: a clash between the determination to increase its power, security, welfare, and prestige as much as possible by its own means, and the dependence on others for those very purposes. Thus, if we look at the principal source of law—treaties—we see that at the same time as such agreements suffer from the weaknesses I have mentioned above, their subject-matter has extended to objects never before regulated by world law (i.e., labor, human rights, etc.), and numerous new subjects of law (i.e., international organizations) have been created by agreements. If we look at the military function of the states—the state as fortress—we see that they try to ensure their security both by expanding their sovereignty as far as they can (especially in the air) or by developing their own weapon systems or armies, and also by participating in military alliances, which involve a radical transformation of traditional territorial sovereignty. If we look at the economic function of the states—the state as provider of welfare—we see that they try to develop their own resources and to acquire additional ones wherever they can get them (for instance, under the sea), but also that they have to join with others in order to promote the welfare of their own citizens or to receive indispensable aid.

---

[22] For a recent discussion of those points, see the *Proceedings of the American Society of International Law*, 1959, pp. 21-45.

In the second place, international law reflects the complexity of states' legal situations in the face of the main issues of contemporary world politics. On the one hand, some of the provisions of the Geneva Conventions on the law of the sea, most of the practices of expropriation, and UN stands on the question of self-determination reflect the alignment over one such issue—a coalition of all those states interested in overthrowing the norms of the nineteenth-century system, against the *status quo* states of the West which are the heirs of this system. On the other hand, in the cold war, it is as if the world were composed of layers of states belonging to different ages of politics. On top, the two superpowers enjoy a large amount of independence (except from one another) and extensive advantages within their respective alliances (bases, status-of-forces agreements). Under this layer, there are those allies of the superpowers who are developing their own deterrent; they continue to depend on a super-power for their ultimate protection, but they are capable of bargaining hard before conceding privileges to it. Next we find other allies who tend to be in the position of more or less gilt-edged satellites (depending on the ideological camp to which they belong): hence outbreaks of neutralism and of fear of war. Fourth and last, we find all those states which have joined no military camp and live in a kind of fictitious nineteenth-century world of territorial sovereignty.

In the third place, law reflects the bizarre coexistence of revolutionary relations, exemplified by the dialectic of the obsolete and the premature, with elements of stability introduced by the "mutual dependence" characteristic of the balance of terror, just at the time when the role of the military in decision-making was becoming greater than ever, and weapons began to live a life of their own, almost distinct from events in the political universe.

The outcome of these and other contradictory impulses and situations is, once again, heterogeneity: the development of overlapping regional institutions and rules. They are evidence of partial integration; but they also show the fragmentation of the legal order which has accompanied the extension of the diplomatic field to the whole planet.

The reactions of theorists to those developments reflect both the heterogeneity of the legal order, and the impact of the changes of the international system on this order. On the one hand, there is little in common between totalitarian theories of law and non-totalitarian theories: we have here both conflict and asymmetry. The former are not scholarly discussions of the international system from the viewpoint of world order: they are instruments at the service of a state strategy. They are not normative examinations of the ideal order and of the gaps between the actual and the ideal: they are policy sciences

showing how the actual should be used or abused in order to reach
the ideal determined by official doctrine. On the other hand, within
the non-totalitarian theories, changes in the international system have
shattered the fragile rapprochement which had taken place previously
between the main tendencies. Both of the nineteenth-century ex-
tremes have disappeared. It has become impossible to believe in a
dialectic of clashing units with a happy ending, and in the vision of
a world which moves inevitably toward law, order, and harmony.
Even the middle group—positivism—has suffered severely from the
marks that the free wills of states have left on world order. Gone is
the common faith in the avoidance of chaos. Dead is the agreement
on the indispensable character of the state as the basis of the system:
theories today range from those that maintain this claim to those
that make anguished pleas for world government. Vanished, also, is
the agreement on the differences between international and domestic
law: theories today range from those that still stress such differences
to those that offer subtle, if unconvincing, demonstrations of the
similarities.

It is characteristic of revolutionary systems that doctrines not only
multiply but often pose as what they are not. Thus, today's deniers or
cynics are either sorrowful (rather than gloating), or else disguised
as "policy-oriented" theorists who dissolve rules and principles into
a maze of processes, messages, and alternatives. Today's utopians are
either straightforward adepts of world government, or outright natural-law revivalists, or natural-law thinkers in pseudo-sociological disguise, or "pure theorists of law" who derive normative order from
empirical chaos by what I would call the parthenogenesis of law. In
the middle, there are persistent, but troubled, positivists and sociolo-
gists of law who—as this author knows—seem more adept at
examing the weaknesses of law than at finding formulas which would
conceal them, as positivism used to do, more adept at maintaining
that it is absurd to separate the legal order from its political roots
than at attempting to close the gap between the aspiration for order
and the practices of chaos.

III

Let us now apply our findings about the role of international law
in various systems to two of the more important theoretical issues of
the discipline of international law: the foundation of obligation, and
the meaning of sovereignty.

(a) The basis of obligation is the same in every legal order: the
consciousness, which prevails among the subjects of the legal order,

of this order's need to realize a common end. Law is not obtained by deduction from a pre-existing natural law or objective law *à la* Duguit; it is a creation toward an end. Thus, the purpose and the legal order cannot be separated, Kelsen's theory notwithstanding. The solidity or authority of a legal order depends on the nature and substance of the common end—which, finally, depends on the group: if the group shows a high degree of community of purpose, and is organized by central power, the binding force of the legal order will be great—not otherwise.

The feeble consciousness of a common end among multiple units which allow no central power to impose its own vision or to promote theirs, weakens the binding force of international law permanently by comparison with domestic law. But there are variations in the degree to which such a common end exists in international politics and consequently variations in the binding force of international law. First, we find variations in *level*: as we have seen, there are, in stable periods, three superimposed groups, with different common ends and, consequently, with an international law of varying binding force. The law of community is strongest because it rests on a common positive purpose. The law of reciprocity is relatively strong because it is the law of a limited partnershp, whose members' common end is a set of mutual interests. The law of the political framework is weakest, for it is the law of a collection of actors engaged in a struggle, and whose common end is both limited to a narrow sphere —the rules of the game—and subordinated to the fluctuations of the balance of power.

Secondly, the binding force of international law is exposed to variations in *time*: it is not the same in stable and in revolutionary systems. The legal order of the nineteenth-century system was both modest and solid. It was modest, both because of the moderation in the scope and means of international relations and because the freedom of action of the units was curtailed by the operation of the balance rather than by law. It was efficient, because it was able, within these limits, both to serve as a restraint on the states and to consolidate their interdependence. Legal theories reflected both this modesty and confidence in the efficiency of the legal order. Contemporary law, on the contrary, has to serve a system in which the extension of international relations would seem to acquire a far wider range of common purposes, but in which heterogeneity has reduced this range drastically. Consequently, there is a divorce between the difficulties of practice and the delirium of theory; and practice is both highly ambitious and relatively inefficient. The increase in the scope of law's subject-matter demonstrates such ambition. But on vital issues, "society" is limited to a few identical or convergent

interests, which are sometimes even too narrow or too flimsy to provide a firm basis for the development of any law. There is today no
strong enough consciousness or representation of a common legal
order of mankind.[23]

Finally, such binding force knows variations in *space*. Given the
narrow range of common ends and the absence of world-wide central power, regional solidarities, institutions, and legal orders have
appeared. They differ, first of all, in their political foundation—i.e.,
the structure of the group: the Soviet bloc is a "Roman" system in
which the common ends are largely imposed by central power,
whereas the Atlantic "community" is really a modern version of the
limited partnership: the range of common ends is far from all-
embracing and cooperation is far from unconditional, but today,
owing to technlogical changes and the revolutionary character of
world politics, such ends require a far greater degree of integration
than in the past; the organizations of the European "Six" shape a
somewhat less narrow or conditional society. These regional orders
differ also in their degree of institutionalization, and in the subject-
matter which they cover. The binding force of law in these systems
depends on all those factors.

(b) Another problem which should be treated in the light of a
theory of the relations between international systems and international law is the problem of sovereignty. Few concepts are as
obscure.[24]

Let us start with the classical definition given by the World Court
in the Wimbledon case. Sovereignty means that the state "is subject
to no other state and has full and exclusive powers within its jurisdiction without prejudice to the limits set by applicable law." Thus,
sovereignty is the situation of the state which has no political superior over it, but is nevertheless bound by international law. Three
consequences follow. First, the exercise of its sovereignty by a state
—for instance, to sign agreements which may restrict its legal freedom of action—does not *exhaust,* and is indeed a demonstration of,

[23] The statesmen have images of world order which are mutually exclusive,
and in which the highest power remains the state; the individual citizens have
no way of breaking the statesmen's monopoly: the citizens' efforts at promoting their transnational common ends through law rarely succeed in transcend-
ing the borders of the state, which continues to fulfill most of their needs and
to be seen as the best protection against outside tempests. Indeed, the development of contemporary law has occurred especially in those areas where
individuals raised demands which the state could not satisfy alone: hence the
law of international functions and economic integration, whose binding force
seems quite strong.

[24] For a sharp analysis, see W. J. Rees, the "The Theory of Sovereignty
Restated," in Peter Laslett, ed., *Philosophy, Politics and Society,* New York,
1956.

its sovereignty. Secondly, the relations between sovereignty and international law are characterized by the principle of domestic jurisdiction: matters not regulated by the former fall within the latter. Thirdly, relations between states are marked by the principle of equality (whatever their size, all states are in the same situation: their only superior is international law), by the duty of non-intervention, and by the right of self-preservation.

The trouble with this set of definitions is that their neatness is an illusion. If we look at the relations between states, we see a broad gamut of situations in between the status of the mythical state-in-isolation which exercises all the privileges of sovereignty without any other limit than that of general international law, and the situation of a member state in a federation. There is in fact a hierarchy of legal statuses according to the amount of sovereignty whose exercise has been given away to, or restricted in favor of, other states or international agencies. The nature and range of this hierarchy vary with each international system. Thus, sovereignty, rather than a reservoir which can be only full or empty, is a divisible nexus of powers of which some may be kept, some limited, some lost. The point at which sovereignty can be assumed to have vanished is a matter of definition. Given such a hierarchy of situations, the equality of states is mythical. If we look next at the relations between states and international law, we find that the definitions are illusory because one of the two terms—international law—is a fuzzy one: the "limit" or "restraint" which such law imposes on states is both ambiguous and shifting. It is ambiguous because of the conditions of elaboration and enforcement of international law, which are the product of the states. It is shifting because the norms of international law vary from system to system.[25]

Thus, the actual substance of sovereignty depends (1) on the international system and (2), in each system on the position of a state on the ladder I have mentioned. In a stable system, such as the nineteenth century's, sovereignty is a fairly clear nexus of powers with sharp edges: the world appears as a juxtaposition of well-defined

[25] The best combination of change over time and ambiguity is provided by the concept of domestic jurisdiction. On the one hand, the area regulated by international law has been drastically expanded in the present system. On the other hand, this increasing "legalization" of interstate relations could become an effective restraint on states only if there existed institutions capable of preventing states from extending the plea of domestic jurisdiction to issues where it does not apply—as well as institutions capable of preventing states from rejecting the plea in those cases where it is still justified. Instead, we find that states successfully invoke the argument even in areas clearly regulated by law (cf. the Interhandel dispute), and refuse to listen to it whenever a problem is of international concern, although it may not be regulated by law (cf. the attitude of the General Assembly of the UN).

units, whose respective rights are neatly delimited, which allow few exceptions to the principle of full territorial jurisdiction, and which have few institutional links among them: cooperation is organized by diplomacy and by the market. In such a system, the limits of sovereignty are essentially set by general international law (customs and general treaties); the ladder is short: the basic distinctions are the double hierarchy I have described previously. In today's revolutionary system, sovereignty is infinitely more complex. First, diversity of legal statuses is extreme, owing to the multiple patterns of military, economic, and political cooperation which introduce various forms of inequality: hence the predominance of treaties over customs, and the prevalence of less-than-universal treaties. Secondly, the sum of powers of which sovereignty is composed as well as the limitations imposed by law are not only in constant flux: they are also increasing simultaneously, because of the intensity of international relations. The same paradox had marked the revolutionary system before Westphalia. Thus, the edges of sovereignty have become blurred. Although the basic legal unit remains the state, powers of action in the world are both widely scattered among states, blocs, and international organizations, and concentrated among the major industrial centers[26] or (in matters of life and death for the planet) the full nuclear powers.

After the dust has settled, a new stable system will probably be one in which a lasting redistribution of many state powers among international and regional actors will have been accomplished: for despite the very general aspiration (especially among the new nations) for a return to a world of sovereign states practicing nonintervention, the traditional substance of sovereignty is barely compatible with the political and technological conditions of the present world. However, we are bound to remain in the dust for quite a while: for a decline of military blocs in the missile age would not make the competition of East and West any less fierce, the emergence of new nations does not make their resentment of their former masters, their demands on the well-endowed states, and their own political uncertainties any less dangerous, the spread of nuclear power does not make the international system any less explosive. We are in the midst of a succession of revolutionary systems—not on the verge of a stable one—and the solidity of international law will continue to remain in doubt.

[26] On the impact of such concentration, see François Perroux, *La coexistence pacifique,* 3 vols., Paris, Presses Universitaires de France, 1958.

6. THE LEGALITY OF UNITED STATES PARTICIPATION IN THE DEFENSE OF VIET NAM

MEMORANDUM OF LAW
LEGAL ADVISER TO THE SECRETARY OF DEFENSE
MARCH 8, 1965

I. The United States and South Viet Nam Have the Right Under International Law To Participate in the Collective Defense of South Viet Nam Against Armed Attack

In response to requests from the Government of South Viet Nam, the United States has been assisting that country in defending itself against armed attack from the Communist North. This attack has taken the forms of externally supported subversion, clandestine supply of arms, infiltration of armed personnel, and most recently the sending of regular units of the North Vietnamese army into the South.

International law has long recognized the right of individual and collective self-defense against armed attack. South Viet Nam and the United States are engaging in such collective defense consistently with international law and with United States obligations under the United Nations Charter.

A. SOUTH VIETNAM IS BEING SUBJECTED TO ARMED ATTACK BY COMMUNIST NORTH VIET NAM

The Geneva Accords of 1954 established a demarcation line between North Viet Nam and South Viet Nam. They provided for withdrawals of military forces into the respective zones north and south of this line. The Accords prohibited the use of either zone for the resumption of hostilities or to "further an aggressive policy."

During the five years following the Geneva Conference of 1954, the Hanoi regime developed a covert political-military organization in South Viet Nam based on Communist cadres it had ordered to stay in the South, contrary to the provisions of the Geneva Accords. The activities of this covert organization were directed toward the kid-

Reprinted by permission of The Yale Law Journal Company and Fred B. Rothman and Company from *The Yale Law Journal*, 75, 1085-1108.

napping and assassination of civilian officials—acts of terrorism that were perpetrated in increasing numbers.

In the three-year period from 1959 to 1961, the North Viet Nam regime infiltrated an estimated 10,000 men into the South. It is estimated that 13,000 additional personnel were infiltrated in 1962, and, by the end of 1964, North Viet Nam may well have moved over 40,000 armed and unarmed guerrillas into South Viet Nam.

The International Control Commission reported in 1962 the findings of its Legal Committee:

> . . . there is evidence to show that arms, armed and unarmed personnel, munitions and other supplies have been sent from the Zone in the North to the Zone in the South with the objective of supporting, organizing and carrying out hostile activities, including armed attacks, directed against the Armed Forces and Administration of the Zone in the South.
> . . . there is evidence that the PAVN [People's Army of Viet Nam] has allowed the Zone in the North to be used for inciting, encouraging and supporting hostile activities in the Zone in the South, aimed at the overthrow of the Administration in the South.

Beginning in 1964, the Communists apparently exhausted their reservoir of southerners who had gone North. Since then the greater number of men infiltrated into the South have been native-born North Vietnamese. Most recently, Hanoi has begun to infiltrate elements of the North Vietnamese army in increasingly larger numbers. Today, there is evidence that nine regiments of regular North Vietnamese forces are fighting in organized units in the South.

In the guerrilla war in Viet Nam, the external aggression from the North is the critical military element of the insurgency, although it is unacknowledged by North Viet Nam. In these circumstances, an "armed attack" is not as easily fixed by date and hour as in the case of traditional warfare. However, the infiltration of thousands of armed men clearly constitutes an "armed attack" under any reasonable definition. There may be some question as to the exact date at which North Viet Nam's aggression grew into an "armed attack," but there can be no doubt that it had occurred before February 1965.

B. INTERNATIONAL LAW RECOGNIZES THE RIGHT OF INDIVIDUAL AND COLLECTIVE SELF-DEFENSE AGAINST ARMED ATTACK

International law had traditionally recognized the right of self-defense against armed attack. This proposition has been asserted by writers on international law through the several centuries in which the modern law of nations has developed. The proposition has been acted on numerous times by governments throughout modern history.

Today the principle of self-defense against armed attack is universally recognized and accepted.[1]

The Charter of the United Nations, concluded at the end of World War II, imposed an important limitation on the use of force by United Nations Members. Article 2, paragraph 4, provides:

> All Members shall refrain in their international relations from the threat or use of force against the territorial integrity or political independence of any state, or in any other manner inconsistent with the Purposes of the United Nations.

In addition, the Charter embodied a system of international peace-keeping through the organs of the United Nations. Article 24 summarizes these structural arrangements in stating that the United Nations Members—

> confer on the Security Council primary responsibility for the maintenance of international peace and security, and agree that in carrying out its duties under this responsibility the Security Council acts on their behalf.

However, the Charter expressly states in Article 51 that the remaining provisions of the Charter—including the limitation of Article 2, paragraph 4, and the creation of United Nations machinery to keep the peace—in no way diminish the inherent right of self-defense against armed attack. Article 51 provides:

> Nothing in the present Charter shall impair the inherent right of individual or collective self-defense if an armed attack occurs against a Member of the United Nations, until the Security Council has taken the measures necessary to maintain international peace and security. Measures taken by Members in the exercise of this right of self-defense shall be immediately reported to the Security Council and shall not in any way affect the authority and responsibility of the Security Council under the present Charter to take at any time such action as it deems necessary in order to maintain or restore international peace and security.

Thus, Article 51 restates and preserves, for Member States in the situations covered by the Article, a long-recognized principle of international law. The Article is a "saving clause" designed to make clear that no other provision in the Charter shall be interpreted to impair the inherent right of self-defense referred to in Article 51.

---

[1] See, e.g., Jessup, *A Modern Law of Nations*, 163 ff. (1948); Oppenheim, *International Law*, 297 ff. (8th ed. Lauterpacht 1955). See generally Bowett, *Self-Defense in International Law* (1958).

Three principal objections have been raised against the availability of the right of individual and collective self-defense in the case of Viet Nam: (1) that this right applies only in the case of an armed attack on a United Nations Member; (2) that it does not apply in the case of South Viet Nam because the latter is not an independent sovereign state; and (3) that collective self-defense may be undertaken only by a regional organization operating under Chapter VIII of the United Nations Charter. These objections will now be considered in turn.

C. THE RIGHT OF INDIVIDUAL AND COLLECTIVE SELF-DEFENSE APPLIES IN THE CASE OF SOUTH VIET NAM WHETHER OR NOT THAT COUNTRY IS A MEMBER OF THE UNITED NATIONS

1. *South Viet Nam Enjoys the Right of Self-Defense.* The argument that the right of self-defense is available only to Members of the United Nations mistakes the nature of the right of self-defense and the relationship of the United Nations Charter to international law in this respect. As already shown, the right of self-defense against armed attack is an inherent right under international law. The right is not conferred by the Charter, and, indeed, Article 51 expressly recognizes that the right is inherent.

The Charter nowhere contains any provision designed to deprive non-Members of the right of self-defense against armed attack.[2] Article 2, paragraph 6, does charge the United Nations with responsibility for ensuring that non-Member States act in accordance with United Nations "Principles so far as may be necessary for the maintenance of international peace and security." Protection against aggression and self-defense against armed attack are important elements in the whole Charter scheme for the maintenance of international peace and security. To deprive non-Members of their inherent right of self-defense would not accord with the Principles of the Organization, but would instead be prejudicial to the maintenance of peace. Thus Article 2, paragraph 6—and, indeed, the rest of the Charter—should certainly not be construed to nullify or diminish the inherent defensive rights of non-Members.

---

[2] While non-Members, such as South Viet Nam, have not formally undertaken the obligations of the United Nations Charter as their own treaty obligations, it should be recognized that much of the substantive law of the Charter has become part of the general law of nations through a very wide acceptance by nations the world over. This is particularly true of the Charter provisions bearing on the use of force. Moreover, in the case of South Viet Nam, the South Vietnamese Government has expressed its ability and willingness to abide by the Charter, in applying for United Nations membership. Thus it seems entirely appropriate to appraise the actions of South Viet Nam in relation to the legal standards set forth in the United Nations Charter.

2. *The United States Has the Right to Assist in the Defense of South Viet Nam Although the Latter Is Not a United Nations Member.* The cooperation of two or more international entities in the defense of one or both against armed attack is generally referred to as collective self-defense. United States participation in the defense of South Viet Nam at the latter's request is an example of collective self-defense.

The United States is entitled to exercise the right of individual or collective self-defense against armed attack, as that right exists in international law, subject only to treaty limitations and obligations undertaken by this country.

It has been urged that the United States has no right to participate in the collective defense of South Viet Nam because Article 51 of the United Nations Charter speaks only of the situation "if an armed attack occurs *against a Member of the United Nations.*" This argument is without substance.

In the first place, Article 51 does not impose restrictions or cut down the otherwise available rights of United Nations Members. By its own terms, the Article preserves an inherent right. It is, therefore, necessary to look elsewhere in the Charter for any obligation of Members restricting their participation in collective defense of an entity that is not a United Nations Member.

Article 2, paragraph 4, is the principal provision of the Charter imposing limitations on the use of force by Members. It states that they—

> shall refrain in their international relations from the threat or use of force against the territorial integrity or political independence of any state, or in any other manner inconsistent with the Purposes of the United Nations.

Action taken in defense against armed attack cannot be characterized as falling wthin this proscription. The record of the San Francisco Conference makes clear that Article 2, paragraph 4, was not intended to restrict the right of self-defense against armed attack.[3]

One will search in vain for any other provision in the Charter that would preclude United States participation in the collective defense of a non-Member. The fact that Article 51 refers only to armed attack "against a Member of the United Nations" implies no intention to preclude Members from participating in the defense of non-Members. Any such result would have seriously detrimental consequences for international peace and security and would be inconsistent with the Purposes of the United Nations as they are set forth in Article 1 of

[3] See, e.g, *6 U.N. Conf. Int'l Org. Docs.* 459.

the Charter.[4] The right of Members to participate in the defense of non-Members is upheld by leading authorities on international law.[5]

D. THE RIGHT OF INDIVIDUAL AND COLLECTIVE SELF-DEFENSE APPLIES WHETHER OR NOT SOUTH VIET NAM IS REGARDED AS AN INDEPENDENT SOVEREIGN STATE

1. *South Viet Nam Enjoys the Right of Self-Defense.* It has been asserted that the conflict in Viet Nam is "civil strife" in which foreign intervention is forbidden. Those who make this assertion have gone so far as to compare Ho Chi Minh's actions in Viet Nam with the efforts of President Lincoln to preserve the Union during the American Civil War. Any such characterization is an entire fiction disregarding the actual situation in Viet Nam. The Hanoi regime is anything but the legitimate government of a unified country in which the South is rebelling against lawful national authority.

The Geneva Accords of 1954 provided for a division of Viet Nam into two zones at the 17th parallel. Although this line of demarcation was intended to be temporary, it was established by international agreement, which specifically forbade aggression by one zone against the other.

The Republic of Viet Nam in the South has been recognized as a separate international entity by approximately sixty governments the world over. It has been admitted as a member of a number of the specialized agencies of the United Nations. The United Nations General Assembly in 1957 voted to recommend South Viet Nam for membership in the Organization, and its admission was frustrated only by the veto of the Soviet Union in the Security Council.

In any event there is no warrant for the suggestion that one zone of a temporarily divided state—whether it be Germany, Korea, or Viet Nam—can be legally overrun by armed forces from the other zone, crossing the internationally recognized line of demarcation between the two. Any such doctrine would subvert the international agreement establishing the line of demarcation and, would pose grave dangers to international peace.

---

[4] In particular, the statement of the first Purpose:
To maintain international peace and security, and to that end: to take effective collective measures for the prevention and removal of threats to the peace, and for the suppression of acts of aggression or other breaches of the peace, and to bring about by peaceful means, and in conformity with the principles of justice and international law, adjustment or settlement of international disputes or situations which might lead to a breach of the peace. . . .

[5] Bowett, *Self-Defense in International Law* 193-95 (1958); Goodhart, *The North Atlantic Treaty of 1949,* 79 Recueil des Cours 183, 202-04 (1951, vol. II), quoted in *Whiteman's Digest of International Law* 1067-68 (1965); Kelsen, *The Law of the United Nations,* 793 (1950); see Stone, *Aggression and World Order,* 44 (1958).

The action of the United Nations in the Korean conflict of 1950 clearly established the principle that there is no greater license for one zone of a temporarily divided state to attack the other zone than there is for one state to attack another state. South Viet Nam has the same right that South Korea had to defend itself and to organize collective defense against an armed attack from the North. A resolution of the Security Council dated June 25, 1950 noted "with grave concern the armed attack upon the Republic of Korea by forces from North Korea" and determined "that this action constitutes a breach of the peace."

2. *The United States Is Entitled To Participate in the Collective Defense of South Viet Nam Whether or Not the Latter Is Regarded as an Independent Sovereign State.* As stated earlier, South Viet Nam has been recognized as a separate international entity by approximately sixty governments. It has been admitted to membership in a number of the United Nations specialized agencies, and has been excluded from the United Nations Organization only by the Soviet veto.

There is nothing in the Charter to suggest that United Nations Members are precluded from participating in the defense of a recognized international entity against armed attack merely because the entity may lack some of the attributes of an independent sovereign state. Any such result would have a destructive effect on the stability of international engagements such as the Geneva Accords of 1954 and on internationally agreed lines of demarcation. Such a result, far from being in accord with the Charter and the Purposes of the United Nations, would undermine them and would create new dangers to international peace and security.

E. THE UNITED NATIONS CHARTER DOES NOT LIMIT THE RIGHT OF SELF-DEFENSE TO REGIONAL ORGANIZATIONS

Some have argued that collective self-defense may be undertaken only by a regional arrangement or agency operating under Chapter VIII of the United Nations Charter. Such an assertion ignores the structure of the Charter and the practice followed in the more than twenty years since the founding of the United Nations.

The basic proposition that rights of self-defense are not impaired by the Charter—as expressly stated in Article 51—is not conditioned by any Charter provision limiting the application of this proposition to collective defense by a regional arrangement or agency. The structure of the Charter reinforces this conclusion. Article 51 appears in Chapter VII of the Charter, entitled "Action With Respect to Threats to the Peace, Breaches of the Peace, and Acts of Aggression," whereas

Chapter VIII, entitled "Regional Arrangements," begins with Article 52 and embraces the two following articles. The records of the San Francisco Conference show that Article 51 was deliberately placed in Chapter VII rather than Chapter VIII, "where it would only have a bearing on the regional system."[6]

Under Article 51, the right of self-defense is available against any armed attack, whether or not the country attacked is a member of a regional arrangement and regardless of the source of the attack. Chapter VIII, on the other hand, deals with relations among members of a regional arrangement or agency, and authorizes regional action as appropriate for dealing with "local disputes." This distinction has been recognized ever since the founding of the United Nations in 1945.

For example, the North Atlantic Treaty has operated as a collective security arrangement, designed to take common measures in preparation against the eventuality of an armed attack for which collective defense under Article 51 would be required. Similarly, the Southeast Asia Treaty Organization was designed as a collective defense arrangement under Article 51. Secretary of State Dulles emphasized this in his testimony before the Senate Foreign Relations Committee in 1954.

By contrast, Article 1 of the Charter of Bogota (1948), establishing the Organization of American States, expressly declares that the Organization is a regional agency with the United Nations. Indeed, Chapter VIII of the United Nations Charter was included primarily to take account of the functioning of the Inter-American System.

In sum, there is no basis in the United Nations Charter for contending that the right of self-defense against armed attack is limited to collective defense by a regional organization.

F. THE UNITED STATES HAS FULFILLED ITS OBLIGATIONS TO THE UNITED NATIONS

A further argument has been made that the Members of the United Nations have conferred on United Nations organs—and, in particular, on the Security Council—exclusive power to act against aggression. Again, the express language of Article 51 contradicts that assertion. A victim of armed attack is not required to forgo individual or collective defense of its territory until such time as the United Nations organizes collective action and takes appropriate measures. To the contrary, Article 51 clearly states that the right of self-defense may be

---

[6] 17 U. N. CONF. INT'L ORG. DOCS. 288.

exercised *"until* the Security Council has taken the measures necessary to maintain international peace and security."[7]

As indicated earlier, Article 51 is not literally applicable to the Viet Nam situation since South Viet Nam is not a Member. However, reasoning by analogy from Article 51 and adopting its provisions as an appropriate guide for the conduct of Members in a case like Viet Nam, one can only conclude that United States actions are fully in accord with this country's obligations as a Member of the United Nations.

Article 51 requires that:

> Measures taken by Members in the exercise of this right of self-defense shall be immediately reported to the Security Council and shall not in any way affect the authority and responsibility of the Security Council under the present Charter to take at any time such action as it deems necessary in order to maintain or restore international peace and security.

The United States has reported to the Security Council on measures it has taken in countering the Communist aggression in Viet Nam. In August 1964 the United States asked the Council to consider the situation created by North Vietnamese attacks on United States destroyers in the Tonkin Gulf. The Council thereafter met to debate the question, but adopted no resolutions. Twice in February 1965 the United States sent additional reports to the Security Council on the conflict in Viet Nam and on the additional measures taken by the United States in the collective defense of South Viet Nam. In January 1966 the United States formally submitted the Viet Nam question to the Security Council for its consideration and introduced a draft resolution calling for discussions looking toward a peaceful settlement on the basis of the Geneva Accords.

At no time has the Council taken any action to restore peace and security in Southeast Asia. The Council has not expressed criticism of United States actions. Indeed, since the United States submission of January 1966, Members of the Council have been notably reluctant to proceed with any consideration of the Viet Nam question.

The conclusion is clear that the United States has in no way acted to interfere with United Nations consideration of the conflict in Viet

[7] An argument has been made by some that the United States, by joining in the collective defense of South Viet Nam, has violated the peaceful settlement obligation of Article 33 in the Charter. This argument overlooks the obvious proposition that a victim of armed aggression is not required to sustain the attack undefended while efforts are made to find a political solution with the aggressor. Article 51 of the Chapter illustrates this by making perfectly clear that the inherent right of self-defense is impaired by "Nothing in the present Charter," including the provisions of Article 33.

Nam. On the contrary, the United States has requested United Nations consideration, and the Council has not seen fit to act.

G. INTERNATIONAL LAW DOES NOT REQUIRE A DECLARATION OF WAR AS A CONDITION PRECEDENT TO TAKING MEASURES OF SELF-DEFENSE AGAINST ARMED ATTACK

The existence or absence of a formal declaration of war is not a factor in determining whether an international use of force is lawful as a matter of international law. The United Nations Charter's restrictions focus on the manner and purpose of its use and not on any formalities of announcement.

It should also be noted that a formal declaration of war would not place any obligations on either side in the conflict by which that side would not be bound in any event. The rules of international law concerning the conduct of hostilities in an international armed conflict apply regardless of any declaration of war.

H. SUMMARY

The analysis set forth above shows that South Viet Nam has the right in present circumstances to defend itself against armed attack from the North and to organize a collective self-defense with the participation of others. In response to requests from South Viet Nam, the United States has been participating in that defense, both through military action within South Viet Nam and actions taken directly against the aggressor in North Viet Nam. This participation by the United States is in conformity with international law and is consistent with our obligations under the Charter of the United Nations.

II. THE UNITED STATES HAS UNDERTAKEN COMMITMENTS TO ASSIST SOUTH VIET NAM IN DEFENDING ITSELF AGAINST COMMUNIST AGGRESSION FROM THE NORTH

The United States has made commitments and given assurances, in various forms and at different times, to assist in the defense of South Viet Nam.

A. THE UNITED STATES GAVE UNDERTAKINGS AT THE END OF THE GENEVA CONFERENCE IN 1954

At the time of the signing of the Geneva Accords in 1954, President Eisenhower warned "that any renewal of Communist aggression would be viewed by us as a matter of grave concern," at the same time giving assurance that the United States would "not use force to disturb the settlement." And the formal declaration made by the United States Government at the conclusion of the Geneva Conference stated that the United States "would view any renewal of aggression in violation of the aforesaid agreements with grave concern and as seriously threatening international peace and security."

B. THE UNITED STATES UNDERTOOK AN INTERNATIONAL OBLIGATION TO DEFEND SOUTH VIET NAM IN THE SEATO TREATY

Later in 1954 the United States negotiated with a number of other countries and signed the Southeast Asia Collective Defense Treaty.

The Treaty contains in the first paragraph of Article 4 the following provision:

> Each Party recognizes that aggression by means of armed attack in the treaty area against any of the Parties or against any State or territory which the Parties by unanimous agreement may hereafter designate, would endanger its own peace and safety, and agrees that it will in that event act to meet the common danger in accordance with its constitutional processes. Measures taken under this paragraph shall be immediately reported to the Security Council of the United Nations.

Annexed to the Treaty was a Protocol stating that:

> The parties to the Southeast Asia Collective Defense Treaty unanimously designate for the purpose of Article IV of the Treaty the States of Cambodia and Laos and the free territory under the jurisdiction of the State of Viet Nam.

Thus, the obligations of Article IV, paragraph 1, dealing with the eventuality of armed attack, have from the outset covered the territory of South Viet Nam. The facts as to the North Vietnamese armed attack against the South have been summarized earlier, in the discussion of the right of self-defense under international law and the Charter of the United Nations. The term "armed attack" has the same meaning in the SEATO Treaty as in the United Nations Charter.

Article IV, paragraph 1, places an obligation on each party to the SEATO Treaty to "act to meet the common danger in accordance with its constitutional processes" in the event of an armed attack. The Treaty does not require a collective determination that an armed attack has occurred in order that the obligation of Article IV, paragraph 1, become operative. Nor does the provision require collective decision on actions to be taken to meet the common danger. As Secretary Dulles pointed out when transmitting the Treaty to the

President, the commitment in Article IV, paragraph 1, "leaves to the judgment of each country the type of action to be taken in the event an armed attack occurs."

The Treaty was intended to deter armed aggression in Southeast Asia. To that end it created not only a multilateral alliance but also a series of bilateral relationships. The obligations are placed squarely on "each Party" in the event of armed attack in the Treaty area—not upon "the Parties," a wording that might have implied a necessity for collective decision. The Treaty was intended to give the assurance of United States assistance to any Party or protocol state that might suffer a Communist armed attack, regardless of the views or actions of other parties. The fact that the obligations are individual, and may even to some extent differ among the parties to the Treaty, is demonstrated by the United States understanding, expressed at the time of signature, that its obligations under Article IV, paragraph I, apply only in the event of *Communist* aggression, whereas the other parties to the Treaty were unwilling so to limit their obligations to each other.

Thus, the United States has a commitment under Article IV, paragraph 1, in the event of armed attack, independent of the decision or action of other treaty parties. A joint communiqué issued by Secretary Rusk and Foreign Minister Thanat Khoman of Thailand on March 6, 1962, reflected this understanding:

> The Secretary of State assured the Foreign Minister that in the event of such aggression, the United States intends to give full effect to its obligations under the Treaty to act to meet the common danger in accordance with its constitutional processes. The Secretary of State reaffirmed that this obligation of the United States does not depend on the prior agreement of all other Parties to the Treaty, since this Treaty obligation is individual as well as collective.

Most of the SEATO countries have stated that they agreed with this interpretation. None has registered objection to it.

When the Senate Committee on Foreign Relations reported on the Southeast Asia Collective Defense Treaty, it noted that the treaty area was further defined so that the "Free Territory of Viet Nam" was an area "which, if attacked, would fall under the protection of the instrument." In its conclusion the Committee stated:

> The Committee is not impervious to the risks which this treaty entails. It fully appreciates that acceptance of these additional obligations commits the United States to a course of action over a vast expanse of the Pacific. Yet these risks are consistent with our own highest interests.

The Senate gave its advice and consent to the Treaty by a vote of 82 to 1.

C. THE UNITED STATES HAS GIVEN ADDITIONAL ASSURANCES TO THE GOVERNMENT OF SOUTH VIET NAM

The United States has also given a series of additional assurances to the Government of South Viet Nam. As early as October 1954 President Eisenhower undertook to provide direct assistance to help make South Viet Nam "capable of resisting attempted subversion or aggression through military means." On May 11, 1957 President Eisenhower and President Ngo Dinh Diem of the Republic of Viet Nam issued a joint statement which called attention to "the large build-up of Vietnamese Communist military forces in North Viet Nam" and stated:

> Noting that the Republic of Vietnam is covered by Article IV of the Southeast Asia Collective Defense Treaty, President Eisenhower and President Ngo Dinh Diem agreed that aggression or subversion threatening the political independence of the Republic of Vietnam would be considered as endangering peace and stability.

On August 2, 1961 President Kennedy declared that "the United States is determined that the Republic of Viet Nam shall not be lost to the Communists for lack of any support which the United States can render." On December 7 of that year President Diem appealed for additional support. In his reply of December 14, 1961 President Kennedy recalled the United States declaration made at the end of the Geneva Conference in 1954, and reaffirmed that the United States was "prepared to help the Republic of Viet Nam to protect its people and to preserve its independence." This assurance has been reaffirmed many times since.

III. ACTIONS BY THE UNITED STATES AND SOUTH VIET NAM ARE JUSTIFIED UNDER THE GENEVA ACCORDS OF 1954

A. DESCRIPTION OF THE ACCORDS

The Geneva Accords of 1954[8] established the date and hour for a cease-fire in Viet Nam, drew a "provisional military demarcation

---

[8] These Accords were composed of a bilateral cease-fire agreement between the "Commander-in-Chief of the People's Army of Viet Nam" and the "Commander-in-Chief of the French Union Forces in Indo-China," together with a Final Declaration of the Conference, to which France adhered. However, it

line" with a demilitarized zone on both sides, and required an exchange of prisoners and the phased regroupment of Viet Minh Forces from the south to the north and of French Union Forces from the north to the south. The introduction into Viet Nam of troop reinforcements and new military equipment (except for replacement and repair) was prohibited. The armed forces of each party were required to respect the demilitarized zone and the territory of the other zone. The adherence of either zone to any military alliance, and the use of either zone for the resumption of hostilities or to "further an aggressive policy," were prohibited. The International Control Commission was established, composed of India, Canada and Poland, with India as Chairman. The task of the Commission was to supervise the proper execution of the provisions of the Cease-Fire Agreement. General elections that would result in reunification were required to be held in July 1956 under the supervision of the ICC.

B. NORTH VIET NAM VIOLATED THE ACCORDS FROM THE BEGINNING

From the very beginning, the North Vietnamese violated the 1954 Geneva Accords. Communist military forces and supplies were left in the South in violation of the Accords. Other Communist guerrillas were moved north for further training and then were infiltrated into the South in violation of the Accords.

C. THE INTRODUCTION OF UNITED STATES MILITARY PERSONNEL AND EQUIPMENT WAS JUSTIFIED

The Accords prohibited the reinforcement of foreign military forces in Viet Nam and the introduction of new military equipment, but they allowed replacement of existing military personnel and equipment. Prior to late 1961 South Viet Nam had received considerable military equipment and supplies from the United States, and the United States had gradually enlarged its Military Assistance Advisory Group to slightly less than 900 men. These actions were reported to the ICC and were justified as replacements for equipment in Viet Nam in 1954 and for French training and advisory personnel who had been withdrawn after 1954.

As the Communist aggression intensified during 1961, with increased infiltration and a marked stepping up of Communist terrorism

---

is to be noted that the South Vietnamese Government was not a signatory of the cease-fire agreement and did not adhere to the Final Declaration. South Viet Nam entered a series of reservations in a statement to the Conference. This statement was noted by the Conference, but by decision of the Conference Chairman it was not included or referred to in the Final Declaration.

in the South, the United States found it necessary in late 1961 to increase substantially the numbers of our military personnel and the amounts and types of equipment introduced by this country into South Viet Nam. These increases were justified by the international law principle that a material breach of an agreement by one party entitles the other at least to withhold compliance with an equivalent, corresponding, or related provision until the defaulting party is prepared to honor its obligations.[9]

In accordance with this principle, the systematic violation of the Geneva Accords by North Viet Nam justified South Viet Nam in suspending compliance with the provision controlling entry of foreign military personnel and military equipment.

D. SOUTH VIET NAM WAS JUSTIFIED IN REFUSING TO IMPLEMENT THE ELECTION PROVISIONS OF THE GENEVA ACCORDS

The Geneva Accords contemplated the reunification of the two parts of Viet Nam. They contained a provision for general elections to be held in July 1956 in order to obtain a "free expression of the national will." The Accords stated that "consultations will be held on this subject between the competent representative authorities of the two zones from 20 July 1955 onwards."

There may be some question whether South Viet Nam was bound by these election provisions. As indicated earlier, South Viet Nam did not sign the cease-fire agreement of 1954, nor did it adhere to the Final Declaration of the Geneva Conference. The South Vietnamese Government at that time gave notice of its objection in particular to the election provisions of the Accords.

However, even on the premise that these provisions were binding on South Viet Nam, the South Vietnamese Government's failure to

---

[9] This principle of law and the circumstances in which it may be invoked are most fully discussed in the Fourth Report on the Law of Treaties by Sir Gerald Fitzmaurice, Articles 18, 20 (UN Doc. A/CN.4/120(1959)), II Yearbook of the International Law Commission 37 (UN Doc. A/CN.4/SER.A/1959/Add. 1), and in the later Report by Sir Humphrey Waldock, Article 20 (UN Doc. A/CN.4/156 and Add.1-3(1963)), II Yearbook of the International Law Commission 36 (UN Doc. A/CN.4/SER.A/1963/Add.1). Among the authorities cited by the Fourth Report for this proposition are: II Oppenheim, *International Law*, 136, 137 (7th ed. Lauterpacht 1955); I Rousseau, *Principes généraux du droit international public*, 365 (1944); II Hyde, *International Law*, 1660 et. seq. (2d ed. 1947); II Guggenheim, *Traité de droit international public*, 84, 85 (1935); Spiropoulos, *Traité théorique et pratique de droit international public*, 289 (1933); *Verdross, Völkerrecht*, 328 (1950); Hall, *Treatise*, 21 (8th ed., Higgins 1924); 3 Accioly, *Tratado de Direito Internacional Publico*, 82 (1956-57). See also draft articles 42 and 46 of the Law of Treaties by the International Law Commission, contained in the Report on the work of its Fifteenth Session (General Assembly, Official Records, 18th Session, Supplement No. 9(A/5809)).

engage in consultations in 1955, with a view to holding elections in 1956, involved no breach of obligation. The conditions in North Viet Nam during that period were such as to make impossible any free and meaningful expression of popular will.

Some of the facts about conditions in the North were admitted even by the Communist leadership in Hanoi. General Giap, currently Defense Minister of North Viet Nam, in addressing the Tenth Congress of the North Vietnamese Communist Party in October 1956, publicly acknowledged that the Communist leaders were running a police state where executions, terror and torture were commonplace. A nationwide election in these circumstances would have been a travesty. No one in the North would have dared to vote except as directed. With a substantial majority of the Vietnamese people living north of the 17th parallel, such an election would have meant turning the country over to the Communists without regard to the will of the people. The South Vietnamese Government realized these facts and quite properly took the position that consultations for elections in 1956 as contemplated by the Accords would be a useless formality.[10]

IV. The President Has Full Authority To Commit United States Forces in the Collective Defense of South Viet Nam

There can be no question in present circumstances of the President's authority to commit United States forces to the defense of South Viet Nam. The grant of authority to the President in Article II of the Constitution extends to the actions of the United States currently undertaken in Viet Nam. In fact, however, it is unnecessary to determine whether this grant standing alone is sufficient to authorize the actions taken in Viet Nam. These actions rest not only on the exercise of Presidential powers under Article II but on the SEATO Treaty—a treaty advised and consented to by the Senate—and on actions of the Congress, particularly the Joint Resolution of August 10, 1964. When these sources of authority are taken together— Article II of the Constitution, the SEATO Treaty, and actions by the Congress—there can be no question of the legality under domestic law of United States actions in Viet Nam.

---

[10] In any event, if North Viet Nam considered there had been a breach of obligation by the South, its remedies lay in discussion with Saigon, perhaps in an appeal to the Co-Chairmen of the Geneva Conference, or in a reconvening of the Conference to consider the situation. Under international law, North Viet Nam had no right to use force outside its own zone in order to secure its political objectives.

A. THE PRESIDENT'S POWER UNDER ARTICLE II OF THE
CONSTITUTION EXTENDS TO THE ACTIONS CURRENTLY
UNDERTAKEN IN VIET NAM

Under the Constitution, the President, in addition to being Chief Executive, is Commander-in-Chief of the Army and Navy. He holds the prime responsibility for the conduct of United States foreign relations. These duties carry very broad powers, including the power to deploy American forces abroad and commit them to military operations when the President deems such action necessary to maintain the security and defense of the United States.

At the Federal Constitutional Convention in 1787, it was originally proposed that Congress have the power "to make war." There were objections that legislative proceedings were too slow for this power to be vested in Congress; it was suggested that the Senate might be a better repository. Madison and Gerry then moved to substitute "to declare war" for "to make war," "leaving to the Executive the power to repel sudden attacks." It was objected that this might make it too easy for the Executive to involve the nation in war, but the motion carried with but one dissenting vote.

In 1787 the world was a far larger place, and the framers probably had in mind attacks upon the United States. In the 20th century, the world has grown much smaller. An attack on a country far from our shores can impinge directly on the nation's security. In the SEATO Treaty, for example, it is formally declared that an armed attack against Viet Nam would endanger the peace and safety of the United States.

Since the Constitution was adopted there have been at least 125 instances in which the President has ordered the armed forces to take action or maintain positions abroad without obtaining prior Congressional authorization, starting with the "undeclared war" with France (1798-1800). For example, President Truman ordered 250,000 troops to Korea during the Korean War of the early 1950's. President Eisenhower dispatched 14,000 troops to Lebanon in 1958.

The Constitution leaves to the President the judgment to determine whether the circumstances of a particular armed attack are so urgent and the potential consequences so threatening to the security of the United States that he should act without formally consulting the Congress.

B. THE SOUTHEAST ASIA COLLECTIVE DEFENSE TREATY
AUTHORIZES THE PRESIDENT'S ACTIONS

Under Article VI of the United States Constitution, "all Treaties made, or which shall be made, under the Authority of the United

States, shall be the supreme Law of the Land." Article IV, paragraph 1 of the SEATO Treaty establishes as a matter of law that a Communist armed attack against South Viet Nam endangers the peace and safety of the United States. In this same provision the United States has undertaken a commitment in the SEATO Treaty to "act to meet the common danger in accordance with its constitutional processes" in the event of such an attack.

Under our Constitution it is the President who must decide when an armed attack has occurred. He has also the constitutional responsibility for determining what measures of defense are required when the peace and safety of the United States are endangered. If he considers that deployment of U.S. forces to South Viet Nam is required, and that military measures against the source of Communist aggression in North Viet Nam are necessary, he is constitutionally empowered to take those measures.

The SEATO Treaty specifies that each party will act "in accordance with its constitutional processes."

It has recently been argued that the use of land forces in Asia is not authorized under the Treaty because their use to deter armed attack was not contemplated at the time the Treaty was considered by the Senate. Secretary Dulles testified at that time that we did not intend to establish (1) a land army in Southeast Asia capable of deterring Communist aggression, or (2) an integrated headquarters and military organization like that of NATO; instead, the United States would rely on "mobile striking power" against the sources of aggression. However, the Treaty obligation in Article IV, paragraph 1, to meet the common danger in the event of armed aggression, is not limited to particular modes of military action. What constitutes an adequate deterrent or an appropriate response, in terms of military strategy, may change; but the essence of our commitment to act to meet the common danger, as necessary at the time of an armed aggression, remains. In 1954 the forecast of military judgment might have been against the use of substantial United States ground forces in Viet Nam. But that does not preclude the President from reaching a different military judgment in different circumstances, twelve years later.

C. THE JOINT RESOLUTION OF CONGRESS OF AUGUST 10, 1964 AUTHORIZES UNITED STATES PARTICIPATION IN THE COLLECTIVE DEFENSE OF SOUTH VIET NAM

As stated earlier, the legality of United States participation in the defense of South Viet Nam does not rest only on the constitutional power of the President under Article II—or indeed on that power taken in conjunction with the SEATO Treaty. In addition, the Congress has acted in unmistakable fashion to approve and authorize United States actions in Viet Nam.

Following the North Vietnamese attacks in the Gulf of Tonkin against United States destroyers, Congress adopted, by a Senate vote of 88-2 and a House vote of 416-0, a Joint Resolution containing a series of important declarations and provisions of law.

Section 1 resolved that "the Congress approves and supports the determination of the President, as Commander in Chief, to take all necessary measures to repel any armed attack against the forces of the United States and to prevent further aggression." Thus, the Congress gave its sanction to specific actions by the President to repel attacks against United States naval vessels in the Gulf of Tonkin and elsewhere in the western Pacific. Congress further approved the taking of "all necessary measures . . . to prevent further aggression." This authorization extended to those measures the President might consider necessary to ward off further attacks and to prevent further aggression by North Viet Nam in Southeast Asia.

The Joint Resolution then went on to provide in section 2:

> The United States regards as vital to its national interest and to world peace the maintenance of international peace and security in southeast Asia. Consonant with the Constitution of the United States and the Charter of the United Nations and in accordance with its obligations under the Southeast Asia Collective Defense Treaty, the United States is, therefore, prepared, as the President determines, to take all necessary steps, including the use of armed force, to assist any member or protocol state of the Southeast Asia Collective Defense Treaty requesting assistance in defense of its freedom.

Section 2 thus constitutes an authorization to the President, in his discretion, to act—using armed force if he determines that is required —to assist South Viet Nam at its request in defense of its freedom. The identification of South Viet Nam through the reference to "protocol state" in this section is unmistakable, and the grant of authority "as the President determines" is unequivocal.

It has been suggested that the legislative history of the Joint Resolution shows an intention to limit United States assistance to South Viet Nam to aid, advice, and training. This suggestion is based on an amendment offered from the floor by Senator Nelson which would have added the following to the text:

> The Congress also approves and supports the efforts of the President to bring the problem of peace in Southeast Asia to the Security Council of the United Nations, and the President's declaration that the United States, seeking no extension of the present military con-

flict, will respond to provocation in a manner that is "limited and fitting." Our continuing policy is to limit our role to the provision of aid, training assistance, and military advice, and it is the sense of Congress that, except when provoked to a greater response, we should continue to attempt to avoid a direct military involvement in the Southeast Asian conflict.[11]

Senator Fulbright, who had reported the Joint Resolution from the Foreign Relations Committee, spoke on the amendment as follows:

Mr. Fulbright. It states fairly accurately what the President has said would be our policy, and what I stated my understanding was as to our policy; also what other Senators have stated. In other words, it states that our response should be appropriate and limited to the provocation, which the Senator states as "respond to provocation in a manner that is limited and fitting," and so forth. We do not wish any political or military bases there. We are not seeking to gain a colony. We seek to insure the capacity of these people to develop along the lines of their own desires, independent of domination by communism.

The Senator has put into his amendment a statement of policy that is unobjectionable. However, I cannot accept the amendment under the circumstances. I do not believe it is contrary to the joint resolution, but it is an enlargement. I am informed that the House is now voting on this resolution. The House joint resolution is about to be presented to us. I cannot accept the amendment and go to conference with it, and thus take responsibility for delaying matters.

I do not object to it as a statement of policy. I believe it is an accurate reflection of what I believe is the President's policy, judging from his own statements. That does not mean that as a practical matter I can accept the amendment. It would delay matters to do so. It would cause confusion and require a conference, and present us with all the other difficulties that are involved in this kind of legislative action. I regret that I cannot do it, even though I do not at all disagree with the amendment as a general statement of policy.[12]

Senator Nelson's amendment related the degree and kind of U.S. response in Viet Nam to "provocation" on the other side; the response should be "limited and fitting." The greater the provocation, the stronger are the measures that may be characterized as "limited and fitting." Bombing of North Vietnamese naval bases was a "limited and fitting" response to the attacks on U.S. destroyers in August 1964, and the subsequent actions taken by the United States and South Viet Nam have been an appropriate response to the increased war of aggression carried on by North Viet Nam since that date. Moreover, Senator Nelson's proposed amendment did not purport to be a restriction on authority available to the President but

---

11 110 *Cong. Rec.* 18459 (Aug. 7, 1964).
12 *Ibid.*

merely a statement concerning what should be the continuing policy of the United States.

Congressional realization of the scope of authority being conferred by the Joint Resolution is shown by the legislative history of the measure as a whole. The following exchange between Senators Cooper and Fulbright is illuminating:

> Mr. Cooper. . . The Senator will remember that the SEATO Treaty, in article IV, provides that in the event an armed attack is made upon a party to the Southeast Asia Collective Defense Treaty, or upon one of the protocol states such as South Vietnam, the parties to the treaty, one of whom is the United States, would then take such action as might be appropriate, after resorting to their constitutional processes. I assume that would mean, in the case of the United States, that Congress would be asked to grant the authority to act.
>
> Does the Senator consider that in enacting this resolution we are satisfying that requirement of article IV of the Southeast Asia Collective Defense Treaty? In other words, are we now giving the President advance authority to take whatever action he may deem necessary respecting South Vietnam and its defense, or with respect to the defense of any other country included in the treaty?
>
> Mr. Fulbright. I think that is correct.
>
> Mr. Cooper. Then, looking ahead, if the President decided that it was necessary to use such force as could lead into war, we will give that authority by this resolution?
>
> Mr. Fulbright. That is the way I would interpret it. If a situation later developed in which we thought the approval should be withdrawn it could be withdrawn by concurrent resolution.[13]

[13] 110 *Cong. Rec.* 18409 (Aug. 6, 1964).
Senator Morse, who opposed the Joint Resolution, expressed the following view on August 6, 1964, concerning the scope of the proposed resolution:
Another Senator thought, in the early part of the debate, that this course would not broaden the power of the President to engage in a land war if he decided that he wanted to apply the resolution in that way.
That Senator was taking great consolation in the then held belief that, if he voted for the resolution, it would give no authority to the President to send many troops into Asia. I am sure he was quite disappointed to finally learn, because it took a little time to get the matter cleared, that the resolution places no restriction on the President in that respect. If he is still in doubt, let him read the language on page 2, lines 3 to 6, and page 2, lines 11 to 17. The first reads:
"The Congress approves and supports the determination of the President, as Commander in Chief, to take all necessary measures to repel any armed attack against the forces of the United States and to prevent further aggression."
It does not say he is limited in regard to the sending of ground forces. It does not limit that authority. That is why I have called it a predated declaration of war, in clear violation of article I, section 8 of the Constitution, which vests the power to declare war in the Congress, and not in the President.
What is proposed is to authorize the President of the United States, without a declaration of war, to commit acts of war.
110 *Cong. Rec.* 18426-27 (Aug. 6, 1964).

The August 1964 Joint Resolution continues in force today. Section 2 of the Resolution provides that it shall expire "when the President shall determine that the peace and security of the area is reasonably assured by international conditions created by action of the United Nations or otherwise, except that it may be terminated earlier by concurrent resolution of the Congress." The President has made no such determination, nor has Congress terminated the Joint Resolution.[14]

Instead, Congress in May 1965 approved an appropriation of $700 million to meet the expense of mounting military requirements in Viet Nam. (Public Law 89-18, 79 Stat. 109.) The President's message asking for this appropriation stated that this was "not a routine request. For each member of Congress who supports this request is also voting to persist in our efforts to halt Communist aggressions in South Viet Nam." The Appropriation Act constitutes a clear Congressional endorsement and approval of the actions taken by the President.

On March 1, 1966 the Congress continued to express its support of the President's policy by approving a $4.8 billion supplemental military authorization by votes of 392-4 and 93-2. An amendment that would have limited the President's authority to commit forces to Viet Nam was rejected in the Senate by a vote of 94-2.

D. NO DECLARATION OF WAR BY THE CONGRESS IS REQUIRED TO AUTHORIZE UNITED STATES PARTICIPATION IN THE COLLECTIVE DEFENSE OF SOUTH VIETNAM

No declaration of war is needed to authorize American actions in Viet Nam. As shown in the preceding sections, the President has ample authority to order the participation of United States armed forces in the defense of South Viet Nam.

Over a very long period in our history, practice and precedent have confirmed the constitutional authority to engage United States forces in hostilities without a declaration of war. This history extends from the undeclared war with France and the war against the Barbary Pirates, at the end of the 18th century, to the Korean War of 1950-53.

James Madison, one of the leading framers of the Constitution, and Presidents John Adams and Jefferson all construed the Constitution, in their official actions during the early years of the Republic, as authorizing the United States to employ its armed forces abroad in hostilities in the absence of any Congressional declaration of war. Their views and actions constitute highly persuasive evidence as to the

---

[14] On March 1, 1966, the Senate voted, 92-5, to table an amendment that would have repealed the Joint Resolution.

meaning and effect of the Constitution. History has accepted the interpretation that was placed on the Constitution by the early Presidents and Congresses in regard to the lawfulness of hostilities without a declaration of war. The instances of such action in our history are numerous.

In the Korean conflict, where large-scale hostilities were conducted with an American troop participation of a quarter of a million men, no declaration of war was made by the Congress. The President acted on the basis of his constitutional responsibilities. While the Security Council, under a treaty of this country—the United Nations Charter —recommended assistance to the Republic of Korea against the Communist armed attack, the United States had no treaty commitment at that time obligating us to join in the defense of South Korea. In the case of South Viet Nam we have the obligation of the SEATO Treaty and clear expressions of Congressional support. If the President could act in Korea without a declaration of war, *a fortiori* he is empowered to do so now in Viet Nam.

It may be suggested that a declaration of war is the only available constitutional process by which Congressional support can be made effective for the use of United States armed forces in combat abroad. But the Constitution does not insist on any rigid formalism. It gives Congress a choice of ways in which to exercise its powers. In the case of Viet Nam the Congress has supported the determination of the President by the Senate's approval of the SEATO Treaty, the adoption of the Joint Resolution of August 10, 1964, and the enactment of the necessary authorizations and appropriations.

V. CONCLUSION

South Viet Nam is being subjected to armed attack by Communist North Viet Nam, through the infiltration of armed personnel, military equipment and regular combat units. International law recognizes the right of individual and collective self-defense against armed attack. South Viet Nam, and the United States upon the request of South Viet Nam, are engaged in such collective defense of the South. Their actions are in conformity with international law and with the Charter of the United Nations. The fact that South Viet Nam has been precluded by Soviet veto from becoming a Member of the United Nations, and the fact that South Viet Nam is a zone of a temporarily divided state, in no way diminish the right of collective defense of South Viet Nam.

The United States has commitments to assist South Viet Nam in defending itself against Communist aggression from the North. The

United States gave undertakings to this effect at the conclusion of the Geneva Conference in 1954. Later that year the United States undertook an international obligation in the SEATO Treaty to defend South Viet Nam against Communist armed aggression. And during the past decade the United States has given additional assurances to the South Vietnamese Government.

The Geneva Accords of 1954 provided for a cease-fire and regroupment of contending forces, a division of Viet Nam into two zones, and a prohibition on the use of either zone for the resumption of hostilities or to "further an aggressive policy." From the beginning, North Viet Nam violated the Geneva Accords through a systematic effort to gain control of South Viet Nam by force. In the light of these progressive North Vietnamese violations, the introduction into South Viet Nam beginning in late 1961 of substantial United States military equipment and personnel, to assist in the defense of the South, was fully justified; substantial breach of an international agreement by one side permits the other side to suspend performance of corresponding obligations under the agreement. South Viet Nam was justified in refusing to implement the provisions of the Geneva Accords calling for reunification through free elections throughout Viet Nam since the Communist regime in North Viet Nam created conditions in the North that made free elections entirely impossible.

The President of the United States has full authority to commit United States forces in the collective defense of South Viet Nam. This authority stems from the Constitutional powers of the President. However, it is not necessary to rely on the Constitution alone as the source of the President's authority, since the SEATO Treaty—advised and consented to by the Senate and forming part of the law of the land—sets forth a United States commitment to defend South Viet Nam against armed attack, and since the Congress—in the Joint Resolution of August 10, 1964, and in authorization and appropriations acts for support of the U.S. military effort in Viet Nam—has given its approval and support to the President's actions. United States actions in Viet Nam, taken by the President and approved by the Congress, do not require any declaration of war, as shown by a long line of precedents for the use of United States armed forces abroad in the absence of any Congressional declaration of war.

7. INTERNATIONAL LAW AND THE UNITED STATES ROLE IN THE VIET NAM WAR

By RICHARD A. FALK

I

NO contemporary problem of world order is more troublesome for an international lawyer than the analysis of the international law of "internal war."[1] A war is usefully classified as internal when violence takes place primarily within a single political entity, regardless of foreign support for the contending factions.[2] The insurgents who won the American Revolution were heavily supported by French arms. Wars of national liberation are not new, nor is external support for an incumbent regime. But considerable historical experience with foreign intervention in internal wars has not been adequately incorporated into prevailing doctrines of international law. In an age of civil turbulence and nuclear risk, the requirements of world order make imperative the effort to overcome the consequent confusion.[3]

Reprinted by permission of the author, The Yale Law Journal Company and Fred B. Rothman and Company from *The Yale Law Journal*, 75, 1122-1160.

[1] See generally *Internal War* (Eckstein ed. 1964); *International Aspects of Civil Strife* (Rosenau ed. 1964) [hereinafter cited as Rosenau].

[2] The "internalness" of an internal war is a consequence of the objectives and arena of the violence. There are, of course, a range of different types of internal war. See Rosenau, *Internal War as an International Event,* in Rosenau 45, at 63-64. Rosenau usefully differentiates between internal wars, in terms of whether they are fought primarily to achieve changes in the personnel of the leadership, the nature of political authority, or the socio-political structure of the society.

[3] For helpful exposition see Huntington, "Patterns of Violence in World Politics," in *Changing Patterns of Military Politics* 17 (Huntington ed. 1962); see also Bloomfield, *International Military Forces* 24-46 (1964). See the table classifying examples of internal war in terms of "basically internal," "externally abetted internal instability," and "externally created or controlled internal instability." *Id.* at 28-30. Incidentally, Professor Bloomfield located the war in Viet Nam in the middle category as of 1964.

The central issue is whether an externally abetted internal war belongs in either traditional legal category of war—"civil" or "international." Four sub-inquiries are relevant. What are the legal restraints, if any, upon national discretion to treat a particular internal war as an international war? What rules and procedures are available to determine whether foreign participation in an internal war constitutes "military assistance," "intervention," "aggression," or "an armed attack"? What responses are permissible by the victim of "aggression" or "an armed attack"? Finally, what should be the roles of national, regional, and global actors in interpreting and applying the relevant rules?

If the internal war is regarded as a "civil" war, then the legally permitted response to intervention is restricted to counter-intervention;[4] an intervening nation whose own territory is not the scene of conflict may not attack the territory of a state intervening on the other side.[5] If foreign intervention were held to convert an "internal" war into an "international" war, the intervention could be regarded as an armed attack that would justify action in self-defense proportionate to the aggression. The victim of aggression is entitled, if necessary, to attack the territory of the aggressor, expanding the arena of violence to more than a single political entity.[6] Given the commitment of international law to limiting the scope, duration, and intensity of warfare, it would appear desirable severely to restrict or perhaps to deny altogether, the discretion of nations to convert an internal war into an international war by characterizing external participation as "aggression" rather than as "intervention."[7]

The American outlook on these issues has dramatically changed in recent years. John Foster Dulles is properly associated with the expansion of American undertakings to defend foreign nations everywhere against Communist takeovers by either direct or indirect ag-

---

[4] See *The International Regulation of Internal Violence in the Developing Countries, Proceedings, American Society of International Law,* (April, 1966).

[5] The assertion in the text must be qualified to the extent that the United States decision to bomb North Viet Nam is treated as a law-creating precedent (rather than as a violation).

[6] If the conceptions of "aggression" and "armed attack" are so vague that nations can themselves determine their content, a self-serving legal description of the desired course of state action can be given and is not subject to criticism in a strict sense. A critic would be required to stress that an expansive definition of "armed attack," although not forbidden by prior rules of law, was an unwise legal claim because of its status as a precedent available to others and because of its tendency to expand the scope and magnify the scale of a particular conflict.

[7] It is important to distinguish between the factual processes of coercion and the legal labels used to justify or protest various positions taken by the participants. Aggression is a legal conclusion about the nature of a particular pattern of coercion.

gression. But even Dulles did not propose treating indirect aggression as the equivalent of an armed attack by one country on another. In fact, during the Congressional hearings on the Eisenhower Doctrine in 1957[8] Dulles declared ". . . if you open the door to saying that any country which feels it is being threatened by subversive activities in another country is free to use armed force against that country, you are opening the door to a series of wars over the world, and I am confident that it would lead to a third world war."[9] In my judgment, by bombing North Viet Nam the United States is opening such a door and is setting a dramatic precedent of precisely the sort that Dulles had in mind. Our pride as a nation is now so deeply dependent upon a successful outcome in Viet Nam that our Government seems insufficiently sensitive to the serious negative consequences of the Viet Nam precedent for the future of world order.[10]

The appraisal of a claim by a national government that an act of intervention is "aggression" is a complex task even if performed with utter impartiality. It depends on assessing very confused facts as to the extent and phasing of external participation, as well as upon interpreting the intentions of the participating nations. For instance, one must distinguish in the behavior of an international rival between a program of unlimited expansion through violence and intervention to assure the fair play of political forces in a particular domestic society. In the context of contemporary international politics, a crucial assessment is whether Communism or specific Communist states propose unlimited expansion by using unlawful force or whether they rely upon persuasion and permissible levels of coercion.[11] It is diffi-

[8] The critical section in The Eisenhower Doctrine (1957) is Section 2:
The President is authorized to undertake, in the general area of the Middle East, military assistance programs with any nation or group of nations of that area desiring such assistance. Furthermore, the United States regards as vital to the national interest and world peace the preservation of the independence and integrity of the nations of the Middle East. To this end, if the President determines the necessity thereof, the United States is prepared to use armed force to assist any such nation or group of nations requesting assistance against armed aggression from any country controlled by international communism: *Provided,* That such employment shall be consonant with the treaty obligations of the United States and with the Constitution of the United States.
36 *Dep't State Bull.* 481 (1957).

[9] *The President's Proposal on the Middle East, Hearings before Senate Committees on Foreign Relations and Armed Services,* 85th Cong., 1st Sess., pt. 1, at 28 (1957).

[10] The role of national claims of a unilateral nature in the development of international law is examined in Falk, *Toward a Responsible Procedure for the National Assertion of Protested Claims to Use Space,* in *Space and Society* 91 (Taubenfeld ed. 1964).

[11] This is the main theme of a speech by the Secretary of State. See Rusk, *Address,* 1965 *Proc. Am. Soc. Int'l L.* 247, 249-51.

cult to obtain adequate evidence on the limits of permissible political and para-military coercion.[12] Arguably, even a program of maximum expansion should be countered by self-limiting responses aimed at neutralizing Communist influence on internal wars and at building a world order that minimizes the role of military force.[13] We must also not overlook the welfare of the society torn by internal war. The great powers tend to wage their struggles for global dominance largely at the expense of the ex-colonial peoples.[14] These considerations support a conservative approach to internal wars, an approach treating them as civil wars, and permitting a neutralizing response as a maximum counteraction. And, specifically, if efforts to neutralize Communist expansion[15] in Viet Nam can be justified at all, the appropriate role of the United States is to counter "intervention" rather than to respond to an "armed attack."

The issue of self-determination is also relevant in the setting of internal war. If Communists or Communist-oriented elites can obtain political control without significant external support, it becomes difficult to vindicate Western intervention in terms of neutralizing Communist expansion. Castro's revolution represents a Communist success that was achieved without significant external support until after political control of Cuba was fully established. Part of the objection to American intervention in the Dominican Republic in 1965 arises from the absence of prior foreign intervention. The policies of preventing war, minimizing violence, and localizing conflict seem in these contexts to outweigh the objectives of anti-Communism; the United States serves both its own interests and those of the world

[12] I have discussed these issues in Falk, "On Minimizing the Use of Nuclear Weapons: A Comparison of Revolutionary and Reformist Perspectives," in Falk, Tucker, & Young, *On Minimizing the Use of Nuclear Weapons* 1 (Research Monograph No. 23, Center of International Studies, Princeton University, March 1, 1966).

[13] Everyone would agree in the abstract that it is important to reconcile policies directed at limiting the expansion of adversaries with those aimed at avoiding warfare, particularly nuclear warfare. See Falk, *Law, Morality, and War* 32-65 (1963).

[14] Relative peace is obtained through mutual deterrence at "the center" of the international system. Struggles for expansion are confined to "the periphery" where the risks of nuclear war can be minimized and where the costs of conflict can be shifted from the great powers to the ex-colonial nations.

[15] My own judgment, based on the analysis of the Geneva settlement in 1954, is that the war in South Viet Nam represents more an American attempt at "rollback" than a Communist attempt at "expansion." The Geneva Conference looked toward the reunification of the whole of Viet Nam under the leadership of Ho Chi Minh. The introduction into South Viet Nam of an American military presence thus appears as an effort to reverse these expectations and to deny Hanoi the full extent of its victory against the French. *Cf.* also Lacouture, *Vietnam: Between Two Truces* 17-68 (1966) [hereinafter cited as Lacouture].

community by respecting the outcome of internal political struggles. Unless we respect domestic political autonomy, our adversaries have no incentive to refrain from participating on the side of their faction. The primary objective in relation to internal warfare is to establish rules of the game that allow domestic processes of political conflict to proceed without creating undue risks of a major war. In addition, human welfare and democratic ideals are best served by allowing the struggle between Communist and Western approaches to development to be waged by domestic factions. Recent events in Indonesia, Algeria, and Ghana demonstrate that these internal struggles for ascendancy are not inevitably won by Communists.

Civil strife can be analyzed in terms of three different types of violent conflict.[16] A Type I conflict involves the direct and massive use of military force by one political entity across a frontier of another— Korea, or Suez.[17] To neutralize the invasion it may be necessary to act promptly and unilaterally, and it is appropriate either to use force in self-defense or to organize collective action under the auspices of a regional or global institution. A Type II conflict involves substantial military participation by one or more foreign nations in an internal struggle for control, *e.g.*, the Spanish Civil War. To neutralize this use of military power it may be necessary, and it is appropriate, to take off-setting military action confined to the internal arena, although only after seeking unsuccessful recourse to available procedures for peaceful settlement and machinery for collective security. A third type of conflict, Type III, is an internal struggle for control of a national society, the outcome of which is virtually independent of external participation. Of course, the outcome of a Type III conflict may affect the relative power of many other countries. Hungary prior to Soviet intervention, Cuba (1958-59), and the Dominican Republic prior to United States intervention, typify this class of struggle. It is inappropriate for a foreign nation to use military power to influence the outcome. The degree of inappropriateness will vary with the extent and duration of the military power used, and also with the explicitness of the foreign nation's role.[18] Thus, the reliance

[16] These "types" are analytical rather than empirical in character. In actual experience a particular occasion of violence is a mixture of types, although the nature of the mixture is what makes one classification more appropriate than another.

[17] Border disputes generating limited, but overt, violence by one entity against another are a special sub-type under Type I that may or may not support a finding of "armed attack" or a defensive claim of "self-defense."

[18] See the emphasis on the *covertness* of the United States role in sponsoring the Bay of Pigs invasion of 1961 as an influential factor in the decision to proceed in Schlesinger, Jr., *A Thousand Days*, 233-97 (1965). And note that Schlesinger's opposition to the invasion was based in large part on his belief that it would be impossible to disguise the United States' role. *Id.* at 253-54.

on Cuban exiles to carry out the anti-Castro mission at the Bay of Pigs (1961) is somewhat less inappropriate than the use of United States Marines. Perhaps appreciating this distinction, North Viet Nam relied almost exclusively on South Vietnamese exiles during the early years of the anti-Diem war.[19]

These three models are analytical tools designed to clarify the nature and consequences of policy choices. Reasonable men may disagree on the proper classification of a particular war, especially if they cannot agree on the facts. An understanding of the controversy over the legality of United States participation in the war in Viet Nam seems aided by keeping in mind these distinct models.

The United States is treating the war as a Type I conflict. I would argue, for reasons set out in the next section, that the war belongs in Class III. But if this position entailing non-participation is rejected, then the maximum American response is counter-intervention as is permissible in a Type II situation.

Two general issues bear on an interpretation of the rights and duties of states in regard to internal wars of either Type II or III. First, to what extent does the constituted elite—the incumbent regime—enjoy a privileged position to request outside help in suppressing internal challenges directed at its control?[20] Traditional international law permits military assistance to the incumbent regime during early stages of an internal challenge. However, once the challenging faction demonstrates its capacity to gain control and administer a substantial portion of the society, most authorities hold that a duty of neutrality or non-discrimination governs the relations of both factions to outside states.[21] A state may act in favor of the incumbent to neutralize a Type III conflict only until the challenge is validated as substantial. A crucial question is whether outside states can themselves determine the point at which the challenge is validated, or whether validation is controlled, or at least influenced, by international procedures and by objective criteria of validation. The United States legal position stresses its continuing right to discriminate in favor of the incumbent regime and to deny even the political existence of the National Liberation Front (N.L.F.), despite the *de facto* existence of the N.L.F.

---

19 See, *e.g.*, Warner, *The Last Confucian*, 155 (1963) [hereinafter cited as Warner]; Fall, *The Two Viet-Nams*, 316-84 (rev. ed. 1964) [hereinafter cited as *The Two Viet-Nams*].

20 See, *e.g.*, Garner, *Questions of International Law in the Spanish Civil War*, 31 *Am. J. Int'l L.* 66 (1937).

21 See generally Thomas & Thomas, *Non-Intervention: The Law and Its Impact in the Americas*, 215-21 (1956); see also Lauterpacht, *Recognition in International Law*, 199-201, 227-33 (1957); Falk, "Janus Tormented: The International Law of Internal War," in Rosenau, 185, 197-209.

over a long period and its effective control of a large portion of the disputed territory.[22]

A second question partially applicable to Viet Nam is whether it is ever permissible to discriminate in favor of the counter-elite. The Communist states and the ex-colonial states of Asia and Africa assume that there are occasions warranting external participation in support of the insurgent faction. The Afro-Asian states argue that political legitimacy is established by an international consensus expressed through the formal acts of international institutions, rather than by the mere control of the constituted government.[23] This theory of legitimacy sanctions foreign military assistance to an "anti-colonialist" struggle. The extent to which this new attitude alters traditional international law is at present unclear, as is its full relevance to the conflict in Viet Nam. The argument for applicability to Viet Nam would emphasize the continuity between the 1946-54 anti-colonial war in Viet Nam and the present conflict. It would presuppose that the diplomatic recognition of South Viet Nam by some sixty countries conferred only nominal sovereignty, and that the Saigon regime is a client government of the United States, which has succeeded to the imperialistic role of the French. This approach implies that external states such as North Viet Nam, China, and the Soviet Union have "the right" to render support to the N.L.F.

These notions of permissible discrimination in favor of the constituted elite or the challenging counter-elite complicate considerably the legal analysis of participation in a Type III conflict and blur the boundaries between Types II and III. Any adequate statement of the international law of internal war, must acknowledge this complexity, and admit along with it a certain degree of legal indeterminancy.[24]

II

The vast and competent literature on the war in South Viet Nam provides an essential factual background for an impartial approach to

[22] For a description of the extent of the N.L.F.'s governmental control see Burchett, *Vietnam: Inside Story of The Guerilla War* 223-26 (1965); for legal argument see Lauterpacht, *op. cit. supra* at 175-238.

[23] The legal status of a counter-elite in a colony is certainly improved by the repeated condemnations of colonialism in the United Nations and the recent passage of formal resolutions calling for decolonialization. Factors other than claims to be the constituted government are regularly taken into account in assessing claims of legitimacy in international relations.

[24] For the theoretical background on legal indeterminacy in international law see Lauterpacht, "Some Observations on the Prohibition of 'Non Liquet' and the Completeness of the Law," in *Symbolae Verzijl*, 196-221 (1958); Stone, "Non Liquet and the Function of Law in the International Community," 35 *Brit. Yb. Int'l L.* 124 (1959).

the legal issues presented in the Memorandum of Law prepared by the State Department.[25] It is impossible to summarize all of the relevant facts, but it may be useful to indicate certain lines of reasoning that account for part of my disagreement with the official legal analysis. This disagreement reflects my interpretation of the internal war as primarily a consequence of indigenous forces. Even more, it stems from my concern for taking into account certain facts entirely excluded from the Memorandum, such as the pre-1954 war against the French and the repression of political opposition by the Diem regime.

It must be kept in mind that the present conflict in Viet Nam originated in the war fought between the French and the Vietminh for control of *the whole* of Viet Nam, which was "settled" at Geneva in 1954.[26] Although the intentions of the participants at Geneva were somewhat ambiguous, the general view at the time was that the Geneva agreements anticipated reunification under the leadership of Ho Chi Minh by 1956 to coincide with the French departure. France came to Geneva a defeated nation; the Vietminh held two-thirds or more of the country.[27] Had elections been held, it is generally agreed that reunification under Ho Chi Minh would have resulted, however one interprets the suppression of political opposition in the North or intimidation in the South.[28] Independent observers also agree that the anticipation of the prospect of peaceful reunification led Hanoi to observe the Geneva arrangements during the two years immediately following 1954. The undoubted disappointment caused by the refusal of the French and the Americans to make Saigon go through with the elections helps explain the resumption of insurrectionary violence after 1956.[29]

---

[25] Among those most helpful see Lacouture, *The Two Viet-Nams;* Fall, *Vietnam Witness 1953-66* (1966) [hereinafter cited as *Vietnam Witness*]; Shaplen, *The Lost Revolution* (rev. ed. 1966) [hereinafter cited as Shaplen]; Lancaster, *The Emancipation of French Indo-China* (1961) [hereinafter cited as Lancaster]; Warner.

[26] The settlement was not very realistic. It failed to take into account Saigon's exclusion or the American opposition to the Geneva solution. No responsibility was imposed upon the French to assure compliance with the terms of settlement prior to their withdrawal. See Warner 142-43.

[27] For a general account see *Lancaster* 290-358; *Vietnam Witness* 69-83; for the fullest account of the Geneva negotiations see Lacouture & Devillers, *La fin d'une guerre* (1960). And see Eisenhower, *Mandate for Change* 322-75 (1963) for official American thinking during this period.

[28] There is agreement that an election held within the prescribed period would have been won by Ho Chi Minh. See, *e.g.,* Shaplen xi, Warner 142-43; Lacouture 32: "The final declaration of the Geneva Conference foresaw, of course, that general election would permit the reunification of Vietnam two years later. And none doubted at the time that this would be to the benefit of the North."

[29] See Lacouture 32-50.

The Vietminh did leave a cadre of 5,000 or so elite guerrillas in the South, withdrawing others, as agreed, north of the Seventeenth Parallel.[30] Those left in the South apparently went "underground," hiding weapons for possible future use. This action seems no more than a reasonable precaution on the part of Hanoi in light of Saigon's continuing objection to the Geneva terms, and in view of Washington's evident willingness from 1954 onward to give Saigon political and military support. Given the terms of conflict and the balance of forces in Viet Nam prior to the Geneva Conference, French acceptance of a Viet Nam-wide defeat, American reluctance to affirm the results of Geneva, and Saigon's repudiation of the settlement, it seems quite reasonable for Hanoi to regard a resumption of the civil war as a distinct contingency. Although a decade of *de facto* independence (affirmed by diplomatic recognition) now gives South Viet Nam a strong claim to existence as a political entity, Hanoi certainly had no obligation in 1954 to respect claims of an independent political status for Saigon.[31] To clarify the diplomatic context in Geneva, it is well to recall that the Vietminh was the sole negotiator on behalf of Vietnamese interests at Geneva in 1954.

Later in 1954 the Saigon regime under Premier Diem ruthlessly suppressed all political opposition.[32] Observers agree that organization of an underground was an inevitable reaction to this suppression, and that the N.L.F. at its inception included many non-Communist elements.[33] It also appears that Saigon was unwilling to negotiate, or even consult, on questions affecting reunification, and was unwilling to normalize economic relations with Hanoi. The great economic strain imposed on North Viet Nam forced it to use scarce foreign exchange to obtain part of its food supply from other countries.[34]

Furthermore, the French military presence soon was replaced by an American military presence prior to the scheduled elections on reunification.[35] The evolution of an American "commitment" to Saigon's permanence and legitimacy contrasts radically with both the expectations created at Geneva in 1954 and the subsequent attitudes

[30] *Id.* at 32-68; cf. *Vietnam Witness* 169-89.

[31] Hanoi was "entitled" to prevent Saigon from establishing itself as a political entity with independent claims to diplomatic status as a sovereign state. A separation of Viet Nam into two states was not contemplated by the participants at Geneva.

[32] See Warner 107-24; Lacouture 17-31.

[33] Fall, *Viet-Cong—The Unseen Enemy in Viet-Nam,* in *The Viet-Nam Reader* (Raskin & Fall eds. 1965) [hereinafter cited as *Viet-Nam Reader*].

[34] Lacouture 34-35, 68.

[35] This is the major thesis of Lacouture, *Vietnam: The Lessons of War,* reprinted from the New York Review of Books, March 3, 1966, p. 1, in *Hearings on S.2793 Before the Senate Committee on Foreign Relations,* 89th Cong., 2d Sess. 655-61 (1966) [hereinafter cited as *Vietnam Hearings*].

of the French. United States involvement in the politics of South Viet Nam increased constantly; it was no secret that the Diem government largely was constituted and sustained in its early months by the United States.[36]

Despite the escalating American political, military, and economic assistance, the Saigon regime proved incapable of achieving political stability. Numerous regimes have come and gone. None has commanded the respect and allegiance of any significant segment of the population. Often in situations of civil war diverse factions are able to establish an expedient working unity during the period of common national emergency. The N.L.F. seems to maintain substantial control over its heterogeneous followers while one Saigon regime after another collapses or totters on the brink. The United States recognized at an early stage that the Saigon regime had to transform its own feudal social structure before it could provide the basis for viable government in South Viet Nam.[37] This is a most unusual demand by an external ally; it bears witness to the fragile and dubious claim of each successive Saigon regime to govern even the parts of South Viet Nam not held by the Vietcong.

In addition, Saigon and the United States seem to have neglected repeated opportunities for negotiations with Hanoi during earlier stages of the war.[38] As late as February, 1965, the United States government rebuked U Thant for engaging in unauthorized negotiations. Until the prospects for a military solution favorable to Saigon diminished to the vanishing point, the United States made no attempt to negotiate a peaceful settlement or to entrust responsibility for settlement to either the Security Council or the Co-Chairmen of the Geneva Conference.[39] This reluctance, when added to the political

[36] For an account of the *covert* dimension of the United States role in the domestic affairs of South Viet Nam see Wise & Ross, *The Invisible Government* 155-64 (1964). There are also references to the exercise of covert influence by the United States in Lacouture, Shaplen, and Warner. American strategies of covert influence in foreign countries are analyzed and described in Blackstock, *The Strategy of Subversion* (1964).

[37] *Cf.* letter of President Eisenhower to Premier Diem on October 23, 1954, *Senate Committee on Foreign Relations, 89th Cong., 1st Sess., Background Information Relating to Southeast Asia and Vietnam* (Comm. Print 1965) [hereinafter cited as *Background Information*]. For a recent reiteration, see *U.S. and South Vietnamese Leaders Meet at Honolulu, 54 Dep't State Bull.* 302-07 (Feb. 28, 1966).

[38] The American approach to a negotiated settlement is recounted and criticized in *American Friends Service Committee, Peace in Viet Nam* 50-67 (1966). Among other observations, this report points out that "a careful reading of the *New York Times* shows that the United States has rejected no fewer than seven efforts to negotiate an end to the war." *Id.* at 51. See also the article by Flora Lewis, in *Vietnam Hearings,* 323-34.

[39] For predictions of an American victory in South Viet Nam, see Raskin & Fall, *Chronology of Events in Viet-Nam and Southeast Asia, Background In-*

losses suffered by Hanoi at Geneva in 1954, makes it easier to comprehend Hanoi's reluctance to negotiate now.[40]

All of these considerations lead me to regard the war in South Vietnam primarily as a Type III conflict, in which the United States ought not to have participated. Because of Hanoi's increasing participation on behalf of the Vietcong, it is arguable, although rather unpersuasive, that this war is properly categorized as an example of Type II, so that the United States could legitimately give military assistance to Saigon, but is obligated to limit the arena of violence to the territory of South Viet Nam. The weakness of the Saigon regime compared to the N.L.F. renders necessary a disproportionately large military commitment by the United States to neutralize the indigenous advantages of the Vietcong and the support of Hanoi.[41] Our disproportionate commitment makes it appear that the United States rather than Hanoi is escalating the war. And this appearance undercuts any defense of our participation as necessary to offset participation on the other side, and thereby give "the true" balance of domestic forces a chance to control the outcome.[42] The State De-

----

formation 377, 388-89, 390-92. As late as October 2, 1963, Secretary McNamara and General Taylor issued an official statement reporting their conclusion that "the major part of the United States military task can be completed by the end of 1965"; and on November 1, 1963 General Paul D. Harkins, U.S. military commander wrote in Stars & Stripes (Tokyo) that "Victory in the sense it would apply to this kind of war is just months away and the reduction of American advisers can begin any time now." The point of quoting these statements is to suggest that as long as a favorable military solution seemed forthcoming at a tolerable cost the United States was not interesed in a negotiated settlement.

[40] An important element in the background of Vietnamese history was the successful resistance movement led by Ho Chi Minh against the Japanese in the closing years of World War II. When the Japanese left French Indo-China, Ho Chi Minh was in control of the entire territory, and was induced to accept the return to power of the French colonial administration in exchange for promises of political independence that were never fulfilled. The recollection of this first phase of the Vietnamese war, when added to the post-1954 experience may deepen Hanoi's impression that its political success depends upon military effort. On negotiating with Hanoi, see also the *Report of the Ad Hoc Congressional Conference on Vietnam, 89th Cong., 2d Sess.* 4-5 (Comm. Print 1966) [hereinafter cited as *Ad Hoc Congressional Conference*].

[41] Bernard Fall, writing on the sort of military superiority that is required to achieve victory over an insurgency, says:

. . . in the past it [victory] has required a ratio of pacification forces versus insurgents that is simply not available in Viet-Nam today [Jan. 1965]. In Malaya, British and Malayan forces have achieved a ratio of 50 to 1; in Cyprus, British forces had achieved a 110 to 1 ratio, and in Algeria the French had reached 10 to 1. The present ratio in South Viet-Nam is 4.5 to 1, and the French ratio in the First Indochina War was an incredibly low 1.2 to 1, which (all other matters being equal) would suffice to explain France's ultimate defeat.

Viet-Nam Witness 291.

[42] Official United States Government statements frequently imply that the

partment Memorandum assumes that the war is a Type I conflict, and argues that American participation is really collective self-defense in response to an armed attack by North Viet Nam upon South Viet Nam. But to characterize North Viet Nam's participation in the struggle in the South as "an armed attack" is unwise as well as incorrect. Such a contention, if accepted as an authoritative precedent, goes a long way toward abolishing the distinction between international and civil war. The war in South Viet Nam should be viewed as primarily between factions contending for control of the southern zone, whether or not the zone is considered a nation.[43] A claim of self-defense by Saigon seems misplaced, and the exercise of rights of self-defense by committing violent acts against the territory of North Viet Nam tends toward the establishment of an unfortunate precedent.[44]

III

The Memorandum of the State Department was submitted by the Legal Adviser to the Senate Committee on Foreign Relations on March 8, 1966.[45] In assessing it, we should keep in mind several considerations. First, the United States Government is the client of the Legal Adviser, and the Memorandum, as is entirely appropriate, is an adversary document. A legal adviser in Hanoi could prepare a comparable document. Adversary discourse in legal analysis should be sharply distinguished from an impartial determination of the merits of opposed positions.[46]

United States must render help to the Saigon regime equivalent to the help given by Hanoi to the N.L.F. If "equivalent" is measured by the needs of the ratio, then it may be as much as 110 times as great as the aid given to the insurgents, whereas if equivalent means arithmetically equal, it will be completely ineffectual.

[43] Hanoi itself takes a conflict-confining position that the war in Viet Nam is a civil war being waged to determine control of South Viet Nam rather than a civil or international war to determine control of the whole of Viet Nam, See, e.g., Policy Declaration of Premier Pham Van Dong of North Viet-Nam, April 14, 1965, in Viet-Nam Reader 342-43 ("Hanoi's Four Points"). See also Program of the National Liberation Front of South Viet-Nam, id. at 216-21 (on Dec. 20, 1960).

[44] But, as of July 1966, the United States has not attacked North Vietnamese centers of population and has made only limited attacks on industrial complexes (oil depots). The unjustified claim of self-defense has been noted, but it is well to appreciate the as yet restrained form of the claim.

[45] An earlier, somewhat skimpy, memorandum, The Legal Basis for U.S. Actions against North Vietnam, was issued by the Department of State on March 8, 1965; for the text see Background Information 191-94.

[46] I have tried to urge a non-adversary role for the international lawyer on several occasions: see Falk, The Adequacy of Contemporary Theories of Inter-

Second, the Legal Memorandum was evidently framed as a response to the Memorandum of Law prepared by the Lawyers Committee on American Policy Toward Viet Nam.[47] The argument of the Lawyers Committee fails to raise sharply the crucial issue—namely, the discretion of the United States to delimit its legal rights and duties by treating the conflict in South Viet Nam as an international war of aggression rather than as a civil war.[48]

Third, the Legal Adviser's Memorandum implies that both the facts of aggression and the legal rules governing self-defense are clear. This is misleading. Except in instances of overt, massive aggression across an international frontier, international law offers very *indefinite* guidance about the permissible occasions for or extent of recourse to force in self-defense. Doctrinal ambiguity is greatest with respect to internal wars with significant external participation.[49] International law offers very little authoritative guidance on the central issue of permissible assistance to the contending factions.[50] To conclude that international law is indefinite is not to suggest that it is irrelevant. On the contrary, if rules are indefinite and procedures for their interpretation unavailable, prevailing national practice sets precedents for the future. In this light, American activity in Viet Nam is particularly unfortunate for the future of doctrines aimed at limiting international violence.[51]

---

national Law—Gaps in Legal Thinking, 50 Va. L. Rev. 231, 233-43 (1964); and a recent paper delivered at the Harris Conference on New Approaches to International Relations, at the University of Chicago, June 1966, with the title, New Approaches to the Study of International Law 3-9 (paper available in mimeographed form, to be published subsequently in conference volume).

[47] See Lawyers Committee on American Policy Toward Vietnam, *American Policy Vis-à-Vis Vietnam, Memorandum of Law,* in *Vietnam Hearings* 687-713.

[48] The Spanish Civil War is a useful historical precedent for the legal treatment of large-scale foreign interventions on both sides of an internal war. For a full analysis see Padelford, *International Law and Diplomacy in the Spanish Civil Strife* (1939). Another way of posing the issue would be to ask whether Cuba, after the Bay of Pigs invasion, might have been entitled to ask the Soviet Union for military assistance, including air strikes against staging areas in the United States. For a critical account of the legal status of American participation in the Bay of Pigs invasion see Falk, *American Intervention in Cuba and the Rule of Law, 22 Ohio St. L.J.* 546 (1961).

[49] I have argued to this effect, in Rosenau 210-40.

[50] By "authoritative guidance" I mean guidance of action by clear, applicable rules of international law that are congruent with community expectations about permissible behavior; the rules must be clear enough to permit identification of a violation without independent fact-finding procedures.

[51] International customary law evolves as a consequence of national claims and counter-claims acquiring through time an authoritative status. States assert these claims and counter-claims to maximize policy considerations in various contexts. For a major exposition of this process see McDougal & Burke, *The Public Order of the Oceans* (1962).

In this section I propose to criticize the legal argument of the Memorandum, taking some issue with both inferences of fact and conclusions of law. I will analyze the consequences of characterizing international participation in Viet Nam as intervention and counter-intervention in an ongoing civil war. Although I will call attention to the shortcomings in the legal position of the United States, my main intention is to approach this inquiry in the spirit of scholarly detachment rather than as an adversary critic.[52] Such detachment is not value-free. I try to appraise the claims of national actors in light of the requirements of world order. My appraisal presupposes the desirability of narrowing the discretion of nations to determine for themselves the occasions on which violence is permissible or that an increase of the scale and scope of ongoing violence is appropriate. I am convinced that it is important for *any* country (including my own) to reconcile its foreign policy with the rules regulating the use of force in international affairs, and that, therefore, it does not serve *even* the national interest to accept a legal justification for our own recourse to violence that we would not be prepared to have invoked against us by other states similarly situated.[53] The international legal order, predominantly decentralized, depends for effectiveness on the acceptance by principal states of the fundamental ordering notions of symmetry, reciprocity, and national precedent-setting.[54]

In analyzing the Memorandum I will adhere to its outline of issues, concentrating on the most significant.

Collective Self-Defense. The Memorandum argues that the United States may, at Saigon's request, participate in the collective self-defense of South Viet Nam because North Viet Nam has made a prior armed attack. But may indirect aggression be treated as an armed attack without the approval of an appropriate international institution? The United States rests its case on the role of Hanoi in the period between -1954 and 1959 in setting up "a covert political-military organization" and by its infiltration of "over 40,000 armed and un-armed guerrillas into South Viet Nam" during the subsequent five years. The Memorandum concludes that "the external aggression from the North is the critical military element of the insurgency,"

[52] An adversary debate may be useful to clarify the legal issues, but an impartial perspective is also needed to help in the process of choosing among the adversary presentations.

[53] America's relative inability to make effective legal protests against further nuclear testing on the high seas and in the atmosphere is partly a result of America's earlier legal defense of its own similar behavior. A legal precedent is created by the effective assertion of a claim to act, and this precedent may be difficult to repudiate, even if the precedent-setter has greater power than does the actor relying upon the precedent.

[54] See Falk, *The Role of Domestic Courts in the International Legal Order* 21-52 (1964).

that "the infiltration of thousands of armed men clearly constitutes an 'armed attack' under any reasonable definition," and that although there may be doubt as to "the exact date at which North Viet Nam's aggression grew into an 'armed attack,' [it certainly] had occurred before February 1965."

This argument is questionable on its face, that is, without even criticizing its most selective presentation of the facts. Consider first the highly ideological character of prevailing attitudes toward the just use of force. The Communist countries favor support for wars of national liberation; the West—in particular, the United States—favors support for anti-Communist wars; and the Afro-Asian states favor support for anti-colonialists and anti-racist wars.[55] Consider also the importance, acknowledged by the United States in other settings,[56] of circumscribing the right of self-defense. The use of force on some other basis—for example, defensive intervention or regional security —moderates rather than escalates a conflict. But the invocation of self-defense as a rationale during a conflict previously contained within a single state tends to enlarge the arena of conflict to include states that are claiming and counter-claiming that each other's intervention in the civil strife is an armed attack. If the infiltration constitutes an armed attack, the bombing of North Viet Nam may be justified. But if North Viet Nam had operative collective defense arrangements with China and the Soviet Union it is easy to project a scenario of escalation ending in global catastrophe. If, on the other hand, infiltration is merely intervention, and appropriate responses are limited to counter-intervention, the area of violence is restricted to the territory of South Viet Nam and its magnitude is kept within more manageable limits.[57]

The argument in the Memorandum also assumes that armed help to the insurgent faction is under all circumstances a violation of international law. As mentioned earlier, at some stage in civil strife it is permissible for outside states to regard the insurgent elite the equal of the incumbent regime and to render it equivalent assistance.[58]

[55] Compare with these claims the prohibitions upon the use of force expressed in absolute terms in Article 2(4) of the United Nations Charter. Self-defense against a prior armed attack appears to be the only permissible national basis for the use of force (without authorization from the United Nations).

[56] See, e.g., avoidance of a self-defense rationale by government officials offering legal justification for the United States claims to interdict on the high seas Soviet intermediate range ballistics bound for Cuba in 1962. Meeker, *Defensive Quarantine and the Law*, 57 Am. J. Int'l L. 515 (1963); Chayes, *The Legal Case for U.S. Action on Cuba*, 47 Dep't State Bull. 763 (1962).

[57] For a fuller rationale see Falk, *supra* note 4.

[58] *Cf.* the study of the international relations of the insurgent groups during the Algerian War of Independence by M. Bedjaoui, *Law and the Algerian Revolution* (1961).

Since no collective procedures are available to determine when an insurgency has proceeded far enough to warrant this status, outside states enjoy virtually unlimited discretion to determine the comparative legitimacy of competing elites.[59] In effect, then, no rules of international law exist to distinguish clearly between permissible and impermissible intervention in civil strife.[60] To call hostile intervention not only impermissible but an instance of the most serious illegality —an armed attack—seems very fortunate. In addition to a tendency to escalate any particular conflict, the position that interventions are armed attacks so broadens the notion of armed attack that all nations will be able to make plausible claims of self-defense in almost every situation of protracted internal war. It therefore seems desirable to confine the armed attack/self-defense rationale to the Korea-type conflict (Type I) and to deny its applicability in Viet Nam, whether the war in Viet Nam is denominated Type II or Type III. The Memorandum's argument on self-defense is also deficient in that it relies upon a very selective presentation of the facts. It ignores Saigon's consistent opposition to the terms of the Geneva settlement, thereby casting in very different light Hanoi's motives for the steps it took in South Viet Nam to assert its claims.[61] It is essential to recall that the pre-1954 conflict was waged for control of *all* of Viet Nam and that the settlement at Geneva was no more than "a cease-fire." President Diem's ruthless suppression of political opposition in South Viet Nam from 1954 onward, in violation of the ban on political reprisals included in the Geneva Agreements, is also relevant.[62]

Furthermore, the injection of an American political and military presence was, from the perspective of Hanoi, inconsistent with the whole spirit of Geneva.[63] The United States decision to commit itself

[59] If "the will of the international community" operates as the true basis of international law, the criteria of legitimacy shift to correspond to the values of the expanded membership in international society.

[60] See Lauterpacht, *op. cit. supra* note 21, at 253-55.

[61] If mutuality is the basic condition for the existence of a legal obligation, it is essential that both disputants accept the terms of settlement. If there is non-acceptance on one side, the other side is in a position to protect its position *as if* the settlement did not exist. In the setting of Viet Nam this would suggest Hanoi was free to pursue its war aims on a pre-1954 basis and ignore the division of the country into two zones. It is ironic that South Viet Nam owes its original political identity entirely to the Geneva Agreements.

[62] *Cf.* Article 15, *Agreement on the Cessation of Hostilities:* "Each party undertakes to refrain from any reprisals or discrimination against persons or organizations for their activities during the hostilities and also undertakes to guarantee their democratic freedoms." *Background Information* 50, 53. See Lacouture 28-31; Burchett, *Vietnam—Inside Story of the Guerilla War* 109-28 (1965).

[63] The operative great power in the area was France. It was not in Hanoi's interest to give up a favorable battle position so that the United States could replace the French military presence. The worsening of their position in the

to maintaining a Western-oriented regime in South Viet Nam upset the expectations regarding the Southeast Asian balance of power; in that respect, it was similar to the Soviet attempt to upset the Caribbean balance of power by installing intermediate-range missiles in Cuba in 1962.[64]

The Memorandum seems to concede that until 1964 the bulk of infiltrated men were South Vietnamese who had come north after the cease-fire in 1954. The use of exiles to bolster an insurgent cause appears to be on the borderline between permissible and impermissible behavior in contemporary international politics. The role of the United States Government in sponsoring the unsuccessful invasion at the Bay of Pigs in 1961 was a far more flagrant example of the use of exiles to overthrow a constituted government in a neighboring country than the early role of Hanoi in fostering an uprising in the South.[65] The claim by the United States to control political events in Cuba is far more tenuous than the claim by North Viet Nam to exercise control (or at least remove the influence of a hostile superpower) over political life in the South.[66] And Castro's regime was domestically viable in a manner that Saigon regimes have never been—suggesting that South Viet Nam presents a more genuine revolutionary situation than does contemporary Cuba. It seems more destructive of world order to help overthrow a firmly established government than to assist an ongoing revolution against a regime incapable of governing.

African countries admit helping exiles overthrow governments under white control.[67] American support for Captive Nations Week is

area as a result of the negotiations at Geneva may explain, in part, their reluctance to negotiate a "settlement" and give up a favorable military position once again.

[64] One influential view of the basis of international order stresses maintaining current balances and expectations. Any attempt to rely upon military means to upset these balances and expectations is perceived and treated as "aggression." The intrusion of Soviet military influence into the Western Hemisphere by attempting to emplace missiles constituted the provocative element. The same military result could have been achieved by increasing the Atlantic deployment of missile-carrying submarines. This sense of "provocative" might also describe the perception of the escalating American military commitment in Southeast Asia.

[65] For an authoritative account of the United States role see Schlesinger, Jr., *A Thousand Days* 206-97 (1965).

[66] The strength of Hanoi's claim arises from the prior struggle to control the entire country, the military victory by the Vietminh in that struggle, the expectations created at Geneva that the elections would confirm that military victory, the delimitation of South Viet Nam as "a temporary zone," and, finally, the refusal by South Viet Nam to consult on elections or to refrain from reprisals.

[67] In the Final Act of the Conference of Heads of States or Governments at Cairo in 1964 the following declaration was made by the forty-seven non-

still another form of support outside of the Communist bloc for exile aspirations.[68] In short, international law neither attempts nor is able to regulate support given exile groups. The activities of Hanoi between 1954 and 1964 conform to patterns of tolerable conflict in contemporary international politics.

The Memorandum contends that subsequent to 1964, Hanoi has increasingly infiltrated regular elements of the North Vietnamese army until at present "there is evidence that nine regiments of regular North Vietnamese forces are fighting in the South." Arguably, the N.L.F. was not eligible to receive external support in the early years of strife after 1954, as its challenge to the government amounted to no more than "a rebellion." But certainly after the Vietcong gained effective control over large portions of the countryside it was *permissible* for North Viet Nam to treat the N.L.F. as a "belligerent" with a right to conduct external relations.[69] This area of international law is exceedingly vague; states have a wide range of discretion in establishing their relations with contending factions in a foreign country.[70]

The remainder of the first section of the Memorandum responds to the Lawyers Committee Memorandum of Law, but is not relevant to the solution of the critical legal questions. It is persuasive but trivial for the State Department to demonstrate that international law recognizes the right of individual and collective self-defense against an armed attack; that non-members of the United Nations enjoy the same rights of self-defense as do members;[71] that South Viet Nam is a political entity entitled to claim the right of self-defense despite its origin as a "temporary zone";[72] and that the right of collective self-

---

aligned powers assembled: "Colonized people may legitimately resort to arms to secure the full exercise of their right to self-determination."

[68] For perceptive discussion of the status of "Captive Nations Week" in international law see Wright, *Subversive Intervention*, 54 *Am. J. Int'l L.* 521 (1960).

[69] See the extent of international recognition accorded the F.L.N. in Algeria during their war against the French, Bedjaoui, *op. cit. supra* note 58, at 110-38.

[70] No clear rules of prohibition nor any required procedures exist which subject national discretion to international review. National discretion consequently governs practice.

For useful discussions stressing the survival under the United Nations Charter of a wider right of self-defense than the interpretation offered here see Bowett, *Self-Defense in International Law* 182-99 (1958); McDougal & Feliciano, *Law and Minimum World Public Order* 121-260 (1961); for a position similar to the one taken in the text see Henkin, *Force, Intervention and Neutrality in Contemporary International Law, 1963 Proc. Am. Soc. Int'l L.* 147-62.

[71] For consideration of this question see Bowett, *op. cit. supra* note 70, at 193-95.

[72] See the first sentence of Article 6 of the Final Declaration: "The Conference recognizes that the essential purpose of the agreement relating to Viet-

defense may be exercised independent of a regional arrangement organized under Chapter VIII of the United Nations Charter.[73] South Viet Nam would have had the right to act in self-defense *if an armed attack had occurred,* and the United States would then have had the right to act in collective self-defense.[74]

It is also important to determine whether the United States has complied with the reporting requirement contained in Article 51 of the United Nations Charter.[75] The United States did encourage a limited Security Council debate during August 1964 of the Gulf of Tonkin "incidents."[76] Furthermore, the United States submitted two reports to the Security Council during February 1965 concerning its recourse to bombing North Viet Nam and the general character of the war. And in January 1966 the United States submitted the Viet Nam question to the Security Council.[77] It seems reasonable to conclude that the Security Council (or, for that matter, the General Assembly) is unwilling and unable to intervene in any *overt* manner in the conflict in Viet Nam. This conclusion is reinforced by the hostility of the Communist states toward American proposals for a settlement.[78] On the other hand, there is no evidence of formal initiative by the members of the United Nations to question the propriety of the United

---

Nam is to settle military questions with a view to ending hostilities and that the military demarcation line is provisional and *should not in any way be interpreted as constituting a political or territorial boundary,"* Background Information 58, 59. (Emphasis added.) For Saigon's relevant conduct see Lacouture 24-31.

[73] For a useful analysis see Bowett, *op. cit. supra* note 70, at 200-48; McDougal & Feliciano, *op. cit. supra* note 70, at 244-53.

[74] That is, it would conform to expectations about what constitutes a permissible claim to use force in self-defense. Despite considerable controversy about the wisdom of the United States' involvement in the defense of Korea, there was no debate whatsoever (outside of Communist countries) about the legality of a defensive claim. There was some legal discussion about the propriety of United Nations involvement. For an argument in favor of legality see McDougal & Gardner, *The Veto and the Charter: An Interpretation for Survival,* in McDougal & Associates, *Studies in World Public Order* 718-60 (1960). In retrospect, however, Korea exemplifies "an armed attack" for which force in response is appropriate, even if used on the territory of the attacking state.

[75] For communications sent by the United States to the United Nations and relied upon to show compliance with the reporting requirements of Article 51 see *Vietnam Hearings* 634-40.

[76] For a description of official United States views see *Promoting the Maintenance of International Peace and Security in Southeast Asia, H.R. Rep. No. 1708, 88th Cong., 2d Sess.* (1964); see Ambassador Stevenson's statement to the Security Council on August 5, 1964, in *Background Information* 124-28.

[77] No action was taken by the United Nations and the debate was inconclusive and insignificant.

[78] Neither China nor North Viet Nam indicate any willingness to acknowledge a role for the United Nations. Of course, the exclusion of China from representation in the United Nations may account for Chinese opposition to a U.N. solution. See also *Ad Hoc Congressional Conference* 5.

States policies. The very serious *procedural* question posed is whether the failure of the United Nations to act relieves the United States of its burden to submit claims of self-defense to review by the organized international community.[79] A further question is whether any international legal limitations upon national discretion apply when the United Nations refrains from passing judgment on claims to use force in self-defense.[80]

The Security Council failed to endorse American claims in Viet Nam, and this failure was not merely a consequence of Soviet or Communist opposition. Therefore, if the burden of justification for recourse to self-defense is upon the claimant, inaction by the United Nations provides no legal comfort on the *substantive issue*—that is, the legality of proportional self-defense given "the facts" in Viet Nam. As to the *procedural issue*—that is, compliance with the reporting requirement of Article 51—the United States may be considered to have compiled *pro forma,* but not in terms of the spirit of the Charter of the United Nations.

The overriding purpose of the Charter is to commit states to use force only as a last resort after the exhaustion of all other alternatives. In the early period after 1954 the United States relied heavily on its unilateral economic and military capability to protect the Saigon regime against the Vietcong. No *prior* attempt was made, in accordance with Article 33, to settle the dispute by peaceful means.[81] Yet the spirit of the Charter requires that a nation claiming to undertake military action in collective self-defense must first invoke the collective review and responsibility of the United Nations. The United States did not call for United Nations review until January 1966, that is, until a time when the prospects for a favorably military solution at tolerable costs seemed dismal, many months subsequent to bombing North Vietnamese territory. As long as a military victory was anticipated, the United States resented any attempt to question

---

[79] To what extent, that is, do states have residual discretion to determine the legality of claims to use force in the event of United Nations inability to reach a clear decision?

[80] The nature of these restraints may be of two varieties: first, the considerations entering into the creation of a precedent; second, the restraints of customary international law requiring that minimum necessary force be used to attain belligerent objectives and requiring the maintenance of the distinction between military and non-military targets and between combatants and non-combatants. One wonders whether these latter distinctions can be maintained in a guerrilla war such as that in Viet Nam.

[81] *U.N. Charter* art. 33(1):
The parties to any dispute, the continuance of which is likely to endanger the maintenance of international peace and security, shall, first of all, seek a solution by negotiation, enquiry, mediation, conciliation, arbitration, judicial settlement, resort to regional agencies or arrangements, or other peaceful means of their own choice.

its discretion to use force or to share its responsibility for obtaining a settlement.[82] American recourse to procedures for peaceful settlement came as a last rather than a first resort. The United States had made no serious effort to complain about alleged North Vietnamese violations of the Geneva Agreements, nor to recommend a reconvening of a new Geneva Conference in the decade of escalating commitment after 1954. Saigon submitted complaints to the International Control Commission, but that body was neither constituted nor intended to deal with the resumption of a war for control of South Viet Nam that was apparently provoked by Saigon's refusal to hold elections.

Further, not until 1965 did the United States welcome the independent efforts of the Secretary-General to act as a negotiating intermediary between Washington and Hanoi.[83] Until it became evident that a military victory over the Vietcong was not forthcoming, the United States Government was hostile to suggestions emanating from either U Thant (or De Gaulle) that a negotiated settlement was both *appropriate* and *attainable*. The State Department's belated offer to negotiate must be discounted in light of its public relations overtones and our effort over the last decade to reverse the expectations of Geneva. The United States negotiating position is also made less credible by our failure to accord the N.L.F. diplomatic status as a party in conflict.[84] This failure is especially dramatic in light of the N.L.F.'s ability effectively to govern territory under its possession and Saigon's relative inability to do so.

The American approach to negotiations lends support to the conclusion that our sporadic attempts at a peaceful settlement are belated gestures, and that we seek "victory" at the negotiating table only when it becomes unattainable on the battlefield. The United States showed no willingness to subordinate national discretion to the collective will of the organized international community. In fact, Viet Nam exemplifies the American global strategy of using military power whenever necessary to prevent Communist expansion and to determine these necessary occasions by national decisions. This militant anti-Communism represents the essence of unilateralism.[85]

---

[82] *Cf.* note 39 *supra*.

[83] *Cf.* note 38 *supra*.

[84] See the recommendations to this effect in *Ad Hoc Congressional Conference* 5.

[85] That is, it represents the claim to use force for purposes determined by the United States. The ideological quality of this unilateralism—its quality as an anti-communist crusade—is suggested by "the understanding" attached by the United States to its ratification of the SEATO treaty limiting "its recognition of the effect of aggression and armed attack . . . to communist aggression." It is very unusual to restrict the applicability of a security arrangement

One must conclude that the United States was determined to use its military power as it saw fit in Viet Nam in the long period from 1954 to January 1966. In 1966 at last a belated, if halfhearted, attempt to collectivize responsibility was made by appealing to the Security Council to obtain, in the words of the Memorandum, "discussions looking toward a peaceful settlement on the basis of the Geneva accords." The Memorandum goes on to observe that "Indeed, since the United States submission on January 1966, members of the Council have been notably reluctant to proceed with any consideration of the Viet-Nam question." Should this reluctance come as a surprise? Given the timing and magnitude of the American request it was inevitable that the United Nations would find itself unable to do anything constructive at that stage. United Nations inaction has deepened the awareness of the Organization's limited ability to safeguard world peace, whenever the nuclear superpowers take opposite sides of a violent conflict.[86] Disputes must be submitted *prior* to deep involvement if the United Nations is to play a significant role.[87] The war in Viet Nam presented many appropriate opportunities—the various steps up the escalation ladder—for earlier, more effective, American recourse to the United Nations. But during the entire war in Viet Nam, the United States has shown no significant disposition to limit discretionary control over its national military power by making constructive use of collective procedures of peaceful settlement.

Proportionality. Even if we grant the Memorandum's contention that North Viet Nam is guilty of aggression amounting to an armed attack and that the United States is entitled to join in the collective self-defense of South Viet Nam, important questions remain concerning the quantum, ratio, and modalities of force employed. Elementary principles both of criminal and international law require that force legitimately used must be reasonably calculated to attain the objective pursued and be somewhat proportional to the provocation. As McDougal and Feliciano observe, "[U]nderlying the processes of coercion is a fundamental principle of economy."[88] This fundamental principle deriving from the restraints on violence found in the earliest

in terms of the ideological identity of the aggressor, rather than in terms of national identity or with reference to the character of the aggression.

[86] For a generalized approach to the problems of international conflict given the structure of international society, see F. Gross, *World Politics and Tension Areas* (1966).

[87] In the Congo Operation the outer limits of United Nations capacity were tested, perhaps exceeded.

[88] McDougal & Feliciano, *op. cit. supra* note 70, at 35.

version of the just war doctrine has two attributes: the effectiveness of the force employed and the avoidance of excessive force.[89]

The United States effort in Viet Nam combines ineffectual with excessive force. The level of military commitment to date seems designed to avert defeat rather than to attain victory. All observers agree that if the other side persists in its commitment, the search for a favorable military solution will be exceedingly prolonged. Since the United States has far greater military resources potentially available, our use of insufficient force violates general norms of international law.[90] At the same time, however, weapons and strategy are being employed to cause destruction and incidental civilian damage without making a proportional contribution to the military effort. This is particularly true of our reliance upon strategic area bombing against dispersed targets of small military value.[91]

The United States has at each juncture also claimed the legal right to engage in disproportionate responses to specific provocations. In August 1964 the Gulf of Tonkin incidents consisted of allegations that North Vietnamese torpedo boats had "attacked" some American warships on the high seas. Although no damage was reported the United States responded by destroying several villages in which the boats were based.[92] This was the first occasion on which force was used directly against North Vietnamese territory and the justifications rested upon a reprisal theory that was largely disassociated from the war in South Viet Nam. Such a disproportionate ratio between action and reaction is typical of great power politics in which superior force is used to discipline a minor adversary. But this exaggerated response violates the legal requisites of equivalency and symmetry between

[89] Implicit in the notion of economy of force is the idea that an unjust and illegal use of force is a futile use. The idea of futility is related to the attainability of a permissible belligerent objective and is difficult to measure. If a negotiated settlement rather than victory is the objective, the amount of force required can only be assessed in terms of the probable intentions of the other side, and these shift in response to many factors, including their assessment of intentions.

[90] Here again a reinterpretation of traditional thinking on war is needed to satisfy the requirements of the nuclear age. American restraint in Viet Nam is explained in part by concern with generating a nuclear war or, at least, provoking a wider war in Southeast Asia. But what legal consequences follow if this inhibition leads to prolonged violence in Viet Nam of an indecisive but devastating form?

[91] The Conference participants were in agreement that the bombings in the north were of little military value, while the diplomatic disadvantages were very serious. Further escalation of the bombings, it was felt, could not be expected to improve the situation. *Ad Hoc Congressional Conference* 4.

[92] For a rather effective presentation of the North Vietnamese version of the Tonkin Incidents see Nguyen Nghe, Facing the Skyhawks (pamphlet printed in Hanoi, 1964). For an attack on the legality of the United States response see I. F. Stone, *International Law and the Tonkin Bay Incidents*, in *Viet-Nam Reader* 307-15. For the U.S. position see references cited note 94 *infra*.

the injury sustained and the response undertaken. Acceptance of mutuality and symmetry is basic to the whole conception of law in a sovereignty-centered social order.[93]

The bombing of North Viet Nam in February 1965 was also originally justified as a "reprisal" for a successful attack by the Vietcong upon two United States air bases, principally the one at Pleiku. Only in retrospect was the justification for attacking North Viet Nam generalized to collective self-defense of South Viet Nam.[94]

No clear legal guidelines exist to measure the proportionality of force used in self-defense. There is also some doubt whether proportionality applies to the belligerent objective pursued or the size and character of the aggression. If we assume that the appropriate quantum of military force is that needed to neutralize the Vietcong (the mere agent, in the American view, of Hanoi), then our military response (given our capability) appears to be disproportionately low. A guerrilla war can be won only by a minimum manpower ratio of 10:1, whereas the present ratio is no better than 5:1. Our present level of commitment of military forces merely prolongs the war; it does not aim to restore peace by means of victory.[95]

If on the other hand, North Viet Nam and the United States are considered as foreign nations intervening on opposite sides of an armed conflict, then in terms of money, materiel, manpower, and overtness the United States has intervened to a degree disproportionately greater than has North Viet Nam.[96] In the early period of the war the Vietcong captured most of its equipment from the Saigon regime and the level of material support from the North was low.

The objective of American military strategy is apparently to destroy enough that is important to Hanoi and the N.L.F. to bring about an eventual *de facto* reduction of belligerent action or to force Hanoi to make a satisfactory offer of negotiations. Are there any legal rules that restrict such a strategy in terms of duration, intensity, or destruction? This question seems so central to the future of international law that it is regrettable, to say the least, that the Memorandum does not dis-

---

[93] *Cf.* Kunz, *The Distinctiveness of the International Legal System, 22 Ohio St. L.J.* 447 (1961).

[94] *Cf.* the White House Statement of February 7, 1965, *Background Information* 146-47; see also *id.* at 148-52 for the context used to justify extending the war to North Viet Nam. No charge is made that the attacks on United States military installations were ordered or performed by North Viet Nam personnel.

[95] *Cf.* note 41 *supra;* see also General Gavin's testimony before the Senate Foreign Relations Committee, *Vietnam Hearings* 270-71.

[96] For an account of some features of the escalation see Mansfield, *et al., Report to Senate Foreign Relations Comm., 89th Cong., 2d Sess., The Vietnam Conflict: The Substance and the Shadow* (Comm. Print Jan. 6, 1966). See also Shaplen xii, xxii; *Vietnam Witness* 307-49.

cuss it. That formalistic document implies that if a state claims to use force in self-defense, and supports its claim with a legal argument, and if the United Nations does not explicitly overrule that claim, international law has nothing further to contribute.[97] I would argue, in contrast, that it is crucial to determine what limiting considerations come into play at this point. It is certainly a regressive approach to international law to assume that if a state alleges "self-defense," it may in its untrammeled discretion determine what military action is reasonably necessary and proportional. The opposing belligerent strategies in Viet Nam seem to call for legal explanation, especially in view of the inability of either side to "win" or "settle" the war; the present standoff causes great destruction of life and property without progressing toward "a resolution" of the conflict.

The Relevance of Commitments to Defend South Viet Nam. The second main section of the Legal Adviser's Memorandum is devoted to establishing that the United States "has made commitments and given assurances, in various forms and at different times, to assist in the defense of South Viet Nam." Much confusion is generated by a very misleading play on the word commitment. In one sense, commitment means a pledge to act in a specified manner. In another sense, commitment means an obligation of law to act in a specified manner.

During 1965-66 the United States clearly came to regard itself as having made a commitment qua pledge to assist in the defense of South Viet Nam. President Johnson expressed this pledge on many occasions. Two examples are illustrative:

> We are in Viet Nam to fulfill one of the most solemn pledges of the American nation. Three Presidents — President Eisenhower, President Kennedy, and your present President—over 11 years have committed themselves and have promised to help defend this small and valiant nation.[98]
>
> We are there because we have a promise to keep. Since 1954 every American President has offered support to the people of South Viet Nam. We have helped to build, and we have helped to defend. Thus, over many years, we have made a national pledge to help South Viet Nam defend its independence.[99]

The present commitment entailing a major military effort is of a very different order than the early conditional offers of economic and military assistance made by President Eisenhower.[100] American in-

---

[97] A state, in effect, satisfies the requirements of international law merely by filing a brief on its own behalf.

[98] N.Y. Times, July 29, 1965.

[99] N.Y. Times, April 8, 1965.

[100] Larson & Larson, *Vietnam and Beyond* 17-29 (1965).

volvement in Vietnam is usually traced to a letter from President Eisenhower to Diem on October 23, 1954, in which the spirit of the undertaking was expressed in the following sentence: "The purpose of this offer is to assist the Government of Viet-Nam in developing and maintaining a strong, viable state, capable of resisting attempted subversion or aggression through military means." The letter contains no hint of a pledge. In fact, the United States conditions its offer to assist with a reciprocal expectation: "The Government of the United States expects that this aid will be met by performance on the part of the Government of Viet-Nam in undertaking needed reforms."[101] It is important to note that the letter contained no reference to SEATO despite the formation of the organization a few weeks before it was written, and that the role of the United States was premised upon satisfactory domestic progress in South Viet Nam.

As late as September 1963, President Kennedy said in a TV interview: "In the final analysis, it is their war. They are the ones who have to win it or lose it. We can help them, we can give them equipment, we can send our men out there as advisers, but they have to win it—the people of Viet Nam—against the Communists. We are prepared to continue to assist them, but I don't think that the war can be won unless the people support the effort. . . . "[102] This expression of American involvement emphasizes its discretionary and reversible character, and again implies that the continuation of American assistance is conditional upon certain steps being taken by the Saigon regime. Even in 1965 Secretary Rusk in an address to the Annual Meeting of the American Society of International Law, provided a legal defense of the United States position in Viet Nam that stopped short of averring a commitment qua legal obligation. Mr. Rusk did not once refer to SEATO in his rather complete coverage of the subject. The crucial explanation of the American presence is contained in the following passage:

> In resisting the aggression against it, the Republic of Viet-Nam is exercising its right of self-defense. It called upon us and other states for assistance. And in the exercise of the right of collective self-defense under the United Nations Charter, we and other nations are providing such assistance. The American policy of assisting South Viet-Nam to maintain its freedom was inaugurated under President Eisenhower and continued under Presidents Kennedy and Johnson.[103]

Each successive increase in the level of American military involvement has been accompanied by an intensification of rhetoric support-

---

101 *Background Information* 67-68.
102 *Id.* at 99.
103 Rusk, *Address, 1965 Proc. Am. Soc. Int'l. L.* 251-52.

ing our presence in Viet Nam. By 1965 President Johnson was, as we observed, referring to Viet Nam as "one of the most solemn national pledges." It is disconcerting to realize that the United States has at each stage offset a deteriorating situation in South Viet Nam by increasing both its military and rhetorical commitment. This process discloses a gathering momentum; at a certain point, policy becomes virtually irreversible. President Johnson's use of the rhetoric of commitment communicates the irreversibility of this policy and conveys a sense of the futility and irrelevance of criticism. If we have a commitment of honor, contrary considerations of prudence and cost are of no concern.[104]

But no commitment qua pledge has the capacity to generate a commitment qua legal obligation. The Administration seems to want simultaneously to invoke both senses of the notion of commitment in order to blunt and confuse criticism. A commitment qua legal obligation is, by definition, illegal to renounce. To speak of commitment in a legal memorandum is particularly misleading. To the extent that we have *any* commitment it is a *pledge of policy*.

Secretary Rusk has injected a further confusion into the debate by his stress on "the SEATO commitment" in the course of his testimony before the Senate Foreign Relations Committee in the early months of 1966.[105] He said, for instance, in his prepared statement: "It is this fundamental SEATO obligation that has from the outset guided our actions in Vietnam."[106] The notion of the obligation is derived from Article IV (1) of the SEATO treaty which says that "each party recognizes that aggression by means of armed attack . . . would endanger its own peace and safety, and agrees that it will in that event act to meet the common danger in accordance with its constitutional processes." It is somewhat doubtful that Article IV (1) can be properly invoked at all in Viet Nam because of the difficulty of

[104] For this reason the Administration is hostile to domestic criticism. It is, above all, unresponsive to this qualitative aspect of our presence in Viet Nam. *Cf.* President Johnson's speech at Johns Hopkins University on April 7, 1965, in *Vietnam Hearings* 640-44.

[105] *Id.* at 567. Secretary Rusk explains to the Senate Foreign Relations Committee that "the language of this treaty is worth careful attention. The obligation it imposes is not only joint but several. That is not only collective but individual.

"The finding that an armed attack has occurred does not have to be made by a collective determination before the obligation of each member becomes operative." *Cf.* the shifting views of SEATO obligation recounted in Young, *The Southeast Asia Crisis, 1963 Hammarskjold Forum* 54. Even Mr. Young, a staunch defender of administration policy, notes that "Until the crisis in Laos in 1961, the United States looked upon SEATO as a collective organization which would take military action, with all eight members participating in the actions as well as the decision." *Id.* at 59.

[106] *Vietnam Hearings* 567; note the absence of reference to SEATO in Rush, *supra* note 103, and in the 1965 legal memorandum, *supra* note 45.

establishing "an armed attack."[107] Secretary Rusk contends, however, that this provision not only *authorizes* but *obliges* the United
States to act in the defense of South Viet Nam.[108]

Ambiguity again abounds. If the commitment to act in Viet Nam is
incorporated in a treaty, the United States is legally bound. Such an
interpretation of Article IV (1) would apply equally to other states
that have ratified the SEATO treaty. None of the other SEATO
signatories acknowledge such "a commitment" to fulfill a duty of
collective self-defense, nor does the United States contend they have
one. France and Pakistan oppose altogether any military effort on
behalf of the Saigon regime undertaken by outside states.

Secretary Rusk later softened his insistence that Article IV (1) imposed a legal commitment qua obligation upon the United States. In
an exchange with Senator Fulbright during Senate hearings on Viet
Nam, Mr. Rusk offered the following explanation:

> The Chairman. . . . do you maintain that we had an obligation
> under the Southeastern Asian Treaty to come to the assistance, all-
> out assistance of South Vietnam? Is that very clear?
> Secretary Rusk. It seems to me sir, that this was an obligation—
> The Chairman. Unilateral.
> Secretary Rusk. An obligation of policy. It is rooted in the policy
> of the treaty. I am not now saying if we had decided we would not
> lift a finger about Southeast Asia that we could be sued in a court
> and be convicted of breaking a treaty.[109]

It seems evident if an armed attack has been established, the treaty
imposes a legal obligation to engage in collective self-defense of the
victim. But in the absence of a collective determination by the
SEATO membership that an armed attack has taken place, it is difficult to maintain that Article IV (1) does more than authorize
discretionary action in appropriate circumstances.

The Memorandum argues that "the treaty does not require a collective determination that an armed attack has occurred in order that
the obligation of Article IV (1) become operative. Nor does the provision require collective decision on actions to be taken to meet the
common danger."[110] This interpretation of Article IV (1) is a blatant
endorsement of extreme unilateralism, made more insidious by its
pretense of "obligation" and its invocation of the multilateral or regional scaffolding of SEATO. Here the legal position of the State
Department displays maximum cynicism, resorting to international
law to obscure the national character of military action. In essence,

[107] See generally SEATO, 3-45, 87-163 (Modelski ed. 1962).
[108] *Vietnam Hearings* 567.
[109] *Id*. at 45; see also *id*. at 7-8.
[110] *Id*. at 567.

the United States claims that it is under an obligation to determine for itself when an armed attack has occurred, and that once this determination is made there arises a further obligation to act in response. This justification for recourse to force is reminiscent of the international law of war prior to World War I, when states were free to decide for themselves when to go to war.[111] The regressive tendency of this position is further intensified by applying it in a situation where there was a background of civil war and where the alleged aggression was low-scale, extended over time, and covert. Under "the Rusk Doctrine" a country alleging "armed attack" seems free to act in self-defense whenever it wishes. The rhetoric of commitment seems connected with the effort to make the policy of support for Saigon irreversible in domestic arenas and credible in external arenas, especially in Saigon and Hanoi, but it has little to do with an appreciation of the relevance of international law to United States action in Viet Nam.

The important underlying question is whether it is permissible to construe an occurrence of "an armed attack" in the circumstances of the internal war in South Viet Nam. If an armed attack can be held to have occurred, then both self-defense and collective self-defense are permissible. The legal status of a claim of collective self-defense is not improved by embedding the claim in a collective defense arrangement. In fact, the collective nature of an arrangement such as SEATO might imply some obligation to attempt recourse to consultative and collective procedures before acting, at least to determine whether an armed attack has occurred and by whom. Under Secretary Rusk's interpretation of the treaty, SEATO members with opposing views on the issue of which side committed an armed attack could become "obligated" to act in "collective self-defense" against one another.[112] Surely this is the *reductio ad absurdum* of collective self-defense.

In terms of both world order and the original understanding of SEATO, the conflict in Viet Nam calls for action, if at all, under Article IV (2).[113] To categorize the conflict under Article IV (1) would seem to require a unanimous collective determination that the assistance given by Hanoi to the Vietcong amounted to an armed attack. Once that determination had been made, it might seem plausible to maintain that the obligation to act in collective self-defense exists on

---

[111] For a general survey of progressive attempts to regulate recourse to war see Wright, *The Role of International Law in the Elimination of War* (1961).

[112] *E.g.*, suppose Laos and Thailand became involved in a conflict in which each state accused the other of being an aggressor—and this is not impossible.

[113] *Cf.* SEATO *op. cit. supra* note 107, at xiv. It is made clear both that internal conflicts abetted by subversion were to be treated under Article IV (2) and that this provision required consultation as a prerequisite to action and had become "a dead letter."

a joint and several basis, and that the United States might join in the defense of the victim of the armed attack without further collective authorization. Unlike the State Department position, the approach outlined in this paragraph requires that a multilateral determination of the facts precede acts of commitment. The United States might help build a more peaceful world by taking seriously the collective procedures governing the use of force which it has taken such an active role in creating.

The Geneva Accords of 1954. The agreements at Geneva were cast in the form of a cease-fire arrangement and a declaration of an agreed procedure for achieving a post-war settlement. The parties to the first war in Viet Nam were the French and the Vietminh, and the agreements were between their respective military commanders. The other powers at Geneva were mere sureties. At Ho Chi Minh's insistence the Saigon regime did not participate; Saigon was evidently dissatisfied from the outset with the terms of settlement.[114] The United States Government was also reluctant to regard the Geneva settlement as binding.[115]

The Final Declaration required elections to be held in July of 1956 "under the supervision of an international commission composed of representatives of the Member States of the International Supervisory Commission."[116] The Memorandum points out that South Viet Nam "did not sign the cease-fire agreement of 1954, nor did it adhere to the Final Declaration of the Geneva Conference" and adds that "the South Vietnamese Government at that time gave notice of its objection in particular to the election provisions of the accords." At the time of the Geneva proceedings, the Saigon regime exerted control over certain areas in the South, and this awkward fact made it unrealistic to suppose that the Geneva terms of settlement would ever be voluntarily carried out. When Diem came to power and the United States moved in to fill the place left vacant by the departure of the French, it became clear, especially in view of the nation-wide popularity of Ho Chi Minh, that the contemplated elections would never be held.[117] In a sense it was naive of Hanoi to accept the Geneva arrangement or to rely upon its implementation.[118]

114 See *Viet-Nam Witness* 74-83. Jean Lacouture has written recently that France bears a heavy responsibility for its failure to secure full implementation of the Geneva "solution" before withdrawing from Viet Nam; in Lacouture's view France's premature withdrawal created a political vacuum immediately filled by the United States. Lacouture 657.

115 *Viet-Nam Witness* 69-83; see Lancaster 313-58 for a general account of the Geneva settlement.

116 See Article 7, *Final Declaration of Geneva Conference, July 21, 1954, Background Information* 58, 59.

117 Lancaster 315-16.

118 *Id.* at 313-37.

Saigon objected to the election provisions from the outset because it hoped for a permanent partition of Viet Nam. But permanent partition was so deeply incompatible with the objective sought by the Vietminh in the war against the French that it is hardly reasonable to expect Hanoi to acquiesce. In a sense, Hanoi's willingness to cooperate with the Geneva arrangement until 1956 is more surprising than is its later effort to revive the war in Viet Nam.

The Memorandum says that even assuming the election provisions were binding on South Viet Nam, there was no breach of obligation arising from Saigon's failure "to engage in consultations in 1955, with a view to holding elections in 1956." The justification offered for Saigon's action is that "the conditions in North Viet Nam during that period were such as to make impossible any free and meaningful expression of popular will." But the election provision in the Final Declaration stated no preconditions about the form of interim government in the two zones, and the type of governmental control existing in the North could have been and presumably was anticipated by those who drew up the Final Declaration. The meaning of "free elections" in Communist countries was well known to all countries including the United States, and the conditions prevailing in South Viet Nam were no more conducive to popular expressions of will.[119] The real objection to the elections was a simple one—namely, the assurance that Ho Chi Minh would win.[120] The Memorandum offers only a self-serving endorsement of Saigon's refusal to go along with the terms of settlement, although they had been endorsed by the United States representative, Bedell Smith.[121]

The Memorandum suggests in footnote 10, that North Viet Nam's remedies, had there been "a breach of obligation by the South, lay in discussion with Saigon, perhaps in an appeal to the co-chairmen of the Geneva conference, or in a reconvening of the conference to consider the situation." In light of the failure of the United States to make use of international remedies which it argues are obligatory for Hanoi, this statement is a shocking instance of legal doubletalk. Footnote 10 ends by saying that "Under international law, North Viet Nam had no right to use force outside its own zone in order to secure its political objectives." This again is misleading. No authoritative rules govern the action of the parties in the event that a settlement of internal war breaks down. Certainly if the settlement is not binding on *all* the parties, no one of them is bound by its constraints. In the absence of the Geneva Accords, Saigon would not exist as a political

---

[119] On the conduct of elections in Viet Nam see Fall, *Vietnam's Twelve Elections,* The New Republic, May 14, 1966, pp. 12-15.
[120] Warner 84-106, 142-43; *cf. Vietnam* 191-94, 210-35 (Gettleman ed.).
[121] For text of Smith's statement see *Background Information* 61.

entity. If Saigon repudiates the Accords, Hanoi would seem to be legally free to resume the pursuit of its political objectives and to ignore the creation of a temporary zone in the South. The principle of mutuality of obligation makes it inappropriate to argue that Saigon is free to ignore the Geneva machinery but that Hanoi is bound to observe it.

Furthermore, international law does not forbid the use of force within a single state. If Hanoi may regard Viet Nam as a single country between 1954 and 1956, its recourse to force in pursuit of political objectives is not prohibited even assuming that its "guidance" and "direction" of the Vietcong constitute "a use" of force by North Viet Nam.

The Memorandum misleadingly implies that the International Control Commission (ICC) endorsed the action of the United States and Saigon and condemned the action of North Viet Nam. Both sides were criticized severely by the ICC for violating provisions of the Geneva Accords.[122] It would appear that the massive military aid given to Saigon by the United States was the most overt and disrupting violation, directly contravening the prohibition on the entry of foreign military forces and new military equipment.[123] According to the reasoning of footnote 10, North Viet Nam's remedy lay in discussion and the Geneva machinery. But a quite different line of legal reasoning is taken to justify American activity:[124] action otherwise prohibited by the Geneva Accords is "justified by the international law principle that a material breach of agreement by one party entitles the other at least to withhold compliance with an equivalent, corresponding, or related provision until the defaulting party is prepared to honor its obligations." One wonders why this "international law principle" is not equally available to North Viet Nam after Saigon's refusal even to consult about holding elections. Why is Hanoi bound by the reasoning of footnote 10 and Washington entitled to the reasoning of reciprocal breach? The self-serving argument of the Memorandum confers competence upon the United States and Saigon to find that a breach has taken place and to select a suitable remedy, but permits Hanoi only to *allege* a breach, and forbids it to take countervailing action until the breach has been impartially verified.

---

[122] For a representative sample see *Vietnam, op. cit. supra* note 120, at 160-90.

[123] *Cf.* Articles 17, 18, *Agreement on the Cessation of Hostilities in Vietnam, Background Information* 28, 34-35.

[124] *Cf.* Department of State White Paper, *Aggression from the North,* in *Viet-Nam Reader* 143-55; for criticism see Stone, *A Reply to White Paper,* in *Viet-Nam Reader* 155-62.

The Authority of the President under the Constitution. I agree with the Legal Adviser's analysis that the President possesses the constitutional authority to use American military forces in Viet Nam without a declaration of war. Past practice and present policy support this conclusion. To declare war against North Viet Nam would further rigidify our own expectations about an acceptable outcome and it would almost certainly escalate the conflict. It might activate dormant collective defense arrangements between North Viet Nam and its allies.

But the Constitution is relevant in another way not discussed by the Memorandum. The President is bound to act in accordance with governing law, including international law. The customary and treaty norms of international law enjoy the status of "the law of the land" and the President has no discretion to violate these norms in the course of pursuing objectives of foreign policy. An impartial determination of the compatibility of our action in Viet Nam with international law is highly relevant to the constitutionality of the exercise of Presidential authority in Viet Nam.

The President has the constitutional authority to commit our armed services to the defense of South Viet Nam without a declaration of war *provided* that such "a commitment" is otherwise in accord with international law. Whether all or part of the United States action violates international law is also a constitutional question. International law offers no authoritative guidance as to the use of force *within* South Viet Nam, but the bombing of North Viet Nam appears to be an unconstitutional use of Presidential authority as well as a violation of international law.

IV

It is appropriate to reflect on the role of the international lawyer in a legal controversy of the sort generated by our role in Viet Nam. The rather keen interest in this controversy about international law results mostly from intense disagreement about the overall wisdom of our foreign policy rather than curiosity about the content of the law on the subject. International law has therefore been used as an instrument of persuasion by those who oppose or favor our Viet Nam policy on political grounds. In such a debate we assume that the United States strives to be law-abiding and that, therefore, it is important for partisans of existing policy to demonstrate the compatibility between law and policy and for opponents of the policy to demonstrate the opposite.

This use of international law to bolster or bludgeon foreign policy positions is unfortunate. It creates the impression that international law serves to inflame debate rather than to guide or shape public policy—an impression fostered by the State Department Memorandum. After a decade of fighting in Viet Nam, the Memorandum was issued in response to legal criticisms made by private groups and echoed by a few dissident members of Congress. It blandly whitewashed the existing government position. The tone is self-assured, the method legalistic, and the contribution to an informed understanding of the issues, minimal. None of the difficult questions of legal analysis are considered. In this intellectual context international lawyers with an independent voice need to be heard.

An international lawyer writing about an ongoing war cannot hope to reach clear conclusions about all the legal issues involved. It is virtually impossible to unravel conflicting facts underlying conflicting legal claims. Of course, we can hope that a legal commentator will acknowledge the uncertainties about the facts and that he will offer explicit reasons for resolving ambiguities in the way and to the extent that he does.[125]

Would it not be better, one is tempted to insist, for international lawyers to avoid so controversial and indeterminate a subject as the legal status of American participation in the war in Viet Nam? I think it important openly to raise this question of propriety, but clearly to answer it in the negative. The scholar has the crucial task of demonstrating the intractability of many, although not of all, the legal issues. Such an undertaking defeats, or calls into serious question, the dogmatic over-clarification of legal issues that arises in the more popular discussions of foreign policy questions. The international lawyer writing in the spirit of scholarly inquiry may have more to contribute by raising the appropriate questions than by purporting to give authoritative answers. He may enable public debate to adopt a more constructive and sophisticated approach to the legal issues.

And, finally, an international lawyer not employed by a government can help modify a distorted nationalistic perspective. An international lawyer is, of course, a citizen with strong views on national policy, but his outlook is universalized by the realization that the function of law in world affairs is to reconcile inconsistent national goals. The international lawyer seeks a legal solution that is based upon an

---

[125] *Cf.* the inscription attributed to "An Old Jew of Galicia" in Milosz, *The Captive Mind* 2 (1953):

When someone is honestly 55% right, that's very good and there's no use wrangling. And if someone is 60% right, it's wonderful, and let him thank God. But what's to be said about 75% right? Wise people say this is suspicious. Well, and what about 100% right? Whoever says he's 100% right is a fanatic, a thug, and the worst kind of rascal.

appreciation, although not always an acceptance, of the position of "the other side" in an international dispute. His goal is a system of world order in which all nations are constrained for the common good by rules and by procedures for their interpretation and enforcement. This implies a new kind of patriotism, one that is convinced that to succeed, the nation must act within the law in its foreign as well as its domestic undertakings.

But are there occasions upon which it would be proper for a nation to violate international law? It may be contended that the United States must act as it does in Viet Nam because the international procedures of Geneva, the United Nations, and SEATO offer no protection to a victim of aggression such as South Viet Nam. The United States is acting, in this view, to fill a vacuum created by the failures of international regulatory machinery. In fact, it is often suggested, the refusal of the United States to act would tempt potential aggressors. Those who emphasize the obligations and ambiguities of power often talk in this vein and warn of the sterility of legalism in foreign affairs.[126] In general terms, this warning is sound, but its very generality is no guide to specific action, especially in the nuclear age. It remains essential to vindicate as explicitly as possible the reasons that might justify violating legal expectations about the use of military power in each instance by documented reference to overriding policies; slogans about peace, security, and freedom are not enough. The analysis must be so conditioned by the specific circumstances that it will not always justify the use of force. I do not believe that such an argument can convincingly be made with respect to Viet Nam, and therefore I affirm the relevance of legal criteria of limitation. If an argument in favor of military intervention is offered, then it should stress the limits and weaknesses of law or the priority of national over international concerns.[127] We would then gain a better understanding of what law can and cannot do than is acquired by the manipulative straining of legal rules into contrived coincidence with national policies.[128]

V

The foregoing analysis points to the following set of conclusions: 1) The United States insistence upon treating North Vietnamese

[126] See generally the writings of the critical legalists, *E.g.,* Kennan, *American Diplomacy 1900-1950,* 95, 96 and 100; Morgenthau, *In Defense of the National Interest* (1951).

[127] Little systematic attention has been given to the rationale and logic for rejecting the claims of the law under certain circumstances in human affairs. The consequence is to lead perceptions into naive over-assertions or cynical denials of the relevance of law to behavior.

[128] There is a role for adversary presentation, but there is a more important need to seek bases upon which to appraise adversary claims.

assistance to the Vietcong as "an armed attack" justifying recourse to "self-defense" goes a long way toward abolishing the legal significance of the distinction between civil war and international war. Without this distinction, we weaken a principal constraint upon the scope and scale of violence in international affairs—the confinement of violence associated with internal wars to the territory of a single political unit.[129] Another adverse consequence of permitting "self-defense" in response to covert aggression is to entrust nations with very wide discretion to determine for themselves the occasions upon which recourse to *overt* violence across international boundaries is permissible.[130] An extension of the doctrine of self-defense would defeat a principal purpose of the United Nations Charter—the delineation of fixed, narrow limits upon the use of overt violence by states in dispute with one another.

2) The United States made no serious attempt to exhaust international remedies prior to recourse to unilateral military power. The gradual unfolding of the conflict provided a long period during which attempts at negotiated settlement could have taken place. Only belatedly and in a *pro forma* fashion did the United States refer the dispute to the United Nations. The United States made no attempt to comply with "the international law principle" alleged by footnote 10 of the Memorandum to govern the action of North Viet Nam. Nor did it attempt during the early phases of the war to subordinate its discretion to the Geneva machinery. No use was made even of the consultative framework of SEATO, an organization inspired by United States initiative for the specific purpose of inhibiting Communist aggression in Southeast Asia.[131] Policies of force were unilaterally adopted and put into execution; no account was taken of the procedural devices created to give a collective quality to decisions about the use of force. Yet the prospect for controlling violence in world affairs depends upon the growth of limiting procedural rules and principles.

3) By extending the scope of violence beyond the territory of South Viet Nam the United States has created an unfortunate precedent in international affairs. Where international institutions fail to provide clear guidance as to the character of permissible action, national actions create quasi-legislative precedents. In view of the background of the conflict in Viet Nam (including the expectation that South Viet

---

[129] One can emphasize the refusal to permit external sanctuary for actors supporting an internal war as a constructive precedent, but its reciprocal operation creates dangers of unrestrained violence. See generally Halpern, *Limited War in the Nuclear Age* (1963).

[130] *Cf.* Henkin, *supra*, note 70.

[131] On the creation of SEATO see SEATO, *op. cit. supra* note 107, introduction, xiii-xix.

Nam would be incorporated into a unified Viet Nam under the control of Hanoi after the French departure), the American decision to bomb North Viet Nam sets an unfortunate precedent. If North Viet Nam and its allies had the will and capability to employ equivalent military force, the precedent would even allow them to claim the right to bomb United States territory in reprisal.

4) The widespread domestic instability in the Afro-Asian world points up the need for an approach to internal war that aims above all to insulate this class of conflict from intervention by the great powers. The early use of peace observation forces, border control machinery, restraints on the introduction of foreign military personnel, and stand-by mediation appears possible and beneficial. Responses to allegations of "aggression" should be verified prior to the unilateral use of defensive force, especially when time is available. Claims of covert aggression might then be verified with sufficient authority and speed to mobilize support for community security actions.

5) In the last analysis, powerful nations have a responsibility to use defensive force to frustrate aggression when international machinery is paralyzed. Viet Nam, however, does not provide a good illustration of the proper discharge of this responsibility. North Viet Nam's action does not seem to constitute "aggression." Available international machinery was not used in a proper fashion. The domestic conditions prevailing in South Viet Nam were themselves so inconsistent with prevailing ideals of welfare, progress, and freedom that it is difficult to claim that the society would be better off as a result of a Saigon victory. The massive American presence has proved to be a net detriment, greatly escalating the war, tearing apart the fabric of Vietnamese society, and yet not likely to alter significantly the political outcome. The balance of domestic and area forces seems so favorable to the Vietcong that it is unlikely that the N.L.F. can be kept forever from political control. The sacrifice of lives and property merely postpones what appears to be an inevitable result. The United States voluntarily assumed a political responsibility for the defense of South Viet Nam that has been gradually converted into a political commitment and a self-proclaimed test of our devotion to the concept of collective self-defense. This responsibility is inconsistent with the requirements of world order to the extent that it depends upon unilateral prerogatives to use military power. The national interest of the United States would be better served by the embrace of *cosmopolitan isolationism*—either we act in conjunction with others or we withdraw. We are the most powerful nation in world history. It is hubris to suppose however, that we are the policemen of the world.[132] Our

---

[132] Even Secretary Rusk has pointed out the limitations upon American power in emphatic terms: "We do not regard ourselves as the policeman of

wasted efforts in Viet Nam suggest the futility and frustration of the politics of over-commitment. We are not the only country in the world concerned with containing Communism. If we cannot find cooperative bases for action we will dissipate our moral and material energies in a series of Viet Nams. The tragedy of Viet Nam provides an occasion for rethinking the complex problems of use of military power in world affairs and calls for an examination of the increasingly imperial role of the United States in international society. Perhaps we will discover the relevance of international law to the *planning* and *execution* of foreign policy as well as to its *justification*. Certainly the talents of the State Department's Legal Adviser are wasted if he is to be merely an official apologist summoned long after our President has proclaimed "a solemn national commitment."

---

the universe. . . . If other governments, other institutions, or other regional organizations can find solutions to the quarrels which disturb this present scene, we are anxious to have this occur." *Vietnam Hearings* 563; and Secretary McNamara stated in an address to the American Society of Newspaper Editors delivered at Montreal on May 18, 1966: ". . . neither conscience nor sanity itself suggests that the United States is, should, or could be the global gendarme." N.Y. Times, May 19, 1966, p. 11.

PART II

INTERNATIONAL ORGANIZATION

8. CONFLICTING CONCEPTS OF THE UNITED NATIONS

By CONOR CRUISE O'BRIEN

THE United Nations organisation has now survived seventeen years, covering several periods of intense international strain, and great specific strains on the structure of the organisation itself. It has survived; it has helped to avert threats to peace and above all, during the worst periods of the Cold War and during actual periods of 'hot war', it has provided a permanent meeting place for great powers which often seemed on the verge of hostilities, and which sometimes were actually engaged in indirect hostilities. Through all this time it has provided, both in the Security Council and, above all, in the General Assembly, a forum where bitterly conflicting opinions could be expressed—a verbal, taking the place of a material, warfare—while in the corridors, through the meetings of permanent representatives and others, and sometimes through the mediation of the Secretary General, compromise solutions were worked out, aimed at preventing the verbal battles from becoming material. It is true that the successes were often equivocal, and that the compromises had often a bitter taste. I shall come, in a moment, to look at these aspects of the matter. At this stage, it is enough to say that the United Nations has achieved a life and an apparent volition of its own—or partly of its own—in a sense that the old League of Nations never knew; that it is universal—or almost universal—in a way that the old League never was, and that it is sensitive to the opinion of smaller countries in a way which, while somewhat more apparent than real, is yet real in a sense that would never even have occurred to the League. This last factor—the sensitivity of the United Nations to the opinions of the smaller, formerly subject, nations—reflects, and is reflected in, the attachment of these countries to the United Nations. It was Hammarskjöld who asserted, in September 1960, speaking of the smaller powers, that 'the organisation is, first of all, their organisation'. This

Reprinted by permission of the author. This article was presented in 1964 as the 21st Montague Burton Lecture on International Relations at Leeds University, England.

statement contained an element of exaggeration, but it did strike a most responsive note among the small nations, with hardly a single exception.

This mutual attachment has become probably the most important single source of strength for the organisation as such. The reason for this is that the great power systems strive, especially in Africa and Asia, for influence over the smaller powers—or to exclude the influence of their rivals, which usually amounts to the same thing—and since these smaller powers like to work through the United Nations, it becomes important for the great powers to be as active and exercise as much authority inside the United Nations as they can. Thus the basic factor in the political life of the United Nations is the triangle of pressures exerted by America and its allies, the Soviet Union and its allies, and the Afro-Asian countries. None of these can afford, as it were, to 'let go' of the United Nations—as Germany and Italy did with the League—and none has power to expel any of the others, as the Western controllers of the League did with Russia. Thus the United Nations has become, as the League never did, a centre of intense, competitive, oblique diplomacy, combined with equally intense open propaganda.

Whatever else may be said about it, the United Nations is an extremely lively organisation, and, as life is the condition of growth, all who count the growth of international institutions as a necessity for human survival must rejoice at the abundant signs of life on the shores of Turtle Bay. Not only is the United Nations lively now, but its continued life may be predicted with reasonable safety. An organisation which has survived the bitterness and confusion of Palestine, Korea, Suez, Hungary and the Congo has demonstrated, among other things, its vital tenacity.

I shall take it, then, as axiomatic that the United Nations—at the very least in its functions as an international forum and centre of mediation—is a necessary human institution and likely to survive as long as organised human society, however long that may be. If we take that for granted, we are enabled to set aside the argument of those who would stifle criticisms of the organisation's imperfections and its sometimes inflated pretensions, by alleging that such criticisms endanger the last, best hope of man. The United Nations, at seventeen, is by no means so fragile as those critics would suggest. On the contrary, it is quite a tough organisation, served by some reasonably tough people and used, in varying ways, by tough, though mostly mildly spoken, representatives of various powers and especially of one power. No light we can shed on the organisation's actual ways of working is likely to bring it to an untimely end, or to prevent the fulfilment of the purposes which it was set up to serve. On the con-

trary, as, like most, if not all, human institutions, its practice has a pronounced tendency to deviate from its professions, it is in the common interest that such light should be shed. It is by the shedding of light that practice is most often encouraged to move up a little closer to profession. In any event, we shall be helping to diminish the area of optimistic illusion which at present has such an unhealthy grip over public opinion in international affairs.

From this introduction I may have given you the impression that I am about to produce some sensational revelations about the inner workings of the United Nations. This is not so. In what follows I shall be doing no more, for the most part, than presenting, and reasoning from, some of the assumptions about the facts of international life at the United Nations which are habitually made by those who work there, whether in the delegations or in the Secretariat. I refer to the assumptions which they make while they are actually working, as distinct from those which spring almost unbidden to their lips when they are addressing outside audiences in their American environment, or in their puzzled homelands.

The first working assumption, which every professional makes, and few professionals publicly refer to, is that if the United States does not want a given course of action to be taken, then the United Nations —that is to say the Security Council, the General Assembly and the Secretariat—will refrain from taking that course of action. The same assumption is not made about any of the other permanent members except in function of their degree of influence, at a given moment, with the United States. The second assumption, the converse of the first, is that any action taken by the United Nations must fit in with the United States' estimate of its own diplomatic interests. The third assumption is the corollary, that extensions of the power and influence of the United Nations are likely to be more at the expense of the Soviet Union and its allies than of the other sovereign members. The fourth is that the United Nations is unlikely to encroach on the interests of America's allies, unless it should be expedient, on a wider view of American interests, for the United States to permit the United Nations to do so. The fifth assumption is that if, in the judgement of the State Department, it is expedient to sacrifice the real or supposed immediate interests of any of America's allies, for the strengthening of America's overall diplomatic position, then the United Nations is likely to act in a manner disrespectful to these particular allies and their interests.

Up to 1958, the sixth assumption—nay the first assumption— would have been that any proposition which the United States desired would become United Nations policy. By 1958, however, at the time of the Lebanon crisis, it became apparent that because of the intake of new members, the United States could no longer carry through any proposition which ran flagrantly counter to Afro-Asian opinion, as a whole. The new sixth assumption then emerged: that any proposition on which the United States and a considerable number of Afro-Asian states can agree will become United Nations policy. This sixth assumption has now become a cardinal one, for practical prognosis, as distinct from academic speculation, about United Nations activity. Major propositions which are intended to be carried are now invariably worked out between the United States and at least some African and Asian delegates before coming to the floor. Naturally other consultations also take place, but the critical ones, as far as voting is concerned, are between the United States and the Afro-Asians. Both the Soviet Union and the Western European powers are, for different reasons, very reluctant to oppose openly a solid American-Afro-Asian consensus, although they will usually strive hard, at different ends, to prevent such a consensus coming into being. This new sixth assumption does differ significantly from the old one, whereby American control over the United Nations was virtually complete. The shift is healthy as far as it goes, in that it encourages the development of real negotiations, instead of pure propaganda demonstrations at the United Nations.[1]

The gap, however, between the two assumptions is not quite so great as one might at first suppose, and this for two reasons. The first is that the United States, through its widespread network of diplomatic and technical aid missions, and the pervasive influence of its

---

[1] Mr. Andrew Boyd (*United Nations: Piety, Myth and Truth,* p. 16) holds the following two assumptions to be 'oversimplified': 'that throughout the U.N.'s first ten years there was an automatic Assembly majority at the disposal of America, and that there is now one controlled by the Afro-Asian members'. The second assumption is indeed oversimplified, if only because it ignores the fact that the Afro-Asian members seldom act as a united group. I cannot see, however, that the first assumption is oversimplified in any serious way. Mr. Geoffrey L. Goodwin, writing of these same ten years, observed that 'the attitude of the U.S. is usually decisive' (*Britain and the United Nations,* p. 218). Mr. Boyd only gives one example to show the limitations on American influence in the period he names. The example given—the case of Palestine (November 1947)—is hardly convincing, since the American administration got its way in that matter, though not without, as Mr. Boyd says, 'exceptional pressure'. *United Nations: Piety, Myth and Truth* is the best introduction to the United Nations which exists, and one of the very few works which give any clear idea of how that institution functions in practice. The only serious weakness of this valuable book is an apparent tendency to underestimate, as here, the importance of American influence in the United Nations, both in the past and now. One of the most realistic comments I have seen on United States influence and attitudes at the United Nations comes from a Canadian observer, K. A. MacKirdy: 'The nation which pays a third of the budget, like the boy who owns the football, wants the game played his way or he will go home' (*Queen's Quarterly,* winter 1961).

great financial, commercial and industrial corporations, has a considerable and probably an increasing say in the foreign policies of a number of Asian and African governments. The second is that the Asian and African countries by no means form a solid block and it is therefore possible for the United States to acquire the necessary accession of Afro-Asian votes for one phase of its policy from one end of the spectrum, and for another phase from the other end. Thus, to take a recent example, the United States, in supporting and deciding military action in Katanga, could have relied, if necessary, on the left and centre of the Afro-Asian group at the Assembly to give, together with the safe Latin-American and other votes, the necessary two-thirds majority in any voting. In the second phase, when it was United States and United Nations policy, just after the end of the secession, to maintain Tshombe and his Government at the head of provincial affairs in South Katanga, the United States could still, if necessary, have found a majority for this policy—but a different and somewhat more vulnerable one, the right and centre, instead of the left and centre, of the Afro-Asian group, combined with the safe votes. Thus, today, by the exercise of a sophisticated kind of parliamentary diplomacy, the United States can get almost as good results as by the cruder methods prevalent up to 1958.

I have deliberately stressed the preponderant American role at the United Nations. I have done so for the sole reason that this is a major fact of international life, well known to all professionally concerned with these matters, but often glossed over, minimised or simply ignored, in public discussion and even, or perhaps especially, in discussions of a serious academic kind. In preparing this lecture I read through a certain number of text-books and similar writings by learned men, sometimes jurists and sometimes political scientists, often attached to, or writing for, some foundation. I was astonished by the regularity with which most of them discussed the deliberations and decisions of, for example, the General Assembly, as if that body were responsive simply to world opinion generally, without the marked specific weighting which it in fact has in favour of the State Department point of view.[2]

In drawing attention to this large and obvious, but relatively neglected, phenomenon it is not at all my wish to denounce the United

---

[2] Professor Benjamin V. Cohen, an eminent legal authority, tells us that the effectiveness of a request addressed to the General Assembly under the 'Uniting for Peace' procedure 'depends primarily upon the extent to which the request expresses the reasoned will and elicits the support of an alert and aroused world-wide conscience' (Cohen, *The United Nations, Constitutional Development, Growth and Possibilities,* p. 19). 'Primarily' this may in some sense be true; 'secondarily' however such a proposition needs to have State Department support, without which it is certain to fail in the Assembly.

States. Any great power which was in a position to exercise such
authority in an international organisation would have made use of its
opportunities, and on the whole I think the other powers would have
made a worse use of it than the United States has done. The United
States, despite certain aberrations on Formosa and Cuba, has never—
so far at least—shown the reckless disregard for the possible consequences of its actions which Britain and France showed at Suez and
the Soviet Union showed in Hungary. On the whole, the United States
administration handled the combined Suez-Hungary crisis through the
United Nations with a caution in relation to its potential foes and a
firmness in relation to its imprudent allies which were what, at the
time, the interests of world peace as well as the particular interests of
the United States probably demanded. Since it is more or less inevitable
in a world of unequal sovereign states, that one great power should
have far greater influence in the international organisation than others,
humanity has probably reason to be glad that the key decisions should
have been in the hands of Eisenhower and Kennedy, rather than of
Eden, Guy Mollet, Macmillan, Chiang Kai-Shek, de Gaulle, Stalin or
Khrushchev. I might add that, of all those named, Khrushchev might
well be the safest second choice.

It will, of course, be pointed out that the United States control over
the United Nations is not, and never has been, absolute, because of
the famous Soviet veto in the Security Council: that is to say, the rule
that decisions of the Security Council require the approval, or at least
the acquiescence, of the five permanent members. As, in principle,
decisions are taken only in the Security Council, while the General
Assembly only has power to *recommend,* this should mean—and
Stalin probably believed' that it did mean—that the United Nations
could never act in a way to which the Soviet Union objected. In
practice, however, once the deep divergence between the blocks
emerged after the war, and once it became apparent—as was the fact
at that time—that the United States had a safe majority in the Assembly, it was natural and possible for the United States and its friends to
build up the authority of the Assembly as against the Security Council. This trend was foreshadowed by Warren Austin as early as
October 1946, when he said: 'the General Assembly wields power
primarily as the voice of the conscience of the world . . . we foresee a
great and expanding area for the General Assembly'.[3] Warren
Austin's prediction of expanding responsibility for the General

---

[3] The Soviet Union, being in a minority, was less impressed by the moral
authority of the General Assembly. 'And it might in fairness be admitted
that if the roles were reversed a not dissimilar attitude would probably be
taken by a minority West' (Geoffrey L. Goodwin, *Britain and the United
Nations,* p. 214).

Assembly came true in 1950. At that time the Truman administration
had judged it expedient to resist the attempt made by the Communist
Government in North Korea to reunify Korea by force, and had very
naturally taken advantage of an ill-advised Soviet absence from the
Security Council to get its decision covered and converted into a
United Nations action by the votes of its allies and supporters on the
Security Council. When the hurried return of the Soviet representa-
tive to the Security Council threatened to obstruct the operation, the
United States took the momentous decision of throwing the matter
into the General Assembly with the 'uniting for peace' resolution. The
safe American majority in the General Assembly enabled the entirely
American-directed action in Korea to be continued under the United
Nations flag.[4]

In 1956, on the other hand, when Soviet troops moved into Hungary, in what seemed to many a clearer case of aggression than the
Korean one, it might have been expected that the 'uniting for peace'
procedure would have been invoked once more to launch a new
United Nations action in resistance to aggression. This was not done,
nor was it ever formally proposed in the Assembly. The reason for
this, of course, was that the United States, which was ready to undertake war against the North Koreans, and risk war against the Chinese,
on the Korean peninsula, was not ready to risk war against the Soviet
Union in Central Europe. This perfectly rational calculation found
expression at the United Nations by rather devious means, and greatly
increased the confusion about what the United Nations is and what
it could be. I remember myself, at the time of my own first arrival at
the United Nations as junior delegate in a minor delegation, the cor-
ridor activities on the Hungarian question, which now seem rather
strange in retrospect. This was before the actual armed Soviet intervention and at a time when the Nagy Government was holding out
under great pressure for its new non-aligned position. At this time,
before the Soviet intervention which crushed the Nagy Government,
it is possible that some kind of United Nations presence in Budapest

[4] Senator Taft, for once in agreement with a Soviet view, questioned the
legality of the United Nations position on Korea, 'because Article 27 of the
Charter clearly provides that decisions by the Security Council on all matters
shall be made by an affirmative vote of seven members including the permanent members. There was no concurring vote by Russia, but we overrode
this objection without considering how it might be used against us in the
future' (*Congressional Record,* 5 January 1951). In the same speech Taft,
with great prescience, declared that it would be 'most unwise' to build up
the power for action of Assembly, adding that 'we should only have one
vote among 60 which sometime in the future, even in the very near future,
may be inconvenient for us' *(ibid.).* Similar, but more lively and even
better founded, apprehensions were entertained by the British Government,
which foresaw the growing anti-colonial tendencies of the Assembly (Goodwin, *Britain and the United Nations,* p. 229).

—the sending of the Secretary General or even a group of his aides—might have induced the Soviet Union to refrain from risking a new and worse Korea; on the other hand, it might not have had that effect at all, but might have left the United Nations, and through it, the United States, in a position of moral commitment to defend Hungary even against the armed intervention of the Soviet Union. The United States Government, after no doubt a very careful assessment of the situation, decided to run no risk. The United States delegation at the United Nations, therefore—a delegation then headed by Henry Cabot Lodge—was active in the corridors in the phase before the Russian intervention, but active not in support of the Nagy Government, but against it. American aides would insistently tell one that Nagy was just as bad a Communist as Khrushchev, that the whole dispute was a falling out of thieves, that the Nagy representatives at the United Nations had an appalling Communist record and so on. It was only after the Hungarian rising had been definitely crushed, and no possibility or danger of effective United Nations and United States intervention remained, that Nagy and his colleagues came to be hailed as heroes and martyrs by the same people who had assiduously smeared them when they may have been within reach of help.

In all this, the policy of the then United States Government, that of Mr. Eisenhower and Mr. Dulles, was rationally defensible. It was rationally defensible not to run a risk of world war over Hungary, as it also was to curb, with the help of the United Nations, the simultaneous sally of rash friends at Suez. All this was quite defensible, but not on any terms which the Republican Administration could consistently and effectively use to its supporters. Mr. Dulles and his friends, after all, had promised to roll back the Iron Curtain, and when it came to the pinch they decided not to roll back, but to climb down. This was a very difficult operation, because millions of Americans, including large immigrant groups, were passionately concerned about Hungary, while those Americans who cared at all about Suez were mainly on the side of Israel, Britain and France—in that order—and detested Nasser. In these circumstances, the Republican Administration used the United Nations and used it very ably, as a lightning conductor. It was the United Nations which, in the public legend, halted Britain and France in Suez; it was the United Nations which, in the same legend, failed to cope with Soviet aggression in Hungary. Hence the myth of the United Nations' double standard: severe on the nations of the West and soft on Communism. In actual fact, of course, what the General Assembly did in both cases was much the same—that is, it passed resolutions calling for a withdrawal of the British and French forces from Egypt, and of the Soviet forces from Hungary. If there was any double standard, it was at the expense of the Soviet Union, whose actions, unlike those of Britain and France, were stigmatised as aggressive and condemned. The British and French obeyed, not so much, one can reasonably assume, because of the voting majority in the Assembly, but because both the United States and the Soviet Union were against them, and there was a risk of having to fight the Soviet Union without American support. The Soviet Union did not obey, because it well knew from the posture of the United States in the early and more critical days, and from the failure of the United States to invoke sanctions under the 'uniting for peace' procedure, that the United States would not intervene in support of Hungary.

These attitudes of the powers were determined by rational, though perhaps mistaken, calculations of their own interests—which did, however, include, and this is important, the common interest in peace —and those of them who could so do, made use of the United Nations to mask their positions. Thus American Republican spokesmen regretted, after the event, that the United Nations had failed in the case of Hungary, and Americans forgot, if they ever realised, that if there was any failure, it was a failure of the United States Government which failed to propose sanctions and dissuaded others from doing so. Similarly, the British Government, withdrawing under Russian and American pressure from its ill-judged Suez venture, made some parade of its law-abiding deference to a decision of the United Nations and emphasised how very different its level of international morality was from that of the Russians, and how defective an instrument the United Nations was for dealing with Russia. In this way, the government of Mr. Eisenhower used the United Nations with great success as a scapegoat, while the government of Sir Anthony Eden, with less success but still with some, used the United Nations as a means of saving what remained of its face. The peace was saved, adventures were liquidated, the public was misled.

In the United States the United Nations came to be thought of as a powerful but suspect almost supra-national body with a mysterious authority over United States policy. This illusion continues to be useful for any American government which finds it necessary to pursue a domestically unpopular line in foreign policy. The government can refer the issue to the United Nations, obtain the decision it wants, and let the United Nations shoulder the unpopularity. In Britain and France, many after Suez thought of the United Nations as a hypocritical and irresponsible mass of small nations applying a double standard and ignorantly intervening in grave matters of policy which should be reserved for experienced statesmen. This, of course, was the reaction of what is called the 'wider public'.[5] Some British and French politicians, who well knew that United States policy was the main factor involved, found it more convenient to denounce the blind hysteria of the United Nations than to complain too much about the stinging and calculated rebuff administered by the senior partner in the NATO Alliance. Similarly today, Lord Home, who resents the policy which the United States has been pursuing in relation to the Congo, does not attack the United States directly, but denounces the United Nations and the supposedly irresponsible smaller powers. The United States Government, of course, perfectly understands what Lord Home is saying; the public at large does not.

Senator Robert Taft, who had in his own country a reputation for being an honest, as well as an able man, said twelve years ago that the United States should use the United Nations as 'a diplomatic weapon'.[6] No spokesman of the United States Government has, I believe, used this language, but successive United States Governments have acted, and with much success, in accordance with the Taft doctrine. The major decisions of the United Nations on Iran, on Palestine, on Korea, on keeping China out of the United Nations and keeping Formosa in China's Security Council seat, on Suez, on Hungary and on the Congo have one thing in common: they were all

[5] Not only of the wider public, and not only in Britain and France. Professor Benjamin V. Cohen believes that 'the irresponsible exercise of voting power by the small and weak states may threaten the future of the United Nations' (Cohen, *The United Nations, Constitutional Development, Growth and Possibilities*, p. 94). This fear prevailed in the League of Nations also. 'The great powers', according to Lord Robert Cecil, 'were obsessed with the wholly unreal danger that the small powers might band together and vote them down' (quoted in Andrew Boyd, *United Nations: Piety, Myth and Truth*, p. 27).

[6] 'But for the present we can only make use of the United Nations as best we may, as a diplomatic weapon, and through it we may hope that perhaps more friendly relations can be established with Russia. But as far as military policy is concerned I see no choice except to disregard the United Nations . . .' (*Congressional Record*, 5 January 1951). It is clear from the general context of this strongly anti-communist speech that Senator Taft, while he genuinely believed in the United Nations as 'a forum for discussion', and a safety-valve, did not envisage a 'diplomatic weapon' primarily as a means for bringing about the problematical 'more friendly relations . . . with Russia' (see above, page 191, footnote 4). A British observer was more explicit about the real functions of the diplomatic weapon: 'And however clear the need to defend Western outposts might seem to ministers and officials, on an issue that might easily appear both obscure and remote to the electorate the moral backing of the U.N. might well be instrumental in rallying the necessary public support [by an] U.N. endorsement of military action by the NATO powers' (Geoffrey L. Goodwin, *Britain and the United Nations*, p. 248). The same observer realised, however, that a diplomatic weapon was something one could cut oneself with. It was not, he wrote, 'impossible to envisage cases in which a two-thirds majority [in the Assembly] against Britain might be mobilized' *(ibid.)*.

in line with United States government policy: in the case of the Congo, United Nations policy changed after a change of United States administration. The only partial exception I can think of is that of Lebanon, in 1958, where the Arab countries, working with the Secretariat, reached agreement, ratified by the United Nations, which fell short of what the United States delegation had hoped for at the outset of the special session in question. In reality, what Lebanon marked was the transition from a state of affairs in which the United States was the sole determinant of General Assembly decisions, to one in which it exercised predominance on condition of working together with the Afro-Asian group—the sixth assumption to which I referred earlier.[7] That is what the case of Lebanon represented in reality, I believe, but it represented something else in the mind of Mr. Hammarskjöld. It represented for him an important stage in the growth of the Secretariat, and especially in the office of the Secretary General, towards independent authority in world affairs. This was the theory of the 'dynamic instrument' of which Mr. Hammarskjöld often spoke.[8] It is not easy to express this theory briefly,

---

[7] 'By 1958, it was noted in Moscow, the Afro-Asian states held a third of the Assembly's seats. This gave them a 'collective veto' since important Assembly resolutions require a majority of two to one and can be defeated by a 'blocking third'. Soviet commentators gleefully argued that 'the American voting machine was no longer working' (Boyd, *United Nations: Piety, Myth and Truth,* p. 38).

[8] *Servant of Peace; A Selection of the Speeches and Statements of Dag Hammarskjöld, Secretary General of the United Nations, 1953-1961,* edited and introduced by Wilder Foote (Harper, New York, 1962). See especially pp. 37, 46-7, 136, 150, 198, 227, 259, 353. The evolution of Hammarskjöld's thought on this matter is too complex to be analysed here. It can, however, be said that in his thinking the 'instrument' tended to become more important and the 'agents' (Council and Assembly) rather less. Compare:

'The Secretary General does not suffer from the fact that he has nobody to refer back to provided that the main organs of the U.N.—the Security Council and the General Assembly—have taken clear decisions on general terms of reference, short of which of course the Secretary General is forced to undertake a kind of policy-making which, from the point of view of member governments I fear may be considered unsound' (Press Conference of 4 April 1957; in *Speeches,* p. 136).

'If negotiations are necessary, or if arrangements with a certain intended political impact are to be made, but member nations are not in a position to lay down exact terms of reference, a natural response of the Organization is to use the services of the Secretary General for what they may be worth' (Statement of 1 May 1960); *Speeches,* p. 259).

The shift in emphasis is remarkable. Failure by the main Organs to provide clear terms of reference is regarded in the 1957 press conference as a regrettable situation from which the Secretary General 'suffers' and in which he may be 'forced' into activities which 'may be considered unsound'. By 1960, the note of misgiving has entirely disappeared and it becomes simply 'natural' that the Secretary General should act without 'exact terms of reference'. But the 1960 line is foreshadowed in some of the earlier statements (*Speeches,* p. 150).

because it developed over the years in Mr. Hammarskjöld's mind, while remaining wrapped in the translucent envelope of his prose style, but roughly speaking, the theory was this: the Secretary General represented the general will of the international community as a whole, independent of the will of any individual member or group of members; where the other organs of the Charter, the Security Council and the General Assembly, had failed to reach agreement or, as more often happened, had reached only ambiguous agreement, the Secretary General, and under him the Secretariat, could be, and ought to be, trusted to act in the general interest of all. In this way, and through such situations, the authority of the Secretary General and the Secretariat were to be gradually built up in the direction, it was hoped, ultimately of a genuinely supra-national authority—a world government.

Now for all of us who are frightened by the anarchy of sovereign states, the Cold War, the armaments race and so on, this is an exceedingly attractive concept, and it has enlisted the loyalty of many able and admirable men and women throughout the world. As I now propose to subject this concept to some criticism, I should perhaps say first that I believe it tends in the right direction, that is to say that the strengthening of a genuine focus of international authority is obviously in the common interest. I do not believe, however, that we are helping the tendency in that direction by pretending that we have already reached a stage which we have not in fact reached: a stage where the Secretary General and the Secretariat can be implicitly relied on as an impartial instrument in the service of the international community as a whole, influenced by no national policies. I believe that the role of the Secretariat, from the foundation of the organisation up to now, has to be seen in relation, not directly to the international community in the rather mystical manner imagined by Hammarskjöld, but in relation to its own immediate and real environment; those buildings on the East River, in which the Security Council, the General Assembly and the other organs work. In that environment, the influence of the United States was, as I have suggested, once supreme, and is now conditionally predominant. In the Secretariat also—that is to say in the executive service of these American-led organs—American influence was once supreme, and is still predominant. The powerful personality of Hammarskjöld partly disguised and to a lesser extent deflected the reality of American pressure on the Secretariat. For a clear view of the basic situation it is therefore well to go back to the days of Trygve Lie.

Trygve Lie possessed neither Hammarskjöld's ability nor his obliquity, and his book *In The Cause of Peace,* so much more candid than anything Hammarskjöld is known to have left us, is still in many ways a better guide to United Nations realities than are Hammar-skjöld's speeches or most textbooks. As regards the Secretariat, Lie tells us that he was 'especially concerned about American recruit-ment'. 'The trouble was', he says, 'that so great a proportion of the staff were of United States nationality, and the United States govern-ment'—he is here referring to pre-McCarthy days—'gave so little help towards choosing among the applicants'. Towards the end of Mr. Lie's tenure in 1952-3, the then American Government turned its attention to this problem, and began to comb out, with Mr. Lie's help, any Americans in the Secretariat who could be suspected of being soft on Communism. Lie, having pointed out that nothing in the Charter or the staff regulations bars a Communist from being a member of the Secretariat, and that every Secretariat member has full freedom for his personal, political and religious convictions, none the less goes on to say that 'if there was even one American Communist in the Secre-tariat, I intend to get rid of him, but quietly and in accordance with the staff regulations'.[9] He refers, a few pages later, without apparently being conscious of an inconsistency and even with some pride, to the fact that he declined to discharge, as the Russians demanded, White Russians employed in the Secretariat, and refused to consider sacking Czechs and Slovaks disapproved by Prague.[10] On the other front, the McCarthyite outcry in the United States continued, and Mr. Lie tells us 'on the one hand the sweeping attacks upon the standing and integrity of the Secretariat were vicious and distorted and out of all proportion to the facts. On the other hand, there was no question in my mind that the cases involving the fifth amendment ought to go, as a matter of sound policy, entirely divorced from the public hue and cry'.[11] This meant in practice that Mr. Lie, who was able to stand up against the pressure of the Russians and their friends—and indeed could not have afforded to give in to it—yielded to the much more powerful pressure of the United States. The F.B.I. installed a kind of inquisition in the Secretariat building; the fifth amendment cases, and others, did go, and Mr. Lie's trusted friend and legal counsel, an American citizen, Abraham Feller jumped out of a twelfth-story window.

The Secretariat inherited by Hammarskjöld was therefore one which contained not only a large number of American citizens, but a particular body of such citizens, a body which had been purged of all who, in the McCarthy time, could be shown to have deviated in some degree from the then very stringent norms of loyalty to the United States. The American survivors of this system would, it could reason-

[9] *In the Cause of Peace,* p. 388.
[10] *Ibid,* p. 394.
[11] *Ibid.* p. 397.

ably be assumed, have a distinct tendency to identify loyalty to the international community with conformity to United States policy, since the penalty for radical nonconformity with United States policy had been shown to be dismissal from the service of the international community. These survivors included the most important people in the Secretariat next to Hammarskjöld—and it was a closer 'next' than the public generally were in a position to see. Hammarskjöld himself, with greater diplomatic resources and cooler judgement than Lie, managed to conduct relations with the State Department with a greater degree of international decorum than Lie had achieved, but the reality of a sort of right of oversight by the State Department over the American Secretariat members—and probably indirectly over other Western members—continued. So, and rigidly, of course, did Soviet control over Soviet citizens in the Secretariat. The difference was that the Americans, under the more supple, but perhaps no less strong, rein of the State Department, remained at the centre, where political decisions were taken, while the Russians, although occupying high-ranking posts, were kept out in the political cold in ignorance of what was really going on. This practice may have originated with the Korean War—that it did prevail then Mr. Lie has recorded —I saw it myself in operation in relation to the Congo, and I believe it is still in force. In Hammarskjöld's time, his closest associates and advisers were all Americans—Cordier, Bunche and (for Congo matters at least) Wieschhoff—and they were all Americans who had the approval—although, in one case, against a background of Congressional criticism—of the State Department. This state of affairs was quite a faithful reflection of the situation in the other organs—the Security Council with its safe (though constitutionally limited) American majority, and the General Assembly with its less safe, but still conditionally reliable, American majority. All this, in turn, reflected the realities of a world in which the United States was the most powerful and the wealthiest country, the greatest in trade and finance, and in diplomatic influence, and of course the greatest contributor to the United Nations. It was entirely natural and quite unavoidable that this influence should permeate also the United Nations Secretariat, which is a service belonging not to some Rousseau-like disembodied general will of the international community, but to the real world, with its real balance of forces.

Hammarskjöld's subtle mind, although quite at home in this real world, conceived the idea that, working through contradictions and ambiguities, in the instructions coming to him from Council and Assembly, he might still make the Secretariat somehow, despite its composition, and its conditions of working, into an instrument genuinely serving the international community in some higher sense. It was a heroic endeavour, and a sincere one, but I am not sure that it was successful. Save for the lonely and transitional issue of the Lebanon, and perhaps the case of Laos—though that is much less certain—it would be hard to think of an issue on which the Secretariat differed to any significant extent from United States policy and succeeded in carrying its point. On what might be called the McCarthy issue, Hammarskjöld bowed, more gracefully and inconspicuously than Trygve Lie, but bowed none the less, to prevailing American opinion. On Suez, naturally enough, and perhaps with more questionable propriety on Hungary, Hammarskjöld worked with the United States and the services of the Secretariat may not have been without importance in enabling the explosive Hungarian issue to be buried. It may be urged, and with truth, that the interests of world peace were involved here, but if the United States had decided to protect Hungary, I think it likely that the United Nations, including the Secretariat, would have asserted that in Hungary, as in Korea, peace could only be defended by resisting aggression.

On the Congo issue, the United Nations was from the beginning and still is generally responsive to American policy. There were some partial or apparent exceptions, which are themselves significant. Thus, when the Republican Administration wanted to seat a Kasavubu delegation as representative of the Congo, at a time when there was no recognised legal government, the Secretariat used its influence against this move. Similarly, when the United States, in concert with Great Britain, wanted to get rid of M. Dayal, the United Nations Representative in the Congo, the Secretary General for a time demurred. Two things, both important, have to be noticed about these exceptions. The first is that it was the United States Government, not the Secretariat, which, in both cases, carried its point; the Kasavubu delegation was seated and Dayal was dropped. The second point is that these happened to be cases on which the Republican Administration acted with relatively little deference to Afro-Asian opinion. It could, I think, be said with truth that when the United States unconditionally controlled the General Assembly, the Secretariat served the United States, and that now that the United States, working in concert with a sizeable section of Afro-Asian opinion, controls the Assembly, so also the Secretariat works for an American-Afro-Asian consensus—with the emphasis still, as it is in the General Assembly, in favour of the United States. The relation of countries like Britain on the one hand and the Soviet Union on the other to this situation is important but intermittent and peripheral. In certain conditions, in particular if United States policy is hesitant and United States public opinion divided, British and French policy may inflect the United States attitude and also and simultaneously that of the Secretariat.

Similarly the Soviet Union strives, with less success, to influence the policies of the Afro-Asian nationalists.[12] The vacillations of United Nations policy in the Congo were mainly due to American hesitations under conflicting Anglo-French and Afro-Asian pressures. When the United States finally makes up its mind to go ahead, however, the United Nations goes ahead also. Thus Andrew Cordier, a senior American on the Secretariat, helped the United States Ambassador to break Lumumba in September 1960. A change in United States policy produced another kind of firm action in Katanga, especially following the despatch of the American Military Mission to Elisabethville and the use of American aircraft to transport United Nations military equipment. The settlement in the Congo—to the degree that we can regard the Congo as being settled—was one determined on in Washington—'Thant Plan' and all—and implemented by the Secretariat through the forces supplied by neutral member nations. The achievement of the United Nations, which may, or may not, have prevented the Congo from becoming the focus of general war, was a rather equivocal success for international action, a partial success for Afro–Asian opinion in relation to the Katanga fraud, a partial defeat for Great Britain, at the very least a major tactical defeat for the Soviet Union, and a triumph—at this moment apparently unqualified—for United States diplomacy. We see therefore that the difference between Senator Taft's concept of the United Nations as a diplomatic weapon for the United States and Hammarskjöld's concept of a dynamic instrument in the hands of the international community is less wide in practice than in theory.

The most hopeful element in all this—the point of growth—is the element of the conditional. United States policy—working through the United Nations—cannot simply dictate, but must bargain for support. This need—combined with the diplomatic competition between the great power blocks in Asia and in Africa—gives to the smaller and weaker countries an influence which they would otherwise not possess. This influence is felt not only in the Assembly but

12 '. . . one of the U.N.'s most striking characteristics is the extent to which it has frustrated the Communist powers' hopes of directing the Afro-Asian anti-colonial movement' (Boyd, *United Nations: Piety, Myth and Truth,* p. 182). There is truth in this, but it must be remembered that the Afro-Asian group at the United Nations is far from being fully representative of the Afro-Asian anti-colonial movement. Many of the African delegates in particular, notably most of those which speak French so well, represent governments which were set up precisely as barriers against the anti-colonial movement, and their philosophy of 'African independence' is very similar to that of Moise Tshombe. It is true, however, that the genuinely 'anti-colonial' governments do also—for different reasons—reject any Communist attempts to give them a lead, and that this is reflected in the United Nations.

in the Security Council, for any potential veto-wielder fears, as Mr. Andrew Boyd has rightly pointed out, 'the sword of Damocles' of the 'Unity for Peace' procedure, and thus the Council has, in Mr. Boyd's words, 'been revived by the Assembly'.[13] The form of this revival has operated to the benefit of the smaller and weaker countries. The influence of these countries—mainly Afro-Asian—tends both towards the mitigation of the Cold War, and towards other unexpected ends—for example, towards a rapid growth in racial equality and therefore in human freedom on a very large scale throughout the world. The part which the United Nations plays in obliging the great powers to carry out their professions regarding racial equality is one of the organisation's greatest contributions. The world, on the whole, is both a safer and a better place than it would be without the United Nations. That, however, is no reason for pretending that the world is already safer and better than it has, in fact, become, or that the United Nations has attained, or is likely soon to attain, a sphere of detached and impartial virtue, remote from the real political environment in which, by many curious and often questionable expedients, we are contriving to live together on this planet.

[13] Boyd, *The United Nations: Piety, Myth and Truth*, pp. 32-3.

9. COLLECTIVE SECURITY AND THE WAR IN KOREA

By ARNOLD WOLFERS

THE action taken by the United Nations in 1950 to halt the attack on South Korea has been heralded as the first experiment in collective security. The implication is that a radical break with the traditional foreign policy of nations has occurred; power politics, we are told, have been replaced by police action of the world community. It is quite likely that many who suffered in the Korean War on our side have been comforted by the thought that they have served the cause of law enforcement by community action, though others who believed that no vital interests of their country were at stake may have found the ordeal harder to bear. Whatever the emotional reaction, it is necessary to investigate dispassionately whether in fact a turning point in world politics was reached when the United Nations flag was unfurled in Korea. On the answer may depend what future policy we and others are entitled to expect of this country.

It may sound like quibbling to ask whether Korea was an example of "collective security." Obviously, the answer depends on the definition of the term. If one chooses to make it include every collective action undertaken for defensive purposes by a group of nations, then the Korean intervention by the United States and its associates falls under the term. Actually, it has become the habit of official spokesmen of our government to use the term in this way. For instance, they speak of NATO as a means of "collective security," although the treaty was legally justified by reference to Article 51 of the United Nations Charter, which explicitly permits "collective self-defense" in cases where the universal collective security provisions of the United Nations *fail* to protect a victim of aggression. But there is nothing new or revolutionary in nations' aligning themselves for purposes of defense against their common national foes. Except for countries pur-

Reprinted by permission of the author and *The Yale Review, XLIII* (No. 4, June 1954) 482-496.

suing a "go it alone" policy, such conduct has been traditional among the members of multistate systems.

This is not what exponents of the principle of collective security have in mind when they urge nations to change the customary direction of their defense policy. They call upon nations to go beyond aligning themselves with each other only to meet the threats emanating from common national enemies and to embrace instead a policy of defense directed against aggression in general or, more precisely, against any aggressor anywhere. Coupled with arrangements to name the aggressor by community decision, nations—instead of reserving their power to defend or enforce their national interests—would be lined up like a police force to strike against any country, friend or foe, that had been declared an aggressor. Such a policy would constitute a radical break with tradition.

Since there are fundamental differences between these two types of collective action, with only one of them constituting a break with traditional national foreign policy, to avoid confusion and misunderstanding the two should be distinguished by the use of different labels. And since "collective security" has become the symbol for a break with power politics, it should be reserved for action that meets this test. It will be used so in this discussion, while other types of multilateral defensive action will be called "collective defense." Aside from semantics then, the problem is whether intervention in Korea represents a radical break with the traditional foreign policy of nation-states and, as a consequence, fulfills the expectations widely held for "collective security."

How serious a break with tradition the policy of collective security would be becomes evident if one considers what risks and sacrifices nations would have to incur in order to make such a policy effective and meaningful. It stands to reason that provisions and commitments for police action would add nothing to the protection that victims of aggression have enjoyed under the old system unless such victims could expect more military assistance than they would have received otherwise. The exponents of collective security have stressed this point. They have assumed that under a system of collective security such as they advocate, overwhelming force would be placed behind the law and at the disposal of a victim of attack. As in municipal affairs, therefore, the power of the police would usually suffice to deter any would-be attacker and thereby serve to maintain the peace rather than merely to punish the offender.

In order that collective security add in this way to the strength of the defense and to the chances of deterrence, it must be assumed that some nations, including one or more of the great powers, will be prepared to resort to force—that is, for all practical purposes, go to war—when, if they had not been devoted to the principle of collective security, they would have remained neutral or fought on the side of the aggressor. Instead of being allowed to reserve their military strength for the exclusive task of balancing the power of countries considered a threat to themselves or their allies, nations committed to a policy of collective security must divert their strength to struggles in remote places or, worse still, take action against friends and allies on whom reliance had been placed for defense against common foes. In extreme cases, a nation might even be called upon to defend and strengthen a foe at the expense of a friend or ally, if the latter were condemned as an aggressor.

If these should seem to be far-fetched contingencies, French experience, as well as possibilities now facing this country, prove them to be anything but theoretical. When Italy attacked Ethiopia, the French were urged in the name of collective security to participate in sanctions, if need be military sanctions, against Italy, a country which had just become a virtual ally against Germany, then considered France's number-one opponent; in the Korean War, France came under pressure to divert more of her strength to the fight with the North Koreans and Chinese aggressors at a time when she already felt too weak at home even to dare consent to German rearmament. A more dangerous situation might arise for the United States if Syngman Rhee should ever make good his threat to seek unification of his country by force. To take police action against him—or even to agree to have the Soviet bloc take such action—would run directly counter to this country's primary defense interests.

In order to be able to assert, then, that collective security has become a living reality, it is necessary to show that one or more countries have in fact proved ready to run the risks and consent to the sacrifices that this radical break with traditional defense policy presupposes. In the instance of Korea, this means inquiring whether there is evidence that such a switch to defense against aggression *per se* was made by the United States and its associates. Before doing so, it may be worth while to ask whether it is possible to conceive of incentives that might be powerful enough to induce nations to change their habits in so radical a fashion.

Those who seek to make a case for collective security, either as having become a reality or as being a practical goal for the future, argue along two lines, one more idealistic, the other more realistic. Nations, it is said, might take up arms against any aggressor anywhere simply because the crime of aggression arouses their moral indignation. The fact that there is such indignation both here and abroad is not in doubt. The desire to see perpetrators of wanton attack stopped and punished is widespread in a world that had so much experi-

ence of brutal attack on weak and peaceful peoples. Yet, it is one
thing to be indignant; another to be prepared to plunge's one's country into war, though it be called police action, and to do so in an age
of increasing wartime horror and destruction. Even aside from narrow nationalist preoccupations which might lessen the ardor for
punitive action on behalf of the world community, there is reason
to doubt whether moral indignation alone can be relied upon to
carry nations into military action when no vital national interests
push them in the same direction. In order to have a chance, it would
rather seem as if collective security itself would have to appeal to
interests of the kind traditionally considered vital to the nation.

According to the more realistic argument, such an interest is in fact
at stake, though nations may still often fail to realize it. The argument rests on what has been called the principle of "indivisible
peace." If aggression is allowed to go unpunished anywhere, it is
said, potential aggressors will be encouraged everywhere, and as a
result no nation will be secure. Instead, if any aggressor anywhere is
stopped or deterred by overwhelming police power, all other potential aggressors will understand the warning and cease to constitute a
threat. Thus, by a kind of detour, nations which for reasons of collective security are forced to divert strength or to weaken alignments
against specific opponents gain more security in the end, even against
their national foes.

This second line of argument has been called realistic because it
rests on security considerations of the kind which have customarily
guided national governments. But the question remains whether the
long-run advantage of deterrence (which is hard to evaluate) can
win out against the very real short-run risks of diversion of strength
and unbalancing of power. Unless it can be shown in the case of
Korea that the United States and its associates actually chose the long-
run advantage at the expense of immediate security, the war in Korea
cannot be called an example of collective security.

In a discussion of Korea, it might appear as if attention would
have to be focused on the United Nations rather than on its members. In a sense this is true. Had no world organization such as the
United Nations existed in 1950, there could have been no question of
police action on behalf of the world community. Collective security
presupposes that the aggressor be named and condemned by means
of some recognized procedure; resort to violence in defense of the
law against such an aggressor must be authorized by an organization
which can claim to speak for the community. Yet no provisions, resolutions, commands, or recommendations of a world organization of
sovereign nations can suffice to make collective security a reality. It
can become real only by the fact of military power being employed

for police purposes; the decision rests with the members who possess such military power and can use it for collective security if they will. In regard to the United Nations, the question is merely whether it did its part in inducing members of the organization to take police action on its behalf and under its auspices.

This is not the place to investigate whether the Charter of the United Nations was aimed at collective security as defined here or offered the best means of inducing countries to act in accordance with this principle. The veto provision certainly allowed members to assume that they would never be expected to participate in police action which would seriously antagonize one or more of the major powers. Furthermore, Article 43 left the implementation of any commitment to participate in such action to subsequent negotiations which have not taken place. It is agreed, however, that when the members of the United Nations subscribed to the purpose of the organization as being "to take effective collective measures . . . for the suppression of acts of aggression," they accepted the principle of common defensive action against any aggressor anywhere. Their legal or at least moral obligation to do so whenever the competent organs of the United Nations order or recommend such action would seem to be beyond doubt, unless one were to assume that the "inherent right of self-defense" permits nations to beg out of any military action which endanger their security. If one accepted this reservation, the Charter could not be said to create much legal embarrassment for members who wanted to avoid the risks of collective security. In the case of Korea, majorities sufficient to reach decisions both in the Security Council and in the General Assembly took all the steps for which they were competent to get police action under way.

The attack by the North Koreans occurred on June 25. On the same day, in the absence of the Soviet delegate, the Security Council determined that a breach of the peace had occurred. It called upon North Korea to withdraw its forces and proceeded to invite its members "to render every assistance to the United Nations in execution of this resolution." Some hours prior to the second meeting of the Council, on June 27, the United States Government announced that it had ordered American air and sea forces to go to the assistance of South Korea for the specific purpose of executing the June 25 resolution of the Security Council. If this was not enough to qualify American intervention as United Nations action, the Security Council identified itself with the action of the United States by voting on the same day that urgent military measures were required. The members were now called upon to furnish assistance of the kind necessary to repel the attack. From then on, the action of the United States and its associates was carried forward in the name of the United Nations, under the United Nations flag, and under a unified United Nations command set up by the United States in accordance with the resolution of the Security Council. Limited to recommendations, the United Nations continued to put what little pressure it could on its members to get them to participate or to make larger contributions; at the same time it sought to influence the United Nations command in the conduct and termination of the war, acting in this respect as a restraining factor.

Aside from this rather marginal though not unimportant role played by the United Nations itself, the character of the action in Korea must be judged by the decisions and acts of the United States and its associates. It would seem permissible, in fact, to concentrate on the conduct of the United States, because the other nations which made contributions to the defense of South Korea might conceivably have done so as friends and allies of the United States, whether this country was acting traditionally in what it considered to be its national interest and that of its friends or was conducting police action on the principle of collective security.

It is not a simple matter to discover whether or not United States intervention in Korea qualifies as collective security in the restricted sense in which the term is used here. The motivations of the chief architects of the policy are not decisive. The devotion of men like Mr. Truman and Mr. Acheson to the idea of collective security as they conceived it is not in doubt, any more than their desire to prevent the United Nations from suffering the same dismal fate which befell the League of Nations at the time of Italy's aggression against Ethiopia.

What is being asked is whether the United States, even if it believed itself to be engaging in police action in conformity with the concept of collective security, did in fact break with traditional national defense policy by accepting the kind of risks which such a break presupposes. If the aggressor had been South Korea rather than North Korea, the answer could not be in doubt. To take up arms against South Korea would have meant siding with this country's chief national enemy, the Soviet bloc, and strengthening the Communist countries at the expense of a country on which the United States could have relied as an ally in the Cold War. No more striking proof could have been given of unqualified American support for police action against any aggressor anywhere. But, the aggressor was Communist North Korea backed by the Soviet Union. It becomes necessary therefore to investigate how intervention in these circumstances looked from the point of view of American security interests as interpreted in Washington at the time.

Speaking negatively first, the United States was obviously not taking up arms against a friend or ally. On the contrary, it was setting out to stop expansion by the Soviet bloc, thus serving what had long been proclaimed to be the major goal of American foreign policy. It might be argued, however, that in extending the "containment" policy to Korea, the United States was diverting military power from Europe, which was considered the chief danger area. As the war proceeded, and American involvement exceeded all early expectations, much fear of such diversion was in fact expressed in Europe. But in this country, the opinion continued to prevail that in terms of the Cold War it would have been much more dangerous even for Europe if Communist aggression had gone unpunished in Asia. Moreover, powerful groups in Congress had long pressed for a stronger stand against Communism in Asia. Thus while the sacrifices in men and resources, borne by the American people in the course of the Korean War, were far in excess of even the most pessimistic initial expectations, they did not include the sacrifice or diversion of defensive military power from the tasks of the Cold War. Instead, the rearmament effort provoked by Communist aggression in Korea led to a multiplication of this power.

The fact that no sacrifice in terms of national protection against a major enemy was involved is not enough, however, to explain why this country should have decided to resort to military force. Except for a radical break with tradition, nations are not expected to take up arms unless there are interests which they consider vital at stake. Accordingly, the apparent absence of any vital American interest in South Korea made it seem as if devotion to collective security alone could have induced the United States to intervene. It was known that our civilian and military leaders did not consider the defense of the 38th Parallel or the preservation of a free South Korea a matter of vital strategic importance to this country, despite the fact that loss of the area to the Communists would have rendered Japan more vulnerable to attack. The Joint Chiefs of Staff had reached this decision at the time American troops were withdrawn from the territory of the Republic of Korea, long before Secretary Acheson made his famous "perimeter" speech. It is also true that the United States was not bound by any treaty of alliance to go to the assistance of South Korea. However, this lack of what might be called a local strategic interest and the absence of any specific commitment to assist South Korea, other than that implied in the United Nations Charter, do not suffice to prove that vital interests were not at stake. The fact is that one can discern a threefold American interest of exactly the kind which, thinking along the lines of traditional power politics, governments would normally consider serious enough to justify military action or even to make it imperative.

In the first place, according to the views prevailing in both political parties at the time of the North Korean attack, any further expansion in any direction on the part of the Soviet bloc constituted a threat to American security. The "containment" policy was under attack not because it went too far in this respect but because it was thought too negative. As a matter of established policy, then, no area adjoining the Soviet Empire was held to be strategically nonvital; any addition to the territory behind the Iron Curtain would threaten to upset an already precarious world balance of power.

In the second place, the United States was vitally interested in proving to its European Allies that they could rely on American military assistance in case of a Soviet attack. NATO, this country's main bulwark against the threat from the East, was weakened by European fears of a resurgence of isolationism in this country. It was strongly felt, therefore, particularly by Secretary Acheson, that if South Korea were left at the mercy of the attacker, all of Russia's weak neighbors—and there were none but weak neighbors—would lose what confidence they had gradually gained that this country meant business when it promised to prevent further Soviet conquest.

As if this were not enough, there was a third reason for this country to be most seriously interested in not allowing a challenge by its number-one enemy to go without military response. The United States was engaged in a vast and strenuous effort to unite the entire free world in a common effort of defense against the Soviet and Communist menace. From most countries, particularly in Asia, it had not succeeded in obtaining commitments of mutual assistance of the kind customarily laid down in treaties of bilateral or multilateral alliance. Therefore, all other non-Communist countries were committed to common defense against Communist aggression only if they could be made to accept the United Nations Charter as such a commitment. Consequently, from the point of view of American security policy, it was of paramount importance that the United Nations be made to serve as a substitute for a formal alliance of the free world. If there was any chance of achieving this result—and subsequent events showed how slim the chance was—it could only be done by demonstrating that under the Charter the United States considered itself committed to take up arms against the North Korean aggressor.

If it be correct, then, to assert that strong American national interests, other than an interest in collective security, pointed in the direction of intervention in Korea, certain conclusions can be drawn concerning the character of this action. In order to avoid misconceptions, certain other conclusions which do not follow from what has been said must also be mentioned.

In the first place, because the resort to violence against North

Korea served to maintain and in fact to strengthen this country's power position relative to its major national opponent, it cannot be considered the kind of break with tradition earlier defined as a prerequisite of effective collective security. However, this does not mean that the Korean action did not represent a drastic change—or call it a break—in United States policy. This country demonstrated its intent to stop Soviet and satellite aggression everywhere, thereby identifying its interests with those of the entire non-Communist world. This is a far cry from earlier isolationist policies which sought national security in withdrawal from areas of conflict. Moreover, the fact that American security interests were at stake does not prove that the Administration or the public would have considered them sufficiently vital to warrant a resort to force if defense of these interests had not coincided with the assertion of the principle of United Nations police action against aggression. Faith in this principle may at least help to explain the almost unanimous support Mr. Truman received at the start of the war.

In the second place, despite the popularity which collective security undoubtedly enjoyed in 1950 and may still enjoy, American military action against a member of the Soviet bloc cannot be taken as evidence that this country would be prepared to follow the same road in the case of an aggressor who was not a member of the Soviet bloc, or in a particular instance, had attacked a member of that bloc. Here the national interest as traditionally understood and the interest in collective security would not coincide; instead, they might run directly counter to each other. One cannot help wondering whether the United States would resort to the same measures if at some future date a Syngman Rhee were declared the aggressor, though only the future can provide a definite answer.

It follows, then, that Korea has not established the practicability or reality of collective security in the sense in which the term is used here. Instead of being a case of nations fighting "any aggressor anywhere" and for no other purpose than to punish aggression and to deter potential aggressors, intervention in Korea was an act of collective military defense against the recognized number-one enemy of the United States and of all the countries which associated themselves with its action. If would-be aggressors have reached the same conclusion, they will not be deterred by the Korean War unless they belong to the Soviet bloc.

This is disheartening news to those who have placed their faith in deterrence through collective security, unless they should believe that aggression by non-Communist countries is out of the question anyway. Disappointment of the high hopes placed on the "first experiment in collective security" should be weighed, however, against possible advantages accruing to this country for not having committed itself by precedent to fight all aggressors everywhere.

While it will always remain a matter of controversy whether a certain commitment or course of action is or is not in the national interest, one may assume wide agreement on the proposition that in the present circumstances this country cannot afford to jeopardize seriously its ability to balance the power of the Soviet bloc. If this be so, any military action against an aggressor would run counter to the elementary rules of prudence if it threatened to tip the balance in favor of the Soviets. It need not do so in the case of every non-Communist aggressor. One can imagine cases of aggression by a non-Communist country against another non-Communist country in which this country would have more to lose from allowing such aggression to be successful than from weakening and antagonizing the aggressor and his friends. In some instances there might be grave danger in allowing violence to continue and spread. But it needs little imagination to see how rare the cases are likely to be in which military intervention against a non-Communist country would favor this country's security position in the Cold War. One need only think of the disastrous consequences which might follow from a resort to force against, say, one of the Arab countries, or against Yugoslavia, or against a member of NATO. These consequences would be particularly grave if a large part of American military strength had to be diverted to such an operation.

A commitment to intervene would be most serious if a non-Communist country launched an attack on a member of the Soviet bloc. While it is to be hoped that this will remain a theoretical contingency, recent fears about Syngman Rhee's intentions and French fears that the West Germans might set out some day to unify their country by force, indicate why it must be taken into consideration. Police action in such instances would necessarily favor the Soviet bloc if it did not lead to Soviet expansion; it would be hard for the United States to remain on the sidelines while one of its erstwhile allies was being defeated by Communist "police" forces. In the present situation, in which this country and the other members of the free world are having the greatest trouble mustering enough strength for their defense against the East, how could their statesmen risk destroying what non-Communist solidarity and common defense positions now exist, even if in doing so they were serving the cause of collective security and future deterrence?

This does not answer the moral question. Some insist that it is the duty of nations to participate in police action because peace and the establishment of the rule of law in the world require that aggressors be stopped or punished. This means placing higher value on such punishment than on national self-defense whenever the two conflict. Against this view it can be argued on moral grounds that when, as today, everything the American people and most free peoples cherish, from independence to their way of life, is in grave danger of Soviet and Communist attack, precedence must be given to the defense of these values. After all, even staunch supporters of collective security are apt to draw a line somewhere beyond which nations cannot be expected to go in their devotion to the cause of police action; they will not expect them to commit national suicide for the sake of serving the long-run interests of the world community. Why not ? ✓

But what about world public opinion? Will people abroad not be shocked to learn that the United States cannot be counted upon to use force against all aggressors, Communist or non-Communist, and will this not make enemies for this country? Where the public stands on this issue is a matter of conjecture. Experience during the Korean War may be revealing, however. This country was given almost unanimous and in most cases enthusiastic moral support by articulate opinion throughout the non-Communist world when it first took up arms to stop the North Koreans. Yet, when the question of taking more forceful action against Red China arose, after that country had been declared an aggressor, condemnation of any such "adventurous" or "militaristic" move was hardly less widespread. Liberal opinion—which had always been most keen to see collective security applied—was now most vigorously opposed to any extension of the war. The reason for this apparent inconsistency is not hard to discover. Punishment of an aggressor is desired but not if it means plunging the nation into a major war, in this case a world war, not even perhaps if it means gravely endangering the immediate security of the nation. "Before the great powers can join in sacrifices of blood and treasure to keep the peace in regions where they have no real interest," wrote Samuel Flagg Bemis prior to the Korean War, "a great transformation of will must take place among the peoples of the nations." This would still seem to hold true, more so, of course, where intervention runs directly counter to these "real interests." Thus, however tempting a system of collective security may appear in the abstract, its implementation in the case of aggressors of considerable military power runs into serious objections on the grounds of morality as well as of procedure.

If it is doubtful, to say the least, whether this country will intervene against any aggressor anywhere, serious disadvantages will accrue to it if the popular label of "collective security" is applied to United States foreign policy. There is first the danger of future disillusionment. There has been some already, because Red China, found guilty of aggression by the United Nations, did not receive the same punishment as North Korea, the weaker country. If the expectation takes root that American military forces will be available against any aggressor anywhere and if in some future instance this expectation is disappointed, the bitterness of the victim of an attack and its friends might have embarrassing consequences.

A second disadvantage has also been borne out by the events. If the American people are made to believe that this country involved itself in a costly and in many ways inconclusive war for no other interest than to serve the cause of collective security, is it surprising that there is resentment against other members of the United Nations who failed to live up to a principle to which they were no less committed than the United States? Such criticism of our friends and allies may be silenced if it is understood that this country in fact did have what were then considered to be very pressing national interests in stopping the North Koreans. It will also be better appreciated that some of the other members of the United Nations, including India, went quite far in backing the United Nations when, in disregard of what they believed to be their interest in neutrality, they voted to authorize the actions of the United States and its associates and to condemn the North Koreans and Chinese as aggressors.

It may be objected that if Korea has not opened the way for a universal system of collective security against all aggression, it has merely served to demonstrate once more the tragic hold that "power politics" has on the nations even of the free world. The United Nations as a security organization, it will be said, can have no place in such a world. However, such conclusions are not warranted. The United States and its associates made good on a policy of "collective defense of the free world" carried out under the authority and control of the United Nations. While the control was weak, it nevertheless brought a restraining influence to bear on one of the world's greatest powers engaged in a bitter and costly defensive struggle. The one great contribution to the development of more lawful conditions in the world which this country can claim to have made in Korea consists therefore in its willingness to recognize the authority of the United Nations over actions which required sacrifices mainly from the American people. If some deplore the way in which the majority in the General Assembly exercised this control, believing that it would have been better for this country and the free world to have fought for victory at all costs, they give testimony thereby to the price countries may have to pay for the advantages of having collective defense operate according to the rules and with the approval of an international organization.

As to the United Nations itself, it has gained stature by the fact of having been able to be useful to the free world in its defense against

Communist aggression without having to give up its universal character and its mediatory potentialities. Obviously, its role has been a more modest one than that contemplated by the exponents of collective security. Instead of being able to order the bulk of its members to fight aggressors, whatever their relations to the aggressor, all the United Nations could do was to name the aggressor, to authorize and recommend action by its members, to lend its name to their action, and to seek to exert influence on the way it was carried out and terminated. This is exactly the role which would fall to the United Nations in cases in which collective self-defense was carried out under Article 51 and preceded action by the Security Council. The similarity is not accidental. If nations will resort to force only against national opponents when it accords with their national defense interests, as was true in Korea, the United Nations must limit itself to functions which are consistent with the needs of collective defense of likeminded countries. This has now been shown to be a practical and beneficial way of using an organization which, it should be added, has many important tasks to perform other than to stop or punish aggression.

10. UNITED NATIONS USE OF MILITARY FORCE

By INIS L. CLAUDE, JR.

THERE are two possible ways of approaching the question of the purposes of the United Nations. One is to concentrate on the Charter—to treat this formal constitutional document as an authoritative and meaningful expression of the goals which the world organization seeks to achieve and toward which it must be presumed to be working. The Charter, of course, was not handed down from on high, but was formulated by states. Thus, this approach appears to suggest that the Charter was, in 1945, a valid statement of a real consensus among the original members as to what the UN should be and do. As for the present, it suggests that the same conception of the UN is held by the expanded membership of the organization—that the consensus has been widened but not substantively altered—or, alternatively, that the UN is an entity sufficiently autonomous to function in accordance with the original consensus, whether or not that consensus, or *any* consensus, still prevails among its members.

The second approach is to focus upon the political interests and purposes of the members of the UN—to proceed upon the assumption that the words of the Charter are less determinative than the policies of the states. Following this approach, we may expect to find that the purposes of the organization are not fixed, but are continuously redefined as states develop new agreements among themselves as to what ends they wish or expect the UN to serve. Moreover, we may expect to find that the organization's purposes are as ambiguous as they are mutable, for it is altogether unlikely that the members have ever been, are now, or ever will be in full agreement concerning the uses to which this international instrument should be put. In these terms, the explorer of the UN's purpose must wrestle with change and conflict, renouncing the expectation of finding the purposes of the organization conveniently spelled out for him.

Reprinted by permission of the author and *The Journal of Conflict Resolution,* VII, 117-129.

Adopting the first course, we may ask what the Charter says with respect to the use of military force. What are the purposes to which 51 states ostensibly subscribed in 1945 and which they, along with 59 additional states, now purport to regard as appropriate and acceptable? The UN is intended to discourage the irresponsible, national use of military force—aggression, in short. It recognizes the legitimacy of defensive action by victims of attack and by other states which may wish to join in that reaction to aggression, but it undertakes to make such defense unnecessary by making offensive action unlikely. In a variety of ways, the UN undertakes to prevent aggression. Its purpose is to deprive states of anything to fight *about*—by inhibiting the development of, and promoting the elimination of, conditions that might make for conflict, and by facilitating the settlement of difficulties that have reached the critical "dispute" stage. By promoting disarmament negotiations, the organization expresses the urge to deprive themselves and each other of anything to fight *with*. Thus far, this analysis suggests that the UN is concerned with the use of force by states, acting on their own. The Charter goes on, however, to say something about the use of force by the UN, or, more accurately, by states acting under its auspices. The two subjects are closely interrelated; provisions calling for the use of force by or on behalf of the UN are integral parts of the scheme for inhibiting aggressive national action and thereby reducing the necessity for individual or collective defensive action. The Charter purports to classify the national use of force under three headings: that which is required, that which is prohibited, and that which is permitted. Insofar as it requires members to provide coercive support for the world organization, the Charter adopts the view that the responsible use of force for international purposes is the ultimate antidote for the irresponsible use of force for national purposes.

The Charter does not in fact go very far in this direction. It pays lip service to the ideal of erecting a collective security system, which would promise to cope with any prohibited use of force by invoking the requirement of collective resistance. But it does not attempt to provide for the actual creation or operation of such a system. At most, it contains a plan for developing a system under which the UN may mobilize collective action against *minor* aggressors in circumstances which find the major powers unanimously disposed to support or at least to tolerate such action. The crucial provisions pertinent to this scheme, Articles 43 and 45, which contemplate agreements on military contingents to be placed at the disposal of the Security Council by states, have become dead letters but have not been formally erased. The Charter does *not,* it should be emphasized, either provide or promise a system for UN action or UN-sponsored action to repress aggression launched or supported by any of the major powers. The famous veto clause of Article 27 expresses the founding fathers' rejection of the attempt to require member states to join forces under the UN banner for resistance to great-power aggression; the "individual or collective self-defense" clause of Article 51, a permissive clause, expresses the judgment of the founding fathers as to what can and must be done under such circumstances. The Charter, in short, prohibits but does not proport to prevent the most dangerous sort of aggression—that undertaken by or under the auspices of a major power.

We might summarize this reading of the Charter by saying that it speaks much more decisively about the use of force by the UN. The purpose of the UN is to discourage the irresponsible, disruptive use of force by states. The organization itself is to use, or to sponsor the use of, force only when—or if—the great powers concur in the implementation of Articles 43 and 45 and subsequently in Security Council decisions regarding particular cases.

Shifting to the second of the approaches to analysis of the purposes of the UN discussed at the beginning, which stresses the policies of states rather than the words of the Charter, one may express doubt as to whether the statesmen who drafted the Charter were as unanimously and as unreservedly dedicated to the creation of an effective peace-preserving organization as they said they were. Equally, one may doubt whether the purposes stated in the Charter are in fact the purposes which all or most member states now wish the UN to pursue and hope that it may realize. There is conflict over the purposes for which the organization is to be used—conflict deriving not from differing interpretations of the Charter but from differing national interests, or conceptions of national interests.

There is no difficulty in securing general condemnation of aggression in the abstract, and agreement that the UN should discourage, if not effectively prevent or suppress, aggression. In concrete terms, however, one state's aggression is always another state's "legitimate use of force to defend vital national interests." What states really want is the imposition of effective international restraint upon the military ventures of "others," not of themselves or of states intimately associated with themselves. It can hardly be imagined that the Soviet Union wishes the UN to be capable of inhibiting Communist conquest of Laos. India presumably does not regret that the organization failed to protect Goa against Indian invasion. The United Arab Republic does not aspire to make the UN an effective guarantor of the integrity of Israel. The United States would have limited enthusiasm for the project of making the UN a bulwark against any possible American attack upon Cuba. With respect to its own resorts to force, actual or potential, every state wants to secure at least the tolerance of the UN, even better the blessing of the UN, and at best such substantial support and reinforcement as the organization might provide.

States vary, of course, in their ability and disposition to use force for the promotion or protection of their interests as they see them. They vary also in the degree to which they conceive their interests as compatible with a stable world order in which respect for the territorial integrity and political independence of all states is enshrined and effectuated as a basic principle. I would argue, for instance, that Washington's view of the national interest of the United States is much more compatible with and conductive to that kind of global system than Moscow's view of the interests and purposes which Soviet policy is to serve. I do not suggest that all states are equally bellicose and aggressive. Nevertheless, it seems to me quite clear that every state has to contemplate the possibility that it might, under some circumstances, feel impelled to take military action that would seem to it absolutely necessary for the protection of vital national interests but might not be regarded as legitimate by the political organs of the UN. States *do* contemplate this possibility; consequently, they do not genuinely commit themselves without reservation to the proposition that they will never resort to force in the face of international disapproval expressed through the UN; consequently, they are not ultimately dedicated to the purpose of enabling the UN—that is, its member states—to control the unilateral resort to military action by any and all states, including themselves.

If I am correct in attributing this attitude to states, then it follows that states must have reservations about conferring upon the UN an extensive legal competence and actual capability to exercise a coercive function. One does not fully endorse the principle of the international use of force unless one fully repudiates the policy of the national use of force, for it must be presumed that a militarily effective UN might frustrate one's state in its efforts to safeguard its vital interests—interests which the state may regard as justifying the national use of force but which a sufficient number of the members of a UN political organ might not so regard.

I submit that this is the actual situation today. We must resist the temptation to take too seriously the simple proposition that the world is divided into two groups of states, one of which (including, most prominently, the Soviet Union) opposes the strengthening of the UN, and the other of which (led by the United States) favors the development of that organization as an international repository of coercive authority and power.

It is easy enough to demonstrate that the Soviets oppose that development. It is perhaps less self-evident that the United States does not favor that development. I would argue, however, that the record shows that the United States favors a UN which can give permissive endorsement and lend moral and perhaps more tangible varieties of support to military actions which we regard as necessary and legitimate; I look in vain for evidence that the United States wishes to equip the UN with either the formal competence or the effective capability to prevent this country and its allies from fighting whenever we may feel it necessary to fight, or to require us to fight when we are not disposed to do so. In the case of Korea, the UN gave an international blessing to, and stimulated the mobilization of multilateral support for, a military reaction to Communist aggression which we felt impelled to undertake. We valued this marginal assistance, and attempted, in the Uniting for Peace plan, to maximize the possibility that such international aid might be rendered to upholders of similarly worthy causes in the future. This was, however, a far cry from endorsing the actual creation of, or expressing the willingness to accept the onerous obligations of, a full-fledged collective security system. The United States has subsequently supported the quasi-military interventions of the UN in the Middle East and the Congo, but these can hardly be characterized as manifestations of, or even as preliminary approaches to, the establishment of a UN capacity to use international military force to squelch illicit national resorts to force.

It might be noted that the United States has, since 1960, stated for the public international record that it regards an effective international coercive mechanism as an essential part of a world system characterized by general and complete disarmament. Perhaps I may be forgiven if I choose to treat this more as an exercise in logic than as a statement of policy. It seems to say that the United States advocates the establishment of a world government—but it should be noted that President Kennedy, in his State of the Union address in January, 1962, described our goal for the future as "a peaceful world community of free and independent states" or "a free community of nations, independent but interdependent" (Kennedy, 1962, pp. 159, 163). Moreover, another spokesman for the Administration declared that: "The ultimate question at issue is whether this small planet is to be organized on the principles of the Communist bloc or on the basis of voluntary cooperation among independent nation-states. . . . We expect this planet to organize itself in time on the principles of voluntary cooperation among independent nation-states . . ." (Rostow, 1962, pp. 835-838). These statements seem to belie the proposition that American policy is dedicated to the creation of a global governmental authority entrusted with supreme coercive power. In any case, the completely disarmed world to which this proposition is linked is not our world. In dealing with the world as it is, and with the UN as it is and seems to be becoming, the United States betrays little enthusiasm for making the use of military force by the UN the central element in plans for the safeguarding of American security and the maintenance of world peace.

The purpose of this paper is not to speculate what the world would be like if it were utterly different from what it is. Focusing on the existing situation and the existing global institution, let us ask what role can reasonably be assigned to the UN in the military-security field.

First, there is the question of the possible use of the UN as a military instrument for dealing with great-power aggression; in our terms, this refers to the possibility of the organization's serving as a defensive bulwark against aggressive action launched by, or supported by, the Soviet Union or Communist China. My response to this is quite negative. We rely, quite properly in my judgment, upon our national power and our alliances for security against this threat. The UN was not designed to cope with this sort of problem, and I see no point in criticizing the organization for not doing what it was not supposed to do, or in regretting its inability to do what it was, from the start, constitutionally debarred from attempting to do. Nor do I see any point in trying to transform the UN into an organization appropriate for this role. The UN is not a NATO, and if we undertake to make it a kind of super-NATO, we may sacrifice its values as a global institution without in fact succeeding in making it a valuable free-world institution. We need not choose between global and free-world organizations. We have both kinds, and we need both kinds, to perform different types of functions. If NATO is defective, the answer is to improve NATO, not to attempt to convert the UN into a NATO-like institution.

I am arguing, in short, that the task of providing a military deterrent against Communist expansionism is a task for a coalition of allies, not for a general international organization that includes Communist states and uncommitted states among its members. The usefulness, actual and potential, of the UN lies in other realms. Conceivably, of course, the UN may lend helpful support to the Western coalition, as it did in the case of Korea. We cannot count on this, however, given the increasing numerical strength of the uncommitted states in the UN. Moreover, I have serious doubts as to whether it would be, on balance, advantageous to the West to have the UN function as a reliable endorser of our position in contests with the Soviet bloc. Insofar as the UN habitually plays that role, it tends to take on the appearance of a pro-Western institution, thereby endangering its potential usefulness as neutral ground, or an impartial instrument, in the Cold War. I shall return to this point later.

Secondly, we might ask whether the UN has a significant capability for dealing militarily with clashes between states which lie outside the alignments of the Cold War and the spheres of interest of the major Cold War antagonists. This is precisely what the UN was intended to have, as is indicated by the plan for making national units available for use by the Security Council, stated in Article 43 of the Charter. The question, then, is whether this plan can or should be revived, or a different scheme be substituted for it. The outlook is not encouraging. The early negotiations regarding the implementation of Article 43 indicated that neither the Western powers nor the Soviet Union trusted the other to participate loyally, without ulterior motives, in a collective UN force (Claude, 1962, pp. 175–190). Since this mutual distrust has become stronger rather than weaker, it seems perfectly evident that any anti-aggression force assembled by the UN would have to exclude units from the major powers and their most intimate allies. This observation suggests a major limiting factor— the persuasiveness of the Cold War. It is extremely difficult to conceive of an international conflict in our time which the Western and Soviet blocs would not regard as at least potentially related to their competitive struggle; in virtually any case that can readily be imagined, UN military action against an aggressive state would be likely to evoke conflicting reactions from the Soviet Union and the United States. Even though these powers might be excluded from participation in the action, they might well find themselves at odds concerning the propriety of the action, the identity of aggressor and victim, and the nature of the political result which the UN should endeavor to promote. The world is too small to provide a wide zone of indifference between the major contestants. In short, an attempt by the UN to deal coercively with almost any conflict would probably be assimilated to an attempt to deal coercively with great-power struggles.

Thus, I see little scope for UN military action in defending one small state divorced from Cold War blocs against another one. Moreover, I see little evidence that the neutralist members of the UN are prepared to institute and effectuate a collective security arrangement among themselves, even assuming that the major powers would be willing to stand dispassionately aside. I would not be willing to advise the leader of any state to base his security policy upon the expectation that a UN force might be mobilized to defend his country against aggression.

What if the UN were equipped with a permanent military force of its own, a force designed to defeat aggressors, and thus ceased to be dependent upon the willingness of states to contribute, or to permit others to contribute, military contingents for UN actions? This possibility seems to me to have no relevance to the problem of restraining great powers. Military power must rest upon a base—a territorial, demographic, social, political, economic, industrial, scientific base. The only base capable of producing and sustaining a military establishment able to match that of a great power is another great power. Concretely, only the United States—or, more broadly, the Western coalition—is able to generate the force required to balance that possessed by the Sino-Soviet bloc. The United States, or the Western coalition, might be rechristened the United Nations, but the change would be both literally and figuratively nominal. The UN is not a New World which can be called in to redress the balance of the old.

Might such a UN force be relevant to the problem of restraining minor aggressors? Possibly—but let us note again how little is really changed by the device of switching from national contingents to an international military organization. Assume that enlistments from major powers are forbidden, so that the question of the force's being internally subverted to the service of one or another of the major powers does not arise. Nevertheless, the critical political issues remain: Who will control the force? Against what state will it be used in a given situation? For what purpose will it fight? Toward what political result will it press? Neither great nor small powers will be indifferent to such issues, or be satisfied with the simple-minded answer that the UN will exercise policy direction and will use the force to achieve the purposes stipulated in the Charter. The retort to this answer is, of course, that the UN is owned and operated by states. Which states will control the UN policy organs that direct the force? The documentary purposes of the Charter are less important than the political purposes of the states which dominate the policy process. There is nothing in the nature of an international military force that makes its use a less contentious issue in a world of political conflict than the use of an assemblage of national units.

More generally, I think we must be on guard against the illusion that a UN fighting force would somehow enable us to escape from national states—from their quarrels and conflicting policies and purposes, from their power. As I have suggested, such a force would not be any less an instrument of states for being labeled an instrument of the UN, for states constitute the UN and their rivalries permeate the policy process of the organization. Moreover, a force which is sustained by the UN is in fact dependent upon states for its sustenance. This is true not only in the general sense that financial support of the UN and its various activities is derived predominantly from states, but also in the more specific sense that the supplies and equipment necessary for transforming a group of men into an effective military unit must come from states. We are back again to the problem of the power base. An army without a country generates no more military power than a country without an army. A UN armed force must be based upon thin air unless it is grounded in dependence upon the very states over which it is supposed to exercise independent authority. Whatever power a UN force might wield would be, in effect, borrowed national power. This is to say that the establishment of a UN force for countering aggression would not in any real sense represent the creation of an autonomous central authority, emancipated from dependence upon the support and cooperation of states and able to function coercively without regard to the policies and attitudes of states.

It might be argued that, given the new technology of warfare, which enhances the significance of ready striking power, the problem of the power base has lost, or is losing, its importance. Thus, the UN might gain an impressive military status simply by acquiring a stock of missiles and nuclear warheads, without the necessity of developing the supportive foundations traditionally required by a military establishment. Leaving aside the question of the willingness of states to endow the UN with such a striking force, I think it is clear that this suggestion reflects an exaggerated notion as to the military significance of a finished and finite supply of weapons and delivery vehicles, divorced from the resources and facilities implicit in the concept of the power base. It relies upon a static conception of military force, at precisely the moment in history when military technology has become unprecedentedly dynamic, when the rate of obsolescence has been dramatically accelerated. The current arms race is not primarily a competition in quantitative accumulation, but in qualitative development of military means; national leaders are not intent upon expanding "over-kill" capacity, but upon keeping up or getting ahead in the quest for innovations that may alter the relative significance of existing weapons. In this setting a static UN striking force, inherently vulnerable because of the impossibility of maintaining secrecy concerning its vital details, would soon become a negligible factor in the global political-military situation. The problem of keeping the UN force up to date, thus eliminating its tendency toward diminishing significance, brings us right back to the issue of the power base.

Moreover, the project of equipping the UN with a self-contained nuclear striking force involves imposing upon the organization all the difficulties and dilemmas associated with the doctrine of massive retaliation. It would be ironical if the United States escaped from the snares of reliance upon massive retaliation, only to saddle the UN with that strategic concept. It is hardly credible that such a political body as the UN would resort to thermonuclear attack whenever international aggression occurred or threatened—or desirable that it should do so. An international military establishment designed to maintain peace and security would require military versatility, the capacity for flexible and graduated response, to the same degree that a major national force requires it. To assert this is to deny that the problem of the power base can be circumvented by providing the UN with a stock of ready-made instruments of thermonuclear destruction, and to reaffirm the dependence of the UN upon its member states. A permanent UN military force for combating aggression is not a substitute for the willing collaboration of states, but simply one of the possible vehicles for such collaboration.

Thus far, my position regarding the possibilities of the use of military force by the UN has been essentially negative. I do not see the task of organizing an effective defense against Soviet aggression as one which can appropriately be assigned to the United Nations. This is a function of a coalition—and of institutions which comprise those states that are willing to associate themselves with the coalition and to contribute whatever they can to its strength. I am doubtful that there is a major role for the UN to play in mobilizing power—whether by pulling together national military contingents or by operating a permanent armed force under its direct authority—for the suppression of aggression outside the framework of the Cold War struggle. What then, if anything, is left as a military function for the UN?

We might find some clues in a perusal of the record of the organization. I think we can set aside the Korean case. Here, the UN endorsed and encouraged joint action against Communist aggression, and came to be clearly associated with one side in what was obviously a major episode of the East-West conflict. The initial enthusiasm for putting the UN into this kind of role, so sharply at variance with the original conception of the UN expressed in the Charter, quickly died away. By the end of the Korean War, the UN was being pushed—by the United States, among other members—into the position of a third party, disengaged from the conflict. It has been vigorously pulled in that direction in subsequent years, as its neutralist members have grown in numbers and matured in their understanding that their neutralism would be violated and endangered if they adhered to an international organization that entered—and brought them with it—into the vortex of Cold War disputes. Korea was an aberration, the expression of an ephemeral urge to make the UN an instrument of collective security in cases falling well within the scope of the Cold War. There is little sentiment among members of the organization for reviving this conception of the UN's function, and it is doubtful that the West can realistically expect or usefully attempt to bring about a development of the UN along these functional lines.

More promising clues are to be found in the string of cases which have involved the use of military personnel under UN auspices for purposes other than doing battle with aggressors—for supervising truces, patrolling borders or armistice lines, observing the degree to which rival parties respect agreed arrangements for stabilizing their relationships, and the like. These cases include UN interventions in the Palestine and Kashmir cases, in Lebanon, and—most notably— in the Suez and Congo crises. These are peace-stabilizing, or peace-keeping, or peace-restoring operations, efforts to aid disputant states in the implementation of political resolves to avoid the outbreak or the renewal of military conflict; they are not measures for the international defeat of determined acts of aggression. We may take UNEF and the military operation in the Congo as the outstanding instances of this sort of UN enterprise.

The late Secretary-General of the UN, Dag Hammarskjöld, functoned in this realm not only as a man of action but also as a man of thought. Having responded to critical needs and grasped opportunities for making the UN significantly useful in emergency situations, by creative improvisation of the UNEF and Congo forces, he turned to the articulation of a most perceptive theoretical analysis of the international political role which the UN had thus assumed. Hammarskjöld's classic statement of what he chose to call the concept of "preventive diplomacy" is contained in his Introduction to the Annual Report submitted to the Fifteenth Session of the General Assembly in 1960 (Hammarskjöld, 1960).

In this essay, the Secretary-General brushed aside the idea that the UN could usefully or safely intervene in "problems which are clearly and definitely within the orbit of present day conflicts between power blocs." The effort to put the UN effectively into such situations would, he feared, be not only futile but dangerous as well—dangerous to the continuing usefulness of the organization in general and of its chief officer in particular. From this, he drew the conclusion that "the main field of useful activity of the United Nations in its efforts to prevent conflicts or to solve conflicts" should be defined as that of taking action to fill vacuums in areas of conflict outside of, or marginal to, the zones already clearly involved in the Cold War struggle, so as to minimize the tendency of—or to diminish the incentive for—great powers to move competitively into those situations. Thus, he hoped that the organization might prevent the widening and aggravation of the bloc conflicts. In these terms, the major political potentiality of the UN is to promote the stabilization of the Cold War, to help the great powers avoid or back away from confrontations that might have disastrous results for themselves and all the rest of the world. It is evident that Hammarskjöld was not engaging in armchair theorizing, but was stating an interpretation of what the UN had been doing, and was doing, in the Middle East and the Congo, and was projecting this same role into the future.

Two points are crucial to the theory of preventive diplomacy:

1. The kind of operation which is envisaged, designed to seal off a zone of trouble from the competitive intrusions of the East and the West, is dependent upon the active or the passive consent of both the major contestants in the Cold War. Hammarskjöld acknowledged this—perhaps not quite explicitly—when he described the UN's role as that of "providing for solutions whenever the interests of all parties in a localization of conflict can be mobilized in favour of its efforts." He hoped that the major powers would tolerate or even support UN ventures in preventive diplomacy because each would recognize its own interest in avoiding new confrontations that might disrupt their delicate relationships. The theory rests upon the assumption that conflict of interest breeds a limited community of interest, particularly in the thermonuclear era. Rival parties have a common interest in preventing their conflict from degenerating into uncontrollable violence. This common interest does not suggest that the conflict is unreal, or is not fundamental and deep-seated, or is diminishing in intensity. Quite to the contrary, it arises precisely because the conflict is a basic one; the community or mutuality of interest is a function of the intensity of the conflict of interest.

It is one thing to assert that the United States and the Soviet Union both *have* a stake in the avoidance of a military showdown, and thus in the encouragement of preventive diplomacy by the UN. It is another thing to assume that both great powers are *aware* of this common interest and prepared to act on the basis of that awareness. Putting Hammarskjöld's point negatively, we can say that the UN cannot hope to develop the function of preventive diplomacy successfully if the major powers do not share the conviction that their own interests would be served thereby. A UNEF or ONUC intervention is something that the UN can do *for* the great powers; it is not something that the UN can reliably do *against* the great powers, or either of them.

This immediately limits the field. It should be recalled that Hammarskjöld spoke of the possibilities of preventive diplomacy in areas *outside* of, or *marginal* to, the well-defined zones of the Cold War. He assumed, realistically, that neither of the major antagonists would look favorably upon UN intervention of the type under discussion within its own sphere of influence. Preventive diplomacy is applicable to the no-man's-land of the Cold War, the in-between area where both contestants may, on grounds of self-interest, give greater weight to the value of avoiding mutual confrontation than to the hope of winning a competitive encounter.

2. The function of preventive diplomacy is essentially *neutralist* in

character. It does not involve neutral mediation in disputes and conflicts between the Cold War blocs—that is also an important political
potentiality of the UN, but it falls under a different heading, and it
calls for diplomatic or legal techniques rather than military or quasi-
military instrumentalities. Rather, preventive diplomacy as such
involves neutral interposition between contestants, using military personnel under UN direction as agents for achieving the neutralization
of a trouble spot—i.e., for insulating the area against the intrusion of
Cold War competition.

Preventive diplomacy is neutralist in method as well as design. It
promises to fill a vacuum with forces contributed by relatively uncommitted states; note that the exclusion of military units from the
major powers or the states most intimately aligned with them has
been a cardinal principle in the constitution of UNEF and ONUC.
Thus, it treats neutralist states as the members of the organization
uniquely eligible for service as agents of the UN in the performance
of its neutralizing function. Preventive diplomacy provides the relatively uncommitted states (I use the qualification in recognition that
neutralism is never absolute) with an opportunity and a challenge to
make their neutralism positive and constructive; it invites them to use
their limited military forces, on behalf of the UN, to do something for
the great powers that the latter could not do for themselves, and
thereby to promote their own interest in the survival of civilization.
Preventive diplomacy, in short, places the major active responsibility
for the military function of the UN upon the smaller and less involved
states. The great powers must *permit* the UN to play the neutral role;
the states that stand most aloof from Cold War alignments must
enable the UN to play that role.

It might be argued that the UN should develop, for the performance of this role, a standing international force, conceived as a continuously available UNEF, an instrument of preventive diplomacy
rather than an army dedicated to the defeat of aggressors. Thus
equipped, the organization would presumably be emancipated from
dependence upon the uncertain willingness of neutralist states to provide units for exercises in preventive diplomacy. I am not convinced
that such a development is either necessary or desirable. Thus far,
the record indicates an impressive willingness on the part of the uncommitted states to do the jobs which preventive diplomacy requires
of them. Moreover, there is substantial doubt that a standing international force would necessarily turn out to be the most appropriate
or most acceptable instrument for dealing with particular cases that
might arise; it may be that every case will be so distinctive as to require a tailor-made UN force. In practical terms, a permanent force
might be inordinately expensive, given the budgetary realities of the

UN. In any case, I suggest that the UN will be able to carry out successful operations of preventive diplomacy only if and when there is wide-spread willingness among its uncommitted members to undertake the military burden, and there is little point in attempting to evade the implications of this reality.

Up to this point, at least, the major difficulty has had to do not with the willingness of neutralist states to serve, but with the willingness of the great powers to be served. The problem of securing the necessary consent of the great antagonists is intimately connected with the issue of the neutral character of the UN in its practice of preventive diplomacy. The great powers will tolerate or support UN action in this realm only if they *want* the neutralization of a given trouble spot and if they *believe* in the neutral character of the UN's activity.

Let us look first at the question of the will of the great powers. In the major cases that have arisen—UNEF and ONUC—the United States has welcomed neutralization. The American stake in the avoidance of new confrontations that might disturb the Cold War situation has been amply recognized. Nevertheless, it is not all clear that either our public or our government is prepared to accept the general proposition that the UN can best serve us—or the world—by operating as a neutral force in global politics. We have valued the UN primarily as an instrument whereby Western victories have been won—or, at least, as a stage upon which Western triumphs have been enacted—and it is not easy to shift to the view that its value to us may be increased as our control over its operations diminishes. Yet, the point stands that the United States has approved and supported the neutralizing function of the UN in the Middle East and Congo cases.

The attitude of the Soviet Union has been different. In the case of UNEF, Soviet disapproval has taken the mild form of passive opposition—refusal to contribute financial support. One might make a case that this is really passive acquiescence. The Congo, of course, makes a much more interesting story. Why did the Soviet Union, after initially supporting the Congo operation, turn against it? A plausible answer is that the USSR did not want the UN to achieve the neutralization of the Congo, but preferred to have a free hand in undertaking to achieve the Communization of the Congo. The Soviet Union supported the UN initiative in the hope that it would contribute to the de-Westernization of the Congo—notably by ousting the Belgians—and then moved to enter its own Soviet elements into the situation. This analysis would suggest that the Soviets did not want to avoid the intrusion of the Cold War competition into the Congo, but welcomed such a competition in the expectation that they would win.

The second problem is that of great-power confidence in the impartial character of the UN: can the organization be trusted to function neutrally in the no-man's-land of the Cold War? The experience of the United States presents no difficulties for us. With considerable reason, we have normally regarded the UN as a pro-Western institution; at worst, it has appeared to function, or to be likely to function, neutrally. Again, the Soviet case is quite different. Starting with a deep-rooted conviction that it confronts a hostile world, the Soviet Union has had a virtually unrelieved experience as a perpetual minority in the UN; from the Soviet vantage point, the UN might, at best —but most improbably—function with genuine impartiality as between East and West. Note that the constant theme of the Soviet attack upon the conduct of the Congo operation is that the ONUC is only spuriously neutral, that the whole affair represents the prostitution of the UN to the service of the Western powers. I am in no position to judge the sincerity of the Soviet assertions, although I must admit to some difficulty in believing that a Russian would not have serious doubts about the impartiality of the UN. We have not helped matters by our inveterate declarations that the UN does, and assertions that it should, serve the anti-Soviet cause—interspersed occasionally with appeals to the Soviets to recognize the "obvious" fact that the UN presides with majestic impartiality over the affairs of all the nations.

Indeed, the Soviets are not alone in interpreting the Congo operation as a move favorable to the West. Note what Ambassador Adlai Stevenson said in an address at Hofstra College on June 5, 1961:

> The Belgian withdrawal was followed by anarchy with which on the one hand the Belgians stepped back and on the other the Russians began to step in. In these circumstances, any direct intervention by the West would have been interpreted as an attempt to reimpose colonialism. Local opinion would have swung over to support the Communists, and the West would have been left in the impossible position of fighting a guerrilla war against a background of implacable local hostility . . . direct Western interventions tend of their very nature to produce a revulsion of local feeling which threatens the effectiveness of the intervention. . . . The result is that in situations such as the Congo, the Western World would be almost powerless if there were no United Nations force available to restore order, [and] check a takeover by an outside power. . . . Direct Western action would only hasten a communist takeover.

Mr. Stevenson went on to say explicitly that the UN had frustrated the Soviet plan to establish control over the Congo, and that the UN is "the only instrument by which the end of the Western system of colonialism can be prevented from opening the doors to the new imperialism of the East" (Stevenson, 1961, p. 70).

I do not mean to be critical of the UN's giving the West a victory which, according to Mr. Stevenson, the West could not have won for itself. My point is that if an official American spokesman can regard the UN's Congo operation as an intervention justified less by its helping both blocs to avoid the dangers of a confrontation than by its helping the West to contain the expansionist thrust of the Communist bloc, it is plausible that a Soviet spokesman should regard the operation as an instance of unneutral, pro-Western, UN activity. Moreover, if we regard the Congo action as a defeat inflicted by the UN upon the Soviet Union, it hardly makes sense for us to expect that the Soviets will refrain from opposing that action, or will help to pay for it, or will be inspired to assist in equipping the UN to act similarly in future contingencies.

The Congo operation has not yet been concluded, although it now appears likely to be brought to a successful conclusion. This possibility might be taken as an indication that preventive diplomacy can, after all, be effectively performed in the face of great-power opposition. Perhaps the Soviet attack upon the operation was never as determined as it was made to appear, or the Soviet hostility was mollified by the alterations of UN policy and personnel which occurred in the course of the operation. In any event, the Soviet Union refrained from carrying out the threat to wreck the organization because of its activity in the Congo. While the outcome of the Congo case may suggest the wisdom of testing the limits of Soviet toleration for operations of this kind, rather than surrendering to announced opposition, it ought not to stimulate the confident assumption that the UN can be regularly used to carry out the function of preventive diplomacy, with or without the support or acquiescence of such a power as the Soviet Union. The extreme difficulties which the Soviet reaction against the Congo operation posed, and the grave risks which the UN encountered in conducting that operation under the political circumstances which developed, should be taken as a warning against adopting that assumption. Regardless of the outcome of the Congo case, it seems, on balance, to confirm the general proposition that the UN can effectively perform the quasi-military role attributed to it under the theory of preventive diplomacy only if, and insofar as, the major powers are impelled by their perceptions of their own interests to welcome UN interposition as a means of helping them to avoid dangerous confrontations, and are convinced that the UN can be relied upon to act in a neutral manner in the exercise of this function.

It appears that the only significant military function which may reasonably be attributed to the UN is that suggested by the theory of preventive diplomacy—the conduct of operations, analogous to UNEF and ONUC, designed to assist the great powers in keeping the Cold War cold. This can be done for the great powers only if they are agreed in wanting it to be done, and only if each of them is confident that the UN will genuinely promote the neutralization of trouble spots, not act in the interest of the other. The outlook for the continuation and development of this role by the UN is discouraging, primarily because of the disaffection of the USSR. If the Soviet Union is not persuaded that it has more to gain from the containment of the Cold War, the prevention of its spreading into new and dangerously explosive situations, than from the waging of the Cold War competition wherever it may spread—and if the Soviet Union is not persuaded that the UN is capable of serving with genuine neutrality as an agent of preventive diplomacy—then it seems to me that it is a major task of American policy, inside and outside of the UN, to promote these convictions on the part of the Soviet Union. If the United States and the Soviet Union can join in accepting and even in valuing the performance of this role by the UN, it seems to me that the organization may contribute significantly to the stabilization of the global situation. If they cannot, the UN may yet contribute valuable services in other realms, but I see no important role for it with respect to the use of military force under international auspices.

REFERENCES

Claude, Inis L., Jr. *Power and International Relations.* New York: Random House, 1962. [See page 215.]

Hammarskjöld, Dag. Introduction to the Annual Report of the Secretary General on the Work of the Organization, 16 June 1959–15 June 1960. General Assembly, Official Records: Fifteenth Session, Supplement No. 1A, United Nations, New York, 1960.

Kennedy, John F. "The State of the Union," *Department of State Bulletin,* 46 (1962), 159-63.

Rostow, Walt W. "The Domestic Base of Foreign Policy," *ibid.,* 46 (1962), 833-9.

Stevenson, Adlai E. "The United Nations, First Step Toward a World Under Law," *ibid.,* 45 (1961), 68-71.

11. CHINA, THE UNITED STATES, AND THE UNITED NATIONS

By LINCOLN P. BLOOMFIELD

I

LIKE a chronic sore that never quite cripples, hurts most of the time, and sometimes becomes dangerously inflamed, the issue of China in the United Nations has plagued United States policy for almost twenty years.

Since January 1950 when the Soviet Union demanded—unsuccessfully—that the Security Council eject the representative of Nationalist China, the question of which regime should represent the "Republic of China"—however that question was procedurally posed —has been an issue at every session of the General Assembly as well as every other UN body of which China is a member.[1]

To date Nationalist China has kept its hold on the Chinese seat. The votes on the Chinese representation issue at the 1966 General Assembly reflected a modest gain on the number of states unwilling to eject the Nationalist Chinese or to act by only a simple majority. Some African states, their eyes opening to the consequences of Chinese penetration, helped to stem what prior to 1966 resembled a steady trend. Fifteen of them voted against the Peking-in-Taipei-out proposal compared with nine in 1965. (The vote was 46 for, 57 against.)

Reprinted by permission of the author and *International Organization,* XX (No. 4, 1966), 653-676.

[1] Of a total of fourteen specialized agencies China is a member of twelve. The exceptions are the Food and Agriculture Organization (FAO), from which China withdrew in 1952, and the International Finance Corporation (IFC). Table 1 below lists the UN bodies which Peking could in theory be invited to join. (In addition, there is a "Chinese" seat in the Eighteen-Nation Disarmament Committee [ENDC].)

But in the Assembly—the bellwether for the Chinese issue[2]—pressures seemed to be actually mounting for a formula that would ultimately enable Peking to take a seat both there and in the Security Council.[3] Since France's decision in 1965 to recognize mainland China,[4] the United States has been the only Great Power supporting Nationalist China. In 1966 Canada and Italy took the initiative to move toward a "two China" solution. Both are close United States allies. If a resolution calling for the seating of Peking *and* the retention of Taipei were ever put forward, one can guess that a more authentic expression of international sentiment would then be registered.

Both the Vietnam war and the growing nuclear capability of Red China have reinforced the pressures to bring Peking in. U Thant has increasingly linked the issues of arms, war, and Chinese seating. In 1965 he said:

Both the Viet-Nam situation and the disarmament *impasse* point once again to the imperative need for the United Nations to achieve universality of membership as soon as possible.[5]

And a new voice was added to the dialogue when Pope Paul VI, addressing the General Assembly on October 4, 1965, urged that it

strive to bring back among you any who may have left you; consider

[2] The Assembly in 1950 adopted a resolution recommending "that the attitude adopted by the General Assembly . . . should be taken into account in other organs of the United Nations and in the specialized agencies." (General Assembly Resolution 396 [V], December 14, 1950.)

[3] Tables 2 and 3 give the record of the General Assembly voting on this issue and the changes therein.

[4] Table 4 below lists the countries recognizing both Chinas.

[5] "Introduction to the Annual Report of the Secretary-General on the Work of the Organization," *UN Monthly Chronicle*, October 1965 (Vol. 2, No. 9), p. 115.

The Secretary-General repeated the call for universality in the introduction to his 1965 annual report:

It is impossible, moreover, to view some of these outstanding problems —whether it is the position of the United Nations in regard to the crisis in South East Asia or the lack of progress in disarmament—without relating them to the fact the United Nations has not yet attained the goal of universality of membership. In the long run the Organization cannot be expected to function to full effect if one fourth of the human race is not allowed to participate in its deliberations. I know that there are serious political difficulties involved in correcting this situation; but I hope that the long-term advantages may be more clearly seen and the necessary adjustments made.

("Introduction to the Annual Report of the Secretary-General on the Work of the Organization," *UN Monthly Chronicle*, October 1966 [Vol. 3, No. 9, section I], p. 121.)

means of calling into your pact of brotherhood, in honour and
loyalty, those who do not yet share in it.[6]

Some observers believe a number of states—possibly including the
United States[7]—preferred to mark time on this issue in 1966 because
of the upheavals in Chinese internal leadership politics. What can be
reasonably predicted is that at some time within the foreseeable
future it is likely that a constitutional majority in the UN General
Assembly will vote to seat the representative of Peking. It may or
may not provide a way to retain under some label the representative
of the exile Chinese regime in Taiwan; some close observers of the
UN seem to believe that it will not.

If that happens, whatever the details, the fat will most assuredly
be in the fire. The United States, having staked its not inconsiderable
prestige since 1950 on keeping Red China out, would suffer a possibly bruising diplomatic defeat. Taiwan, a paramount symbol of
American protection, will urgently require a new status in international law and diplomacy if it is to survive as a political entity.
And assuming that the militant and fanatical leaders of China *do*
decide to accept the invitation—which is by no means certain—the
UN itself will undergo change and even grave crisis.

The United States has virtually exhausted its diplomatic capital on
this issue, and such moves as remain to it are drastic indeed. The
most extreme would be to threaten to withdraw from the United
Nations. While conceivable, particularly if Taiwan is ejected, this
does not appear rational when soberly weighed against the cost of
abandoning to the enemies of the United States the leading position
in a host of multilateral programs.

Less draconian would be the threat of withdrawing financial support, and one can predict substantial pressures to this end in Congress. Such action might give pause to some responsible governments
and even affect their vote. But it seems unlikely to be effective for
long, as UN programs or actions develop which it is in the American
interest to foster—and as others become impatient with what they
will construe as American blackmail to have its way on an unpopular
issue. Certainly in the light of the Article 19 fiasco it would seem
particularly inadvisable for the United States to threaten to withdraw
without meaning it. To have to back down from another untenable

---

[6] "Address of Pope Paul VI to the United Nations," *UN Monthly Chronicle*,
November 1965 (Vol. 2, No. 10), p. 67.

[7] Assistant Secretary of State William P. Bundy was reported to have told
an audience that in view of the current "convulsions" in China, Washington felt this was the wrong time to revise its position "lest it be an
encouragement to the hard-liners in Peking." *The New York Times*, November
29, 1966.)

stand would symbolize to other nations either a diplomatic disaster or, at best, chronic American inconstancy.

We can conclude as a working hypothesis that realistically there seems little the United States might plausibly do that could alter the probability of Peking being seated in the General Assembly within a very few years.

II

The case against representation of the Chinese Communists has been stated many times in the UN and has rested on the Chinese record of aggression and hostility toward its neighbors in Korea, Tibet, and India; on the Communist dedication as a matter of high policy, in contradiction to the purposes and principles of the Charter, to violent revolution in other countries; on the specific Charter requirements for membership; and on Peking's increasingly sweeping conditions for participation.

In recent times there have been signs that the unbendingly firm American position might be under some review although Secretary of State Dean Rusk indicated on September 16, 1966, that since the "basic situation" had not changed, there was no need for the United States to alter its policy.[8] Earlier he had seemed to be shifting the emphasis to United States efforts to prevent the expulsion of the Republic of China from the United Nations or its agencies.[9] At the heart of Washington's dilemma on China policy is the persistent conviction that even if national interests would be better served by a change in United States tactics on this issue, violent political opposition to any change could be expected from the Congress. With the Korean War the Congress became united and voluble on this issue, and it has periodically passed by unanimous vote resolutions reiterating implacable opposition to both recognition and UN seating of Red China. Both major parties as recently as 1964 adopted platform planks in this vein. Private organizations[10] such as the Committee of One Million as well as the AFL-CIO, American Legion, Jewish War Veterans, and others have militantly supported the same view.

But there have been widening cracks in the hitherto solid American political front on the China issue. Various private organizations

[8] News conference reported in *The New York Times,* September 17, 1966.

[9] Statement on China policy delivered March 16, 1966, before a closed session of the Far East Subcommittee of the House Foreign Affairs Committee. (*The New York Times,* April 17, 1966.)

[10] Opinion-forming American groups on both sides of this issue are usefully summarized in "The China Problem," *Intercom,* January-February 1965 (Vol. 7, No. 1), pp. 44-59.

have upheld the principle of UN universality, usually emphasizing the rights of the people of Taiwan as well. These have included most of the major church groups, as well as a variety of other citizens' associations. That public opinion generally shares a somewhat more flexible position than the Congress was implied in polls taken in recent years. A recent survey conducted by the Survey Research Center of the University of Michigan revealed that a large majority of Americans polled favored increased United States-Chinese communications. Over half wished to see ambassadors exchanged. And on the question of what the United States should do if Communist China were admitted to the United Nations, there was almost unanimous agreement (only 5 percent dissenting) that the United States should stay in the United Nations rather than withdraw.[11]

Other polls suggest that the American people are not disposed to favor American sponsorship of Communist Chinese representation, although the percentage opposing, according to an Oliver Quayle poll in early summer 1966, had dropped from 3 to 1 to about 40 percent, and a total of 67 percent of those queried favored admission, might favor it under certain circumstances, or were not sure.[12] They also, however, imply that significant sectors of the articulate American public might favor a new, more flexible policy, provided that it does not imply a betrayal of American commitments to Taiwan. (According to the June 1966 Quayle survey only 12 percent of those queried supported Peking's admission as a *replacement* for Taipei.) This has already been reflected in official statements such as that by Ambassador Arthur J. Goldberg to the effect that the United States is willing to see Peking represented if, among other conditions, it withdraws its demand for the expulsion of Taipei.[13]

[11] "The American Public's View of the U.S. Policy," published as the appendix to A. T. Steele, *The American People and China* (New York: McGraw-Hill, 1966), a volume in the series of the Council on Foreign Relations' project on "The United States and China in World Affairs."

[12] Drew Middleton in *The New York Times*, June 26, 1966. A Gallup poll released in November 1964 found that 57 percent believed Communist China should not be admitted, 20 percent believed it should, and 23 percent expressed no opinion. A special survey by Louis Harris released in the same month found 56 percent opposed to admission, 25 percent in favor, and 19 percent not sure. A National Analysts, Inc., poll in April 1966 showed 57 percent opposed, 25 percent in favor, and 18 percent neutral. However, in 1964, 77 percent believed that the United States should remain in the United Nations if Communist China were admitted, 7 percent would want the United States to pull out, and 16 percent were not sure. For detailed figures also see Alfred O. Hero, Jr., "The American Public and the UN," *Journal of Conflict Resolution*, December 1966 (Vol. 10, No. 4), pp. 436-475.

[13] Speech to National Press Club, April 19, 1966, reported in the *Washington Post*, April 20, 1966. Freedom House, a dedicated anti-Communist organization, publicly adopted a similar line in a statement released June 13, 1966. (*Freedom House News Letter*, July 1966.)

Nineteen hundred sixty-six has already seen a new fluidity in America on the China issue. Washington relaxed mainland travel restrictions for physicians, scholars, and even some tourists and offered to admit Chinese newsmen on a nonreciprocal basis. Peking has so far explicitly rejected such overtures. Hearings before the Senate Foreign Relations Committee saw an impressive procession of witnesses recommend changes in policy. The Ripon Society, a national organization of young Republicans, urged the Republican Party to "fill a leadership vacuum" in developing a more flexible China policy.[14]

All in all, a possibly decisive trend of opinion could be discerned that had as its slogan "Containment Without Isolation." This phrase, used initially by Professor A. Doak Barnett, was repeated within the week by the Vice President of the United States.[15] Perhaps the most unusual feature of the debate was the number of experts supporting American policy in Vietnam, for example, who positively favored membership in the UN as helping to move China toward a more tolerable relationship with the non-Communist world. In dramatic contrast with the past, this proposal was apparently "accepted with equanimity."[16] The question was thus raised in a serious way for the first time whether United States interests might not be better served by favoring Peking's UN presence, or at least not continuing to stake all on blocking it. The new mood was perhaps accurately reflected by a respected former general turned industrialist when he said, "I think we should recognize Red China and move along to get it into the United Nations. I believe we'd have a lot less problems with them if we did."[17]

The most substantial clue to a possible shift in United States policy was Washington's support of the Italian proposal for a committee to make recommendations to the 1967 General Assembly for "an equitable and practical solution" to the Chinese representation question. That the committee plan failed to carry[18] was perhaps less significant than the increasing official flexibility it denoted.

III

It is one thing to decide that United States policy needs reconsidering. China policy has become a sort of albatross we wear around our

[14] *New York Times*, April 7, 1966.

[15] *Ibid.,* March 14, 1966.

[16] E. W. Kenworthy in *The New York Times,* March 11, 1966.

[17] Lieutenant General James M. Gavin (Retired), Chairman of the Board of Arthur D. Little, Inc., in speech at Northeastern University, Boston, Massachusetts, reported in *ibid.,* April 15, 1966.

[18] The vote was taken on November 29, 1966. There were 34 in favor, 62 against, with 25 abstentions.

neck, and it is natural to wish to be freed of its weight. It is something quite different to estimate what is likely to happen if Peking does enter the UN. What, for example, would be the probable impact of Communist China in the UN? What kinds of actions are open to the United States that might minimize the disadvantages and maximize the advantages of Peking's admission from the standpoint of United States interests?

The first international forum where Peking's role might be significantly altered could well be a conference on Vietnam. If such negotiations were protracted, the pressures to bring China into all the centers of international discourse—including the UN—would surely mount. Within the UN the point of primary action is the 121-Member General Assembly. There a crucial technicality has since 1961 been the bulwark of the American parliamentary opposition: the ruling that the seating of Communist China is an "important question" which under Article 18 of the Charter requires a two-thirds vote.[19] In November 1966 this proposal carried again with 66 (54.6 percent) in favor and 48 (39.7 percent) opposed, plus 7 abstentions. Its transcendent importance as a tactic is clear when one considers the vote at the 1965 session to *seat* Peking—47 to 47. But on December 20, 1965, on a different issue which previous Assemblies had also ruled to be an "important question"—the removal of military bases from non-self-governing territories—the twentieth Assembly voted to decide the matter by a simple majority—an ominous precedent.

A favorite question among lawyers has long been whether seating Peking is a simple matter of "representation"—the procedural acceptance of credentials of one or another delegation from a state already a Member—or whether, as many people suppose, it is a question of electing a new Member. New membership is the basis for the frequently quoted criterion from Article 4 of "peace loving" for newly admitted states. This in turn has been linked to the question of bilateral United States-Chinese diplomatic relations. As a practical matter the United States may in the end decide to hold its nose and swallow both pills—recognition and UN representation. But if Washington ever came to acknowledge Peking's right to a seat in the UN, it would not be legally obliged to extend diplomatic recognition. Certainly it would not have to enter into active diplomatic relations: Such countries as Albania, Cambodia, Cuba, and Mongolia, with which the United States has no diplomatic relations, are active Members of the UN today.

---

[19] General Assembly Resolution 1668 (XVI), December 14, 1961. The vote then was 61 (58.6 percent) in favor of the United States position and 34 (32.7 percent) against.

The weight of expert opinion at the present time seems to prefer to regard the problem as one of credentials. If this is upheld, the veto that applies to new membership would thus not apply, and it would not be possible to veto Peking's seating in the Security Council. Worse yet, the credentials approach could, by substituting one delegation for another, bring about the result that above all others would be anathema for United States policy. In the absence of a very persuasive formula Taipei's representatives would be excluded from one UN body after another by act of accepting those from Peking. It is this kind of scenario that has in recent years inspired the talk of a "two China" solution. (It was earlier feared that Taipei would lose its Council seat if and when the incumbent Nationalist representative Tsingfu Tsiang vacated it. With commendable foresight a deputy was quietly accredited and on Mr. Tsiang's demise in 1965 the seat thus remained filled. Perhaps the most fascinating thing about the maneuver was that the Soviet representative made no objection.)

The basic legal question is whether Peking can be regarded as a "successor state" under international law. Has China split into two states? If it can be so viewed, a possible out becomes visible for Taiwan, as simply a second "successor" to pre-1949 China. Since the heart of the American policy dilemma is to find a suitable formula for ensuring Taiwan's continued representation whatever befalls, this version of the "two China" approach looks interesting—or would if both Chinas had not violently opposed any scheme that undermined their respective claims to a monopoly on representation of "China." For it is they who insist the matter is one of two governments claiming to be the legitimate representative of a single state. Barring a clear reversal of the form in which the issue so far has been presented, it will arise again technically as a question of whether to seat Peking's delegates as most properly representing the "government of China."

The nature of things in the UN favors this issue being confronted first in the General Assembly. Practically, if China were seated *and* deigned to show up—a large "if"—it is highly unlikely that the process would stop short of complete membership. The Long March would have at last ended, via the caves in Yenan and the palaces of Peking, in New York, Geneva, Rome, Bangkok—in short, in the 36 organs, committees, and specialized agencies of the United Nations system where Nationalist China is now entitled to sit.

IV

Shortly before mainland China fell to Mao Tse-tung's troops in 1949 some "guidance documents" were prepared by various elements of the State Department with a view to minimizing the appearance of

an American defeat. Some officials undertaking this sensibly pruden-
tial task were subsequently publicly vilified on the premise that to
anticipate defeat must be to wish for it. Fears that motives may be
similarly misconstrued may dangerously inhibit the needed planning
regarding the UN problem. Let us, however, take the planner's
necessarily most pessimistic assumption and ask what concrete effects
China's presence might have on the UN and its workings.

This question can only be answered in the context of the evolving
political and parliamentary situation in the UN in recent years. The
aspect bearing most on Chinese participation is the growing numerical strength and cohesion of the Afro-Asian group, now commanding
a clear majority among the membership and coming close to two-
thirds if the Soviet bloc is added. Observers have noted two conflicting trends here. The first is a tendency toward stands the West
considers radical on racial and economic issues. The countervailing
trend is toward greater maturity and responsibility on the part of a
few of the new states.

The most portentous effect of introducing Red Chinese spokesmen
into this setting could be the magnification of the first of these trends.
Peking outside the UN has sought to polarize the *tiers monde* around
revolutionary programs, anti-Western postures, and—most ominous
of all—racial tensions. There is no reason to believe that all of these
would not spill over in the UN in ways that might embarrass and
even harm the United States.

Peking in the UN could be expected to try to assert leadership of
at least the extremist states among the Afro-Asians. As a new power
center and rallying point Peking could act as a catalyst, precipitating
out of a still rather amorphous situation the reality of a coherent
radical movement. Enough states in the bloc have assorted grievances
against the United States to furnish a ready-made opportunity for
China to endow their periodic blackmail attempts with a multiplier
effect.

This exacerbation of already existing tendencies could well increase the American sense of frustration, of being besieged by exigent
and irresponsible demands. It is not inconceivable that a United
States increasingly on the defensive in the UN would move to the
right, so to speak, to occupy the lukewarm posture toward the Organization held by the United Kingdom in recent years (with the British
moving in turn toward the openly skeptical French stance).[20] Looking
back to recent years, it is difficult to find any votes of genuine significance where Chinese membership would have made a substantial
difference, other than increasing the already huge majorities for issues

[20] I owe this suggestion to my colleague Lucian W. Pye.

of concern to the Afro-Asian majority. But one difference would have been a probable Chinese breach in the gentlemen's agreement not to press votes during the 1964 Assembly. Another certainly would have been in the introduction of condemnatory resolutions covering virtually any United States action; if Peking is seated, Washington might have to work energetically in some cases to fend off critical expressions.

Chinese participation in the Assembly might have other effects, however, not all of which are negative from the Western standpoint. In a contest for leadership of the Afro-Asian caucus with India or the United Arab Republic, China might not do very well; some even predict a breaking away of African nations under those circumstances in order to preserve their nonalignment. These tensions in the relationship have already been reflected in such recent Chinese policy contretemps as the collapse of preparations for the Algerian conference of Asian and African leaders, the backlash of the attempted Communist coup in Indonesia, 1965's crude—and unexecuted— hostile gestures toward India, and the succession of African states that are coming to appreciate the threat to their integrity implied in local Chinese operations. Assembly membership might of course give China a handy device for repairing the damage through forensics and daily diplomatic intimacy. But these events have demonstrated that there are limits to Chinese political capacities. A China that is historically turning inward[21] may not act as much of a positive force in the UN.

Perhaps the most intriguing factor of all arises out of Sino-Soviet politics and the struggle for leadership of Communist movements, of revolutionary drives, of discontent with the status quo anywhere. If Rome and Byzantium, so to speak, are put together publicly in a setting where stands and postures symbolically bespeak a country's sympathy for the developing countries, one can foresee fascinating demonstrations of polemical warfare as Moscow and Peking vie for favor. For here they must vote on concrete programs usually of a moderate liberal-reformist nature, on which Peking's austere dialectics would presumably forbid "going along." Here increasing divergencies might develop between the search for stability on the part of the nonaligned, and the current interest of the Chinese Communists in instability and subversion. Here Moscow's growing *embourgeoisement* must ultimately clash with Peking's revolutionary *élan*. In all of

[21] See, for example, Morton H. Halperin, *Is China Turning In?*, Occasional Paper No. 12 (Cambridge, Mass.: Center for International Affairs, Harvard University, December 1965), with comments by Lincoln P. Bloomfield, William H. Gleysteen, Milton Katz, Ithiel de Sola Pool, Dwight H. Perkins, and Marshall Shulman.

this, given the nonbinding character of the Assembly's actions, it does not necessarily follow that American interests would be seriously jeopardized.

But there are drawbacks to public Sino-Soviet competition. This is an age and a time when a Soviet-American détente begins to look like the grail we seek if an enduring peace is to be had. It is at least possible that public monitoring and harassment by ideological purists from Peking would wither at birth the shoots, tender at best, of United States-Soviet understanding on issues bearing on survival. Moscow's flirtations with the West could be gravely inhibited by the insistent presence of a doctrinaire *amah*. If the Soviets are further educated in the process, we can applaud. But meanwhile a larger prize may elude us.

The other great secular trend in the UN is a steady move back toward use of the Security Council. Both Moscow and Washington find it periodically useful for delicate diplomatic operations—such as the successful Kashmir cease-fire in the fall of 1965—where the Assembly would be clumsy and even unmanageable. The denouement of the constitutional crisis over financing peacekeeping implied greater use of the Council. And indeed it *has* been used to initiate UN field operations in the Congo, Lebanon, Cyprus, and most recently Kashmir. Can we say with any assurance that the India-Pakistan fighting would have been ended as it was in September 1965 or the Cyprus force extended for three months as it unanimously was in March 1966—or some future explosion quickly defused—with Peking in China's Council seat? The occupant would seem far more likely to bear a close family resemblance to Moscow in the 1940's and 1950's.

Peacekeeping issues seem to have been of particular interest to Peking, perhaps because Communist China was on the receiving end of the largest one of all—Korea. Two contemporary authors have documented the increasing divergence of Russian and Chinese attitudes with regard to peacekeeping starting as early the 1956 Suez crisis, when the Soviet Union was content to abstain on the vote to establish a force, while China was outspokenly suspicious.[22] The authors are not certain that China would have voted against the operation which was strongly supported among the underdeveloped nations; but since 1958 the divergence has been more marked. The Soviet Union abstained on the establishment of the United Nations Observer Group in Lebanon (UNOGIL), but Red China called the

[22] See Morton H. Halperin and Dwight H. Perkins, *Communist China and Arms Control* (Cambridge, Mass.: East Asian Research Center, Center for International Affairs, Harvard University, 1965), p. 149.

mission an "instrument of U.S.-British intervention" in the Lebanon situation.[23]

Again, during the Congo crisis beginning in July 1960, the Soviet Union initially voted in favor of sending UN troops to assist the Congolese government. The Communist Chinese, however, talked of United States imperialism operating "under the UN flag"[24] and consistently opposed the entire operation. And after the long financial crisis, Soviet willingness to consider peacekeeping functions under Security Council control and Moscow's stated intention (long unfulfilled) to make a voluntary contribution toward the United Nations Emergency Force (UNEF) and the UN Operation in the Congo (ONUC) deficit in return for setting aside Article 19, was denounced by China as cooperation with "imperialism" in the suppression of world revolution. The Chinese Communists appear to fear in these precedents a possible UN role in Vietnam, and they can obviously no longer count on the Soviet Union to save the day in the UN. The result of all this might be a renewed Western attempt to use the Assembly—but it would be a very different Assembly from that of 1950 and the Uniting for Peace Resolution.

Of the several other UN actions subject to the great-power veto one more needs to be flagged: the election of a Secretary-General. One has only to recall the bitter Soviet attacks on both Trygve Lie and Dag Hammarskjöld toward the end of the tenure of both to appreciate the excruciating difficulties involved in getting agreement on their successors without China—and on Mr. Thant's replacement *with* China, if that is the prospect for 1971.

In the disarmament realm the ready availability of China would probably increase pressures on both China and France to sign the test ban treaty and join the Geneva disarmament talks. But perhaps too little attention is given to the likelihood that its presence could be very disruptive. On the plausible assumption that both countries pursue a prestige policy and therefore must possess a force in being before negotiating about it, one can conclude that the Geneva talks are likely to go further and faster without them. This need not necessarily spell futility for those negotiations. If the countries with sophisticated nuclear systems can agree among themselves on arms control or disarmament measures, the pressures of world opinion can then be applied to the nonparticipants. There is nothing to suggest that obstructive participation by China and/or France would necessarily lead to a more desirable conclusion, except insofar as negotiations serve as an educative process (as they have for the neutral Mem-

---

[23] *Ibid.*, p. 150, citing the *People's Daily* of June 19, 1958.
[24] *Ibid.*

bers). On balance, the Chinese presence for the moment seems unhelpful—but could be essential if the superpowers agreed.

As for the specialized agencies the degree of cooperation or obstruction that can be expected will depend in each instance on the specific Chinese interests, if any, these organizations can serve. It has become obvious that Peking has no resources to spare for other than marginal operations in the Third World.[25] Perhaps much of the recent disenchantment of some African countries and Cuba can be directly tied to their disappointment on this score. Foreign Minister Chen Yi has been quoted as referring contemptuously to "bread from Moscow and Washington,"[26] but the Chinese failure to deliver in this area severely limits the amount of influence that can be exerted.

At the same time, Peking would probably wish to occupy positions from which to influence the aid and development process. The UN Economic Commission for Asia and the Far East (ECAFE) might be paralyzed in its work with a belligerent and obstructive China in its midst. The Asian Development Bank is one of world diplomacy's most promising gestures to Asia. Communist China might become its largest single recipient; indeed, the largest single potential claimant to UN development and technical assistance funds across the board could, at least in theory, be Peking.

This prospect is virtually guaranteed to give nightmares to appropriations committees who must vote the funds, officials who must defend them, and international civil servants who must work with the Chinese. But several things should be remembered. For one thing, UN aid involves more people than money, and if China accepts the foreign personnel, it can only help break down the Chinese wall of isolation. For another, a policy of carrot and stick, if that is what we are to follow, is at some point going to have to involve a carrot. The whole process may be perhaps less traumatic if the United States does not attempt to relive its missionary role with the present generation of Chinese but uses multilateral machinery for the purpose.

Finally, what of the Secretariat? Having survived the early years of Soviet obstructionism, the Secretariat, it may be argued, is perhaps not in real danger from the Chinese. But there will be disruption whatever happens, whether from the need to create new positions or the displacement of the 50-odd present Chinese officials that is sure to be demanded by Peking. Above all, the Chinese Communists sent to work in the UN will be charged with a mission reflecting the fanatical

[25] A recent survey indicates that in 1965 Peking pledged only $50 million in aid compared with $330 million the previous year. (Seymour Topping, *The New York Times*, February 16, 1966.)

[26] Quoted by Seymour Topping, "Southeast Asia Isn't Scared by Chinese Dragon," *The New York Times Magazine*, January 16, 1966, p. 13.

world view of their masters. The absorption of large numbers of indoctrinated Chinese Communists can only have a disruptive and stultifying effect on the Secretariat.

It should be assumed that Chinese Communists, although doubtless confined to the Headquarters district, will, like the Soviets, use any opportunity for espionage. There is no classified American information available to the Secretariat. But within the UN there is material of a highly sensitive nature to UN operations themselves, notably when peacekeeping missions are under way. Precautions now observed to restrict such papers to trustworthy and reliable UN employees, whatever their nationality, would have to be reinforced. A kind of Gresham's law could result in lowering the quality of Secretariat employees. And, to take perhaps the most practical piece of bureaucratic fallout from Chinese entry, many more documents would have to be translated into Chinese than at present, multiplying the present Niagara of paperwork—and its cost.

In offering these estimates I have not been unmindful of the often heard argument for UN membership as a civilizing process for the isolated and blinkered men of Peking. This possibility must of course be measured against the predictable disruptions. Within the context of "containment without isolation" it seems reasonable to believe that release of the Chinese from isolation, while painful for others, cannot help but insert correctives into their frankly lunatic picture of the West and specifically of the United States. Practically any influence that might reduce Peking's extreme ethnocentrism and make its international performance more "political," so to speak, is a clear plus. This process has had beneficial effects over time on Soviet and East European diplomats and can be an asset to the cause of peace. China is said by those who know it best to be trying to impose "a course that would lead to a continuous aggravation of the international situation and ultimately to war."[27] Any potentially beneficial influence should not be rejected.

But it should not be overvalued for people acting under extraordinary discipline, and it may be hard to discern in the midst of short-term disruption, wrecking operations, and continued slanderous reporting to those back home alert for signs of deviationism. Above all, it should be understood that the UN is not going to serve as a reform school for Peking any more than it has for Moscow; at best it can be a marginal aid in the urgent process of bringing China to terms with the established order. If consolation is wanted, some of the most clear-eyed observers believe that UN participation can be part of a

[27] *Pravda*, November 28, 1966.

realistic relationship once the present Chinese leadership passes from
the scene.[28]

V

There is no ambiguity about the position of the Chinese Nationalist regime on the representation question, including its refusal to
consider anything smacking of recognition of "two Chinas." When it
comes to Peking's attitudes, however, the picture is somewhat
blurred. For one thing, Peking's relations so far with the UN have
been minimal and generally antagonistic on both sides. Direct communication between the two has been rare. The Communist regime
initially acted as all other successful revolutionary regimes do and in
November 1949 repudiated the UN delegation still representing
China, soon sending the Secretary-General credentials for a Chinese
delegation to the fifth Assembly. The delegation was not accredited,
and China's attitudes have been increasingly bitter ever since. The
whole situation became profoundly exacerbated when Chinese troops
entered the Korean War. Chinese representatives have periodically
been invited to attend certain UN debates but only once came (in
1950 when the Security Council took up Peking's complaint of
"armed invasion of the island of Taiwan"). Other invitations were
extended in connection with the prisoner-of-war issue (which in fact
took the Secretary-General to China in January 1955) and with the
dispute the same year over the offshore islands. In rejecting these
invitations Peking declared that all decisions taken by the United
Nations would be considered "null and void."[29]

There are grounds for believing that Peking could have been
seated before now if its attitude had been more conciliatory. But on

[28] See, for instance, Donald S. Zagoria, "China's Strategy—A Critique,"
Commentary, November 1965 (Vol. 40, No. 5), pp. 61-66. Recently translated
secret Chinese source material indicates the view that although the United
States shows no present sign of "sincerity," "the far-reaching view of the relationship between the two countries is optimistic and some day this problem
will arrive at a satisfactory solution." (J. Chester Cheng [ed.], *The Politics of
the Chinese Red Army—A Translation of the Bulletin of Activities of the People's Liberation Army* [Stanford, Calif.: Hoover Institution on War, Revolution, and Peace, 1966], p. 486.) But for the Americans to pin their hopes on
"peaceful evolution" is a pipe dream, according to an editorial in *Jen-min
Jih-pao,* reprinted in *The New York Times,* April 7, 1966.

[29] Exchange of cablegrams between the Secretary-General and the Minister
of Foreign Affairs of the People's Republic of China (UN Document S/3358).
The Chinese regime has referred to United States policy as the "one-and-a-half
China" policy since it virtually admits Chinese suzerainty over Taiwan. See
Cheng, *The Politics of the Chinese Red Army,* p. 487.

the specific issues that represent concrete obstacles to a seat for Peking, Chinese responses have become increasingly uncompromising and imperious. The bill of particulars has been presented by Foreign Minister Chen Yi:

> The United Nations must rectify its mistakes and undergo a thorough reorganization and reform. It must admit and correct all its past mistakes. Among other things it should cancel its resolution condemning China and the Democratic People's Republic of Korea as aggressors and adopt a resolution condemning the United States as aggressor; the UN Charter must be reviewed and revised jointly by all countries, big and small.[30]

As for Taiwan, or any version of a "two China" solution,

> China will not participate in any international conference, organization or undertaking in which representatives of the Taiwan local authorities are participating, no matter by what name they call themselves.[31]
> China will never enter into any relations with the United Nations and any conference connected with it before restoration of her legitimate rights in the United Nations and the expulsion of the Chiang Kai-Shek clique from the organization.[32]

When in January 1965 Indonesia became the UN's first temporary dropout, Peking applauded, characterizing the UN as a United States tool for supporting "reactionary," "imperialist" groups. Unless the UN were drastically reorganized, said Premier Chou En-lai,

> A revolutionary United Nations may well be set up so that rival dramas may be staged in competition with that body which calls itself the United Nations but which, being under the manipulation of United States imperialism, is capable only of making mischief and can do nothing good.[33]

An intriguing and perplexing question is how seriously to take Peking's belligerent assertions. Some apparently consider that the polemics of Chinese leaders are to be fully believed and that it would be the height of folly not to assume that they mean precisely what they say.[34] At the other extreme are those who either ignore their statements or dismiss them as propaganda.

[30] Press conference, September 29, 1965 (New China News Agency).

[31] Quoted in "The China Problem," *Intercom*, Vol. 7, No. 1, p. 25.

[32] Foreign Ministry statement, December 1, 1965, reported in *The New York Times*, December 2, 1965.

[33] *Ibid.*, January 26, 1965.

[34] See *The Economist*, August 20, 1966 (Vol. 220, No. 6417), pp. 709-710, quoted approvingly by President Lyndon B. Johnson in his speech of August 30, 1966, reported in *The New York Times*, August 31, 1966.

It seems wisest not only to take the statements very seriously indeed but also to understand the psychology involved. The Chinese Communists are Asians whose race was historically given to feelings of superiority but was humiliatingly dealt with by lesser (i.e., Western) breeds (as anyone who lived in pre-1949 China can attest). Since taking power they have been treated as pariahs. They now behave in a way extraordinarily similar to the way others have when excluded from clubs. "I didn't want to join your miserable club anyway," or "I'll form my own club," or "If you want me back you'll have to crawl" seem somehow more natural to the circumstances than "I'm sorry, you were right all along, I'm grateful you finally will let me in, and I promise to behave on your terms." Some United States officials refer to this interpretation of Chinese psychology as a "neurosis" theory, rejecting it because they believe it rests on the assumption—which I do not share—that membership "will reform" Peking.[35] The neurosis can, I think, be readily demonstrated, however cloudy the prognosis for its cure.

A more tangible explanation is found in Peking's own private admission that if China joined the UN

> we cannot have a majority in voting; formally the difficult situation may be moderated to some extent, but the struggle that arises will become more violent and we shall lose our present freedom of action.[36]

On balance, it probably ought to be assumed that China may not in reality be posing insuperable obstacles to taking its "rightful" seat if offered, although it may in face-saving fashion arrange a humiliating and anxious wait before showing up. If the scenario unfolds as most predict, the General Assembly will be the first to vote Peking in. It may or may not have worked out a formula for keeping Taiwan in; present indications are that few are concerned that this be done, perhaps underestimating the strength of American feelings in this matter. Peking will doubtless make Taiwan's complete ouster a condition for taking its seat; the present representatives of the Republic of China could be expected to insist on remaining. There being no grounds for expulsion, we can anticipate great confusion, unpleasantness, and undoubtedly the creation of a committee to find ways out of the parliamentary labyrinth.

It can also be assumed that Peking would insist on all the perquisites of membership including the Chinese seat in the Security

---

[35] See the address "The United States and Communist China" by Assistant Secretary of State William P. Bundy made before the Associated Students of Pomona College at Pomona, California, on February 12, 1966, in Department of State *Bulletin*, February 28, 1966 (Vol. 59, No. 1392), p. 316.

[36] Cheng, *The Politics of the Chinese Red Army*, p. 480.

Council before deigning to arrive. These two conditions could keep the mainland Chinese out for a matter of years. But, like the Soviets in August 1950, they may equally well decide that exigent political interests, above all, the chance for such intimate contact with Afro-Asians and with gut issues affecting the latter, override other considerations.

VI

Underlying all the problems of tactics and parliamentary diplomacy is a fundamental question of principle: What kind of organization is the UN in fact? What kind ought it to become?

It is not now a universal body in which all countries and people are represented. Neither is it an organization composed exclusively of "good," "peace-loving," "like-minded" nations—although American policy on Chinese representation has traditionally pretended that it was. It does increasingly behave like a universal organization containing every region and range of ideology—but it still excludes certain nations. We can surely proceed on the assumption that any moral distinction between those in and those outside is without foundation and has been since the day the Soviet Union joined.

One sometimes forgets that China is not the only case that reduces the UN's claim to be universally representative, for the divided states of Germany, Korea, and Vietnam are also on the outside. The United States has generally opposed admission of both halves of these countries as Members because it would appear to confirm both the legitimacy of the Communist regimes and the permanence of the divisions. West Germany, Monaco, South Korea, South Vietnam, the Vatican, and Switzerland are now represented by observers; U Thant has suggested that the time has come to accept observers from other non-Member nations (though for a time he carefully excluded East Germany), to maintain contact with the world which "would surely lead to a better understanding of the problems of the world and a more realistic approach to their solution."[37] East Germany itself recently created a minor stir by proposing that it become a Member, and in the fall of 1966 Soviet Foreign Minister Andrei Gromyko proposed that both Germanies be admitted.[38] U Thant has several times stated that the greatest impediment to the serious involvement in the Vietnam question by the UN is the fact that of all the parties

[37] "Introduction to the Annual Report of the Secretary-General on the Work of the Organization," *UN Monthly Chronicle*, Vol. 3, No. 9, section I, p. 121.
[38] Address to the General Assembly's 1413th plenary meeting, September 23, 1966, reported in *The New York Times*, September 24, 1966.

heavily engaged in the conflict only one—the United States—is a
Member of the Organization.[39]

The "successor state" notion mentioned earlier might cut two ways
here. It would clearly be politically undesirable for the divided
countries to be admitted to the UN on grounds that they are all
de jure successors to earlier single states. But in all three cases, at war
or at peace, successor governments are exercising *de facto* control
over halves of the territories and are so recognized by numbers of
their peers. In law, admission to the UN of both halves of the three
countries would not have to imply acceptance of any change in status
for those that do not recognize them although it might give Moscow's
German puppet, for instance, more standing than Bonn and consequently Washington might be prepared to tolerate. The device of
successor states was in fact used when the United Arab Republic
broke up (but was not employed to bring in Pakistan after the partition
of India). Perhaps a special form of "provisional membership" would
ensure that the future disposition of all three was clearly acknowledged to be *sub judice,* as it were, and without prejudice thereto.

A serious case can probably be made that in the long run American
interests would be better served by having all nations represented in
the UN by their effective governments regardless of whether we
approve of those regimes or not. It seems at least arguable that this
country would benefit from the ability to confront and deal, publicly
or within the UN, with the representatives of all states including those
with which it has no direct diplomatic relations. Many values inhere
in requiring them, as the United States is required, to account for and
justify themselves in public confrontation before the rest of the international community. All in all, it would probably be wise to conclude
that, other things being equal, membership in the UN is not a right
but rather an obligation none should be permitted to escape.[40] If this
were the American philosophic view of the UN, the details of individual membership would be likely to fall into place.

On the assumption that a new strategy might supply some much
needed new tactics, a gesture along these lines by the United States
might regain for it the fast-disappearing initiative on this question.
Well before the climactic moment the United States itself could
announce that it is time to take a new look at what the Organization
has in fact become and to act on that fact by setting up seats for *all*
states now out. On this premise it would call for scrapping Article
107 with its inhibitions on UN involvement in post-World War II
settlements.

[39] *The New York Times,* April 30, 1966.
[40] Some of these points were rehearsed in Lincoln P. Bloomfield, "The UN
at Twenty and After," *Headline Series,* October 1965 (No. 173).

A UN which included both Germanies could be charged to examine the issues involved in ultimate German settlement, issues no one else seems to have been able to deal with successfully. Such a *bouleverse-ment* becomes somewhat more thinkable when one considers the possible virtue in having put the Vietnam matter before the UN twelve years ago; surely from the American standpoint the results could not have been much worse. But perhaps its greatest value would be to bury China under Germany, so to speak, while arguing with both statesmanship and realism that the world is too small and too dangerous to attempt to build a community on less than a universal basis. An automatic effect of a "universal representation policy" would be to keep Taiwan in; the onus for coming into the UN would be on the Communist Chinese. Finally, if West Germany were not willing to apply, perhaps a majority could be persuaded not to accept East Germany.

At this writing one inclines to be skeptical that from a political standpoint American policy could undergo such a basic shift, particularly given Congressional pressures. Moreover, the idea of universal organization is an abstract good only, while the problems of the divided countries are all too real, and the policy makers enmeshed in them unlikely to welcome any new complication. And as far as the application of universalism to China itself is concerned, for all the calls for realism in China policy it should be evident from this analysis that realism includes some fairly stark forecasts about the effect on the UN of Peking's membership.

But my central point is that American wishes in this matter may not be determinative for much longer. If the assumption is correct that China will be admitted anyway sooner or later, and probably sooner, there is urgent need for the United States to recover the tactical ground it has already lost to derive whatever redeeming virtues can be found in the situation, and to minimize the eventual damage done. My analysis has indicated that seating Peking would bring serious problems. It has not indicated that the problems would be fatal or that the difficulties presented could not be overcome.

The issue for the United States, therefore, apart from a more basic reassessment of universality I have suggested, is essentially one of tactics in the face of an unpromising parliamentary situation. The central issue of tactics is the need to keep Taiwan represented in the UN. The subsidiary issue is the need to keep Peking as long as possible from China's Security Council seat, even if seated in the Assembly.

Logic is entirely on the side of considering the "two Chinas" to be two states, whether called China or not. On any grounds of equity Taiwan, with a population larger than that of 85 other UN Members, has as much right to be represented in the UN as the 700 million Chinese on the mainland, regardless of what sort of government either group currently lives under. The "two China" approach has twice been urged by Ceylon but rejected by the Afro-Asians and Albanians. If it is not going to be accepted, one should perhaps think in novel terms. It is particularly important to develop United States policies for a post-Chiang era in Taiwan that reflect durable American principles of diplomacy and politics. One theoretical possibility would be a UN trusteeship over Formosa under Article 81 of the Charter. Another would be a UN plebiscite on the island to give the inhabitants the right of self-determination they have never in the past enjoyed (the choices to them being independence, UN trusteeship, or annexation to mainland China). Precedents exist in the Saar, the quasi plebiscite under UN auspices in Malaysia, and, perhaps before we are through, Vietnam.

These suggestions may seem infeasible now, particularly if Chiang Kai-shek rejects any compromise. But to save the island of Taiwan from being forced, in a reversal of roles, into itself becoming the political and legal outcast, United States strategy ought to be to identify Taiwan as much as possible with UN-sponsored procedures and actions. Happily, American power makes impossible Taiwan's takeover by Peking, and the suggested policies can be pursued despite Peking's intransigence. But it is becoming politically imperative to devise formulas for ensuring broad support for such policies, which in turn could increase pressures on Peking to moderate its stand.

As to the Security Council seat, the United States would undoubtedly press to have the Nationalist Chinese remain there. I have indicated the unlikelihood that if Peking is voted a seat in the Assembly it can be kept off the Council. In the light of this the preferred United States strategy ought to be to aim at a compromise under which Taiwan would keep full membership in the Assembly under whatever name is appropriate, with efforts concentrated on keeping the Council seat vacant until, to give one possible suggestion, the International Court of Justice could resolve the question of legal membership.

One cannot be either sanguine or enthusiastic about any of the options open to American diplomacy on this thorny issue. It need only be recalled that China was the one major foreign policy matter which, according to Theodore Sorensen, President John F. Kennedy deliberately postponed to his second term.[41] It is an admitted mark of desperation even to suggest some of the possible approaches sketched out here. But time is running out.

[41] Theodore C. Sorensen, *Kennedy* (New York: Harper & Row, 1965), p. 755.

TABLE 1ᵃ

UN BODIES ON WHICH CHINA SITS OR MIGHT SIT

Security Council
Military Staff Committee (inactive)

General Assembly
Seven Main Committees of the Whole:
    First (Political and Security) Committee
    Special Political Committee
    Second (Economic and Financial) Committee
    Third (Social, Humanitarian, and Cultural) Committee
    Fourth (Trust and Non-Self-Governing Territories) Committee
    Fifth (Administrative and Budgetary) Committee
    Sixth (Legal) Committee
General Committee
Peace Observation Commission (largely inactive)
Committee Established Under General Assembly Resolution 1181 (XII) (Question of Defining Aggression)

Subsidiary Bodies
Trusteeship Council (becoming inactive)
Economic Commission for Asia and the Far East (ECAFE)
Statistical Commission
Population Commission
Technical Assistance Committee (TAC)
Social Commission
Commission on Narcotic Drugs
Executive Board of the UN Children's Fund (UNICEF)
Executive Committee of the Program of the UN High Commissioner for Refugees (UNHCR)
Economic and Social Council (ECOSOC)ᵇ
UN Conference on Trade and Development (UNCTAD) Trade and Development Boardᵇ

Specialized Agencies
International Atomic Energy Agency (IAEA)
International Labor Organization (ILO)
UN Educational, Scientific and Cultural Organization (UNESCO)
World Health Organization (WHO)
International Bank for Reconstruction and Development (IBRD)
International Monetary Fund (IMF)
International Development Association (IDA)
International Civil Aviation Organization (ICAO)
Universal Postal Union (UPU)
International Telecommunication Union (ITU)
World Meteorological Organization (WMO)
Intergovernmental Maritime Consultative Organization (IMCO)
Food and Agriculture Organization (FAO)ᵇ

ᵃ Source: "A New China Policy—Some Quaker Proposals," A Report Prepared for the American Friends Service Committee (New Haven, Conn.: Yale University Press, 1965), p. 37.

ᵇ (Membership seats not now held by Nationalist China but open to Chinese membership in the future.)

TABLE 2ª

Year	Total UN Member-ship	To Consider	Not to Consider	Abstention	Absent	Sponsor
1951	60	11 (18.7%)	37 (61%)	4	no roll call	Soviet Union
1952	60	7 (11.7%)	42 (70%)	11	0	Soviet Union
1953	60	10 (16.7%)	44 (73.3%)	2	4	Soviet Union
1954	60	11 (18.3%)	43 (71.7%)	6	0	Soviet Union
1955	60	12 (20%)	42 (70%)	6	0	Soviet Union
1956	79	24 (30.4%)	47 (59.4%)	8	0	India
1957	82	27 (32.9%)	48 (58.6%)	6	1	India
1958	81ᵇ	28 (34.6%)	44 (54.3%)	9	0	India
1959	82	29 (35.4%)	44 (53.7%)	9	0	India
1960	98	34 (34.7%)	42 (42.9%)	22	0	Soviet Union

From 1951 through 1960 the vote was on a United States proposal not to put the question on the agenda.

Thereafter placing the item on the agenda was not contested. The Assembly voted each year to regard the matter as an "important question" requiring a two-thirds majority. The votes below are on the substantive question of seating the Communist Chinese delegates and removing the Nationalist Chinese delegates.

		To Seat	Not to Seat			
1961	104	36 (34.6%)	48 (46.1%)	20	1	Soviet Union
1962	110	42 (38.7%)	56 (50.9%)	12	0	Soviet Union
1963	111	41 (36.9%)	57 (51.4%)	12	1	Albania
1964		General Assembly session postponed				
1965	117	47 (40.2%)	47 (40.2%)	20	3	Cambodia, Albania. Algeria, Congo (Brazzaville), Cuba, Ghana, Guinea, Mali, Pakistan, Rumania, Somalia, Syria
1966	121	46 (38%)	57 (47.1%)	17	1	(same as 1965 minus Ghana and Somalia and plus Mauritania)

ª Adapted from "The China Problem," *Intercom,* Vol. 7, No. 1, pp. 32-33.
ᵇ Egypt and Syria formed the United Arab Republic.

TABLE 3

1) Voting to Admit in 1963 (41)

Afghanistan	Denmark	Mongolia	Sweden
Albania	Finland	Morocco	Syria
Algeria	Ghana	Nepal	Tanganyika
Bulgaria	Guinea	Norway	Tunisia
Burma	Hungary	Pakistan	Uganda
Burundi	India	Poland	Ukraine
Byelorussia	Indonesia	Rumania	United Arab Republic
Cambodia	Iraq	Somalia	United Kingdom
Ceylon	Laos	Soviet Union	Yemen
Cuba	Mali	Sudan	Yugoslavia
Czechoslovakia			

2) Voting to Admit in 1965 (47)

The Members listed above with four exceptions and ten additions.

Exceptions: Indonesia—withdrew from the UN in 1965
Laos—did not vote in 1965
Burundi—abstained in 1965
Tunisia—abstained in 1965

Additions: Central African Republic—voted "No" in 1963
Congo (Brazzaville)—voted "No" in 1963
Ethiopia—absent in 1963
France—voted "No" in 1963
Kenya—new Member
Mauritania—abstained in 1963
Nigeria—abstained in 1963
Sierra Leone—abstained in 1963
Singapore—new Member
Zambia—new Member

3) Voting to Admit in 1966 (46)

The changes in 1966 from 1965 were as follows:
Burundi, which abstained in 1965, voted "Yes."
Central African Republic, which voted "Yes" in 1965, voted "No."
Indonesia, which had withdrawn in 1965, voted "Yes."
Morocco, which voted "Yes" in 1965, abstained.
Senegal, which abstained in 1965, voted "Yes."
Sierra Leone, which voted "Yes" in 1965, voted "No."
Singapore, which voted "Yes" in 1965, abstained.

Of the 46 Members maintaining diplomatic relations with Communist China, all voted for admission in 1966 except:

Laos-absent (also in 1965)
Morocco-abstained (voted "Yes" in 1965)
Netherlands-abstained (also in 1965)
Tunisia-abstained (also in 1965)

Of 58 UN Members maintaining diplomatic relations with *Nationalist* China in 1966, 48 voted against seating Communist China and expelling the Nationalist delegates. The remaining ten abstained.

TABLE 4a

COUNTRIES WHICH RECOGNIZE AND HAVE DIPLOMATIC RELATIONS WITH:

PEOPLE'S REPUBLIC OF CHINA   REPUBLIC OF CHINA

UN MEMBERS	Sudan	UN MEMBERS	Luxembourg
	Sweden		Madagascar
Afghanistan	Syria	Argentina	Malawi
Albania	Tanzania	Australia	Maldive Islands
Algeria	Tunisia	Belgium	Malta
Bulgaria	Uganda	Bolivia	Mexico
Burma	Ukraine	Brazil	New Zealand
Byelorussia	United Arab	Cameroun	Nicaragua
Cambodia	Republic	Canada	Niger
Ceylon	United Kingdom	Chad	Panama
Congo (Brazzaville)	Yemen	Chile	Paraguay
Cuba	Yugoslavia	Colombia	Peru
Czechoslovakia	Zambia	Congo	Philippines
Denmark		(Leopoldville)	Portugal
Finland		Costa Rica	Rwanda
France	NON-UN MEMBERS	Cyprus	Saudi Arabia
Ghana		Dahomey	Sierra Leone
Guinea	German Demo-	Dominican	South Africa
Hungary	cratic Republic	Republic	Spain
India	(East Germany)	Ecuador	Thailand
Indonesia	Korean People's	El Salvador	Togo
Iraq	Democratic	Gabon	Turkey
Kenya	Republic (North	Greece	United States
Laos	Korea)	Guatemala	Upper Volta
Mali	Democratic Repub-	Haiti	Uruguay
Mauritania	lic of Vietnam	Honduras	Venezuela
Mongolia	(North Vietnam)	Iran	
Morocco	Switzerland	Italy	
Nepal		Ivory Coast	NON-UN MEMBERS
Netherlands		Jamaica	
Norway		Japan	Republic of Korea
Pakistan		Jordan	(South Korea)
Poland		Kuwait	Republic of
Rumania		Lebanon	Vietnam
Somalia		Liberia	(South Vietnam)
Soviet Union		Libya	

a Source: *China, the United Nations and United States Policy,* A Report of a National Policy Panel established by the United Nations Association of the United States of America (New York: United Nations Association of the United States of America, October 1966), Appendix E.

COUNTRIES WHICH RECOGNIZE NEITHER PEOPLE'S REPUBLIC OF CHINA
NOR REPUBLIC OF CHINA

UN MEMBERS	NON-UN MEMBERS
Austria	Andorra
Burundi	Bhutan
Central African Republic	Federal Republic of Germany
Ethiopia	Liechtenstein
Gambia	Monaco
Guyana	San Marino
Iceland	Western Samoa
Ireland	
Israel	
Malaysia	
Nigeria	
Senegal	
Singapore	
Trinidad and Tobago	

12. REGIONAL ORGANIZATION AND THE REGULATION OF INTERNAL CONFLICT

By LINDA B. MILLER

I

ARE regional and global approaches to world order compatible or competitive? Policy-makers and scholars pose this question with increasing frequency. Yet too often assessments of the relative capabilities of regional and general international organizations fail to distinguish the different demands such issues as threats to the peace or modernization create for widely divergent institutions. Enthusiasm for regionalism waxes and wanes with events. As Inis Claude observes, "The advocacy of regionalism can be, and often is, as doctrinaire and as heedless of concrete realities as the passion for all-encompassing organization."[1]

The realities of contemporary internal violence suggest that international regulation of intrastate disorder is desirable. Internal disorders, in the form of armed insurrections, bloodless military coups, colonial revolts, or factional disputes, are prevalent in the less industrialized sections of Asia, Latin America, Africa, and the Middle East. The attempts of countries in these regions to modernize their societies generate social and political unrest and invite violent or subviolent civil strife.

These disorders may reveal a desire to achieve political change when previously legitimate means of effecting change have broken down or when the goals of dissident groups cannot be realized by legitimate means.[2] Revolutions, civil wars, coups, or mere threats of force attest to issues of policy or ideology; disagreements over foreign-policy, constitutional, ethnic, racial, or economic questions may spark violence that creates new issues for domestic and external parties.[3] Nation-building and insurgency are closely linked: the lack of a basic

Reprinted by permission of the author and *World Politics,* XIX (No. 4, July 1967), 582-600.

[1] *Swords Into Plowshares* (New York 1964), 95.
[2] Cyril E. Black, in Cyril E. Black and Thomas P. Thornton, eds., *Communism and Revolution* (Princeton 1964), 7ff.
[3] *Ibid.,* 9-12.

national consensus about the means and ends of government may raise doubts as to the legitimacy of the formal government in power; or bureaucratic inefficiencies may call into question the capacity of ruling groups to govern.[4]

Different kinds of internal violence create different international concerns. Conflicts that subside quickly or remain confined within national boundaries may arouse some interest on a regional basis and little or no attention on a global scale. Protracted disorders that may spill over territorial boundaries stimulate global interests in peaceful change and human rights. When struggles for internal supremacy are seen by local and foreign participants as parts of larger conflicts of a racial or ideological character, the potential or actual threat to global and regional stability is increased.

Competitive external interventions have become the familiar mode for larger powers who view internal conflicts as a means of extending their own national influence at the expense of cold-war adversaries or regional competitors. Thus the steadily expanding war in Vietnam has dramatized the extent to which the line between international and internal conflicts may be erased by the actions of third parties who regard civil disorders as threats to political values. The lack of substantive rules of conduct in civil strife increases the likelihood of unregulated third-party interventions. The specter of unilateral military responses to internal violence raises the most serious issues for world order. Few would disagree with Richard A. Falk who argues that "civil strife constitutes the major challenge to those convinced that decisions to use military power in world affairs should not be matters of national discretion."[5] Nevertheless, since the effective control of force remains on the national level, the prospects for international regulation of internal conflict depend upon the self-restraint of third parties.

Such a fragile basis for world order is unsatisfactory to those who would give primacy to transnational interests. Therefore it is not surprising that some scholars have attempted to postulate a series of "legal" restraints that might serve as guides for policy-makers. Falk, for example, has proposed that the legitimacy of particular interventions be based on whether they rest on prior principles that express "patterns of general community consent or merely reflect *ad hoc* political majorities of the moment." Thus unilateral interventions in which one nation intervenes in the internal affairs of another, as did the Soviet Union in Hungary, would rank lower on the scale of

[4] Lucian Pye, in Harry Eckstein, ed., *Internal War: Problems and Approaches* (New York 1964), 158, 164.

[5] "The International Regulation of Internal Violence in the Developing Countries," American Society of International Law, *Proceedings* (April 1966), 59.

legitimacy than regional interventions in which a group of states forms a juridical entity and imposes a combined will on a dissenting member, as did the OAS with Cuba. Still higher on the scale would come collective interventions under the aegis of the UN, as in the Congo or Cyprus.[6] Falk would give to the UN greater legislative competence to intervene in domestic affairs, authority that would enable the Organization to move into *any* civil disorder threatening world peace or abusing human rights. In some instances the UN might become the sole authority in modernizing countries experiencing civil upheaval.[7] Regional interventions would occupy a middle position between undesirable unilateral interventions and desirable but perhaps unattainable, UN interpositions.

The structural and political realities of regional organization indicate that the possibilities for attaining effective management of civil strife through regional efforts are limited. Nevertheless, it is useful to stipulate the *feasible* responses for regional actors even if these responses fall short of *desirable* ones.

II

It is important to differentiate both types of internal conflict and patterns of regional organization. The term "internal war" is not helpful in this context, since many internal disorders are not "wars" in a traditional sense. Moreover, "internal war" is rendered still less precise by its occasional use as a description of conflicts in which "Communist" states participate.[8] It would be advantageous if scholars could develop categories that permit clear distinctions between diversified internal conflicts.[9] In the absence of widely accepted categories, observers must select those pertinent to the scope of a particular inquiry. From the standpoint of international organization, three types of internal conflict are significant: colonial wars, internal conflicts involving a breakdown of law and order, and proxy wars and internal conflicts involving charges of external aggression or subversion.

Two types of regional organization are of potential consequence in the regulation of internal conflict: (1) groupings of states such as the

---

[6] Falk, in Roland Stanger, ed., *Essays on Intervention* (Columbus 1964), 40-41.

[7] *Ibid.,* 40-44.

[8] See, for example, Roger Hilsman, "Internal War: The New Communist Tactic," in Franklin Mark Osanka, ed., *Modern Guerrilla Warfare* (New York 1962), 452-63.

[9] For an extended discussion of this point, see Linda B. Miller, *World Order and Local Disorder: The United Nations and Internal Conflicts* (Princeton 1967), Introduction.

Organization of American States and the Organization of African Unity, with a continental or hemispheric basis, a set of decision-making institutions, and established procedures for pacific settlement of disputes; and (2) collective defense arrangements such as NATO, SEATO, and the Warsaw Pact, whose geographical bases conform to strategic needs rather than natural boundaries and whose nonmilitary functions are virtually undeveloped. Regional organizations of both types are arenas in which competing governmental interests are acted out. When these interests converge, a consensus may emerge on appropriate responses to internal violence. These responses, whether they involve attempts to isolate an internal conflict, to foster negotiations between disputants, or to impose a settlement, develop pragmatically in each case. The British Commonwealth is a more anomalous type of "regional" organization. Despite the fact that the Commonwealth is unlike other organizations, it may attempt similar functions when internal strife breaks out in a member state, if political circumstances permit. The Commonwealth's lack of cohesion, apparent throughout Rhodesia's conflict with Britain, is a major impediment to effective action.

Few precedents are discernible in the practice of regional organizations in civil disorders, but some frequently observed deficiencies have proved to be highly relevant. In Asia, there is no regional grouping of stature and comprehensive authority. The recently formed Asian and Pacific Council (ASPAC) has no institutional structure and is limited to a few countries in the area. Even more restricted is Maphilindo, a grouping that has remained an expression of intent rather than a viable foundation for regional activities. In Africa, the existing OAU lacks military resources and is torn by periodic ideological splits. In the Middle East, the Arab League's membership is incomplete and the competition for dominance between Egypt and Saudi Arabia affects every regional undertaking. In Latin America, the U.S. continues to dominate the OAS and seeks to have American conceptions of Communist threats to the hemisphere prevail. Similarly, preeminent American power plus divergent attitudes toward the degree and quality of Communist involvement have characterized the responses of NATO and SEATO to intraregional civil strife.

Past attempts of regional organizations to regulate varieties of internal violence illustrate these deficiencies and others that preclude effective contributions to world order.

III

The chief colonial wars since 1945 have unfolded in parts of the world where regional organization is either precarious or nonexistent.

Throughout the postwar period, the organizational focus of decolonization has remained the United Nations. The destabilizing effects of the new nations' transition to self-rule have colored the relations of the Europeans nations with the Soviet Union and its allies, as well as intra-alliance relations in the West. The lengthy struggles of indigenous groups in Indonesia, Algeria, and Angola have involved third-party states and international organizations in asymmetrical conflicts in which incumbents have enjoyed an initial preponderance of power. These revolutionary wars have taken place in territories in which the metropolitan power remained distant, geographically and politically. Each European power in turn has confronted nongovernmental cliques determined to end foreign domination. The Dutch, French, and Portuguese governments sought to isolate these conflicts in hopes that concessions short of outright independence would be sufficient to quell disorder. Each colonial power vigorously opposed formal internationalization of the conflict, fearing that the UN (and later the OAU, in the case of Angola) would serve to confer status on the rebelling faction and to expose repressive administrative policies.

Insurgent groups in Indonesia, Algeria, and Angola have favored UN involvement (and now OAU participation) for the reasons the European states opposed it: first, as a means of enlisting sympathy for rebel goals; and second, as a means of enhancing bargaining positions and compensating for military weaknesses. In all three colonial wars, the UN's efforts (and those of the OAU) to confine hostilities, to restore order, to foster self-determination, and to encourage viable political settlements have been hampered by the reluctance of incumbents and insurgents to legitimize each other, to accord the recognition implied in acceding to negotiations. In each case, the international organizations have expressed a definite preference for change favorable to insurgents.

The vestiges of white rule in southern Africa constitute the last barrier to an independent continent. A "colonial" war that could dwarf the violence of preceding African conflicts is a distinct possibility. Can the OAU be expected to play a constructive role in securing the black majority's rights and in preventing uncontrolled bloodshed? The record of the OAU in the Angolan revolt is instructive.

Unlike many of the intra-African issues, the Angolan colonial war has served to unite the states of Black Africa on policy. The formation of the OAU in 1963 provided new impetus for a sanctionist approach to Portugal, but African leaders have sought a wider forum for their denunciation of Salazar's administration—hence their concentration on securing UN resolutions and UN investigations rather than exclusive OAU discussions. Lacking the military capabilities to intervene with force in Rhodesia, Angola, Mozambique, or South West Africa, the African states have tended to act individually in such matters as training rebels or recognizing a specific indigenous regime as the *de jure* authority. The OAU as an organization, apart from the actions of certain of its members, has not "regulated" the Angolan conflict in any sense; in fact, the revolt has diminished. The OAU members have cast themselves as a group in the role of negotiators for the rebels in their dealings with Portugal. These talks, urged in numerous UN resolutions, have foundered on the issue of self-determination for Angola. But the fact that the OAU has considered itself a party to the conflict and has been accepted as such by the UN may be a valuable precedent.

In view of the ideological splits that have plagued the OAU since its establishment and the continuing military weakness of the organization, it is difficult to foresee a more interventionary OAU role even in circumstances of policy agreement. It would appear that both regional and global approaches to change in southern Africa are dependent on shifts in the commitments of Western states, notably the United States and Britain. The African states continue to lack sufficient power to "impose" a settlement on Portugal or South Africa, even if the combined will of the OAU membership would favor an attempt to do so. Moreover, the pattern of settlement in the Indonesian and Algerian wars indicates a bilateral framework for eventual solutions rather than a regional one. Feasible OAU responses would involve continued diplomatic pressure on other UN members in presentations that stress violations of human rights and the compatibility of regional and global concerns. In addition, the thirty-eight members of the OAU might adopt more uniform procedures for urging all African states to refrain from trading with either Portugal or South Africa. The many examples of extensive trade between the new states and the "colonial" powers are impressive. Only if other economic arrangements can be devised so that the losses from an end to such trade are shared will the new African states be willing to adopt firm practices.

A severe outbreak of organized resistance to the South African regime, rather than sporadic incidents of civil disobedience, would involve the UN as well as the OAU. A potential source of disagreement between the two organizations might develop over the question of border-sealing. From the UN's perspective, such a move might increase the chances for isolating the disorder. But from the OAU's viewpoint, border-sealing would favor the police actions of the incumbents and prevent the external assistance needed to topple the white government. Thus border-sealing, while feasible, might not be desirable. In this instance, competitive means might mask compatible goals.

The role of security pacts in colonial wars appears even more restricted. In the Indonesian and Algerian conflicts, NATO served as a minor channel through which the United States could direct pressures against the Netherlands and France when it wished to do so. In the Angolan rebellion, the United States shifted its initial position in the UN and came to accept the *principle* of an arms embargo against its NATO ally Portugal. But since the alliance itself is in chronic disarray, it is unrealistic to expect "NATO" policies on colonial matters that appear less critical now than in the 1950's.

IV

The declining importance of prolonged struggles for independence has been accompanied by an upsurge in virulent forms of postcolonial civil disorder. These conflicts, often characterized by a breakdown of law and order, create a complex set of policy choices for third parties, both individual states and regional or global organizations. A compatibility of ends and means between the UN and the interested regional association cannot be assumed. Friction or tension between field operations of the UN and those of regional organizations may be the price of a mutual concern for stability. The Congo, Dominican, and Cyprus disorders have found international organizations deeply involved in seeking to halt violence and to promote political solutions.

The relatively uncomplicated roles played by these organizations in the colonial wars contrast sharply with the intricacies of their prolonged participation in the breakdowns of law and order. These conflicts have confronted international organizations with an array of parties whose interests transcend the colonial pattern of incumbents and insurgents. In countries as diverse as the Congo, the Dominican Republic, and Cyprus, a common instability arising from a lack of adequate preparation for full self-rule (as opposed to colonial or dictatorial rule) has marked the disintegration of political processes.

To an important extent, regional organizations and the UN have shared compatible goals in these disorders. Both have tried to restore and maintain international peace and security, pursuant to their principles and purposes. Both have tried to prevent external interventions from escalating local violence into superpower conflagrations. In attempts to realize their goals, both have been limited by inadequate means and by the attitudes of individual member states with narrower national interests in the outcome of internal strife. Similar limitations have plagued the efforts of international organizations in colonial wars and internal conflicts involving charges of external aggressions or subversion. But special hazards have accompanied the involvement of international institutions in upheavals that have exposed the weaknesses of the social fabric in developing societies with minority groups of a mixed racial or linguistic heritage. The nature of the breakdowns of law and order has required the formation of a consensus within each organization. In each case, a commitment to a definite outcome has developed within each institution when local and external parties have evaded political solutions.

By the time the Organization of African Unity was formed in May 1963, the post-independence breakdown of law and order in the Congo had passed through several critical stages. From the beginning of tribal violence and the subsequent collapse of central authority in Léopoldville, African statesmen individually and collectively had sought to exercise some influence on events. Hammarskjöld and later President Kennedy and U Thant expressed the hope that the Black African states might play a constructive role in securing a political settlement of the Congo's turmoil. But the expectations of these officials rested on two assumptions, both of which proved unrealistic: that the African states could unite sufficiently to take a concerted approach toward the rival Congolese leaders, especially Tshombe and Lumumba, and that in matters of tactics and strategy African political figures would step aside in favor of U.S.-UN management. The initial response of the Africans to Hammarskjöld's principles for the operation of ONUC was favorable. Lacking military capabilities and a continental organization through which to act, African leaders endorsed a UN peacekeeping operation as a means of preventing direct superpower exploitation of the situation. Individual African statesmen took the lead in drafting Security Council resolutions that led to ONUC's establishment, and they contributed contingents quickly.

The Congo crisis soon threw the disagreements among African leaders into sharp relief. A central issue concerned the appropriate attitude for the UN to adopt toward Katanga's continued secession, and toward Tshombe personally. Severe differences separated Nkrumah and Touré, who wished to see the secession crushed, from representatives of the former French colonies, who were prone to regard the rebel leader as a bulwark against communism in Africa. This early divergence between the "conservative" Brazzaville group and the more "radical" Casablanca group proved to be the precursor of other cleavages that threatened to prevent the formation of an African regional organization. Neither grouping proved to be rigid in structure; the Brazzaville group itself split in August 1961. The military coups in Africa in 1965-1966 have produced new configurations, with Ghana now a "conservative" state in contrast to its earlier "radical" posture.

As conflict in the Congo persisted in 1961-1962, the activities of a more moderate group of African states, among them Nigeria, began to be prominent in Hammarskjöld's Advisory Committee and later in the UN Conciliation Commission. By the time the Addis Ababa conference convened to chart the course of the new African organization, it was apparent that the "bloc" configurations represented by Casablanca, Monrovia, and Brazzaville had become dysfunctional. Linked by the common but negative bond of anticolonialism, eager for a distinctively African association that would replace the imposed decentralization of the colonial era, the thirty-six states adopted a charter that revealed the need to avoid extreme positions. Faced with problems of internal security as well as of economic underdevelopment and the absence of a historical tradition of cooperation, the assemblage approved a constitutional document that placed emphasis on the legitimacy of existing regimes in Black Africa and the "illegality" of white-dominated governments in southern Africa.

Barely a year after its founding, the OAU was strained by the establishment of the Kasavubu-Tshombe government in July 1964. While Tshombe's return as head of a "Government of National Reconciliation" had been accomplished by legitimate means, he remained, for some African leaders at least, a "Belgian lackey" and a "white man's puppet." The Belgian-American airlift in November intensified the views of these dissenters. Prior to the rescue mission, the OAU's Conciliation Commission had failed in its efforts to negotiate the release of rebel-held prisoners in Kwilu and Kivu provinces. The vituperative Security Council debates on the airlift exposed cracks in the facade of African unity. The impotence of the OAU in circumstances of intra-regional civil conflict was demonstrated unmistakably as Ghana, the UAR, and Algeria intervened on behalf of the rebels, while other African states urged a recognition of Tshombe's government. The Security Council's compromise resolution called for a conciliatory role for the OAU.[10] But as the time for ONUC's withdrawal neared, the African organization did not command enough respect to make its influence felt, despite its pacific settlement procedures. African leaders, in failing to agree on the choice of a regime to govern the Congo or to endorse leaders already selected, prevented effective OAU participation.

V

In the Dominican Republic's lengthy civil strife the American military intervention shaped not only the course of the upheaval but also the responses of the OAS and the UN. The role of the United States

[10] Security Council Resolution S/6129, December 30, 1964.

throughout the course of the disorder was so pronounced, so pre-dominant that some observers may question the utility of discussing the Dominican instance in the context of regional control of internal conflict. Yet it is precisely the way in which the U.S. used the OAS in an attempt to legitimize its own actions that gives the episode its importance.

From the initial stages, different characterizations of the circum-stances leading to the American intervention were advanced by Presi-dent Johnson, former Dominican President Juan Bosch, and compet-ing Dominican forces engaged in the struggle.

The dispatch of American airborne units and Marine reinforce-ments to the Dominican Republic on April 28, 1965, was explained by President Johnson on that day as a measure to "give protection to hundreds of Americans who are still in the Dominican Republic and to escort them safely back to this country."[11] The same reason was cited in a letter dated April 29 sent to the President of the UN Secu-rity Council explaining the American action.[12] But on May 2, Presi-dent Johnson, in answering widespread criticism of the intervention, stated that "the revolutionary movement took a tragic turn. Com-munist leaders, many of them trained in Cuba, seeing a chance to increase disorder, to gain a foothold, joined the revolution. They took increasing control. And what began as a popular democratic revolu-tion, committed to democracy and social justice, very shortly moved and was taken over and really seized and placed into the hands of a band of Communist conspirators."[13] The President produced no evidence to support his assertion; but on May 5, the State Department released a list of fifty-five "Communist and Castroite" names to sup-port the Johnson administration's claims of Communist takeover. The list, denounced by Bosch and rebel leaders, was also ridiculed by other governments and individuals critical of the American action.

The extent of hemispheric hostility to the unilateral American in-tervention emerged when the United States sought to involve the OAS in a peacekeeping role. An American draft resolution calling for a ceasefire was adopted on April 30 by the Council of the OAS with no negative votes.[14] Similarly, a second draft resolution intro-duced by the U.S., in conjunction with Argentina, Brazil, Colombia, Guatemala, Mexico, and Peru, at the Tenth Meeting of Consultation of Ministers of Foreign Affairs, a resolution calling for the establish-

[11] White House press release, April 28, 1965; reprinted in *Department of State Bulletin,* LII (May 17, 1965), 738.

[12] U.N. Doc. S/6310, April 29, 1965.

[13] White House press release, May 2, 1965; reprinted in *Department of State Bulletin,* LII (May 17, 1965), 744.

[14] Resolution of the Council of the Organization of American States, April 30, 1965, U.N. Doc. S/6315, May 1, 1965.

ment of an OAS committee to investigate "all aspects of the situation in the Dominican Republic" and to assist in the arrangement of a cease-fire, was adopted on May 1.[15] But prolonged negotiations were required to secure the adoption of an American draft resolution to establish an inter-American peacekeeping force. The creation of a regional military force, endorsed by the five-nation peace committee sent to Santo Domingo pursuant to the May 1 resolution, was opposed by Mexico, Uruguay, Chile, Ecuador, and Peru, states with social and political systems more advanced than those in many other Latin American states. These states, fearful that the American intervention might be a foretaste of other U.S. interventions in Latin American states experiencing domestic unrest, condemned the American action in the Dominican Republic and voted against the resolution. They decried the intervention as illegal under Article 17 of the OAS Charter[16] and scored the United States' failure to consult the OAS before taking its action. Their negative votes were not sufficient to defeat the plan; intensive behind-the-scenes discussions produced a bare two-thirds majority for the American proposal, as amended by five other Latin American states who recorded the view that approval of OAS intervention in the Dominican Republic should not be construed as approval of the initial American intervention. Venezuela abstained on the resolution.

Approved by thirteen states plus a representative of the Dominican Republic (although the country had no legitimate government at the time), the resolution provided for an international force to be established incorporating United States forces present in the Dominican Republic and units to be contributed by other members of the OAS. The resolution stipulated that the force would operate under the authority of the Tenth Meeting of Consultation and would have as its purpose "that of co-operating in the restoration of normal conditions in the Dominican Republic, in maintaining the security of its inhabitants and the inviolability of human rights, and in the establishment of an atmosphere of peace and conciliation that will permit the functioning of democratic institutions."[17] The Security Council,

[15] Resolution of the Tenth Meeting of Consultation of Ministers of Foreign Affairs, Organization of American States, May 1, 1965, U.N. Doc. S/6319, May 3, 1965.

[16] Article 17 of the OAS Charter states: "The territory of a state is inviolable; it may not be the object, even temporarily, of military occupation or of other measures of force taken by another state, directly or indirectly, under any grounds whatever."

[17] Resolution of the Tenth Meeting of Consultation of Ministers of Foreign Affairs, Organization of American States, May 6, 1965, para. 2, U.N. Doc. S/6333, Rev. 1, May 7, 1965.

under Article 54 of the Charter,[18] was informed of passage of the OAS resolution, as it had been informed of other actions taken by the regional body in the Dominican conflict.

The preference of the United States government for OAS consideration of the Dominican disorder rather than United Nations involvement stemmed from America's dominant position in the OAS and its disinclination to encourage the Soviet Union or Cuba to exploit the American military presence on the island for propaganda purposes. Thus when the Security Council debated the Dominican question in sixteen meetings from May 3 to May 25, the American representative argued that the OAS should continue to exercise primary responsibility for attaining a permanent cease-fire and promoting a political solution to the disorder. In a series of statements to the Council, Adlai Stevenson defended the American intervention as necessary: "When hours and even minutes counted—there was no time for deliberate consultation and for the organization of international machinery which did not yet exist."[19] He repeated the claims of the U.S. government that its intervention was justified on humanitarian and legal grounds and stressed its interest in securing a settlement in accord with the wishes of the Dominican people.

The predictable Soviet and Cuban denunciations of the American position were echoed by British, Bolivian, and French criticisms. The United States succeeded in preventing the passage of a Security Council resolution that would have condemned its actions and given U Thant and the Council more extensive responsibilities in the Dominican conflict. While debate in the OAS and the UN continued, the United States shifted its support from the military junta it had placed in power to a coalition regime, in a belated acknowledgment of the depth of non-Communist endorsement of the rebel cause. Throughout the next few months, the rebel forces continued to press for an enlarged UN role rather than OAS mediation, which they regarded as partial to the Dominican military forces manipulated by the United States. Each local party to the internal conflict sought to use one of the interested international organizations to advance its cause against its opponents.

The eventual settlement of the Dominican conflict, the establishment of a provisional government after a cease-fire, and the inquiries into violations of human rights took place under OAS aegis. Frequent reports of "confusion" between the regional body's functions and

[18] Article 54 states: "The Security Council shall at all times be kept fully informed of activities undertaken or in contemplation under regional arrangements or by regional agencies for the maintenance of international peace and security."

[19] U.N. Doc. S/P.V. 1200, May 5, 1965, 12.

those of the UN observer on the scene were voiced in Security Council debates and in the press. U Thant on several occasions expressed concern over the precedents that the OAS actions might set for relationships between the UN and regional organizations. The Charter articles setting forth the desirable balance between regional and UN activities are ambiguous. They emphasize the need for Security Council authorization when regional enforcement action is undertaken, but they do not clarify what kinds of action shall be considered "enforcement." The United States, arguing that the OAS actions in the Dominican Republic did not constitute "enforcement," claimed the primacy of the regional organization. Apart from legal questions, the conflict raised, but did not resolve, a practical issue: the compatibility of functions between regional organizations and the UN in civil strife. Might it be desirable to consider allotting *peacekeeping* functions to one organization and *peacemaking* functions to the other? What function should each organization assume? Can a feasible combination be found?

The widespread distaste for the American intervention was evident as few Latin American countries endorsed a United States plan for a permanent inter-American peace force. Aside from Brazil, only the military dictatorships of Honduras, Nicaragua, and Paraguay contributed troops; Costa Rica contributed police. The initial intervention raised doubts about the purposes of regional organization in the hemisphere; the subsequent establishment of the inter-American force and the OAS assumption of responsibilities for securing a specific settlement ran the risk of hindering the organization in the performance of other political tasks.

VI

The capabilities of security pacts in circumstances of intraregional civil strife remain untested. When disturbances between the Greek and Turkish communities erupted on Cyprus in December 1963, it appeared that NATO might lead in the search for a settlement of the internal conflict. The British and American governments clearly preferred a regional approach to a global one. The British proposed a three-month, NATO-recruited peacekeeping force of 10,000 men under British command with political guidance from a committee of ambassadors, as well as the appointment of a mediator from a North Atlantic non-NATO country.

Turkey reluctantly assented to the plan, Greece accepted it with some reservations, but the Greek Cypriots rejected it. American support for the British plan was subject to temporary suspension of the two contested treaties and avoidance of any Security Council control. The U.S. hoped to prevent Soviet intrusion into the affair via Council vetoes. The Cypriot president, Archbishop Makarios, then demanded that the proposed force be made responsible to the Security Council, that Turkish troops be excluded from its composition, and that mediation be confined to Britain, Greece, and Turkey (with the Turkish Cypriot minority barred from the talks). He also urged that a Commonwealth force be established rather than a NATO one. Shortly thereafter, the United States yielded to Makarios' demand that the force be "linked" to the UN via "reports." After additional negotiations between U Thant, American and British officials, and the Archbishop, the U.S. abandoned its earlier position and, with Britain, endorsed an appeal to the Security Council.

Speculation on alternatives to the course adopted are worth pondering. Could the U.S. and British negotiators have given Makarios a choice of a NATO force or no force at all and risked Soviet intervention in the Cyprus dispute? Would Makarios have invited the Soviets to intervene directly, and would they have done so? Could the two Western powers have arranged to have the Council meet in order to authorize a force whose composition and instructions were agreed upon in advance by the parties? The Archbishop's refusal to accept a regional peacemaking force or continuation of the British force on Cyprus marked a defeat for Anglo-American diplomacy. It was clear that his rejection did not derive from the military deficiencies of these proposals but from his conviction that the UN would serve as the most reliable mechanism for realization of his internal political goals. Controlling eighty percent of the island's population, the Archbishop defined the problem as one of "self-determination" in an attempt to court the sympathies of the new states who might be expected to support anticolonialist positions in the General Assembly.

The evidence suggests that instances of a breakdown of law and order may pose the most intractable problems for regional organizations and for the UN. One issue that remains unsettled is the character of the desirable relationship between the two types of organization. Since it can be assumed that political rather than legal considerations are uppermost in the minds of policy-makers, any clarification of these ill-defined relationships that would require advance commitments to use one or the other type of organization first or exclusively appears remote. The demands placed on the UN in breakdowns of law and order are comparable to those placed on regional organizations when they become involved in similar conflicts. It is clear that rival local factions will attempt to use these organizations, against one another if necessary, in order to realize internal political aspirations. Also, it is apparent that the different members of regional organizations may disagree on the nature of outside threats or external control in individual conflicts and may withhold the support needed to promote collective peacekeeping actions or negotiations between disputants. As a result, it is possible that a regional organization may become overcommitted, politically, if its members cannot agree on a single candidate or group of individuals among many to perform the order-giving functions of government.

The efforts of regional organizations to foster peaceful solutions to internal disorders may be unrewarding if the type of settlement proposed ignores the fact that the very outbreak of violence indicates the lack of a national consensus needed for orderly government. Recommendations that call for the establishment of new political structures must take national histories and traditions into account. If a solution is proposed in regional decision-making councils that is not suited to the politics of the country in disorder, tensions may be exacerbated rather than eased. The more extensive the role of the international organization, the greater the uncertainties that hamper attempts to secure cease-fires and lasting accommodation between local adversaries. Less ambitious but no less desirable tasks for regional actors to perform in breakdowns of law and order include adequate fact-finding procedures and selective border-sealing or supervision while violence works itself out. These activities would be extremely valuable, given the frequent inability of the UN to undertake them. In addition, such responses would underscore the compatibility of regional and global approaches, a compatibility threatened by elaborate peacekeeping operations that appear competitive.

VII

The interests that have limited the effectiveness of international organizations in colonial wars and in conflicts involving a breakdown of law and order have assumed still greater proportions in proxy wars and conflicts involving charges of external aggression or subversion. The actions of third-party states—the superpowers in Greece, Guatemala, Hungary, Lebanon, Laos, and Vietnam, and Egypt and Saudi Arabia in Yemen—have heightened the threat to regional and global stability when internal violence has erupted in these countries. International organizations as political institutions have represented at best a partial embodiment of national objectives for third parties. They have served chiefly as forums for debate and propaganda. Occasionally, the UN and regional organizations have undertaken investigations or observation missions, but patterns of response have developed excluding large-scale peacekeeping operations or responsibilities for obtaining political settlements.

The policy preferences of the United States and the Soviet Union continue to be crucial in determining whether regional and global approaches to these conflicts are perceived as compatible or competitive. Throughout the postwar period, American, Soviet, and, more recently, Chinese policy-makers have exercised wide discretionary powers in classifying internal conflicts as externally initiated, abetted, or controlled. Major U.S. foreign policy "doctrines"—the Truman, the Eisenhower, and the Johnson-Rusk—have had as a prime purpose the delineation of "subversive" threats or "aggressive" intentions that the United States commits itself to combat by whatever means —unilateral, regional, or multilateral—it selects. Similarly, Russian and Chinese policy statements have argued that "wars of national liberation" or "people's wars" against "imperialist oppressors" are not subject to international review procedures that might assess the legitimacy of interventions and counterinterventions. Since the Chinese leadership is not represented directly in the UN or in regional organizations, its doctrines and actions are removed still further from review than are those of the United States and the Soviet Union.

The superpowers, both in the UN and in their respective alliances, have adopted flexible criteria for estimating the dangers created by each other's interventions in internal conflicts. Understandably, security pacts have served as the most convenient vehicles for the superpowers in their efforts to legitimize interventionary courses of action. Yet the internal stresses and strains of their defense systems— NATO, SEATO and the Warsaw Pact—have confronted the U.S. and the Soviet Union with the need to "go it alone" if they choose to intervene on a massive scale in conflicts like Vietnam. The increasing reluctance of formal allies to support superpower interventions in internal conflicts, of which Vietnam is the most notable example, has reduced one value of security pacts to the superpowers. At the same time, the lessened tension between the superpowers themselves has called the rationale of such alliances into question.

Throughout the postwar period, the superpowers have used a variety of instrumentalities to secure endorsement of their own policy goals as well as to prevent unfavorable shifts in the world balance of power. When internal conflicts involving charges of subversion or external aggression have appeared to presage detrimental shifts, the United States and the Soviet Union have employed security pacts and the UN to explain the selection of direct intervention, lesser forms of manipulation, or, in some cases, abstention. The United States used the UN, prior to NATO's formation, as the mechanism for exposing what it termed a Soviet-inspired foreign challenge to Greek independence and sovereignty. The announcement of the Truman Doctrine reaffirmed the already evident U.S. policy of meeting such challenges with unilateral or collective defense responses rather than with UN measures.

In the 1954 Guatemalan disorder, the U.S. successfully used the OAS as a Latin American NATO, while the Soviet Union argued for Security Council primacy. In the 1956 Hungarian uprising, the U.S., preoccupied with intra-NATO ramifications of the Suez crisis, used the UN as an instrument for expressing its desire to avoid intervention. The Soviet Union, defending its unilateral intervention in Hungary, cited the Warsaw Pact in a transparent effort to adduce "regional" legitimacy for its actions. In Lebanon, the U.S. approved UN observation, while it supported the incumbent Chamoun regime with a unilateral intervention.

Repeatedly, the superpowers have denounced each other's interventions or defended their own by referring to Article 51 of the UN Charter.[20] In no disorder has the tendency to allege "self-defense" against "armed attack" produced greater controversay than in the Vietnam war.[21] In no instance has the failure to develop mandatory review procedures for arguments based on Article 51 been more dangerous. The United States, in asserting that infiltration from North Vietnam to assist insurgents constitutes "an armed attack" that justifies its large-scale intervention on behalf of incumbents in South Vietnam as "self-defense," has underscored the impotence of regional security pacts as well as the UN in proxy conflicts. Despite American attempts to place its intervention in a SEATO context, many states in the region, as well as outside it, have denied the validity of this characterization. Apart from the legal ramifications of such questionable arguments, the political consequences for international organizations are serious.

The absence of agreement on definitions of aggression, self-defense, and armed attack hinders, but need not preclude entirely, the development of review procedures in the UN or in regional organizations whereby member states might subject to careful scrutiny the claims and counterclaims made under Article 51. Without such scrutiny, unilateral interventions can continue to transform internal disorders

[20] Article 51 states: "Nothing in the present Charter shall impair the inherent right of individual or collective self-defense if an armed attack occurs against a Member of the United Nations, until the Security Council has taken the measures necessary to maintain international peace and security. Measures taken by Members in the exercise of this right of self-defense shall be immediately reported to the Security Council and shall not in any way affect the authority and responsibility of the Security Council under the present Charter to take at any time such action as it deems necessary in order to maintain or restore international peace and security."

[21] For a lucid analysis of the legal aspects of American intervention in Vietnam, see Falk, "The International Regulation of Internal Violence in the Developing Countries," 63-67.

into proxy wars with no chance of effective international regulation. With such procedures, the salience of regional organizations as centers for debate, conciliation, negotiation, or even selective interpositions would be enhanced.[22]

Clearly, it is in the interest of the developing countries to press for the institutionalization of review procedures since the larger powers cannot be expected to do so. Relevant discussion in the OAU and the OAS might demonstrate the compatibility of regional and global approaches in enforcing a pause in fighting during which parties could move toward negotiations. Collective defense arrangements, by definition, will tend to favor a revision or maintenance of the status quo favorable to one or the other superpower, an objective that may be incompatible with the aims of international organizations in specific instances. The Afro-Asian states and the Latin American states who wish to avoid client status may improve their chances by forming organizations that avoid alliance connotations.

VIII

The preceding discussion has emphasized the internal and external limitations that characterize the responses of regional organizations to civil strife. Some limitations—for example, restricted memberships, jurisdictions, and resources—are equally significant in attempts to regulate the three types of internal conflict considered. Others, especially ideological splits, may be more relevant to one type of conflict than to the other two. Colonial wars, internal conflicts involving a breakdown of law and order, and proxy wars and internal conflicts involving charges of subversion or external aggression confront regional organizations with demands they are not well equipped to meet. The line between the three types of disorders is fluid, of course. A colonial war may be but the first step toward a breakdown of law and order, and then a proxy war. The perceptions of leaders of third-party states rather than objective tests may be most important in determining the classification of internal conflicts and, hence, the compatibility or competitiveness of regional and global approaches. These approaches appear to be most compatible in the colonial wars and potentially most competitive in the breakdowns of law and order.

The coincident interest of global and regional organizations in proxy wars is the maximization of pressures that will restrain the superpowers, China, or smaller revisionist powers in the modernizing areas from counterinterventions in civil strife. The present resources

---

[22] For a provocative discussion of this point, see Oran R. Young, *The Intermediaries: Third Parties in International Crises* (Princeton 1967), chap. 3.

of regional groupings like the OAU and OAS permit investigatory activities that present little risk and, too often, are of little value in civil strife. The resources of security pacts, on the other hand, are impressive militarily but of peripheral political value in promoting peaceful change in modernizing countries.

Barring desirable changes in the direction of stronger autonomous regional groupings, the prevailing pattern of *ad hoc* responses to internal conflicts is likely to persist. A restructuring of regional organization would facilitate the regulation of internal conflict on a sub-global basis. As already suggested, the smaller states, whose territories are targets for competitive unilateral interventions, might well take the lead in establishing new organizations that exclude the superpowers from membership. But if countries in disorder are to avoid foreign interventions, third-party states must exercise greater restraint in using internal conflicts for the achievement of national policy goals. Both changes in the international system are desirable for purposes of conflict management. Both are feasible only if a large number of states give priority to them.

13. INTERNATIONAL ORGANIZATIONS AND INTERNATIONAL SYSTEMS[1]

By WOLFRAM F. HANRIEDER

A N international system is a pattern of relations among the actors
in world politics which is characterized by the scope of actor
objectives and the means available and applied for their realization.
This set of ends-means relationships reflects the tasks imposed on
the system by its members, their political demands and physical
capabilities, and the nature of the forces which operate within and
among them.

An international organization may be defined as an institutionalized arrangement among members of the international system to
solve tasks which have evolved from systemic conditions. The organization therefore reflects the attributes, aspirations, and preoccupations of its members. Inasmuch as the organization represents a
pattern of relations formed by the regular interaction of its members,
it may be regarded as a subsystem, or *structure*, of the international
system.[2] Examples of other systemic structures would be the balancing operations of the "classical" balance-of-power system, nuclear
deterrence postures, the procedures and restraints of international
law, the interdependencies of international trade, alliances, the rou-

Reprinted by permission of the author and *The Journal of Conflict Resolution,* X (No. 3, September 1966), 297-313.

[1] This essay is a revised version of a paper delivered at the annual convention of the American Political Science Association, September 1964. I am grateful for research support received from the Center of International Studies at
Princeton University and for the generous counsel of my colleagues at the Center, especially Gabriella Rosner Lande and Richard A. Falk. [Author's note]

[2] In performing its designated functions, which presumably affect the conditions of the system by solving tasks, the organization may also be viewed as an
actor of the international system. Depending on the analytical purpose and
vantage point, an international organization may therefore be viewed either as
an *actor*, along with other actors in the system including the members of the
organization, or as one of many possible *structures* through which the members of the system address themselves to tasks and projects which arise from
the ends—means relationships of the system.

tines of diplomatic communications, and so forth. Clearly, the efficacy and relevance of different types of structures, which may be institutionalized or not, can be expected to change along with transformations of the conditions and tasks of different historical international systems. In short, the members of an international system may turn to different types of task-solving structures, depending on the historical circumstances prevailing in the system and how they are perceived by members of the system.

In what follows, I shall be concerned with three of the many possible functions that public international organizations may be intended to perform: collective security, peaceful change, and pacific settlement. In particular, I want to explore the permissive conditions and patterns of relationships that should prevail in the international system if an international organization is to perform successfully in these three task areas. It is the purpose of this essay to spell out the ideal analytic precepts for the three functions, and to contrast those ideal analytical suppositions with the conditions of historical international systems in terms of their compatibility, dissonance, or irrelevance.

The ideal preconditions to be postulated for collective security, peaceful change, and pacific settlement operations also represent a patterned interaction among the actors in world politics and their ends–means relationships; that is to say, the relationships among actors in these three task areas may also be viewed as systems, although limited to specific functions.[3] I shall, therefore, be concerned with two types of systems. The first is the international system as the comprehensive multifunctional aggregate of patterns of relationships covering a wide variety of interactions among the members of the system. Of this type of system, I shall focus on two examples: analytical propositions about the classical balance-of-power systm, and the concrete historical international system from World War II to the present. The second type of system represents functionally specific "task systems" concerned with projects of collective security, peaceful change, and pacific settlement.

The role and chances of success of an international organization in these task areas are necessarily affected by how closely the actual conditions of international systems approximate the ideal circumstances required for the three functional subsystems. Before examining such degrees of congruence or dissonance we must specify some of the prerequisites for a functioning collective security, peaceful change, and pacific settlement system. The rather sharp differentiation among the

[3] For a persuasive argument to break down the aggregate of relationships represented by the global international system into systematically treated "issue-areas," see Rosenau (1963).

three functional systems which results from this analytical separation should not obscure the fact that one cannot expect to come across a "pure" case of collective security or peaceful change in an empirical setting. Nor can one anticipate that the ideal prerequisites for these functional systems are ever met in a concrete historical situation. Still, the formulation of the concepts of collective security, peaceful change, and pacific settlement as "ideal" analytical types should permit useful comparisons among them and illuminate the contrast between their ideal prerequisites and the limitations and opportunities posed by concrete historical circumstances.

I. The Three Task Systems

1. THE COLLECTIVE SECURITY SYSTEM

Collective security is based on the premise that the members of the system deter and stifle aggression by threatening to apply or by actually applying military, economic, or diplomatic sanctions to the offending party. The system rests on the principle of "one for all and all for one" and differs from a defensive alliance in that it seeks to prevent aggression from *within* the system, whereas a defensive alliance envisages a collective response to a party *external* to the alliance. The advance identification of friend, and sometimes of foe, in an alliance is incompatible with a collective security system, which presupposes impartiality and flexibility of attitudes on the part of the members until the aggressor is identified. This in turn requires that an effective collective security system come as close as possible to universal membership of states; that the members commit themselves in advance to a specified response to a specified challenge; and that they reject bilateral localized wars.

In a functioning collective security system the combined capabilities of the restrainers must always be, as a minimum precept, greater than those of the aggressor. Although this is a logically sufficient precondition, the operational requirements of the system actually call for a significant *preponderance* of power on the part of the restrainers. The system is built on the propositions that aggression does not pay because of the overwhelming power which can be brought against an aggressor; that a potential aggressor is deterred by this realization; and that, therefore, the system is brought into action infrequently. In other words, it is expected that the system should *deter* rather than *act*. When the power ratio between potential aggressors and potential restrainers approaches an equilibrium these assumptions are called into question. A corollary to these considerations is the desirability of some degree of disarmament and some measure of arms control to prevent a unilateral technological breakthrough. Ideally, a collective security system requires considerable diffusion of power among the members. Both diffusion of power and universality of membership are conducive to the anticipated *un*balancing of power through which a potential or actual aggressor is to be contained. While the system should be capable of institutionalized and centralized *management* of power when aggression takes place, the *distribution* of power among the members should be diffuse.

A collective security system is essentially a system for the management of *means*. Strictly speaking, the members of the system and its institutional organ need not be concerned with the *substance* of the issue over which aggression is committed. It is not necessary, for the performance of collective security functions, to consider the intrinsic merits of the dispute. The system is "involved in the penalization of disturbers of the peace, without too much consideration of the factors which make the peace susceptible of disturbance," and the members must be willing to curb an aggressor "without regard to any underlying sympathies they may have for claims of frustrated justice that may be enunciated by the assailants. As a general proposition, peace through justice must be the watchword of collective security. However, its provisional rule of action can hardly be any other than peace *over* justice" (Claude, 1956, pp. 289 and 262; also see chs. 11 and 12). Indeed, neutrality with respect to the merits of the issue and abstention from substantive judgment are necessary so that the members can muster the flexibility of alignment and the unbalancing of power required to contain an aggressor.

Lack of concern with substantive issues also implies that the operations of a collective security system tend to favor the status quo, especially with respect to territory. While the members of the system need not inherently seek to perpetuate the existing state of affairs, "the essential commitments of a collective security system necessitate the willingness of nations to fight for the status quo" (Claude, 1956, p. 261).

The concept of territorial inviolability is important for the system in another respect. The trigger of aggression which actuates the system is difficult to define legally and often hard to establish operationally. An act of aggression is most easily established when it involves physical transgressions which violate clearly established territorial boundaries. Consequently, a functioning collective security system is most unambiguously called into action when one state violates the territory of another. In such a situation there is no need for the collective security organization to be concerned with the *internal* sociopolitical conditions of the parties involved. The system becomes actuated by a clear-cut, physical, instrumental event: the use of proscribed means by an aggressor. Because of the "external" nature of the event, it is possible to regard states as monolithic units whose aspirations and domestic political predispositions can remain unexamined. Therefore, a collective security system is not required to interfere in matters of domestic jurisdiction. This is, of course, a corollary to the proposition that the system is not concerned with the substantive merits or the underlying grievances of the dispute over which aggression is committed.

In sum, a collective security system is a system for the management of means; it is actuated by a proscribed event without regard to the merits of the underlying issue and the internal conditions of the members.

2. THE PEACEFUL CHANGE SYSTEM

In important respects a peaceful change system offers the starkest contrast to the collective security system. The meaning of the term "peaceful change" is not easily circumscribed because of its broad and elusive implications and the not always consistent, or even explicit, attributes given to it in the literature. It is generally agreed, however, that concern with peaceful change entails consideration of ends, purposes, aspirations, and projects, in addition to the concern that these objectives be pursued through nonviolent means. Attitudes toward change in the international system are necessarily value-laden, and issues arising from the advocated or impending transformation of the status quo require substantive evaluations of what constitutes a desirable dynamic international order. Frederick Dunn defined peaceful change as being "concerned both with changes in the distribution of rights and possessions and changes in the laws which govern the acquisition of rights and possessions" (1937, p. 3), and Inis Claude contrasts pacific settlement, as being concerned with "disputes *within* the legal order," with peaceful change as being concerned with "disputes *about* the legal order" (1956, p. 228; emphasis in original).

Although a collective security system and a peaceful change system may well be interdependent for their respective operations, important differences exist between them. Most importantly, perhaps, these two systems can be distinguished by the differing emphasis they place on considering the *substance* of issues. While a collective security system is primarily a system for the management of *means,* a peaceful change system cannot help but face up to the intrinsic aspirations reflected in the issues and address them with a substantive response; in important respects the latter system is a management of *ends.*

The two systems also reflect differing attitudes *vis-à-vis* the status quo. In a functioning peaceful change system the members agree on the inevitability, and perhaps the desirability, of change. This attitude must more or less explicitly take cognizance of the sociopolitical and economic aspirations of member states. To recognize the relevance of grievances, ambitions, and projects to international order requires not only a substantive commitment with respect to national aspirations but also entails concern with the *internal* conditions of members. Consequently, peaceful change operations should be initiated at the incipient stage of conflict situations: "peaceful change, as distinguished from collective security, is any successful adjustment in the international status quo brought about *before* a specific 'dispute' involving force or the threat of it arises" (Haas, 1962, pp. 286–287; emphasis added).

In sum, a peaceful change system is a system for the management of ends and projects; it requires a positive attitude with respect to change, a substantive evaluation of aspirations, and concern with the internal disposition of states.

3. THE PACIFIC SETTLEMENT SYSTEM

Whereas the prime instruments of the collective security system are sanctions of one variety or another, pacific settlement relies chiefly on such devices as good offices, inquiry, mediation, arbitration, and conciliation. These methods depend less on institutional structures than do those of a collective security system. However, the more novel instruments of pacific settlement or pacific "perpetuation" of disputes—truce organizations, plebiscite groups, paramilitary multi-national forces and organizational "presence" as keepers of the peace, etc.—in fact presuppose some measure of institutional organization.

The operational prerequisites of a pacific settlement system are in important ways a hybrid between those required for collective security and those required for peaceful change. The desirability of a roughly equal distribution of power among the members in the collective security system is somewhat less relevant in a pacific settlement system. To be sure, the disputants whose conflict is being mediated by a third party should presumably be of equal power. If the imbalance of power between the disputants were too great there would be less incentive for the stronger party to consent to arbitration, other things being equal. Especially if the arbitrator is an international organization it should, for maximum effectiveness, represent the preponderance of power and influence of the members of the system. The likelihood of this preponderance increases the more equally power is distributed among the members. As in the collective security system, the grouping of powers in alliances tends to undermine the mediating functions of a pacific settlement system, since it implies advance identification of potential opponents. At the same time, the system can conceivably work if there are at least three alliance groupings, the minimum number of units necessary for arbitration and mediation functions. This in turn presupposes that the members hold heterogeneous attitudes on the substantive merits of the issue mediated. The necessary presence of a neutral third party—nation-state, alliance, or international organization—presupposes that some actors in the system are able to conceive of a third alternative attitude in addition to the two conflicting ones represented by the disputants. The pacific settlement system is therefore more ambivalent regarding the desirability of actor homogeneity (with respect to both power and attitudes) than either a collective security or a peaceful change system.

This ambivalence of attitudinal requirements is also reflected in another way. Claude suggests, for example, that

> ... the pacific settlement approach has been characterized by emphasis upon the problem of discouraging resort to war as a means of solving disputes. It appears that war, even though it has been interpreted in functional terms, has been recognized as a problem in itself; the task is not so much to settle the quarrel as to prevent the adoption of violent means for its settlement. The pacific settlement physician finds himself engaged as seriously in curing the addiction to a false remedy as in curing the original disease (1956, p. 223).

In other words, consistent with their middle position between collective security and peaceful change, pacific settlement functions involve both ends and means relationships: the system is not as much concerned with the substantive dimension of a dispute as is peaceful change, but neither does it envisage a purely instrumental response like the means management of collective security.

A collective security system is not operationally concerned with the merits of the underlying issue but condemns unauthorized violence as a method of resolution. A pacific settlement system assumes "the moral ambiguity of a situation of conflict; avoiding an initial judgment on the moral merits of the positions held by disputants, it applies pressure equally to the two parties to adopt positive moral attitudes conducive to an agreed solution" (Claude, 1956, p. 256). The collective security system ignores substantive merits but is unambiguously clear in proscribing unauthorized means. Pacific settlement is ambivalent as to the merits and implicitly encourages bargaining and compromise solutions. Consequently, the pacific settlement system seeks to prevent violence by providing reasonable alternatives, "functional equivalents," for the solution of issues—conciliation forums, arbitration machinery, face-saving devices, cooling-off periods which may clear up misunderstandings, and so forth.

Pacific settlement operations also tend to take some cognizance of the internal predisposition of states. The assumption that war may be caused by ignorance or misunderstanding, or that it may result from irresponsible or cynical national leadership, tends to focus the concerns of the system on the nature of societies or the character of specific groups in society. While collective security "contemplates the indiscriminate punishment of entire populations for the misdeeds of their governments," in the assumption of pacific settlement "kings, dictators, diplomats, militarists, financiers, and arms manufacturers have shared the opprobrium of the accusation that they are the rascals who lead unwitting people to the slaughter for their private ends . . ." (Claude, 1956, pp. 290 and 227). Pacific settlement does not share the monolithic image of nation-states implicit in a collective security system; but neither does it fully share the willingness of an operative peaceful change system to address serious social grievances with an unequivocal and carefully considered response which rejects scapegoat theories of social discontent.

4. THE CONTINUUM OF TASK SYSTEMS

It follows from the preceding discussion that, in important respects, the conditions and attitudes conducive to the functioning of the three task systems can be ordered along a continuum[4] (see Table 1). One reason for arranging (and defining) these task-systems along a continuum is to underline the *gradual* transition from the conditions and assumptions of one system to those of another. (In a concrete historical situation an international organization may of course be concerned with the operational implications of all three task areas simultaneously; because of the differences between these implications, however, there is the more reason to point to their possibly contradictory impact on organizational functions.)

[4] The contrast between the two ends of the continuum is suggestively similar to the one between two fundamentally different approaches to the study of international politics, analyzed by Singer (1961). The first approach looks at international relations from a global vantage point and highlights the compulsive features of the international system, which are viewed as imposing inescapable restraints and necessary attitudes on the actors. This "systemic" perspective treats nation-states as essentially monolithic units whose internal makeup is generally irrelevant for understanding their external conduct. The other approach stresses the relevance of internal predispositions and the complex internal basis of actor activity, and tends to relegate environmental conditions to a secondary analytical place. The parallels between the first approach and collective security preoccupations, and between the second and peaceful change preoccupations, are obvious. The methodological characteristics of either approach also are germane to analyses of collective security or peaceful change functions. For a fuller treatment of the problems raised by this dual perspective in considering actor aspirations, see Hanrieder (1965a).

There is, first, a progression as to the degree to which the operations of the three systems rest on an assessment of the internal condition and predispositions of the members. Because of the external and instrumental nature of the trigger of aggression which actuates the collective security system, that system can regard members as monolithic units. The peaceful change system, on the other hand, must be sensitive to the domestic conditions and preoccupations of the members and assume some degree of responsibility and jurisdiction for the pace and direction of aspirations and the methods employed for their realization. The operational concerns of the pacific settlement system can be placed at a half-way point between the two ends of the continuum.

A second element in the continuum, closely related to the first, is a progression along a *zweckrational-wertrational* line, in Weber's terms.[5] A collective security system embodies an instrumental, *zweckrational* response in the sense that it should be operational without the members coming to terms with the substantive, intrinsic, *wertrational* aspects of a conflict situation. While the purpose of the system is of course based on an intrinsic ultimate value—namely, that peace is desirable—its operational requirements do not logically demand substantive assessment of an issue. The peaceful change system on the other hand, is involved in substantive, *wertrational* assessments and concerned with management of ends, projects, and aspirations. Again the pacific settlement system occupies a middle position between the two ends of the continuum.

A third element in the continuum pertains to the degree of immediacy and urgency of the issues addressed by the three systems. A collective security system becomes actuated by *aggression,* the last and most serious step in the escalation of a conflict situation; pacific settlement intercedes at the stage of *confrontation* between conflicting interests; and peaceful change is involved at the incipient stage of aspirations, that of interest verbalization and *formulation.* Clearly, this continuum is again closely related to the other two sets of progressions: from collective security to pacific settlement to peaceful change, the focus of concerns and operations moves closer to the underlying sources of the conflict.

There is, finally, the important progression from operational preoccupation with the status quo in the collective security system to that of concern with transformation in the peaceful change system, with the pacific settlement system again occupying an intermediate position.

---

[5] For a summary statement, see Parsons *et al.* (1961), pp. 1063-1065.

TABLE 1

	COLLECTIVE SECURITY	PACIFIC SETTLEMENT	PEACEFUL CHANGE
Operational concern with internal conditions	low	medium	high
Value response which actuates the system	*zweckrational-* instrumental	mixed	*wertrational-* substantive
Degree of urgency and of conflict escalation addressed	aggression	confrontation	incipiency
Operational attitudes toward system transformation	status quo	compromise	change

II. THE BALANCE-OF-POWER SYSTEM AND THE THREE TASK SYSTEMS

Space limitations do not permit an examination of the relationships between the three task systems and the *historical* circumstances of the classical balance-of-power system of the eighteenth century. Nonetheless, it may be useful to consider very briefly the degrees of compatibility between the three task systems and *analytical* postulates of a balance-of-power system as formulated, among others, by Morton Kaplan (1957), Richard Rosecrance (1963), and Inis Claude (1956, 1961, 1962).[6]

1. COLLECTIVE SECURITY

On both normative and analytical grounds an ideally functioning collective security system is frequently regarded as being the *opposite* of a balance-of-power system. It is argued, for example, that a collective security system seeks to bring about an *un*balancing of power whenever an aggressor is to be restrained by the power combination of the other members in the system. At that time, the restraining members are to *abjure* neutrality and treat the aggressor as the com-

---

[6] Claude suggests that a balance-of-power system, a collective security system, and world government be viewed as "systems related to each other as successive points along a continuum and differing most fundamentally in the degree of centralization of power and authority which they imply. In this view, balance of power represents the extreme of decentralization, a kind of *laissez-faire* arrangement in the sphere of power politics. . . . Collective security falls next in line along the scale of centralization, representing an effort to deal with the power problem by superimposing a scheme of partially centralized management upon a situation in which power remains diffused among national units" (1961, pp. 220-221).

mon enemy.[7] The balance-of-power system, on the other hand, is taken to rest on the capability and willingness of members to preserve the neutrality of alignment which allows a flexible shifting of power constellations.[8]

The nonneutral stance of the restrainers in a functioning collective security system is spurious, however, and subject to an important qualification. It is true that the members are expected to treat the offender as the common enemy in an established case of aggression. Prior to the act of aggression, however, the members should ideally be neutral with respect to the issue over which aggression is committed, in order to avoid preconceived "opinions" which would make it difficult to abjure neutrality once aggression has taken place. A collective security system operates on the assumption that the members oppose the act of aggression qua aggression, regardless of their attitudes on the issue itself. (To be sure, the system can be expected to work best when the attitudes of the members are neutral, or in agreement, with respect to the issue. But this condition is not logically required for the functioning of a collective security system.)

As in the collective security system, the members of a balance-of-power system are to respond to a physical, instrumental event, that of a shifting of power, which must be compensated for by other shifts of power, primarily through realignments. The members in both systems are expected to react almost automatically and to ignore the underlying reasons for the *casus operandi* which actuates the system. Aggression in one system, and a shift of power in the other, triggers the systemic response.

Another important similarity is the desirability of homogeneous membership in both systems. It is a generally accepted analytical proposition that an ideally functioning balance-of-power system should have homogeneous membership. Not only is it desirable that the members have similar "political cultures"; they should also be of approximately equal strength. Both precepts are important for the neutrality of alignment which allows the flexible equilibrating necessary to keep the system going (see Kaplan, 1957, pp. 22-36; and Burns, 1957). This homogeneity is also desirable in a collective security system. The difference between the ideal power patterns in the two systems is in the degree of *centralization of power management:* low in the balance-of-power system, high in the collective security system. Both systems, however, require a diffusion of power among the members. Moreover, both systems work best when the means available to the members are within moderate and stable limits. A balance-of-power system would most likely become unstable if mem-

---

[7] Cf. Russell (1961), pp. 630-636, esp. p. 633, in a rejoinder to Claude (1961).
[8] For an analytical statement, see Kaplan (1957, pp. 22-36).

bers were engaged in an armaments race or if they had to fear far-reaching technological breakthroughs. A collective security system also functions best when coupled with at least partial disarmament (see Claude, 1956, pp. 266-67; also Burns, 1958).

The two systems are also similar in that their operational requirements presuppose that the members can regard each other as monolithic units, without distinctions on the basis of regime, ideological orientation, race, and so forth. If this is not possible both systems break down because the necessary flexibility and open-mindedness of realignment (in the balance-of-power system) and the abjuring of neutrality in case of aggression (in the collective security system) are undermined.

Hence, the operational precepts of the two systems are different in only two major respects. War is an acceptable and perhaps necessary equilibrating instrument in the balance-of-power system; it is proscribed in a collective security system except as an authoritative collective response in case of aggression. The degree of centralization of the management of power is high in a collective security system and requires an institutional body for actuating the system; management of power is diffused in a balance-of-power system and equilibrating is expected to take place mechanically, without an institutionalized structure.

In sum, the differences between the operational prerequisites for a balance-of-power system and a collective security system are not nearly as pronounced as is implied in normative exhortations to replace the machinations of a balance-of-power system with the ordered processes of a collective security system. In fact, the attitudes required of the members in either system, and the required diffusion of power among them, are strikingly similar.

2. PEACEFUL CHANGE

If it is legitimate to place the three functional systems along the continuum I have suggested, the *dissimilarities* between the balance-of-power system and a peaceful change system should follow, by extension and analogy, from the significant *similarities* between the balance-of-power system and the collective security system.

An important distinction between the balance-of-power system and the peaceful change system is the difference between the operationally required attitudes toward change. The equilibrating operations in the balance-of-power system are based on, or lead to, an interest in the continuation of the system itself; the balance-of-power system is basically a status quo system. The peaceful change system, on the other hand, institutionalizes the readiness to encourage or permit change not only in the existing *inter*national distribution of rights and possessions but also, at least implicitly, in the existing *intra*national domestic distribution.

The different attitudes toward change in the two systems tend to reinforce their differing emphasis on considering the internal conditions of their members. A peaceful change system requires substantive responses to sociopolitical and economic aspirations which unavoidably rest on evaluations of the internal processes of member states. Unless there were general agreement on the desirable outcome of such issues among the members of a balance-of-power system, each nation would tend to distinguish among the others on that basis. This would prevent the flexible shifting of alignments in the system.

Another important distinction beween the two systems is the degree of institutionalization required for their operations. A balance-of-power system works on Adam Smith's principle of the "invisible hand." The system is self-adjusting and operates best when the members are allowed to pursue their self-interests, which are presumed to be essentially identical. Like the precept of a *laissez-faire* economy, the interaction and aggregation of properly pursued self-interests are expected to lead to the common interest. The equilibrating that seeks to compensate for shifts in the power pattern of the system responds "to *overt* changes in the equilibrium of forces, and [does] not form itself until power relations [are] in process of alteration" (Rosecrance, 1963, p. 52; emphasis added). A peaceful change system, on the other hand, is intended to come into play earlier, at the incipient stage of conflict. This makes it difficult to leave the regulation of forces of transformation to automatic, self-adjusting mechanisms. Attitudes toward ends, projects, and aspirations cannot be expected to equilibrate themselves as automatically as responses to overt shifts in power patterns. If the peaceful change system is to act effectively, it can hardly dispense with an institutional forum in which the members can formulate and organize a collective response.

3. PACIFIC SETTLEMENT

The intermediary point occupied by the pacific settlement system in the collective security-peaceful change continuum makes it harder to compare with the balance-of-power system.

With respect to concern with the internal conditions of the members, the resemblance between the two systems is ambiguous. Pacific settlement cannot regard states as monolithic units, as is possible in the balance-of-power system, but it is not committed to such a full and continuous cognizance of the aspirations and internal conditions of the members as is the peaceful change system. Similarly, the degree of complementarity is blurred on the *wertrational-zweckrational* aspect of the value responses that actuate the two systems.

Diffusion of power is desirable in both balance-of-power and pacific settlement operations. Diffusion and approximate equality of power multiply the chances that disputants in a pacific settlement system will prefer concilation and mediation to violent solutions; compromise is more attractive and dictation or self-abnegation less likely. As mentioned previously, however, diffusion is not as stringently required in the pacific settlement system as it is in the balance-of-power system, and lasting alliances need not necessarily render the system inoperative as long as at least three coalition "groups" are present to perform mediating functions for one another.

III. THE POSTWAR INTERNATIONAL SYSTEM AND THE THREE TASK SYSTEMS

1. COLLECTIVE SECURITY

The limitations imposed on collective security functions by the conditions of the postwar international system have been analyzed in a great number of commentaries. Here I shall merely summarize the most salient of these obstacles and restate them within the framework of my previous discussion.

First, the United Nations, the institutional framework established for collective security operations, presupposed a harmony of interests within the Big Five directorate of the permanent members of the Security Council. The developing bipolarity of conflict, of perceived interests, and of ideology between the Soviet Union and the Western powers shattered the concert envisaged by the framers of the Charter. Moreover, the expanded, worldwide dimensions of the postwar international system led the Cold War antagonists to assess most conflicts arising in the system in the light of their effect on the East-West struggle.

Secondly, the bipolarization of tensions and perceived interests between East and West was coupled with a bipolarization of capabilities. Power, rather than being diffused, was concentrated in the hands of two superpowers, setting them apart and above the weaker members of the system.[9]

Third, the UN was handicapped in its collective security functions by the nature of the state system in the postwar world. The framers

[9] The bipolar distribution of power among the members of the international system became even more symmetrical when the Soviet Union acquired nuclear weapons and delivery systems. However, this development held conflicting implications for the overall pattern of the international system. On the one hand, the dyadic *power* pattern between the United States and the Soviet

of the Charter apparently had assumed that it would be possible to draw rather clear distinctions between domestic and international affairs. The validity of this assumption is an important element in a working collective security system, because the system is called into action most unambiguously when the transgression involves the violation of territorial sovereignty. In many parts of the world this condition could not be met. Especially in conflict situations between colonial powers and their colonies, and among the new states, it was frequently difficult to draw meaningful distinctions between internal and external dimensions of a conflict. The political, social, economic, and administrative conditions in many of these new states in the system were such that the traditionally neat boundaries between sovereign entities could not be readily drawn. Moreover, while the conflict in some of these states raged over the control of the internal political structure, the outcome was assessed by the super-powers in a global context because the nature of the regime emerging from the domestic contest tended to determine its external attitudes and consequently affected the Cold War balance of power.

Finally, the UN organization itself became a forum which the superpowers sought to exploit for their respective national policies and in which they sought to marshal the support of the membership for Cold War projects. The organization was therefore prevented from mustering the flexibility of alignment against an aggressor which is required for collective security; it could not even be expected to exhibit a united moral front in cases of aggression, to say nothing of taking effective action.

In light of the contradictions between the conditions of the postwar international system, and those conducive to a working collective security system, it is not surprising that the UN failed in this task area. However, "collective" security functions were performed in the international system by alternative structures. For example, the

---

Union became more symmetrical; on the other hand, the previously more cohesive alliance systems of the two superpowers showed signs of loosening toward the late fifties and early sixties. (See Liska, 1962; Hanrieder, 1965b.) This fragmentation was, at least in part, a consequence of nuclear symmetry. Particularly the Western alliance began to show the strains imposed upon it by the "balance of terror" which called into question the credibility of a nuclear response by the alliance leader in case of aggression against its smaller allies. The security interests of the superpower and the smaller allies began to diverge and, coupled with economic and political regionalism in Western Europe, the Western alliance was exposed to strong centrifugal tendencies. (See Osgood, 1961 and 1962.) Bipolarity between the Cold War blocs was further eroded by the emergence of a large number of uncommitted new nations in Africa and Asia and the developing schism between the Soviet Union and Red China. The implications of these developments for UN functions in the task areas of peaceful change and pacific settlement will be discussed below.

restraints imposed by the nuclear balance of terror and by the two Cold War alliance blocs undoubtedly contributed substantially to the stability of the postwar world. This is one of the most poignant ironies of the postwar international order: the most stabilizing factors rested on conditions that vitiated a successful universal collective security system. The bipolar distribution of nuclear and conventional capabilities, undoubtedly a stabilizing influence for its deterrence effects, was antithetical to a collective security system, which ideally requires diffusion of power (albeit with centralized *ad hoc* management in the event of aggression). The postwar world was stable, at least in part, for the same reasons that made it extremely difficult to operate a successful collective security system.[10]

Despite the severe limitations placed upon the UN by the conditions of the international system, the organization did not wholly succumb to the deadlock threatened by the contrast between the real world and the collective security system envisaged in the Charter. Four different organizational attempts to escape the impasse can be distinguished.

First, the organization was of course not paralyzed entirely. A small number of *"ad hoc* concerts" between the superpowers, in cases which did not involve a direct confrontation of interests between East and West, provided some opportunities for organizational activity and relevance. On such occasions as the Kashmir, Indonesia, and Palestine disputes, the superpowers apparently considered it impolitic to take opposing stands, and this consequently allowed the UN to fulfill limited *ad hoc* functions.

A second route of escape was a shift of authority from the Security Council to the Assembly. Since the Council was immobilized by the veto, the Assembly was to activate the institutional mechanism to organize against aggression. Delegation of enforcement to the United States during the Korean conflict and the subsequent Uniting for Peace Resolution are examples of this alternative, which has been appropriately labeled "permissive enforcement." Ernst Haas (1955, p. 47) suggests that

> . . . the striking and unique feature of permissive enforcement lies in the fact that it could be directed *against* one of the guarantors of collective security. . . . Its purpose is the mobilization of the United Nations membership, or a portion of it, against the expansive design of any member state, including a permanent member of the Security Council, i.e., against one of the super-powers and its global bloc.

---

[10] For a strong argument that bipolar power and interest patterns stabilized the postwar international system, see Waltz (1964).

The unique set of circumstances which allowed permissive enforcement began to change already during the course of the Korean conflict, and it is difficult to envisage contingencies which would allow its recurrence.

A third organizational response to the collective security impasse, in contrast to permissive enforcement, attempted to *exclude* the superpowers (and their Cold War interests) from conflict situations. Buttressed by the executive leadership of the Secretary General and by military contingents from small and neutral states, this approach sought to isolate and neutralize conflicts by shielding them from Cold War influences. This worked fairly well in the Suez crisis of 1956, but it was less effective under different circumstances in the Congo operation, where the superpowers could not be excluded as successfully.

A final and perhaps most important alternative to collective security functions was that of "balancing." The concept of "balancing" in the UN rests on an intricate negotiating process wherein the Afro-Asian members, as neutral mediators, trade their support on Cold War security issues for the superpowers' support on colonial, social, and economic issues. In particular, the superpowers sought to enlist the symbol of the UN for their Cold War projects by supporting the neutrals' projects of colonial emancipation, human rights, and economic development. This bartering relationship

> . . . hinges on a balancing process among the members because it takes its departure from the *de facto* polarization of the nations around a pro-American, a pro-Soviet, and an uncommitted focus. The efforts of the uncommitted bloc or blocs provide the initiative to which the two antagonists have to adjust, thus setting up a pattern of compromise. Balancing of influence and power is of the essence in this process, since the conciliation efforts of the uncommitted bloc are likely to be taken seriously by the super-powers, not because of good will, but in order not to alienate allies or offend important neutrals [Haas, 1955, p. 55].

UN operations in the area of "balancing" are of particular significance because they reflect, and rest upon, the gradual loosening of the postwar bipolarity of the international system. For one thing, some of the balancing operations of the UN in cross-functional issue trading presuppose a *tri*polarization of interests between the Communist bloc, the West, and the underdeveloped members of the organization. This suggests that UN influence through balancing operations has depended upon a *combination* of bipolar and tripolar patterns: bipolar as to tension, interest, and power patterns between East and West, and tripolar with respect to the varying interests and projects pursued by the three interest "groups."

Furthermore, UN balancing operations had an effect on bargaining processes among the members of the Western Cold War allliance. As mentioned previously, the nuclear standoff between East and West prevented institutionalized collective security while it stabilized the international system. Nuclear bipolarity, however, also produced fissures in the Western alliance by eroding previously more congruent security interests among the Western powers. The resulting tensions within the Western alliance were sharpened by differing attitudes on the pace of colonial emancipation and by the conflicts which developed between the United States and some Western European allies because of political and economic regionalism in Western Europe. To the extent that these differences could not be fully resolved on the level of Western regional organizations, but had to be further compromised at the UN level in order to obtain a united Western voting posture, the world organization contributed to the adjustment of interests not only *among* but also *within* regional interest groups (see Haas, 1956). In addition to its immediate effects in the area of collective security, nuclear bipolarity thus had important secondary effects in the international system. These repercussions tended to "loosen" bipolarity and therefore aided the UN in its role as an interest broker in interregional and intraregional issue bartering.

2. PEACEFUL CHANGE AND PACIFIC SETTLEMENT

Clearly, in its balancing operations the UN shifted its functional preoccupations from collective security projects to those more akin to peaceful change and pacific settlement.[11] Although, for all practical purposes, its collective security functions were tacitly abandoned, the UN (in contrast to the League) managed to retain or obtain some relevance and influence in contemporary international politics by expanding into alternative functional areas. In terms of the series of continua which I suggested for viewing the differences between collective security, pacific settlement, and peaceful change, this means that the focus of organizational projects shifted from the *zweckrational,* external, status-quo end of the continuum to the *wertrational,* internal, dynamic end. Because of the differing assumptions, attitudes, and objective requirements which are reflected at the opposite ends of these progressions, the degree of compatibility between organiza-

[11] In the following pages I shall consider peaceful change and pacific settlement projects in conjunction, since my primary purpose is to indicate the general direction of UN functions along the various continua I have suggested. In detailed analytical treatments it would be desirable to distinguish more specifically between peaceful change and pacific settlement cases. In particular, it may be useful to place specific cases on the four continua *separately,* rather than along one aggregate continuum which combines the four types of progressions.

tional projects and the conditions of the international system began to shift significantly.

Most importantly, perhaps, the UN's balancing operations began to involve projects and issues which required a substantive, *wertrational* judgment of the aspirations and grievances presented in its forum. Especially issues in the areas of colonial emancipation, economic development, and human rights called for declarations and commitments as to what the world ought to be like and how the organization could aid in its transformation. As an operational corollary, the organization could not help but take into account—and to some extent become involved in—the internal political conditions of member states. To have done otherwise would have meant abdication of the organization's relevance not only in the field of collective security but also in the area of peaceful change and pacific settlement.

With respect to peaceful change and pacific settlement projects, the Cold War bipolarization of power and interests held conflicting implications. On the one hand, the Cold War could not be kept out of peaceful change operations any more than it had been possible to bracket out the East-West conflict from collective security projects. Even in peripheral situations which did not involve a direct confrontation of interests between East and West, the organization's chances of success in reaching settlements and in restoring peaceful conditions were dependent upon the implicit or explicit approval of the superpowers. A reverse process of "permissive enforcement" based on the consent of the United States and the Soviet Union, one which might be called "permissive engagement," was the prerequisite of the organization's involvement. Generally, lack of authority and of effective independent military, financial, and political resources prevented the UN from operating within the spheres of influence established by the superpowers. The UN failed to affect significantly the outcome in Hungary, Tibet, and Cuba, and it took a hands-off attitude *vis-à-vis* Berlin. These facts attest to the stringent limits imposed on UN influence and "presence" in Cold War contests that could seriously affect the power equilibrium between the major antagonists.

Even so, on issues such as Palestine, the former Italian colonies, the Togo trust territories, and West Irian, the UN managed to exert considerable influence. Particularly striking is the fact that its limited success in the peaceful change area, and especially in the area of colonial emancipation, was made possible not so much in spite of, but because of, Cold War tensions. For example, the shift of influence from the Council to the Assembly and the blurring of functions between the two bodies was in good part an outgrowth of the collective security impasse imposed by the Cold War. This provided the growing number of smaller powers with the opportunity and the parliamentary lever to exert a disproportionate influence (in terms of actual power) over UN functions; their role as mediators in the Cold War conflict further enhanced their advantage in a setting of multilateral diplomacy, cross-functional balancing, and egalitarian voting procedures. The organization's influence in the creation of new states accelerated this trend while allowing it to be active in this most important aspect of peaceful change functions. At the root of these permissive conditions was the fact that both East and West, in their Cold War competition over the allegiance (or at least neutrality) of the new states, were committed to advocating and supporting forces of change, modernization, and economic development.

On the whole, the heterogeneous membership of the postwar international system, which posed such problems for collective security, presented certain limited opportunities to the United Nations in the area of peaceful change and pacific settlement. The organization's opportunities in these areas depended largely upon its *balancing* operations, and hence on those conditions of the international system which allowed balancing. It may be useful, in conclusion, briefly to reiterate the obstacles that hampered UN *collective security* functions, but also to stress the positive effect of these strictures on UN balancing operations as a prerequisite for *peaceful change* and *pacific settlement* functions.

Balancing presupposes Cold War bipolarization of interests: this is the mainspring of the bartering relationships of balancing. If the superpowers had reached a fundamental Cold War settlement, or had lost interest in enlisting the organization for Cold War projects, the most important element in the bartering pattern would have evaporated.

Even the bipolarization of power between East and West aided in balancing. The restraints imposed by the nuclear balance of power (which contributed to the demise of permissive enforcement) provided incentives for the superpowers to carry on their Cold War contests through political rather than military structures of the international system, and the UN served as one of these alternative structures. A rough equilibrium of power between the superpowers also allowed the smaller mediators greater influence than with a less symmetrical power distribution. Furthermore, balancing operations are most effective if there is a polarization of possible sources from which technical assistance, economic aid, and support on colonial issues can be extracted—sources which can be played against each other by the mediators.

Another aspect of the heterogeneous membership of the postwar international system which proved troublesome for collective security tasks served as an important element in balancing operations: the nature of the state system in the underdeveloped part of the world and the North-South polarization of economic development and industrial capacity. Without this disparity the superpowers, and the United Nations *qua* broker, would have been deprived of the important bargaining element of economic aid and technical assistance. The fact that underdevelopment and aspirations of colonial emancipation tended to coincide reinforced this pattern. Again, the bipolarization of the Cold War conflict, and especially its ideological dimensions, aided in balancing operations. It induced the two superpowers to vie for the support of the underdeveloped world with two competing ideologies which were presented as guidelines for the building of viable nationhood and for rapid economic development and equitable social reforms. In large measure, the Cold War patterns of the international system which proved so forbidding for collective security functions at the same time provided the United Nations with limited opportunities for peaceful change and pacific settlement operations, and saved the world forum from complete paralysis and irrelevance.

REFERENCES

Burns, Arthur Lee. "From Balance to Deterrence: A Theoretical Analysis," *World Politics*, 9, 4 (July 1957), 494-529.
———. "The International Consequences of Expecting Surprise," *World Politics*, 10, 4 (July 1958), 512-36.
Claude, Inis L., Jr. *Swords Into Plowshares*. New York: Random House, 1956.
———. "The Management of Power in the Changing United Nations," *International Organization*, 15, 2 (Spring 1961), 219-35.
———. *Power and International Relations*. New York: Random House, 1962.
Dunn, Frederick S. *Peaceful Change*. New York: Council on Foreign Relations, 1937.
Haas, Ernst B. "Types of Collective Security: An Examination of Operational Concepts," *American Political Science Review*, 49, 1 (March 1955), 40-62.
———. "Regionalism, Functionalism, and Universal International Organization," *World Politics*, 8, 2 (January 1956), 238-63.
———. "Dynamic Environment and Static System: Revolutionary Regimes in the United Nations," in Morton A. Kaplan (ed.), *The Revolution in World Politics*. New York: Wiley, 1962, 267-309.
Hanrieder, Wolfram F. "Actor Objectives and International Systems," *Journal of Politics*, 27, 1 (February 1965a), 109-32.
———. "The International System: Bipolar or Multibloc?" *Journal of Conflict Resolution*, 9, 3 (September 1965b), 299-308.
Kaplan, Morton A. *System and Process in International Politics*. New York: Wiley, 1957.
Liska, George. *Nations in Alliance*. Baltimore, Md.: Johns Hopkins Press, 1962.
Osgood, Robert E. *NATO: The Entangling Alliance*. Chicago: University of Chicago Press, 1962.

————. "Stabilizing the Military Environment," *American Political Science Review,* 55, 1 (March 1961), 24-39.

Rosecrance, Richard N. *Action and Reaction in World Politics.* Boston: Little, Brown, 1963.

Rosenau, James N. "The Functioning of International Systems," *Background,* 7, 3 (November 1963), 111-17.

Russell, Ruth B. "The Management of Power and Political Organization: Some Observations on Inis L. Claude's Conceptual Approach," *International Organization,* 15, 4 (Autumn 1961), 630-36.

Singer, J. David. "The Level-of-Analysis Problem in International Relations," *World Politics,* 14, 1 (October 1961), 77-92.

Waltz, Kenneth N. "The Stability of a Bipolar World," *Daedalus,* 93, 3 (Summer 1964), 881-909.

Weber, Max. "Types of Rationality," in Talcott Parsons *et al.* (eds.), *Theories of Society.* Vol. II. Glencoe, Ill.: Free Press, 1961, 1063-65.

14. COLLECTIVE SECURITY AND THE FUTURE INTERNATIONAL SYSTEM

By ERNST B. HAAS

THE purpose of this essay is to think about the future as it concerns the maintenance of peace by the United Nations. What will be the shape of the international system fifteen or twenty years hence? Will that system contain forces more (or less) likely to allow for the operation of collective security by the United Nations? Which of these forces will be the result of domestic conditions in the member states? Which forces will flow from purely international pressures, as filtered through the institutions of the UN?

In approaching this issue, it is useful to think in terms of three ways of dealing with the future. One involves the construction of utopias. Another uses various types of projections. A third—and this is the mode attempted here—makes use of selective developmental models in a systemic setting. The result is neither prophecy nor prediction. It is merely contingent forecasting based on articulate assumptions, established trends, and probable logical connections between these.

More generally, such models require us to spell out a baseline for our projection: a starting date and a list of acting units that produce the inputs of which the trends are composed. The model also requires a specification of the units whose transformation is to be studied. Thus in the case of the UN, the units producing the inputs would be nation-states; the units being transformed might be international

This article is a much shortened version of a monograph published under the same title by the Social Science Foundation, University of Denver, January, 1968. The reader is advised to consult that monograph for more elaborate explanations of the methodological and conceptual aspects of the study, the qualifications and limits implied by the methods and concepts chosen which space limits did not permit me to develop fully here. Further, the full study includes examples and supporting literature that had to be excluded in this version. I gratefully acknowledge the financial support of the Institute of International Studies of the University of California (Berkeley) in the preparation of the original study. In addition the paper owes a great deal to the comments and thoughts of Wolfram F. Hanrieder with whom it has been a pleasure to work for many years. Kathleen M. Wilson did much research and all of the editorial work for the paper. The responsibility for mistakes is mine alone. [Author's note]

organizations, regional organizations, or the same nation-states, as the hypothesis may require.

Further, such models require us to spell out the operating characteristics of the unit, the recurrent features of behavior and structure which give it its peculiarity. Put differently, if we proceed in this fashion we have to set up ideal types of units whose life makes up the bulk of our concern. Next, we have to specify the key variables which we expect to operate as causative agents in bringing about change. Continuing with our example of the influence of nation-states on the future of the United Nations, such key independent variables might be the pace and kind of technological-scientific innovation and diffusion, the institutionalization of social engineering, the relationship between equality and meritocracy, or the number-density ratio of cities, populations, and agriculture. Finally, we must conceptualize the process whereby the key variables postulated are thought to affect the inputs produced by the acting units on the unit whose transformation is being projected. This may lead us to an incremental theory of change or to a revolutionary one. In either event, a process theory is required to explain the way in which innovation takes place, how its results are diffused, and to tell us when the diffusion results in new inputs producing structural change. I propose to opt for an incremental theory of change as more nearly describing the normal pattern.[1]

This theory of change is closely akin to the one embedded in the pluralist model of American society and politics. I am convinced that the international system performs in many ways analogously to this model even though its component units are not necessarily pluralistic. The developmental model appropriate for an incremental theory of change makes use of the notion of a "requisite" future state of affairs. I shall posit a future international arrangement as a "requisite" and ask myself which of the currently visible variables of change must work out in a certain way in order to meet the requisites of the future so specified. In this fashion, we gain some clarity as to what would have to happen in the attitudes and behavior patterns of nations to make possible the kind of United Nations sketched for, say, the 1980s.

---

[1] My conception of the incremental process follows roughly the scheme developed by David Braybrooke and Charles E. Lindblom, *A Strategy of Decision* (New York: The Free Press, 1963). The way in which this concept of change is incorporated into a theory of political decision-making and change in social structure is illustrated by Robert A. Dahl and Charles E. Lindblom, *Politics, Economics and Welfare* (New York: Harper, 1953); Ralf Dahrendorf, *Class and Class Conflict in Industrial Society* (Stanford: Stanford University Press, 1959); Ralf Dahrendorf, "Recent Change in the Class Structure of European Societies," in S. Graubard (ed.), *A New Europe?* (Boston: Houghton, Mifflin, 1964).

I. The Reconciliation Model of the International System

The construct chosen carries the label "reconciliation model."[2] It was developed by David E. Apter to describe the evolution of national states grappling with innovation and its diffusion, with ways and means of modernization and its political implications. Apter's purpose is to view the future of national states as determined by the selective developmental projection of key variables. The enterprise rests on an explicit functional logic but makes no claim as to applicability to international relations.

Among other plausible possibilities—an international social system model, a primitive system model, and various learning models—the reconciliation model was selected because it rests on a number of intellectual operations associated with "functionalism" and "functional analysis" which I have found useful for mapping international system change.

A reconciliation model of politics features bargaining as its main decision-making technique, rather than coercion, ideological fervor, or traditional sanctions. The decisions made by its concrete institutions are always based on the kind of bargaining which implies that all antagonists remain in the game and continue to adhere to its rules *even though* no single actor ever wins a complete victory. The learning ability of large human aggregates, jockeying for advantage to realize their interests, may be very modest in such a setting; yet the adaptive powers of the constituent units are considerable because the stakes are rarely very comprehensive and the calculus of survival can afford to be quietly rational.

A reconciliation model of politics can be specified further in terms of the values most commonly professed by its citizens and subjects and by the structuring of authority in it. Social values can be dichotomized as being "consummatory" or "instrumental" in nature. Consummatory values imply a devotion to the integral realization of strongly held beliefs; instrumental values involve a constant calculation of the adjustment of the proper means to achieve limited ends, and a willingness to settle for an approximation to one's beliefs. The reconciliation model, then, clearly presupposes the prevalence of instrumental values. Authority can be viewed as being structured hierarchically or pyramidally. A hierarchical social system is divided into horizontal layers of status and power such that it is very difficult for individuals to pass upward to higher layers. A feudal or a caste-dominated society is rigidly hierarchical. A pyramidal ordering of

[2] The term and the concept is borrowed and adapted from David E. Apter's work. See his *The Politics of Modernization* (Chicago: University of Chicago Press, 1965).

authority, however, allows for some upward passage toward the apex of power on the part of individuals and groups initially located on or near the base of the pyramid. Reconciliation models are pyramidal.

But the international system would be hierarchical if *all* decisions were authoritatively made by the super-powers and if no smaller state were ever permitted into the inner decision-making circle. I suggest that the General Assembly be regarded as the base of the pyramid of authority, the Security Council (including its non-permanent members) as the apex, and variously weighted committees and commissions in the intermediate ranges. The essence of the reconciliation model is the fact that no one group clearly rules to the exclusion of the demands of others, even though there may be less than perfect political participation, in law or in fact.

Now, a reconciliation version of the political system, just like any other version, must meet certain "functional" and "structural" requisites so that the system may survive. This is a formal way of saying that severe strains are imposed by clashing demands, none of which are ever fully satisfied, and yet none is supposed to be so stringent as to lead to the secession or rebellion of a dissatisfied constituent unit. The "functional requisites" of a reconciliation model of politics dictate that coercion be minimal, that there be a clear source of shared norms and a strong central symbolic referent, a mechanism for integrating the system which highlights public participation, and a source of identification with the system based on satisfaction. The "structural requisites" of the model demand that the political process highlight accountability to the public, possess a wide basis of recruitment, be flexible in the enforcement of norms, possess a mechanism for allocating resources which satisfies the constituents, and have a relationship with consent groups which gives them a sense of belonging.[3]

Our task now is the adaptation of this model to international relations. Because it is a bargaining model it assumes no radical breakthrough toward a world community either in terms of world federation or conquest by a single nation. The values professed in the practice of diplomacy and war—short of total conflict—are highly instrumental. Authority is structured in an essentially pyramidal fashion. Let me stress that we are talking about *international* systemic qualities here; the constituent units, the member states, may well be devoted to consummatory values and feature a hierarchical structure of authority. But a reconciliation model of the international system holds that relations among the units will be characterized by instru-

[3] These formulations are all from Apter, *ibid.,* chaps. 7, 11. As Apter uses the term, a reconciliation system is a more comprehensive rubric than "democracy." Democracies are a species of the genus "reconciliation system," but the genus would include such less-than-completely democratic polities as Britain and France during the nineteenth century, as well as contemporary Mexico, India, Turkey, the Philippines, and Senegal.

mental behavior and pyramidal authority relations *despite* the possible prevalence of the other characteristics at the national level.

The United Nations, in the past as now, illustrates my point. Certainly the bulk of its members are not reconciliation polities. Yet the systemic characteristics of the ensemble meet the reconciliation requisites, and the UN has functioned as a reconciliation polity. We posit that the projected UN will be a reconciliation system, albeit under great strain because the functional requisites will be subjected to new and powerful demands while the structural requisites may be unable to adjust.

In the 1980s as in the past, the international system will continue to exist and be given regulative tasks even though it will probably not succeed in changing the internal characteristics of its constituent units. The United Nations will remain highly "accountable" and not very "authoritative" vis-à-vis its member states. It will make new norms only in areas where the members continue to experience common or converging needs, and it will enforce these norms selectively and flexibly. Resources made available to the United Nations will probably increase, but their distribution will be subject to the same bargaining process which has existed so far and will not rest on an automatic and calculated international technocratic development plan. International civil servants will be recruited, as heretofore, on the basis of their technical skills *and* in proportion to the influence of their home government on the politics of the organization through a geographical representation formula subject to renegotiation. Consent groups, whether governments or private associations, cannot be coerced and must be coopted to ensure their support for organizational objectives. In this sense, then, the future international system will have the same characteristics as the present one. Because no one state will dominate it and all wish to remain in the game, it is condemned to be a bargaining system achieving sporadic and *ad hoc* reconciliation of national objectives.

In view of this projection, can we expect the UN to practice collective security in the 1980s as it has been practiced since 1945? What would have to happen to the various factors certain to make for social change nationally and internationally so as to make possible the practice of collective security? Or, given the likelihood of certain kinds of change and the survival of a reconciliation system, is the practice of collective security going to be possible at all?

II. Systems and Environments in History

THE COMPONENTS OF SYSTEMS

We differentiate historical systems from one another in terms of these variables: the number of actors, the internal characteristics of the actors, the relative power of the actors, the goals they pursue, the methods they adopt, and the outcomes of their conflicting goals and methods which they impose on the common structures they have set up, i.e., the "tasks" assigned to international organizations. We hold that the outcomes are determined by the sum of the other variables; a major change in one of the several "input" variables will result in a different pattern of outcomes, thus resulting in a different type of system. Historical systems may be related to one another through the "feedback" effects of earlier outcomes on the actors, thus yielding new inputs, new outputs, new task patterns, and different international structures. But systems may also change because of autonomous developments in the character of the actors. In the history of the United Nations, at any rate, autonomous systems change has been a more pronounced phenomenon than change due to feedback effects. Still, both processes are at work and we conceptualize systems change as a continuous phenomenon due to both impulses.

(1) Number and Character of Actors. We shall confine the notion of "actor" to states which appear as members of universal international organizations: the League of Nations and the United Nations. The number grew from about 50 in the early life of the League to the present 123 in the UN. But the character of the member states changed even more dramatically and frequently. We are concerned, as before, with the impact of social and economic modernization of the nature of political regimes. Hence we shall continue to use Apter's typology, as amended, for establishing the distribution of key characteristics among actors in the historical international systems. The key types of polity are: reconciliation systems, mobilization systems, modernizing autocracies, authoritarian systems, modernizing oligarchies, and traditional oligarchies.[4]

A national reconciliation system was described above. Its values are preponderantly instrumental, its authority structure pyramidal, its government possesses much information regarding the society and economy, and uses little coercion against it. Norms are sanctioned by the constitution and custom, history serves as a symbolic referent, integration is achieved by a bureaucracy working in close conjunction with private groups, and national identity rests on the satisfaction of the populace, which is "participant" in character. Government is

---

[4] *Ibid.* I have not used the system Apter calls "Military Oligarchy" because I believe that the forces it represents are just as frequently carried by non-military oligarchies of dedicated intellectuals. I have instead adopted the distinction established by Edward Shils between "Modernizing" and "Traditional" oligarchies. See Shils, *Political Development in the New States* (Gravenhage: Mouton, 1962), pp. 67, 75, 85. In addition, I have taken the liberty to re-label the system Apter calls "Neo-Mercantilism" as "Authoritarianism."

highly accountable, elites are recruited on the basis of individual skill and merit as well as on the basis of access, enforcement of norms is flexible, resource allocation rests on market forces or wide consultation with private enterprise, and consent groups are coopted into the governing structure.

A mobilization system is the exact opposite. Consummatory values predominate and the authority structure is hierarchical. The single "party" serves as the source of norms and the integrative mechanism. A "political religion" provides symbolic referent and national identity. There is little accountability, recruitment into the elite rests on loyalty to the party, norms are rigidly enforced, resources allocated according to a plan, and consent groups manipulated. All national energies are "mobilized" to achieve dramatic and rapid modernization.

A modernizing autocracy attempts to attain rapid modernization by more modest means. The traditional ruler seeks to use and adapt traditional symbols, norms, integrational mechanisms, and sources of identity to cajole his subjects into modernity. Authoritarian systems are milder and more relaxed forms of mobilization systems; sometimes they emerge after a harassed populace has succeeded in overthrowing a mobilization system which had failed to plan and manipulate consent groups successfully. Authoritarian systems hinge around the person of a "presidential monarch," an "elected ruler" who claims legitimacy on the basis of popular acclaim but who surrounds himself with the trappings of a court. Instrumental values dominate, but the authority structure tends to be hierarchical. Moderate amounts of coercion are used. The president himself attempts to be the source of new, modernizing, and progressive norms; he seeks to shape the new tradition, using a single party and a bureaucracy as the integrative device. National identity rests on the people's identification with the "new tradition" and also on the degree of satisfaction they experience. Personal merit and skill are important in recruitment, some accountability is maintained, and norms are enforced with moderation. While consent groups are both coopted and manipulated, the allocation of resources preserves a large sphere to private enterprise and mixed corporations.

A modernizing oligarchy is led by a junta of dedicated civilians or military people, ruling over subjects of largely pre-modern people only dimly aware of their formal citizenship in a state. The authority structure is hierarchical in principle but far less efficient and rigorous in practice than that of the authoritarian system. Values are consummatory at the verbal level but tend toward the instrumental in practice. Formal links between government and society and economy are tenuous; the civil or military bureaucracy is neither large nor

efficient, though committed to modernization. There is no accountability, consent groups are ignored, the enforcement of norms is rigid
in principle but haphazard in practice, and recruitment to the elite
rests on bureaucratic or personal identification with the junta seizing
power. Modernizing oligarchies have little staying power; they readily
develop into authoritarian or mobilization systems. By way of contrast, a traditional oligarchy is a system in which a small group of
people, related in terms of family and status, control the government,
society, and economy, while the people live in tribal or village units
under traditional rules and are outside the political system altogether.

(2) Distribution of Power. In classifying historical periods in
terms of the relative international distribution of power, we must
bear in mind two aspects of that elusive notion "power." We must
specify the *kinds* of power we mean, such as nuclear capability,
conventional military capability, economic-industrial capacity, and
the ability to launch effective ideological, propaganda, and subversive
offensives. We must then ask ourselves whether these kinds of power
were distributed symmetrically, heterosymmetrically, or asymmetri-
cally among the actors. A period in which all kinds of power were
so distributed that two actors or two blocs shared them about evenly
is characterized by symmetry. A period in which some third force
possesses the kinds of power which *reduce* the aggregate ability of
the major blocs to maneuver freely on the international stage in *equal
proportions* is one of heterosymmetry. Finally, a period in which the
third force or forces reduce the capability of the major centers in
unequal proportions would be characterized by an asymmetrical distribution of power.

Further, we must specify how the distribution of these kinds of
power is clustered around poles or into blocs. When single states
"lead" or "dominate" (through alliances or otherwise) large seg-
ments of the globe we speak of a polar distribution, bipolar from
1947 until 1955, tripolar in the immediate aftermath of the Bandung
Conference, and multipolar since the mass admission of African
nations. Note that this multipolarity implied the introduction of a
heterogeneous distribution of power *even though* the third pole possessed neither the nuclear nor the conventional military capability to
cut into the slices possessed by the United States and the Soviet
Union. Symmetry was destroyed because of the ideological-subversive
capability of the third bloc and because of its ability to make claims
on the economic-industrial capacity of the large powers. With the
possible decline in the ability of single states to "lead" alliances, we
may have to start speaking of "multibloc" clusterings of power in
preference to "poles." The change in terminology obviously implies
much more than a mere shift in words: a multibloc system permits

far more room for maneuver and adjustment than a multipolar one because international agreements would have to be pre-negotiated within each bloc before full acceptance by all the blocs.[5]

With the specification of these categories relating to the nature of the units and their relative power, we have described some environmental aspects of historical systems. We now turn to the aims of the actors and to the methods they employ, thus describing the inputs into the system. When we finally deal with the task thus imposed on international organizations, we shall be describing the system's outputs.

(3) Aims of States. Broadly speaking, the objectives of national foreign policy have always been classified as "revisionist" or "status quo"-oriented. States either wish to keep things as they are or work for a change favoring their goals. In talking about actor objectives in these terms we have in mind the substance of politics.

The legitimacy of existing political boundaries is one such issue. States demanding territorial adjustments, cessions of provinces, the removal of colonial administrations, and tribal reunification are revisionists; governments taking their stand on the legitimacy of borders at any one point—a position usually cloaked in the phrase "respect for international obligations and treaties"—are not. The expansion of a specific ideology, whether by conquest or propaganda linked with externally-supported subversion, is another aspect of the same larger issue. The immediate relevance of this issue to the practice of collective security hardly requires comment. Another issue is international economics. Should there be a "natural" division of labor between raw material producers and industrial countries? Should there be a concerted effort to make everybody industrialize? Is the most-favored-nation clause an instrument of economic oppression or a device to assure equality? A revisionist state aims at the reduction of the superiority of the industrialized West; the West itself has taken a status quo position much of the time. The universal protection of human rights, through international legal obligations and possibly intervention, is another issue area. Revisionists stress such a role; status quo powers emphasize the domestic character of such questions. One may quibble over whether the disarmament and arms control question is a sub-aspect of the territorial and ideological security issue or whether it should be considered as an issue in its own right. Revisionists stress the danger of arms—the arms of other powers— while status quo powers emphasize the need for caution and the

[5] This terminology and the concepts summed up by it were developed by Wolfram F. Hanrieder in "The International System: Bipolar or Multibloc?" *The Journal of Conflict Resolution*, Vol. IX, No. 3 (September, 1965), pp. 299-308.

demands of security. Finally, the promises and dangers of science and its relationship to social change has emerged as an international issue area; status quo countries here tend to defend the promise of science and the need for unfettered diffusion of techniques and ideas while the revisionists are more alive to the implicit dangers. Note, however, that on this issue it is the developed countries who act as the revisionists.

(4) Methods of States. Little need be said about the methods which states use to attain these objectives. What matters to us is which methods are predominant in any one historical system. The types of methods available do not change very rapidly. In the period which concerns us, means have included the marshaling of national armaments (both nuclear and conventional), strategic planning and counter-planning, the eventual institutionalization of the nuclear balance of terror, and reliance on it in the methods of the super-powers. It has also included the fostering of conventional capability for the fighting of local and/or limited wars on the part of the super-powers no less than on almost everybody else's part. In the inevitable confrontations which ensued, the dominant methods have been alliance-building, threat, and appeasement. The ideological dimension has seen the flowering of systematic propaganda, large-scale "international information" programs designed to praise the home state and to defame the opponent, the encouragement of dissident movements in the opponent's territory, and the support of subversive activity. In the realm of economics, the methods have included bilateral and multilateral technical assistance, international lending, emergency relief, and the granting of long-range development funds. Human rights have been extolled, by and large, as a way to hurt the opponent's image and to cater to the ideological commitments of third blocs. Disarmament negotiations have been featured to eliminate threats perceived symmetrically by all parties as well as to score propaganda points. Large-scale scientific conferences and much technical work by international agencies, including international inspection, have been the way of dealing with the issue area of science.

(5) Tasks of International Organizations. The purpose of this whole involved exercise is to determine how various combinations of environmental forces, aims, and methods of states mingle so as to produce "typical" task combinations for international organizations of universal membership. We shall examine actual periods of history and then seek to project probable changes in independent variables as the causative agents of a future system. The mixture of tasks which will concern us comprises the following ingredients.

Collective security is an ingredient of each historical system. Do security decisions rest on a big power consensus, on bargaining with third forces, on overwhelmng majority support? Are bargains struck which involve other issue areas? How important are collective economic decisions favoring the revisionists in shaping collective security policy? Must human rights be protected in the process? Do third forces extract disarmament or national self-determination concessions in voting for a United Nations police force? In other words, our objective is to determine whether collective security decisions rest on a combination of variables which bring in the other issue areas, thus widening the scope of bargaining, discussion, and international activity, or whether the maintenance of collective security is an isolated task unrelated to the growth or decline of overall United Nations activity. Our hypothesis, not unexpectedly, holds that the autonomy of the collective security task declines in proportion to the increase in the multipolarity and heterosymmetry of the power constellation.

These, in gross terms, are the variables to be examined when we sketch a given historical system. But how does one system "die," so to speak, and another "enter life"? How do we explain transitions from one to another?

SYSTEMS CHANGE AND HISTORICAL SYSTEMS

Transitions from one historical system to another are rarely clear to the actors themselves. The finding that we have arrived at a "new" system is the property of the observer. How then do political leaders find out about this? After all, the character of the system is determined by their behavior. Transition from one system to another, therefore, must imply some kind of changed behavior. It is crucial to discover whether this changed behavior is the result of something learned by the decision-maker as a consequence of his international experiences—or whether it is not.

Two alternative models of explaining international systems change exist and both are equally plausible; but only one relies on a species of learning theory that can be linked up with the perceptions and experiences of actors in international organization. It is a kind of "learning" strange to psychologists and psychologically-oriented students of socialization processes because it has little to do with the essentially nonrational—or at least nonpurposive—behavior patterns of subjects whose adjustment is measured in terms of intensity of or the timing of stimuli. It is a kind of learning which presupposes that actors make decisions that are "rational" for them in the sense that they are designed to achieve a definable political objective; but they may ultimately be "irrational" in the sense that the personal frame of reference of the decision-maker may correspond to all the well-known

Lasswellian psychopathologies. This, however, would not matter for us. Insofar as the frame of reference yields articulate statements about the actor's desires and the objects desired from the international scene we can undertake a systematic analysis of how these desires change with experience. Learning, therefore, is a rational process of redefining objectives and changing methods as leaders discover that persistence with the initial aims is self-defeating or overly costly. Hence international bargaining may serve as a "school" in which such lessons are learned. Yet it is important to remember that we are not assuming that "learning" involves conversion to a new belief system, dramatic shifts in values, or convergences that will suddenly yield love whereas the previous picture had been one of mutual hostility. The school of international bargaining yields no documented case of positive reenforcement that translates into a warm community of objectives.

Considered from the vantage point of the international system itself, we can express the functional-rational learning process differently. The initial objectives of states are the explicit purposes which lead to demands made of other states in international organizations. In order to gain acceptance of these purposes, a price has to be paid to the purposes of other states, perhaps in a different issue area. The purpose, once accepted by the organization, becomes its immediate task and its program is built around it. The program, however, cannot be fully realized because of faulty planning, inadequate power, low budgets, or national opposition. Disappointment and the hope for better performance in the future is a consequence unintended by those who first framed the task. The lessons of what could and could not be done is "fed back" into the national states. They put forward new purposes. These can either increase or decrease the task of the organization. In either event, learning has taken place through the feedback process triggered by unintended consequences. Reformulated purposes may become "functional" for system transformation; hence we speak of them as "functions."

This model of international system transformation credits the international organization with the capacity to produce feedbacks capable of changing the environment. There is an alternative model which puts the emphasis on autonomous changes at the national level. Developments in the various social, economic, and political sectors making up the environment are conceived as proceeding more rapidly and decisively than the national learning of international feedbacks. New demands will then also be put on the system's structures. These will still encounter other new or opposing demands. The structures may not gain any net power at the expense of the member states but will be transformed just the same because the new mix of demands will result in a different task for the organization. The point which bears repetition here is the absence of any learning on the part of the national decision-makers. The new task is purely the result of needs experienced at the national level and does not follow a previous period of related experience connected with the earlier task of the organization. The phenomenon of reevaluated national purpose is lacking.

System transformation can be explained with either model. In the actual history of the United Nations and the specialized agencies, the second model comes closer to describing the truth. It is largely responsible for having given us a succession of reconciliation systems. But what are the limits of peaceful transition from one kind of reconciliation system to another? They can, in part, be explained by the frame of reference decision-makers are sensitive to in formulating goals. Actors make their decisions according to three possible frames of value.[6]

Material policy objectives may be derived purely from internal referents, as is the case in seeking routine commercial and technical relations. But non-material values encountered at home as well as abroad also fall into this frame of reference provided their realization does not depend on any forces outside the state. Hence the idealistic devotion to higher living standards, natural law, peaceful change, and the like leads to policy demands of purely internal relevance. The New Dealer who preached international Keynesianism (without making specific claims that foreigners change their systems of banking) as well as the Isolationist of the 1930's responded to internal referents.

An external referent dominates the making of policy whenever a given value demands a change of behavior on the part of foreign nations. Foreign policy based on a crusading ideology is the obvious example. Territorial revisionism is another. A policy devoted to reconstructing the world economic system is a third. Any policy which places the foreigner in a position desired by the home state, either in fact or in advocacy, responds to an externally-focused value referent.

Finally, policy can be based on a systemic referent. No normative implication attaches to the impulse: it is simply perceived as existing. Most commonly, the systemic reference implies the desire of the state to safeguard its existence, granting the prevalence of a probably hostile system. Armament policies, in the absence of specific territorial or ideological claims, derive from such a referent. But accommodation in the United Nations—once that institution is taken for granted —may also be regarded as a systemic response.

[6] Wolfram F. Hanrieder, "Actor Objectives and International Systems," *Journal of Politics,* Vol. XXVII (1965), pp. 109-132.

These three frames of reference have very different implications for system transformation. Internal and external value referents are imbued with consummatory qualities. They refer to cherished beliefs, styles of life, and hallowed traditions. Systemic referents are highly instrumental and policies based on them lend themselves to bargaining and accommodation. It follows that international systems made up of states whose leaders respond to systemic frames of reference are more adaptable than others. Systems made up of a large number of countries devoted to violent policies involving external referents find it difficult to carry on negotiations. The League of Nations suffered accordingly after 1931. In brief, the peaceful transition of international systems is facilitated by two conditions: (1) the actors, or at least the most powerful, should respond to a systemic frame of value reference; (2) the actors should overwhelmingly be devoted to internal frames of value reference making no dramatic claims on foreigners.

With these conceptual and methodological apologetics out of the way, we can now summarize the characteristics of the various reconciliation systems which have prevailed since 1945:

TABLE 1

INTERNATIONAL SYSTEMS
1945-1965

PERIOD	AIMS OF STATES	POWER DISTRIBUTION	TASKS OF INTERNATIONAL ORGANIZATIONS
1945-1947	Victors: preserve new political status quo, colonial system, global free enterprise. Dissenters: not heard.	Unipolar victor group.	Collective security through Big Power concert; emergency relief for victims of World War II; promote world trade rules stressing non-discrimination and unfettered investment; promote arms reduction.
1948-1951	West: preserve total status quo. East: expand into Europe and Asia; support nationalist and communist revolts.	Tight bipolar symmetrical.	Collective security through authority delegated to U.S. and its allies; technical assistance; some regional economic planning for industrialization; Western-controlled human rights advocacy.

1952-1955	West: preserve *territorial* status quo; cater to third forces otherwise. East: aid nationalist and communist revolts. Others: profit from cold war to further national and economic development.	Tripolar hetero-symmetrical.	Collective security through third-world mediation between East and West: more technical assistance; more general human rights advocacy; more varied technical services for under-developed countries.
1956-1960	West: adapt to third force by winning or neutralizing it; spur global economic growth. East: adapt to third force by winning or neutralizing it; support decolonization. (excludes China) Others: profit from cold war to further national and economic development; contain cold war and nuclear arms; dislodge colonial powers.	Loose bipolar hetero-symmetrical.	Collective security through cautious supra-national leadership of UN Secretary-General; much more extensive economic aid; ambitious technical aid programs; collective intervention for decolonization and human rights.
1961-1965	West: same as above with Europe more eager to adapt than U.S.; mute cold war. East: same as above with U.S.S.R. most eager to adapt; mute cold war; reduce involvement in new countries while stressing decolonization. (excludes China) Others: same as above (with three different blocs of unaligned states); reorganize world trade and finance system.	Multipolar hetero-symmetrical.	Collective security through supranational leadership *and* Big Power concert; massive human rights promotion and decolonization; new world trade norms; arms control; implications of science explored; great expansion of investment aid to developing countries.

III. THE UN AND COLLECTIVE SECURITY

We should now proceed to analyze the past and future of collective security in terms of this conceptualization. But what is "collective security"? We follow the basic distinction between "collective security" and "peaceful change" elaborated by Hanrieder in the preceding selection. Our concern is exclusively with collective security, and we define this concept operationally. We ask: What kind of technique did the UN use under what circumstances? What was the environmental constellation of forces when the technique was adopted? What kind of consensus did the members display in adopting a certain technique? How often and under what circumstances was the technique successful? In doing so we admit that the ideal requisites are rarely met and that the diplomatic understandings are transitory. But since cases continue to be submitted to the UN, and are sometimes successfully dealt with, we are forced to ask the larger questions if we are concerned with the future as a resultant of the past.

The period 1945-1965 witnessed 108 disputes posing a possible threat to peace. Only 27 of these were not referred to any international organization. This gives us a referral score of 75 percent, distributed as follows:

Referred to United Nations:	45	(42%)
Referred to regional organizations:	26	(24%)
Referred to United Nations and regional organizations:	10	(9%)

We derive our conclusions on collective security in operation from the 55 disputes referred to the United Nations.[7]

Before presenting the data for these 55 disputes, we must make plain what was counted in each instance and how certain judgments were made.

[7] The following procedure was used in arriving at the total of 55. Certain obviously related complaints were counted as one dispute even though complaints were lodged at separate times. Thus the Tunisian, Moroccan, and Algerian effort to dislodge the French was counted as one "North African" dispute. Complaints of violations of established truce arrangements (as in Palestine and Kashmir) were not counted as separate disputes; but a general breakdown of a truce by way of a new major campaign was (as in Suez and the India-Pakistan war of 1965). Generalized propaganda complaints (e.g., the use of bacteriological warfare in Korea) were not counted at all; usually they occurred in the context of a more specific dispute which was counted, even though they may have appeared as separate UN agenda items. In terms of periodization, a dispute was counted only once, during the period when it originated, even though it may have carried over into the next period.

CODING THE DISPUTES

(1) Objective Information on UN Action. Disputes were coded as to which organ of the UN was involved: the Security Council, the General Assembly, or both. In addition, we differentiated between the different types of action which each of these organs could adopt; naturally, a single dispute could be scored as having featured one, some, or all of these types of action. A given dispute was coded as "no action" if none of the UN organs was able or willing to adopt a resolution concerning it.

(2) Hostilities. We also coded each dispute as to whether hostilities were involved, another operation involving no judgment. International hostilities as well as civil war were included, and in some instances both of these forms of violence were involved.

(3) Power Status of Parties. Disputes were classified as to the power possessed by the parties and with respect to their position in the world alliance system. Thus we used the following categories: (a) disputes involving a major power (defined as a permanent member of the Security Council); (b) disputes involving two minor powers who are aligned within the same bloc; (c) disputes involving two minor powers who are members of opposing blocs; (d) disputes involving two minor powers, one of whom is aligned and the other unaligned; and (e) disputes involving two minor unaligned powers.

(4) Type of Issue. Disputes were coded as (a) cold war, (b) colonial, and (c) other, which need not accord with the way the parties themselves saw their dispute.

(5) Type of Polity. Wherever feasible, the parties were classified in terms of the nature of their domestic political system. The categories employed were taken from the Apter typology, as amended by me and described above.

(6) Type of Consensus in the UN. Consensual categories involve heavy conceptual judgments which take us some distance away from the factual scene and the explicit perceptions of the parties. These judgments flow from conceptual commitments on my part derived from the observational stance represented by the motion of a reconciliation system. They include first and foremost the institutional question of which decisional format was used to determine UN action: unanimity of the great powers in the Security Council, a two-thirds majority vote in the General Assembly, an initiative of the Secretary-General which is more or less rigorously ratified by either the Security Council or the General Assembly, or a prolonged bargaining pattern in either organ in which a "third bloc" of some kind figured prominently. Secondly, a consensual category includes the question of the identity of the participating actors and of the pattern

in which they group themselves in arriving at a collective decision. We distinguish between these seven consensual patterns:

(a) Majority Will. The most uncomplicated consensual picture obtains when the necessary constitutional majority in the General Assembly opts for a given course of action without special bargaining or extensive manipulation on the part of a big power.

(b) Concert. A decision is based on a concert if the minimal legal requirement for an affirmative vote in the Security Council is met. A concert can take the form of the unanimous vote of the permanent members or manifest itself in the abstention of one or more.

(c) Permissive Enforcement. Collective security takes the form of a decentralized and largely national effort whenever the General Assembly "delegates" to a state or to a group of states the power to restrain or punish aggression. In such a situation the state which carries out its national policy under the aegis of the UN is "permitted" to use force in the name of the organization or engage in demonstrations of international authority short of force.

(d) Balancing. A consensus based on balancing can be organized either in the General Assembly or the Security Council. Balancing described a situation in which a bloc of uncommitted or unaligned states (with respect to the dispute in question) intercedes between the major disputants and makes them accept a compromise formula.

In recent years a form of balancing has been discernible in the Security Council even in the absence of a previous permissive enforcement situation. Balancing there can be said to occur whenever the major powers take opposing positions *initially* with respect to action appropriate to a dispute. The balancing countries then attempt to introduce a resolution which will encompass some minimum common denominator spanning the gulf between the major power positions in the hope of persuading one side to abstain rather than vote against the course of action suggested. The eventual consensus thus involves a minimalist resolution offered by the unaligned country sufficiently acceptable to one side as to make abstention possible.

(e) Permissive Engagement with Majority Will. The consensual formula featuring "permissive engagement" refers in all cases to the role the Secretary-General assumed after 1956. He did the "engaging" for the UN; he took the initiative in bringing the dispute to the attention of the members, and he usually proposed a specific course of action. This took the form of truce supervision, police forces, personal mediation, or the creation of his institutionalized "presence" in the troubled area. In some cases, the military and civilian organizations created to deal with the dispute were under the personal command of the Secretary-General.

But he still needed a consensus among the members to do this if he wanted to avoid the difficulties associated with the financial crisis. One type of permission to engage the UN can be given by the General Assembly acting through the two-thirds voting formula, thus sidestepping the possibility of a major power's opposing this course of action. This is what occurred in the Suez and Hungarian disputes.

(f) Permissive Engagement with Concert. On the other hand, there have been situations in which the permanent members of the Security Council have been willing to permit the Secretary-General to engage the UN in peace-keeping. Clearly, a tighter control over the UN's chief administrator can be exercised if this consensual formula applies because he is held accountable to a smaller body and to states able to back their attitudes with action.

(g) Permissive Engagement with Balancing. The characteristics of a consensus based on mediation and bargaining between and among major powers and blocs in order to arrive at agreement with respect to a UN action apply here once more. Some state or group of unaligned states has to assume a balancing role in order to obtain the necessary legal support for a resolution. This can occur either in the Security Council or in the General Assembly. Again, however, the added ingredient is the role assumed by the Secretary-General in proposing action and in offering his services for implementing measures in the field.

(7) Degree of Success of UN Action. The success the UN may or may not have achieved is the dependent variable of the whole enterprise. We must know which combinations of independent variables, mediated by what form of consensus in the organization, has produced successful outcomes. We must also know whether the pattern of success varies with the historical system. One criterion of success is the frequency with which the UN succeeded in stopping hostilities once they had broken out, in most instances through the medium of a truce supervision organization. In the 55 disputes studied, hostilities occurred in 32 instances. Hostilities were stopped, largely as a result of UN action, in 10 cases.

Another measure of "success" is the frequency with which the UN managed to dispose of the major issue which caused the dispute in the first place. Here we ask when and how often the parties to the dispute accepted the form of action adopted by the UN and settled their difference on that basis. Our 55 disputes break down as follows with respect to the settlement of the issue:

Settled on the basis of the UN resolution:	7
Settled in part on the basis of the UN resolution:	11
Settled wholly outside the UN:	13
Unsettled:	24

THE EXTENT OF REFERRAL AND SUCCESS

Table 2 presents the list of disputes which we have identified as "successfully" handled after being referred to the UN. Table 3 summarizes the disputes in which hostilities were prominent. The success scores of the variables used are summarized on Table 4.

TABLE 2

DISPUTES REFERRED TO UN
1945-1965

Period	Number	Disputes Referred to But Not Settled by UN	UN Settles or Helps Settle
1945-1947	11	French withdrawal from Levant Franco government in Spain Status of Trieste Kashmir Palestine South African race policies Revision of 1936 Suez Canal/Sudan agreement	Azerbaijan Balkans Corfu Channel Indonesia
1948-1951	6	Berlin blockade Communist coup in Czechoslovakia Hyderabad Iran oil nationalization	Korea Withdrawal of Republic of China troops from Burma
1952-1955	3	North African decolonization Future status of Cyprus Guatemala	None
1956-1960	10	Hungary Syria/Turkey border Laos civil war Tibet South Tyrol U-2 flights	Suez war Lebanon/Jordan unrest Nicaragua/Honduras border Thai/Cambodia border
1961-1965	25	Civil unrest in Oman Cuba (Bay of Pigs) Cuban intervention in Dominican Republic Goa Iraq/Kuwait (U.K.) Portuguese colonies in Africa Cuban missile crisis U.K./Venezuela border Dominican intervention in Haiti	Congo West Irian Bizerta Southern Rhodesia Aden/Yemen border Cambodia/South Vietnam (U.S.) Stanleyville air rescue India-Pakistan war

Malaysia/Indonesia
Senegal/Portugal border
Yemen civil war
Cyprus civil war
Greece/Turkey hostile
    acts
Panama Canal
U.S./North Vietnam
    (Gulf of Tonkin)
U.S. intervention in
    Dominican Republic

TABLE 3

DISPUTES INVOLVING HOSTILITIES REFERRED TO UN
1945-1965

Period	Number	UN Fails in Maintaining Truce or Stopping Hostilities	UN Succeeds in Maintaining Truce or Stopping Hostilities
1945-1947	4	Balkans	Indonesia Kashmir Palestine
1948-1951	1	None	Korea
1952-1955	3	North African decolonization Future status of Cyprus Guatemala	None
1956-1960	5	Hungary Tibet Laos civil war	Suez war Lebanon/Jordan unrest
1961-1965	19	Bizerta Cuba (Bay of Pigs) Goa Portuguese colonies in Africa Cuban missile crisis Civil unrest in Oman Dominican intervention in Haiti Malaysia/Indonesia Senegal/Portugal border Yemen civil war Aden/Yemen border Cambodia/South Vietnam (U.S.) Stanleyville air rescue U.S./North Vietnam (Gulf of Tonkin) U.S. intervention in Dominican Republic	Congo West Irian Cyprus civil war India-Pakistan war

TABLE 4

UN Performance: Settling Issues
(IN PERCENT)

Period	Organ			Action Taken[a]											Issue			Power of Parties				
	Security Council	General Assembly	Both	Direct neg. and/or ref. to reg. org.	Inquiry	Collective mediation or conciliation	Single mediator	Adjudication	Cease-fire ordered	Truce supervision established	Enforcement, boycott, embargo	Police force	Secretary-General's "Presence"	Committee of experts	Colonial	Cold War	Other	Big Power	Small powers, same bloc	Small powers, different blocs	One unaligned, other allied	Both unaligned
1945-1947 Average=36%	43	—	25	38	43	57	0	100	33	33	25	—	0	—	25	75	0	40	—	100	100	0
1948-1951 Average=33%	20	—	100	50	100	100	—	0	100	100	100	—	—	—	0	33	50	40	—	—	—	0
1952-1955 Average=0%	0	0	—	0	—	—	—	—	—	—	—	—	—	—	0	0	—	0	—	0	—	—
1956-1960 Average=40%	50	0	50	33	33	40	100	100	100	100	—	100	60	—	100	0	75	25	100	—	25	100
1961-1965 Average=32%	25	33	50	40	40	56	50	—	50	33	67	67	43	0	55	17	13	42	0	0	29	50
1945-1965 Average=33%	29	13	47	36	43	57	40	67	58	56	50	75	46	0	42	26	29	36	25	33	33	25
Number of Cases Total=55	31	8	15	25	16	23	5	3	12	9	8	4	13	1	19	19	17	28	4	3	12	8

Legend: — no cases occurred
[a] no action taken in 19 cases

TABLE 4 (Continued)

UN PERFORMANCE: SETTLING ISSUES
(IN PERCENT)

Period	Type of Consensus							Domestic Political System of Parties											
	Majority will	Concert	Permissive enforcement	Balancing	Permissive engagement with majority will	Permissive engagement with concert	Permissive engagement with balancing	Reconciliation/ Reconciliation	Reconciliation/ Mobilization	Reconciliation/ Modernizing Autocracy	Reconciliation/ Authoritarian	Reconciliation/ Traditional Oligarchy	Reconciliation/ Modernizing Oligarchy	Modern Autocracy/ Mobilization	Modern Autocracy/ Modern Autocracy	Traditional Oligarchy/ Mobilization	Traditional Oligarchy/ Traditional Oligarchy	Modern Oligarchy/ Modern Autocracy	Too many to work
1945-1947 Average=36%	0	60	100	0	—	—	—	33	75	—	—	0	—	—	—	—	—	—	0
1948-1951 Average=33%	—	100	100	100	—	—	—	0	50	—	—	—	—	—	—	—	—	—	0
1952-1955 Average=0%	0	—	—	—	—	—	—	0	0	—	—	—	—	—	100	—	—	—	0
1956-1960 Average=40%	0	—	—	0	50	50	100	0	33	—	—	—	0	0	—	—	100	—	—
1961-1965 Average=32%	50	33	—	80	50	0	50	0	20	0	100	0	100	0	100	0	0	100	50
1945-1965 Average=33%	17	50	100	63	50	25	67	10	40	0	100	0	50	0	100	0	50	100	30
Number of Cases Total=55	6	12	2	8	4	4	3	10	20	3	2	2	2	1	1	1	2	1	10

Legend: — no cases occurred

TABLE 5

UN Performance: Stopping Hostilities
(In Percent)

Period	Organ			ActionTaken[a]											Issue			Power of Parties				
	Security Council	General Assembly	Both	Direct negative/Referral to regional organization	Inquiry	Collective mediation or conciliation	Single mediator	Adjudication	Cease-fire ordered	Truce supervision established	Enforcement, boycott,embargo	Police force	Secretary-General's "Presence"	Committee of experts	Colonial	Cold War	Other	Big power	Small powers, same bloc	Small powers, different blocs	One unaligned, other allied	Both unaligned
1945-1947 Average=75%	100	—	50	75	75	75	100	—	100	100	100	—	100	—	100	0	100	—	—	0	100	100
1948-1951 Average=100%	—	—	100	—	—	100	—	—	100	100	100	—	—	—	—	100	—	100	—	—	—	—
1952-1955 Average=0%	0	0	—	0	—	—	—	—	—	—	—	—	—	—	0	0	—	0	—	0	—	—
1956-1960 Average=40%	—	0	50	50	33	40	—	—	100	100	—	100	50	—	100	0	100	33	—	—	0	100
1961-1965 Average=21%	8	50	40	13	0	38	100	—	33	67	50	100	14	—	22	0	40	11	50	—	17	50
1945-1965 Average=31%	20	20	50	31	33	50	100	—	67	89	80	100	33	—	31	9	63	20	50	0	25	75
Number of Cases Total=32	15	5	12	16	12	18	4	—	12	9	5	4	12	—	13	11	8	15	2	2	8	5

Legend: — no cases occurred
* no action taken in 7 cases

TABLE 5 (Continued)

UN PERFORMANCE: STOPPING HOSTILITIES
(IN PERCENT)

Period	Type of Consensus							Domestic Political System of Parties								
	Majority will	Concert	Permissive enforcement	Balancing	Permissive engagement with maj. will	Permanent engagement with concert	Permanent engagement with balancing	Reconciliation/ Reconciliation	Reconciliation/ Mobilization	Reconciliation/ Modernizing Autocracy	Reconciliation/ Authoritarian	Reconciliation/ Modernizing Oligarchy	Modern Autocracy/ Mobilization	Traditional Oligarchy/ Traditional Oligarchy	Modern Oligarchy/ Modern Autocracy	Too many parties to work
1945-1947 Average=75%	—	100	0	—	—	—	—	100	0	—	—	—	—	—	—	100
1948-1951 Average=100%	—	—	100	100	—	—	—	—	100	—	—	—	—	—	—	—
1952-1955 Average=0%	0	—	—	—	—	—	—	0	0	—	—	—	—	—	—	0
1956-1960 Average=40%	—	—	—	0	50	0	100	—	40	—	—	—	—	—	—	—
1961-1965 Average=21%	0	25	—	0	50	0	100	100	20	0	50	0	0	0	0	20
1945-65 Average=31%	0	57	50	17	50	0	100	75	31	0	50	0	0	0	0	29
Number of Cases Total=32	3	7	2	6	4	3	3	4	13	2	2	1	1	1	1	7

Legend: — no cases occurred

WHICH DISPUTES ARE SUCCESSFULLY SETTLED?

What of the efficacy of the UN organs used and the types of action taken? The combined use of the Security Council and the General Assembly brings results most frequently; the General Assembly used in isolation is ineffective. None of the methods of pacific settlement and/or enforcement is useless. But only collective mediation/conciliation worked in more than half of the instances in which it was used. Truce maintenance is reasonably effective and various recommended enforcement measures have been of utility half of the time, though the Secretary-General's "presence" has not. Adjudication has been effective, but then it was used in only three instances.

Settlement occurs most frequently in the context of colonial issues, but the prophets of doom were wrong in holding that cold war disputes—by definition—are incapable of solution by the UN. A success score of one in four is not total ineffectiveness. It has also been suggested that the UN is good only for settling disputes among small states. The record proves this assertion wrong. Over one-third of the disputes involving a major power has been successfully settled; in fact, the success score is *lowest* for small power antagonists which are allies and for pairs of small unaligned nations.

The corresponding figures for disputes which involved hostilities are given on Table 5. The combined use of Security Council and General Assembly for the stopping of hostilities and the establishment of a truce is the most effective approach. The use of single mediators has been found equally effective in maintaining a truce. Indeed, there are very few cases in which the order to honor a truce was not obeyed by the parties, though occasional violations did occur. Police forces have been effective whenever they were created.

The picture is different when we examine the kinds of issues which called forth UN efforts to halt hostilities. Cold war-related hostilities cannot be readily stopped by the UN. Hostilities unconnected with any of the major schisms of world politics are most frequently brought to a halt. Once a major power is involved in hostilities, the UN is not very often successful in inducing it to stop. However, it is successful in bringing war between two unaligned countries to a halt in three out of four cases. Still, the UN is more often successful in inducing the major powers to stop fighting than in controlling small nations who are members of opposing alliances. It is simply not true that the practice of collective security has been doomed by the dominance and lack of responsiveness of the great powers, the omnipresence of cold war issues, the role of ideology in world affairs, the advent of nuclear weapons, or any of the other developments held to be incompatible with the assumptions of the statesmen who negotiated the UN Charter in 1945.

The data suggest no trend of a cumulative pattern, of new successes inducing better performance in later periods. Performance in regard to the settlement of issues has remained fairly stable, with the temporary improvement in the period 1956-1960 apparently dissipated by the crisis over permissive engagement triggered by the Congo dispute. UN success in halting hostilities has declined sharply over the years. Collective security as an institutionalized organizational task has shown no sign of producing any kind of cumulative patterns of satisfaction, acceptance, or growth. Nor can we conclude that a cumulative pattern of satisfaction can be correlated with type of action, issue, or the power of the parties.

Obviously, the Security Council's effectiveness in stopping hostilities has suffered over the years. The General Assembly remains ineffective (the 50 percent score in 1960-1965 being accounted for by the West Irian case) and recourse to both organs shows no net growth. The efficacy of bilateral negotiations, inquiry, and collective mediation/conciliation has declined sharply. Single mediators were effective during the first and the last periods. Truce maintenance and enforcement had been very successful until the most recent period. Police forces have retained their very high success scores, but the efficacy of a "presence" has declined. Not unexpectedly, UN successes with respect to all types of issues have declined, though "other" disputes have declined the least and colonial issues remain more amenable to UN intervention than cold war ones. Finally, the major powers are less amenable to accepting UN intervention in their wars now as compared to the previous periods, and the same is true of pairs of unaligned states and especially of situations involving one unaligned and one allied nation.

Clearly, the UN has shown more ability to function effectively with respect to settling certain kinds of disputes than in stopping wars. Colonial disputes of all kinds are the most likely to be settled successfully even if a major power is a party. Wars among pairs of unaligned states are stopped most readily, but with respect to the settlement of disputes the power of the parties seems to make little difference. Methods for the pacific settlement of disputes have become less effective over the years as mild enforcement measures, police forces, and the Secretary-General have increased in potency— with the proviso that all this is true more for Hammarskjöld than for U Thant.

TYPES OF CONSENSUS AND SETTLEMENT OF DISPUTES

These statistics have neglected the intervening variable of the consensual pattern, the manner in which the member states reach agree-

TABLE 6

UN Settlement of Disputes: Power Distribution, Consensus, Issues[o]

Power Distribution	Majority Will		Concert			Permissive Enforcement	Balancing		Permissive Engagement with Majority Will		Permissive Engagement with Concert		Permissive Engagement with Balancing	
	clnl.[a]	other[b]	clnl.[c]	c.war[d]	other[e]	c.war[f]	clnl.[g]	c.war[h]	clnl.[i]	c.war[j]	c.war[k]	other[l]	clnl.[m]	other[n]
Unipolar victor group	—	0 of 1	1 of 1	2 of 2	0 of 2	1 of 1	—	—	—	—	—	—	—	—
Tight bipolar symmetrical	—	—	—	—	1 of 1	1 of 1	—	1 of 1	—	—	—	—	—	—
Loose bipolar heterosymmetrical	0 of 2	—	—	—	—	—	—	—	—	—	—	—	—	—
Tripolar hetero-symmetrical	—	0 of 1	—	—	—	—	—	0 of 1	1 of 1	0 of 1	0 of 1	1 of 1	—	1 of 1
Multipolar hetero-symmetrical	1 of 2	—	1 of 3	—	1 of 3	—	3 of 5	1 of 1	1 of 1	0 of 1	0 of 1	0 of 1	—	0 of 1

Legend: clnl. = colonial
c.war = cold war
— = no cases occurred

[a] North African decolonization
Future status of Cyprus
Portuguese colonies in Africa
Southern Rhodesia

[b] Franco government in Spain
South Tyrol

[c] Indonesia
Bizerta
Senegal/Portugal border
Panama Canal

[d] Azerbaijan
Corfu Channel

[e] Kashmir
Palestine
Withdrawal of Republic of China troops from Burma
Dominican intervention in Haiti
Greece/Turkey hostile acts
India-Pakistan war

[f] Balkans
Korea

[g] South African race policies
Portuguese colonies in Africa
Southern Rhodesia
Aden/Yemen border
Stanleyville air rescue

[h] Korea
Tibet
Cambodia/South Vietnam (U.S.)

[i] Suez war
West Irian

[j] Hungary

[k] Laos civil war
Cuban missile crisis

[l] Thai/Cambodia border
Yemen civil war

[m] Congo

[n] Lebanon/Jordan unrest
Cyprus civil war

[o] Disputes on which UN could reach no consensus:
French withdrawal from Levant
Status of Trieste
Revision of 1936 Suez Canel/Sudan Agreement
Berlin blockage
Communist coup in Czechoslovakia
Hyderabad
Iran oil nationalization
Guatemala
Syria/Turkey border
U-2 flights
Cuba (Bay of Pigs)
Cuban intervention in Dominican Republic
Goa
Iraq/Kuwait (U.K.)
Civil unrest in Oman
U.K./Venezuela border
Malaysia/Indonesia
U.S./North Vietnam (Gulf of Tonkin)
U.S. intervention in Dominican Republic

ment on a course of action. I suggest that a causal understanding of why the UN succeeds or fails must attempt to link the power distribution of the system, the consensual patterns which prevail, and the type of issues to which they apply. This information is summarized on Table 6. What does it suggest?

A consensus based on majority will has emerged predominantly on colonial questions, twice on "other" questions which were of very little importance to world politics, and never on cold war matters. No past, present, or future importance should be attached to this way of approaching world security, not even in an increasingly multibloc systemic setting.

The concert has proved the most viable and effective approach, irrespective of international systemic conditions. It has been successful in all types of issues, even on cold war matters where the major powers were looking for a *modus vivendi*. If we project a future in which both cold war and colonial issues will decline in incidence, it is important to note the relative degree of success which attends the concert on "other" issues during the multipolar system which has prevailed most recently. Since even during the height of the cold war (1947-1951) the United States and the Soviet Union managed to agree on some disputes outside either's sphere of major interest, the same possibility might be kept in mind if China were to assume a seat on the Security Council.

Balancing has gone through two distinct phases. The first involved simply the negotiated settlement of the Korean conflict, with a portion of the UN membership "balancing" between the aggressor and the UN Command carrying out the earlier mandate of the organization. This type of consensus depends on a previous permissive enforcement decision and therefore is obsolete. Thus attention must be focused on the five cases of balancing which occurred under the very different circumstances of the most recent period. In three out of five colonial disputes, the consensus produced effective UN action; it worked in one cold war dispute in which the Soviet Union and the United States wished to minimize the damage, but it failed in the effort to save Tibet from China. There would seem to be no reason to suppose that in a multibloc or multipolar setting this approach to persuading the major powers—while ignoring the Secretary-General—could not increasingly apply to disputes which bear no relationship to the cold war or the colonial revolution.

The various patterns of permissive engagement did not come into existence until 1956. This is not due entirely to Dag Hammarskjöld's tenets regarding the role of the Secretary-General and the drive toward a UN which is less of a conference of states and more akin to a supra-national entity. It also required a loosening of the bipolar

TABLE 7

UN Stops Hostilities: Power Distribution, Consensus, Issues[m]
(in percent)

Power Distribution	Majority Will	Concert		Permissive Enforcement	Balancing		Permissive Engagement with Majority Will		Permissive Engagement with Concert		Permissive Engagement with Balancing	
	clnl.[a]	clnl.[b]	other[c]	c.war[d]	clnl.[e]	c.war[f]	clnl.[g]	c.war[h]	c.war[i]	other[j]	clnl.[k]	other[l]
Unipolar victor group	—	100% (N=1)	100% (N=2)	100% (N=1)	—	—	—	—	—	—	—	—
Tight bipolar symmetrical	—	—	—	100 (N=1)	—	100% (N=1)	—	—	—	—	—	—
Loose bipolar heterosymmetrical	0% (N=2)	—	—	—	—	—	—	—	—	—	—	—
Tripolar hetero-symmetrical	100 (N=1)	—	—	—	—	0 (N=1)	100% (N=1)	0% (N=1)	0% (N=1)	—	—	100% (N=1)
Multipolar hetero-symmetrical	—	50 (N=2)	0 (N=1)	—	67% (N=3)	100 (N=1)	100 (N=1)	—	0 (N=1)	0 (N=1)	100 (N=1)	100 (N=2)

Legend: clnl. = colonial
c.war = cold war
— = no cases occurred

a North African decolonization
Future status of Cyprus
Portuguese colonies in Africa

b Indonesia
Bizerta
Senegal/Portugal border

c Kashmir
Palestine
Dominican intervention in Haiti
India-Pakistan war

d Balkans
Korea

e Portuguese colonies in Africa
Aden/Yemen border
Stanleyville air rescue

f Korea
Tibet
Cambodia/South Vietnam (U.S.)

g Suez war
West Irian

h Hungary

i Laos civil war
Cuban missile crisis

j Yemen civil war

k Congo

l Lebanon/Jordan unrest
Cyprus civil war

m Disputes with hostilities on which UN proved unable to reach a consensus:
Guatemala
Civil unrest in Oman
Cuba (Bay of Pigs)
Goa
Malaysia/Indonesia
U.S./North Vietnam (Gulf of Tonkin)
U.S. intervention in Dominican Republic

system, a more heterogeneous membership, and the tendency toward tripolar and multipolar diplomatic alignments outside the UN. Because issues and blocs were thus diffused and multiplied, the Secretary-General acquired the ability to maneuver for support, construct different coalitions of supporters on different issues, and thus succeeded in gaining permission to "engage" the organization in collective security.

Among the various manipulative options open to the Secretary-General, it appears that reliance on majority support in the General Assembly is the least reliable; it is unlikely to recur very often. Nor has the concert been often used with success, though there is no reason to suppose that the major powers will not permit the Secretary-General to "engage" them in local squabbles of no importance to their basic policy objectives. Balancing, finally, emerges as the most prominent formula, particularly in post-colonial situations of the kind likely to be with us for some time in which the super-powers are anxious merely to keep each other from profiting from the turmoil without having other specific aims.

The same conclusions are supported by a tabulation of the consensual and issue patterns underlying the ability of the UN to stop hostilities, as summarized on Table 7.

COLLECTIVE SECURITY AND TYPES OF POLITIES

This brings us to the major question which suggests itself to students of reconciliation systems: What kinds of polities tend to accept UN decisions on settling disputes and stopping hostilities? Do reconciliation polities respond more frequently than other kinds of polities? Briefly, does the success of the international reconciliation system depend in some measure on the behavior of national reconciliation polities? Answers are suggested by Tables 8 and 9.

The data on Table 8 suggests that the success of the international reconciliation system *owes nothing* to the internal political mores and institutions of the member states. Table 9 changes this conclusion somewhat. When actual hostilities are involved, the UN success score for pairs of reconciliation polities rises to 50 percent, and for disputes involving reconciliation polities on one side and various systems on the other the score reaches 75 percent. We must bear in mind, however, that each of these clusters includes only four cases. The score for disputes between reconciliation polities and mobilization systems remains about the same. Both tables support unequivocally the conclusion that a unipolar or tight bipolar nuclear power distribution is conducive to successful collective security operations

TABLE 8

UN Settlement: Power Distribution, Polities, Issues[a]
(in percent)

Power Distribution	Reconciliation/ Reconciliation		Reconciliation/ Mobilization			Reconciliation/ Modernizing Autocracy/ Authoritarian/ Modernizing Oligarchy		
	clnl.b	otherc	clnl.d	c.ware	otherf	clnl.g	c.warh	otheri
Unipolar victor group	50 (N=2)	0 (N=1)	—	75 (N=4)	—	0 (N=1)	—	—
Tight bipolar symmetrical	0 (N=1)	0 (N=1)	—	33 (N=3)	100 (N=1)	—	—	—
Loose bipolar hetero-symmetrical	0 (N=1)	—	—	0 (N=1)	—	—	—	—
Tripolar hetero-symmetrical	—	0 (N=1)	100 (N=1)	0 (N=4)	100 (N=1)	—	0 (N=1)	—
Multipolar hetero-symmetrical	—	0 (N=3)	100 (N=1)	0 (N=3)	0 (N=1)	40 (N=5)	—	50 (N=2)

Legend: clnl.   = colonial
        c.war = cold war
        —   = no cases occurred

[a] Some disputes were not tabulated. The following cases involved too small a sample of pairs of possibilities and were therefore excluded: Nicaragua/Honduras border, Thai/Cambodia border, Cambodia/South Vietnam (U.S.) (all successfully settled by UN); Cuban intervention in Dominican Republic, Dominican intervention in Haiti, Yemen civil war (none successfully settled).

The following disputes each involved more than three parties and could therefore not be summarized in terms of polity patterns: Congo, Southern Rhodesia, Stanleyville air rescue (all successfully settled); Franco government in Spain, Palestine, South African race policies, North African decolonization, Civil unrest in Oman, Portuguese colonies in Africa, U.S. intervention in Dominican Republic (none successfully settled).

[b] French withdrawal from Levant
Indonesia
Iran oil nationalization
Future status of Cyprus

[c] Kashmir
Hyderabad
South Tyrol
U.K./Venezuela border
Cyprus civil war
Greece/Turkey hostile acts

[d] Suez war
West Irian

[e] Azerbaijan
Balkans
Corfu Channel
Status of Trieste
Berlin blockade
Communist coup in Czechoslovakia
Korea
Guatemala
Hungary
Laos civil war
Tibet
U-2 flights
Cuba (Bay of Pigs)
Cuban missile crisis
U.S./North Vietnam (Gulf of Tonkin)

[f] Withdrawal of Republic of China troops
from Burma
Lebanon/Jordan unrest
Malaysia/Indonesia

[g] Revision of 1936 Suez Canal/Sudan
Agreement
Bizerta
Goa
Senegal/Portugal border
Aden/Yemen border
Panama Canal

[h] Syria/Turkey border

[i] Iraq/Kuwait (U.K.)
India-Pakistan war

TABLE 9

UN STOPS HOSTILITIES: POWER DISTRIBUTION, POLITIES, ISSUES[a]
(IN PERCENT)

Power Distribution	Type of Polity and Issues							
	Reconciliation/ Reconciliation		Reconciliation/ Mobilization			Reconciliation/ Modernizing Autocracy/ Authoritarian/ Modernizing Oligarchy		
	clnl.b	otherc	clnl.d	c.ware	otherf	clnl.g	otherh	
Unipolar victor group	100 (N=1)	0 (N=1)	—	100 (N=1)	—	—	—	
Tight bipolar symmetrical	—	—	—	100 (N=1)	—	—	—	
Loose bipolar heterosymmetrical	0 (N=1)	—	—	0 (N=1)	—	—	—	
Tripolar hetero-symmetrical	—	—	100 (N=1)	0 (N=3)	100 (N=1)	—	—	
Multipolar hetero-symmetrical	—	100 (N=1)	100 (N=1)	0 (N=3)	0 (N=1)	67 (N=3)	100 (N=1)	

Legend: clnl. = colonial
c.war = cold war
— = no cases occurred

[a] Cases excluded from Table 8 were excluded here also.

[b] Indonesia
Future status of Cyprus

[c] Kashmir
Cyprus civil war

[d] Suez war
West Irian

[e] Balkans
Korea
Guatemala
Hungary
Laos civil war
Tibet
Cuba (Bay of Pigs)
Cuban missile crisis
U.S./North Vietnam (Gulf of Tonkin)

[f] Lebanon/Jordan unrest
Malaysia/Indonesia

[g] Bizerta
Senegal/Portugal border
Aden/Yemen border

[h] India-Pakistan war

between reconciliation and mobilization systems. Further, both tables also permit us to conclude that a multipolar power distribution is conducive to successful collective security in cases involving a reconciliation polity scrapping with a modernizing oligarchy, modernizing autocracy, or authoritarian system.

The responsiveness of parties to disputes to UN action is only one side of the coin. We have an additional test for dealing with the problem of whether reconciliation polities are required to assure the functioning of collective security in a reconciliation-type UN. We must also inquire as to who furnishes the money, the troops, and the facilities in disputes involving hostilities. The answer is simple: without the disproportionate contribution in men on the part of the small Western democracies and India and without the heavy financial and transport contribution of the United States, none of the major peacekeeping operations could have been mounted. In short, it requires the good will of reconciliation polities to keep the peacekeeping activities of the UN intact.

THE FUTURE OF COLLECTIVE SECURITY

Our purpose in engaging in this exercise remains a projection of the future of collective security. But what can the past be squeezed into suggesting here? Clearly, the experience of the UN has been very discontinuous, and little evidence was uncovered which indicated a progressive and cumulative movement in a particular direction. Collective security was successfully practiced during the first period and again during the fourth, with the score declining during the most recent era. The institutionalization and legitimation of permissive engagement was suggested by the record of the fourth period; the most recent experiences of the UN argue a retreat from that position. What then can we project?

We can use the record of the past and probable outlines of the future system of international relations to exclude certain possibilities. Cold war disputes will decline in frequency but prove unamenable to collective security if the major powers are directly involved. Colonial disputes will disappear after the Portuguese and South African situations have been resolved, though their resolution will tax collective security procedures to the utmost. The Congo may turn out to have been nothing but a suggestive overture when Portugal's and South Africa's time comes. Consensus based on majority will and permissive enforcement will not recur in view of the multibloc character of the system. This leaves us with the likelihood of many post-colonial territorial disputes in the Afro-Asian world, ideological "international" civil wars in Latin America and Africa, and routine minor disagreements anywhere. The consensual patterns will be confined to concerts and balancing. The central question for the UN is whether such consensual arrangements will also feature permissive engagement and the attendant institutionalization of an autonomous supranational force.

The future of collective security can also be envisaged by correlating the two consensual formulas likely to prevail with the degree of urgency or fear experienced by the major powers. This juxtaposition is illustrated in the matrix below.[8] The disputes placed in squares 1,

---

[8] I am greatly indebted to Mr. Peter Madian's undergraduate honors thesis in the Department of Political Science at the University of California (Berkeley) for this way of conceptualizing the future of peacekeeping forces. Norman

2, 4, and 5 involved reasonably energetic and successful UN operations and suggest that the major powers must at least experience some
sense of urgency if action is to be taken on the basis of an energetic
concert or the more passive balancing. The matrix also suggests very
strongly that three kinds of disputes will not trigger any future collective security operations. First, direct confrontations between the
major blocs will remain outside the scope of successful UN action.
Second, post-colonial disputes considered to present few dangers to
world peace will also be neglected. Finally, local disputes of little
import with respect to world peace will not result in successful UN
action whenever the parties are members of opposing blocs.

CONSENSUS FOR UN ACTION

		Concert	Balancing	None
	High	1 Early Congo India-Pakistan war	2 Later Congo Later Korea	3 Cuban Missile Crisis
PERCEPTION OF DANGER BY SUPER-POWERS	**Med.**	4 Early Kashmir Early Palestine Indonesia Bizerta	5 Cyprus Lebanon Cambodia/South Vietnam	6 Malaysia/Indonesia U.S. in Dominican Republic Later Kashmir Later Palestine
	Low	7 Haiti/Dominican Republic Laos civil war Yemen civil war	8 Portuguese Africa	9 Goa Guatemala Tibet

Padelford offers a similar projection in his "Financing Peacekeeping: Politics
and Crisis," *International Organization* (Summer, 1965). Padelford, taking into
account all we have said about the political limits on future peacekeeping
operations, sees a "negotiating area" from which future *ad hoc* forces will
derive their authorization. These will involve truce supervision missions, small
police forces, and even UNEF-type operations. The consensual basis will be the
passive acquiescence or resistance of countries like France and the Soviet
Union and the enthusiastic (or at least moral) support of the small Western
countries and India.

IV. GLOBAL TASKS AND THE UN OF THE FUTURE

The use of developmental models for forecasting now reaches its limits: we can project the future only in terms of the concepts and mechanisms we have applied to the analysis of the past, not because there are no others but because there are too many possibilities. Whatever rigor in analysis has been present so far is now sacrificed to the exploration of future trends in terms of broad possibilities that remain somehow linked to what is visible in the international system and its environment at the present time. The tentative character of the speculations associated with this approach hardly require emphasis.

We might well wonder why there was moderate satisfaction in most countries with the UN even though its rate of success was confined to one case in three.[9] I argue that this surprising finding can be accounted for on two grounds: First, since few national elites show any commitment to a future of world government, conquest by a single nation, or isolationism, *there was no alternative to the UN.* Second, it must be understood that collective security since 1956 has been practiced in the context of a tacit bargaining pattern which also included peaceful decolonization, international economic development aid, and the protection of human rights. In a sense, politics has become less "political" as the member countries were becoming preoccupied with issues almost as important to them as military and territorial objectives. National self-determination has ceased to be a purely political slogan; it has come to be understood also as a program including economic and human rights (though the rights are collective rather than individual). The practice of collective security which happened to satisfy Western objectives could be indirectly legitimated by paying a price to non-Western countries in the currency of the other issue areas; Soviet collective security objectives responded to the same logic, though to a much lesser extent. In other words, not every security issue had to be settled so as to satisfy each major nation or bloc because compensating advantages could be and were provided by the UN in other issue areas sometimes of greater importance to many nations. Relative satisfaction with the collective security task could be sustained because of an inter-functional and inter-regional tacit bargaining process.

---

[9] An amazing amount of dissatisfaction with collective security operations was revealed in the Carnegie Endowment's multi-volume series of national studies of the UN, dissatisfaction symmetrically distributed among Western industrialized and Afro-Asian and Latin American underdeveloped countries. Yet the authority of UN decisions did not decline. For a review and an evaluation of this material, see Haas, "The Comparative Study of the United Nations," *World Politics,* Vol. XII, No. 2 (January, 1960).

This process was the result of rapidly changing social and economic forces within the member states, especially in the Afro-Asian and Latin American regions. Modernization, investment, industrialization, urbanization, the need for new sources of energy, immense population growth, public health, basic literacy, crash programs of technical education, and agricultural productivity all figure in these trends. The multi-pronged drive for modernization obviously had its origin in frustrations and dissatisfaction, but the efforts to meet the demands for modernization produced new frustrations and dissatisfactions—"economic and social imbalances"—which also make themselves felt in the foreign policy demands espoused by states. During the past ten years, these overlapping and contradictory pressures provided a field of maneuver and accommodation at the UN.

The next ten or twenty years may deny the UN such a field of maneuver because each of these areas of action is acquiring an autonomous legitimacy in the minds of the world's leaders, thus requiring fewer bargains and compromises across regions and functions from which the practice of collective security might benefit. Collective security will have to stand on its own feet—and the limiting conditions we discovered suggest the built-in obstacles here. Why this is so must now be shown. It calls for a discussion of the environmental forces clamoring for action, the types of polities likely to prevail in the future, the international distribution of power twenty years hence, and the kinds of issues that will preoccupy the UN of the future—thus giving us the substantive areas in and among which policy compromises must take place.

THE ENVIRONMENT OF THE FUTURE

That the domestic setting of policy will be vastly different twenty years from now is a truism. The use of synthetics and of automation will replace natural commodities as well as men. Leisure will abound and so will religious and quasi-religious activities designed to fill the void of time or monotony of work. Space flights will be routine, weapons systems will come to include non-killing devices, fertility control will have been perfected, many diseases eliminated. The list continues almost endlessly. But so do the social and economic problems—unsolved ones from our era and additional ones begotten by massive technological-scientific change. The demand for controlled and accelerated social change in the third world will continue to grow. The developed world will suffer from a surfeit of success in not being able to reconcile democracy and pluralism with relative deprivation for the less skilled and educated in the face of ever-rising levels of consumption. Mass movements of discontent may grow as a result of improved education in all parts of the world. And the search for new methods of social control will go on in proportion.

What types of polities are likely to prevail in the mid-1980s? No oligarchies and modernizing autocracies will survive by 1985. My projection is therefore confined to reasonably confident assertions as to the number of reconciliation, authoritarian, and mobilization polities and to likely alternatives in the more doubtful cases.

Established reconciliation systems in industrialized countries will survive, and they are likely to become even looser and more flexible in social texture and political cohesion as the disintegrative logic of technology and leisure time acquires momentum. None will survive in Africa and few in Asia. Some of the Latin American countries (Chile, Venezuela, Uruguay, for instance) will succeed in cementing the reconciliation pattern which already prevails. The European communist nations will have become more relaxed and benign authoritarianisms or even begin to approach a reconciliation polity as they experience the same technological-social syndrome already visible in the West. Mobilization polities in Africa will become fewer as their inefficiency and lack of flexibility combine to make them objects

TABLE 10
DISTRIBUTION OF POLITIES BY TYPE IN UN OF 1985
(Number of Countries)

	Probable			Likely Alternatives			
	Reconciliation	Authoritarian	Mobilization	Reconciliation/Authoritarian	Reconciliation/Mobilization	Authoritarian/Mobilization	TOTAL
Europe	21	5	0	4	0	0	30
W. Hemisphere	10	1	1	3	3	8	26
Australasia	4	2	0	0	0	0	6
Asia	4	6	6	7	1	7	31
Africa	0	16	3	2	0	21	42
Total	39	30	10	16	4	36	135
Percentage of UN Membership	28%	22%	8%	12%	3%	27%	100%

New member states by 1985: Rhodesia, Angola, Mozambique, S.W. Africa, Belize, Fiji, Pacific Trust Territory, Solomon Islands, Papua/New Guinea, West Germany, East Germany, Vietnam, South/North Korea, Aden, Oman/Trucial Coast, "China" will be the Peking regime, Korea, with the exclusion of Taiwan. I am unable to assert a "probable future" for 42% of the 135-member UN projected. For example, I consider it equally likely that Tunisia and Cyprus will either be reconciliation or authoritarian polities; the chances of Algeria being a mobilization or authoritarian polity are equally good, etc. Hence the projection is limited to stating the likely alternatives.

of popular discontent and overthrow; they will give rise to authoritarian regimes. The Asian communist states, however, will survive as mobilization polities. Authoritarian regimes will increase in number and show a great diversity of styles and institutions, but they will resemble one another in seeking to control and channel the scope and pace of modernization in order to avert the implications of some of the factors listed above. Table 10 summarizes my speculations.

If because international reconciliation systems do not require a fixed number of national reconciliation polities to permit successful adjustment and bargaining and a minimum of a dozen or twenty such regimes to permit peacekeeping operations, these forecasts permit the projection that many crucial requisites of a future reconciliation-type UN can be met. Reconciliation polities will account for a minimum of 28 percent and a maximum of 43 percent of the membership; mobilization systems for a minimum of 8 percent and a maximum of 38 percent. The Soviet Union will not be a mobilization regime, though its place in the lineup will be taken by China. Authoritarian regimes will be ample in number and power for any balancing operations. All past systems suggest that such regimes make acceptable role-players in collective security operations. We shall have to see whether the social change patterns suggested in and among these countries will also meet the additional requisite of satisfaction through tacit inter-functional bargaining.

THE FUTURE INTERNATIONAL DISTRIBUTION OF POWER

This brings us to the kind of power distribution likely in 1985. Instead of being multipolar, the new system will be a multibloc arrangement. The leadership role of such nations as the United States, Soviet Union, India, Egypt, Ivory Coast, and Ghana will be much less pronounced. An increasing and more uniform amount of technological, industrial, and human skill development will tend to diminish capability differentials within regions. However, the blocs will not be identical or equally cohesive in all kinds of issues. A reduction of influence in the realm of economic capability will not be symmetrically distributed among East and West in the sense that both blocs lose equal increments to a third bloc, simply because there will be no single "third" bloc any longer. Furthermore, both blocs may lose different and unequal amounts of influence in the ideological and military realms, again to various blocs. Inter-functional and inter-regional bargaining will become much more complex, defying an easy reckoning of gains and losses. In short, the system of the future will be characterized by a multibloc asymmetric power distribution.

Let us project the probable blocs which will exist for purposes of economic development issues and economic-financial bargaining. There will be a Latin American Community, a Caribbean grouping, and a viable Central American Common Market. There will also be a self-contained East and Southeast Asian communist bloc, one or more African blocs, and a heterogeneous socialist Asian grouping. Together these will comprise the "developing nations" bloc within the UNCTAD of the future, confronting an industrialized bloc made up of a West European Community, Japan, a United States-Canadian component, and the European communist nations. Neither of the two super-groups will be very cohesive.

Considered in ideological-military terms, the blocs may be slightly different. On the communist side, there will be a European alliance somewhat looser and more egalitarian than the Warsaw Pact Organization and some kind of Asian communist alliance. These will correspond ideologically to the "Marxism" appropriate to the successors of Lenin's and Mao's states. Relations between these two need not be hostile. NATO may disappear to give rise to a West European alliance with its own nuclear deterrent and a separate United States military establishment, or it may linger on without much to do as the cold war changes in character and technology.

It is easier to think about future ideological than military groupings in the third world. None of the conceivable groupings there will possess the power, cohesion, unity of purpose, or strong central institutions which the communist and Western military and economic blocs possess now. Personal rivalries aside, it makes sense to think of two mutually antagonistic African blocs: one of authoritarian and another of mobilization polities, one reasonable friendly to the West, the other to China. Perhaps the same trend would be true of Latin America, though it is doubtful that an alliance of mobilization regimes will be permitted by the United States. It makes more sense to forecast a military-ideological grouping of reconciliation and authoritarian polities, retaining much looser ties with the United States than those maintained by the OAS now, and a number of isolated and bellicose mobilization polities. If Maoism remains forceful, we may forecast in Asia a defensive military-ideological grouping of authoritarian and reconciliation polities, including India, Indonesia, Malaysia, Iran, and the Philippines, and a few genuine neutrals, such as Burma, Nepal, and Afghanistan. If China were to become preoccupied with other matters, no military-ideological formations of any significance will emerge in Asia.

In the UN we would then have a minimum of six military blocs, or a maximum of ten, with a considerable number of neutral states. The cohesion of each is more than doubtful, as their central institutions will vary from tacit understandings among equals to more elaborate bonds. Even if we assume a certain amount of nuclear proliferation, their military capacities will differ greatly. It is quite conceivable that some of the cheaper new weapons systems will be in general use and be employed effectively in domestic and regional counter-insurgency operations. This obviously would contribute to the internal stability of rapidly modernizing nations and to bloc strength. What matters most in the present context is that the military, economic, and ideological inputs of nations will no longer form a tight and coherent bundle and that blocs differentiated on a functional rather than consistent geographic basis will appear as role-players in the UN of the future.

The implications for collective security go beyond the change in the bargaining pattern. In the past, such regional entities as the OAS and the OAU have occasionally carried out pacific settlement tasks delegated to them by the UN. Conversely, the OAU and the Arab League have also engaged in aggressive acts violating the Charter, and the same has been said of SEATO. Neither possibility will prevail in the future with the obsolescence of the existing military alliances and the corresponding UN voting blocs.

ISSUE AREAS IN THE FUTURE

The only typical decolonization questions left over from the previous periods in UN history are those referring to the Portuguese in Africa and the future of South Africa. While the period from 1960 to 1965 can be given the label "decolonization era" because so much of the UN's energy was taken up with the implementation of the General Assembly's declaration on the complete termination of colonialism, little of this task will be left for subsequent periods. The resolution of the remaining "hard core" questions will probably not follow the pattern of reasonably peaceful change. In fact, the immediate future may well involve the application of the full panoply of collective security procedures to Africa. This done, the decolonization task of the UN will be accomplished, and the ideological and legal justification for the application of Chapters VI and VII of the Charter to this kind of situation will no longer prove feasible. The oppression of ethnic groups by the young state of Africa and Asia will not be treated as threats to world peace, despite the fact that practice is the reverse during the current period when the oppressor is white.

This means that the apparent increase in the competence and authority of the organization triggered by the decolonization issue will be given no opportunity to solidify or expand. Decolonization completed, the successor states are likely to be exceedingly jealous of the very powers they had denied their colonial antagonists and thus block the carry-over of the UN constitutional evolution into the next system.

But is not the argument over national self-determination also a human rights issue? Is it impossible to suppose that the claims to human freedom and dignity voiced in the context of decolonization will be heard more and more in the UN and be applied to all member states? It is not only possible but likely. I suspect, however, that the issue of human rights in the next system will no longer profit from being carried along by the prevalence of other issues.

In the past, the increased emphasis on the international protection of human rights owed its salience to the cold war and the colonial revolution. The cold war was responsible for the ILO conventions dealing with freedom of association, the right of collective bargaining, and forced labor because these texts were initially sponsored by Western governments in order to embarrass the communist nations. The colonial revolt was the godfather of the ILO convention dealing with discrimination in employment, the UNESCO convention on discrimination in education, and the 1965 UN convention on the elimination of all racial discrimination. Since texts that do not owe their origin to some other and more salient issue area are unlikely to succeed in penetrating the international environment, the legitimacy now closely associated with certain rights in the decolonization nexus is not destined to last. Even though racial discrimination and the suppression of voluntary organizations are certain to recur, we must be skeptical of their salience in triggering concern or UN action. The experience of the ILO suggests that only reconciliation polities of recent origin and certain modernizing oligarchies tend to be responsive to international criticism, primarily in order to demonstrate their respectability. Because the future international system is likely to be inhabited by a very large number of authoritarian polities we cannot rely on the continuation of the pattern of responsiveness. Neither an autonomous expansion of the human rights task nor the possibility of trade-offs with security concerns can be foreseen.

What about economic development and financial aid as future issues? I think that we are on the threshold of a dramatically different approach to economic issues which will have broad implications for this issue area and its link with other tasks. Hitherto, UN economic aid, financed largely by the Western industrial powers, has not been an autonomous issue area. The UN economic development machinery has expanded strikingly from the initially conservative IBRD and the modest technical assistance operations of the TAB to the much more powerful Special Fund and more generous lending and granting agencies now clustering around the Bank. Additional autonomous UN planning and research agencies are developing rapidly. At the same time, the scattered and self-preoccupied aid policies of the specialized agencies have been centralized and coordinated through the UN Development Program. These developments were a component of a tacit bargaining process between the West, the Soviet bloc, and the underdeveloped nations. The primary concern of the dispensers of aid—the West and the Soviets—was rooted in the interplay between the cold war and the colonial revolt. It was therefore closely connected with collective security concerns and peacekeeping operations. Economic aid—bilateral and multilateral— was a method found useful to advance national objectives and to buy support in the third world. In order to maintain such a pattern, even a greatly multilateralized one, the economic aid task should *not* become autonomous and self-generating but remain tied to the other concerns. Otherwise there can be no tacit bargaining. However, the events of the last few years suggest that this task is about to become autonomous and self-generating as symbolized by the emergence of UNCTAD and UNIDO.

Is the field of disarmament and arms control in space and on earth likely to offer opportunities for inter-functional bargaining in the future? The lessons of the past allow very little optimism here. There have been almost continuous disarmament negotiations since 1945, yet in no sense have they constituted a task area or provided an issue which has been successfully pulled into a tacit bargaining pattern involving other issues and tasks. The future course of events seems here clearly delineated by the past. Substantively, the only agreements actually concluded have been arms control measures of a self-enforcing character, confirming the technological *status quo*. Because these agreements are largely self-enforcing, no role of any kind has accrued to the UN except the capacity to register, *ex post facto,* ventures into space. We can only guess that with the diffusion of scientific and technological capability, other countries will come to share the fears of the super-powers and also submit to the same minimal restraints implied by IAEA inspection of nuclear facilities, but this implies no trade-off possibilities from which collective security can profit.

This review of issue areas leaves us with one very speculative and uncharted sea of possibilities: the impact of science and technology generally. Do the probabilities enumerated earlier constitute areas of shared concern which might lead to demands and inputs on the part of various emerging blocs so as to trigger a new inter-functional tacit bargaining pattern? Could one suppose that the eagerness of the Atlantic nations to obtain a financial basis for peacekeeping might be tacitly bartered for Indian or Indonesian desire to obtain more UN support in population control? Or that an American concern over the consequences of uncontrolled automation may be countered with demands for certain new types of investment aid by African nations, thus creating a bargaining situation in which collective security could find a new niche? Obviously, some reliance on science fiction becomes crucial in this kind of speculation, and our experience with space technology, science, and exploration furnishes a few indications for optimistic conjecture.

Outer space exploration suggests several possible new tasks when the dangers and the promise of this venture are examined. Thus far the UN-sanctioned rules have merely made space safe for peaceful national exploration; in Wolfgang Friedmann's terms, they have confirmed the "law of coexistence," not the "law of cooperation." The dangers of minimal regulation, however, are not confined to the obvious military implications but also evoke fears of wholly unforeseen chemical, genetic, and epidemiological catastrophes. On the other hand, outer space could conceivably be harnessed to the solution of some of the Earth's economic and population problems, possibilities not amenable to simple national initiatives.

The perfection and increasing use of communications satellites throws into relief another set of possibilities. International assignment of radio frequencies and a World Weather Watch have been accomplished, but by the mid-1980s actual control over the weather is conceivable. No nation will trust another to control the weather. If one nation were to attempt it, a new international bargaining situation is created that will permit some inter-functional activity until the WMO acquires the task of controlling the weather. Communications satellites also permit the United States, Russia, and China to compete simultaneously for ideological support in everyone's living room, tent, adobe hut, and igloo. "It may be no exaggeration to say that priority in establishing the satellite communication system may determine whether, fifty years from now, Russian or English is the main language of mankind. The TV satellite is mightier than the ICBM, and intercontinental TV may indeed be the ultimate weapon."[10] We might add that this is true especially when it is pressed into service by UNESCO for crash teaching in developing areas. In such a situation, the major and minor powers may suddenly acquire converging interests in UN control over all TV broadcasting, and such an interest might conceivably keep open issues for some inter-functional bargaining.

[10] Arthur C. Clarke as quoted by Lincoln Bloomfield "Outer Space and International Cooperation," *International Organization* (Summer, 1965), p. 608. See also Howard J. Taubenfeld (ed.), *Space and Society* (Dobbs Ferry: Oceana, 1964) and Rita and Howard J. Taubenfeld, *Man and Space* (Dallas: Southern Methodist University, 1964).

No scenarios can be sketched for the implications of genetic manipulation, the farming of the ocean bottom, motivation control by way of drugs, asymmetric population growth, the application of new sources of energy, and universal pollution of air and water, to name a few obvious issues of the future. The political implications of each is enormous. Who can affirm with certainty that they may not lend themselves to a new inter-bloc bargaining pattern in which trade-offs benefiting the mundane practice of collective security can be found? But it is also conceivable that the recognition of dangers and benefits in the science of the future may lead to energetic international action that remains entirely autonomous and self-contained, thus being successful *because* it remains aloof from a political world order and generalized bargaining—to the detriment of peacekeeping.

Our survey leads to the conclusion that the opportunities for inter-functional and inter-regional bargaining will be more restricted in 1988 than in 1968. As far as domestic change impulses and inputs into the international system are concerned, we have seen that the bulk of presently interconnected issue areas will probably have become autonomous two decades hence. We have suggested that the shape of the future regional blocs will yield a political power constellation in which the familiar inter-bloc bargaining pattern will not survive. And we must be hesitant in affirming that functional equivalents will be found for the obsolescence of familiar trade-off patterns.

And so we reach the end of the prophetic road. *The UN of 1985 will be a reconciliation system.* The heterogeneity of the environment, the prevailing polities, the distribution of power, and the structural and functional characteristics of relations between the nations and the international organization *do* meet the requisites posited. But, because most of the tasks of the organization will be autonomous, *the mingling of inputs and the production of outputs will not satisfy the requisites as well as does the present system. The UN then will be a reconciliation system unable to carry out the collective security task as well as does the current UN.* Future consensual patterns based on *ad hoc* concerts are possible and even likely, but these may well tend toward a dictatorship of the big powers. Balancing is even more necessary for successful collective security but less likely precisely because of the changing pattern of inter-functional and inter-regional bargaining. If the Security Council harbors the danger of big power dominance, the General Assembly hides the peril of flabby majorities without the collective will to act. No sermonizing in favor of "flexible" policies that call for moving between the two will provide a stable output pattern. What is good for most UN tasks is bad for collective security. The local forces of change will bring about a clustering of issue areas under which the institutionalization of world order itself is likely to become a subordinate function. And the possible increases in human welfare cannot count on a companion benefit in world peace.

SELECT BIBLIOGRAPHY

Alker, Hayward R., Jr., and Bruce M. Russett, *World Politics in the General Assembly*. New Haven, Conn.: Yale University Press, 1965.

Asher, Robert E., *et al.*, *The United Nations and Promotion of the General Welfare*. Washington, D.C.: The Brookings Institution, 1957.

Bailey, Sydney D., *The General Assembly of the United Nations*. London: Stevens & Sons Ltd., for the Carnegie Endowment for International Peace, 1960.

Boyd, Andrew, *United Nations: Piety, Myth, and Truth*. Penguin, 1962.

Bloomfield, Lincoln P., *The United Nations and U.S. Foreign Policy*, 2nd rev. ed. Boston: Little, Brown, 1967.

Claude, Inis L., Jr., *Swords Into Plowshares: The Problems and Progress of International Organization,* 3rd ed. New York: Random House, Inc., 1964.

_____ , *The Changing United Nations*. New York: Random House, 1967.

Dallin, Alexander, *The Soviet Union at the United Nations*. New York: Frederick A. Praeger, 1962.

Etzioni, Amitai, *Political Unification*. New York: Holt, Rinehart and Winston, 1965.

Friedmann, Wolfgang, *The Changing Structure of International Law*. New York: Columbia University Press, 1964.

Gardner, Richard N., *In Pursuit of World Order: U.S. Foreign Policy and International Organizations*. New York: Frederick A. Praeger, 1964.

Goodspeed, Stephen S., *The Nature and Function of International Organization*. New York: Oxford University Press, 1959.

Haas, Ernst B., *Beyond the Nation-State: Functionalism and International Organization*. Stanford, Calif.: Stanford University Press, 1964.

Higgins, Rosalyn, *The Development of International Law Through The Political Organs of the United Nations*. London: Oxford University Press, 1963.

Kaplan, Morton A. and Nicholas deB. Katzenbach, *The Political Foundations of International Law*. New York: John Wiley & Sons, 1961.

Kelsen, Hans and Robert W. Tucker, *Principles of International Law,* 2nd rev. ed. New York: Holt, Rinehart and Winston, 1966.

Lindberg, Leon, *The Political Dynamics of European Economic Integration.* Stanford, Calif.: Stanford University Press, 1963.

Luard, Evan, ed., *The Evolution of International Organizations.* London: Thames and Hudson, 1966.

McDougal, Myres S. and Florentino P. Feliciano, *Law and Minimum World Public Order.* New Haven: Yale University Press, 1962.

Padelford, Norman J. and Leland M. Goodrich, eds., *The United Nations in the Balance.* New York: Frederick A. Praeger, 1965.

Rosner, Gabriella, *The United Nations Emergency Force.* New York: Columbia University Press, 1963.

Stoessinger, John G., *The United Nations and the Superpowers.* New York: Random House, 1965.

Stone, Julius, *Legal Controls of International Conflict.* New York: Rinehart and Co., Inc., 1954.

"less than honorable techniques"
whose responsibility?
mutual respect. > how did he show it?
to his opponents?

some say begin to build unity out of disunity,
others disagree.

"no one should tamper with the senate,
who does not love that
kind of institution."